Microeconomics for Public Managers

Microeconomics *for* Public Managers

BARRY P. KEATING AND
MARYANN O. KEATING

A John Wiley & Sons, Ltd., Publication

This edition first published 2009
© 2009 Barry P. Keating and Maryann O. Keating

Blackwell Publishing was acquired by John Wiley & Sons in February 2007.
Blackwell's publishing program has been merged with Wiley's global Scientific,
Technical, and Medical business to form Wiley-Blackwell.

Registered Office
John Wiley & Sons Ltd, The Atrium, Southern Gate, Chichester, West Sussex,
PO19 8SQ, United Kingdom

Editorial Offices
350 Main Street, Malden, MA 02148-5020, USA
9600 Garsington Road, Oxford, OX4 2DQ, UK
The Atrium, Southern Gate, Chichester, West Sussex, PO19 8SQ, UK

For details of our global editorial offices, for customer services, and for information
about how to apply for permission to reuse the copyright material in this book please
see our website at www.wiley.com/wiley-blackwell.

Library of Congress Cataloging-in-Publication Data

Keating, Barry, 1945–
Microeconomics for public managers / Barry P. Keating and Maryann O. Keating.
p. cm.
Includes bibliographical references and index.
ISBN 978-1-4051-2543-7 (hbk. : alk. paper)—ISBN 978-1-4051-2544-4
(pbk. : alk. paper)   1. Microeconomics.   2. Public administration.
3. Nonprofit organizations.   I. Keating, Maryann O.   II. Title.
HB172.K45 2009
338.5024′351—dc22
2008023251

A catalogue record for this title is available from the British Library.

Set in 10.5/12pt Times by Graphicraft Limited, Hong Kong
Printed and bound in Singapore by Markono Print Media Pte Ltd

1   2009

Contents

Figures

Tables

Preface

The three primary goals of *Microeconomics for Public Managers* are:

1 to direct future nonprofit and public administrators, with or without introductory economics classes, to managerial techniques based on microeconomic theory;
2 to assist students in realizing the unique constraints and institutional framework in which these organizations operate;
3 to review skills needed to interpret the contribution of economics to public administration and stimulate interest in ongoing research.

This is not a public-policy text, although policy-makers benefit from mastering the microeconomic tools that economists use. Focusing on markets and firms, this text sifts through microeconomics for useful applications in nonprofit and public administration. The role of nonprofits and government in product and factor markets is integrated with economic theory, not merely included as an add-on to the profit-seeking sector. Market failure and public goods are introduced early into the analysis.

Students in public administration who may lack a background in statistics and economics dread required courses using economic tools. This text is designed to reduce this anxiety. Calculus is neither used nor required. Regression and forecasting is reviewed but optional at the discretion of the instructor. Indifference curves are introduced, but welfare analysis is confined to consumer and producer surplus. The text level is targeted between a principles and an intermediate class in microeconomics; we assume a grasp of algebra. The text is therefore less rigorous than that needed for Ph.D. policy programs. We attempt to introduce microeconomic reasoning and the logic it provides to students with a declared interest in public administration. This vocational approach to microeconomics is somewhat more managerial than theoretical, with a specific type of rigor, based on techniques, applications, and a full discussion of costs. The text aspires to provide a deeper understanding of the institutional uniqueness of the nonprofit and government sectors compared with a traditional microeconomics text.

In our experience, students in public administration tend to have strengths in economics, mathematics/statistics, or management experience, but not all three. The text is sufficiently challenging for students lacking competency in at least one of these areas. Economists, teaching courses for which this text is aimed, are required to overcome student resistance to economic theory. Although students go forth into economic theory reluctantly, they rejoice at knowing that others have ploughed the same fields, yielding useful tools. Applications directly related to a student's field and relatively simple exercises provide incentives to learn and reinforce economic concepts.

Over 40 Applications are presented based on current administrative issues and research and several exercises at the end of chapters reinforce each concept.

The text is divided into four parts using a traditional microeconomic framework:

I   Institutional Setting
II   Consumer Theory and Public Goods
III   Production Theory and Public Administration
IV   Input Markets and Cost–Benefit Analysis.

Concluding Notes, essentially learning objectives, end each chapter; however, students still need to read the full text and be introduced to the material in classroom lectures. The list of Key Terms for each chapter includes those terms italicized in bold and defined in the body of the text. An instructor's manual, including PowerPoint slides, chapter notes, and End of Chapter Exercise answers, is posted online.

Acknowledgments

The authors are indebted to those economists, on whose shoulders we stand and who have worked to create and define the economic concepts presented. Specific theoretical understanding has been provided by Professors Holt Wilson, John T. Croteau, James Rakowski, Gordon Tullock, and James Buchanan. We are grateful as well to the editors of Wiley–Blackwell for their support and encouragement and to several anonymous reviewers. We must thank our students at the University of Notre Dame and Indiana University South Bend, for sustaining our interest in public and nonprofit administration over several decades. Finally, any blame for errors in understanding and presentation rests with us.

Organizational Alternatives

This text is designed as a required text for upper division undergraduate or first year graduate students. Given a full semester, an instructor can easily supplement with additional readings, case studies, and applications. In an accelerated class, several chapters may be omitted. Chapter 11 can be skipped if students in your program are required to complete a class in cost–benefit analysis. The Appendix on Regression in Chapter 1 and the sections on Forecasting at the end of Chapter 4 may also be omitted. Instructors could assign but not lecture on Part I if students have work experience or course background on nonprofit and government institutions. Policy-oriented classes need to supplement the text with lectures and additional assignments in indifference curve analysis and taxation.

It is the desire of the authors that instructors, using this text, continue to delight in the insights provided by microeconomics and share their enthusiasm with those who will shortly be entrusted with nonprofit/government decisions.

Part I

Institutional Setting

1
Managerial Economics in Public and Nonprofit Administration: An Overview

1.1   INTRODUCTION

Nonprofit and government organizations, justified by custom and tradition, predate the corporate sector historically. They teach, heal, provide social services, and lift people's spirit with recreational, musical, and artistic outlets. These are not flawed businesses to be tolerated whenever the market fails. They have standing in and of themselves, although they cannot show a profit and have difficulty in demonstrating cost-effectiveness, quality, and relevance to long-term Gross National Product.

Any business manager crossing over into the nonprofit and public sector has much to learn. As compared with business executives, nonprofits and public administrators wield less authority, answer to a wider range of shareholders, lack a straightforward performance measure such as profit, are under greater public scrutiny, and have fewer resources to achieve their objectives.

Misunderstandings about the nonprofit and public sectors have serious repercussions. Board members may treat their positions less professionally than their corporate board memberships. Donors neglect to use their influence. Talented administrators, particularly those with business backgrounds, end up frustrated and ineffective because they do not have a handle on the complexity of the nonprofit and public sectors (Silverman and Taliento, 2006). Robert Rubin, former U.S. Treasury Secretary, experienced these differences first hand as described in Application 1.1.

APPLICATION 1.1
Crossing into Government Administration from the Profit-seeking Sector

Robert E. Rubin, U.S. Treasury Secretary under President Clinton, offers several observations about the differences he experienced on becoming a government administrator after 26 years at Goldman Sachs, an investment bank, where he rose to co-senior partner.

Rubin observes that anyone going from head of a large firm in the profit-seeking sector to a cabinet position can be misled by the similarities. In both cases, the person is administrating a large, hierarchically structured organization. However, if one does not recognize the differences, he or she will not be effective in government for the following reasons:

1   In business the chief focus is on profitability. Government has no simple bottom line but a vast array of interests and priorities, some of which are in conflict.
2   Government decision-making is vastly more complex and the decision-making power of the government administrator is more limited. Almost every major decision must be approved

after an extensive interagency process. This permits decision-making power to be far more centralized in profit-seeking firms than in government.

3   A profit-seeking CEO has the power to hire and fire based on performance, to pay bonuses, and to promote capable people. In government, an employee can be dismissed for gross incompetence, but the cost is seldom worth the effort.
4   In government, structural reorganization requires legislation.
5   The key to a top NFP administrator's success is one's relationship with key committees and politicians, and this takes enormous time and thought. Internal oversight of U.S. profit-seeking boards is less intrusive on a day to day basis.

Because of these differences between profit-seeking and government firms, Rubin concludes:

1   Profit-seeking firms have much to offer government firms in improving efficiency in both processes and operations. However, the inherent complexity of government administration remains.
2   In spite of the prejudice many profit-seeking managers have against government administrators, they have much to learn from the way government works. Those who learn how to manage complicated interagency governmental processes have a crucial set of skills less likely to be as well developed in business.

Source: Robert E. Rubin and Jacob Weisberg, *In An Uncertain World*, New York: Random House, 2003.

Like any firm, public and nonprofit organizations create something of value that individuals and groups of individuals are willing to purchase. Public administrators, managing these institutions, wish to avoid politicization and provide the best service for the least cost. However, some organizations are more effective than others. This difference is in part explained by the microeconomic underpinnings of each organization.

With few exceptions, firms producing a good or service are included in one of the following economic sectors:

1   the profit-seeking sector;
2   the government sector; or
3   the nonprofit sector.

This book concerns the second and third sectors, accounting for more than 20 percent of total U.S. employment. Approximately 13 percent of all workers are

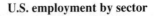

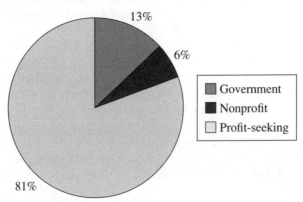

Figure 1.1   U.S. employment by sector (estimated). Precise employment figures by sector are presently unavailable. The sector percentages here are based on Table 1.1 data but adjusted to account for agricultural and self-employed workers excluded from that data. The healthcare industry, for example, spans across the profit-seeking, government, and private nonprofit sectors. U.S. Department of Labor data differentiates between private and public non-agricultural employment but not between the profit-seeking and private nonprofit sectors.

employed by government and 7 percent by nonprofit firms. Figure 1.1 outlines the relative sizes of the three sectors in which the total labor force is employed. Our goal in this book is to show how economics, a social science dealing with scarcity and choice, is relevant to the nonprofit and government sectors.

Consider for a moment the following fantasy. Imagine lounging on a deck chair at your local swimming pool on a sunny summer afternoon. Only the periodic whistle of the lifeguards disturbs the serenity of blue sky and water. Small children in the pool cry "Look at me!" and teens flirt by the concession stand. A few trees and a fence shut out the rest of the world. The only serious decision you face is whether to continue dozing in your chair or plunge into the water for a few laps.

Permit us to draw you back into the world of economics. Most likely the pool of your fantasy is not in the profit-seeking sector, unless located in a private home or hotel. Using valuable real estate for a stand-alone pool is generally inconsistent with profit maximization. A *profit-seeking firm* is one that seeks to maximize profit and shareholders' wealth. Is the pool of your fantasy operated by the government or by a private nonprofit? Both represent the focus of this text. We use the term *not-for-profit (NFP)* to include firms in both the nonprofit and government sectors. A private *nonprofit firm* is a non-government organization providing benefits for members or clients within the community. Note that we use the term "firm" for all three types of legal institutions: profit-seeking, nonprofit, and government. In economics, a firm is a producing unit of society, and all three types of institutions create value in the form of goods and services. However, the government and nonprofit sectors share common economic characteristics that differ from firms in the profit-seeking sector in two important ways:

1 NFP firms receive part of their revenue from a source other than from the sale of output to users.
2 These alternate sources of revenue, whether from donations or taxation, affect firm behavior and administrative decisions.

Public administration is the broad study and practice of implementing policy within a government or quasi-government organization. Increasingly, the term public administration implies the management of all NFP firms providing certain goods and services called public goods. This text, designed for government and private nonprofit administrators and students, is less concerned with policy formation but more with policy interpretation and implementation within an organization. Whenever organizations are somewhat autonomous, administrators set fees, decide on output, and make management decisions.

From birth onward, we are in constant association with NFP firms: hospitals, churches, schools, civic and fraternal associations, cooperatives, retirement communities, etc. These institutions are the foundation on which the whole economy rests; they are the necessary socializing institutions that create the environment and legal arrangements under which business transactions take place. The very fabric of society is stitched together with the thread of these firms, public and private. They are not businesses; they neither seek profit nor intend to maximize profits. They are not households. Public and private NFP firms are organized to produce a given outcome, and like any firm they sometimes fail. Many of us were disillusioned with disaster relief provided in 2005 after Hurricane Katrina. It seems as if every sector of the economy was incapable of responding effectively. Some lessons and suggestions for dealing with future catastrophes are discussed in Application 1.2.

APPLICATION 1.2
Lessons from Hurricane Katrina

It is easy to criticize each sector of the U.S., government, private non-profit, and profit-seeking, associated with disaster relief in the aftermath of the devastation to New Orleans and its outlying areas caused by Hurricane Katrina in 2005. However, Trent Stamp, President of Charity Navigator, suggests that even if the federal government through its Federal Management Agency appears to have failed in its ability to handle the Katrina disaster, the role of private charities in future disasters is more vital than ever.

Lean staffing and volunteer labor limit private nonprofit response. After Katrina, the New Orleans Red Cross office was flooded, half its employees lost their homes, and two employees lost family members. Yet, private charities with donor dollars evacuated residents, served meals, provided cash assistance, and is rebuilding communities. In the midst of the disaster, mistakes were made on the one hand by too hastily distributing debit cards and providing redundant services and on the other hand by too slowly assisting people in distress.

Stamp suggests that nonprofit and government organizations can learn from their mistakes. He suggests that particular agencies recognize their comparative advantage, refer clients to other charities, cooperate with other agencies rather than be territorial, and refrain from soliciting funds for services for which they have no experience.

Disaster relief procedures should be based on general principles for dealing with unexpected circumstances. After Katrina hit, food, stored 70 miles away in Baton Rouge, failed to reach New Orleans on flooded roads. NFPs must construct worst-case not merely most-likely scenarios. After the September 11, 2001, terrorist attacks, in order to avoid excessive hoarding of funds, organizations initiated "pay as your go" policies in which funds have to be raised and allocated separately for each catastrophe. The unintended consequence was to prevent charities from shifting funds to assist after Hurricane Rita followed Katrina in just four weeks. Thus, it would be imprudent to devise new rules based exclusively on the Katrina experience.

Source: Trent Stamp, "Charities Must Heed the Lessons From Hurricane Katrina," *Chronicle of Philanthropy*, 18 (21), August 17, 2006, 28.

The following three assumptions are the basis of the intersection between the study of economics and NFP firm management:

1   Unlike profit-seeking firms, NFP firms do not focus on what is earned, but rather on what they do. The output of the organization is important independently of income earned by the sale of its output. In fact, the output is important whether or not it earns any income at all.
2   NFP firms operate with internal and external constraints that distinguish them from profit-seeking firms. Although human behavior is a constant, administrators and clients of NFP firms are motivated and rewarded differently than executives and customers of profit-seeking firms.
3   NFP firms allocate scarce resources and create value. As such, they should be operated so as to provide the most benefits at minimum cost. The study of economics provides administrators with tools to do this.

Students earning a Masters in Business Administration (MBA) expect to apply their training over a range of profit-seeking industries. Of course, some training must be specific to that industry; managing a factory producing steel is different from managing a firm in the fashion industry. Similarly, the experience and training of healthcare administration is different from that of educational administrators, and both are different from social services and the arts. The study of public administration economics respects the ideals and mores of diverse professionals, their unique rules and regulations, and their standard procedures. Nevertheless, economic theory of a general NFP firm offers insight into how organizations operating across a wide variety of industries can be most effective.

What specifically can economics offer those who study and work in public and nonprofit administration? Public administrators need to internalize five essential economic concepts:

1   The nature of public versus private choice and a clearer understanding of differences and similarities between profit-seeking and NFP firms.
2   A heightened awareness of scarcity with respect to unlimited wants.
3   The primary focus of the organization, with which he or she is associated, is the provision of a specific good or service intended by the sponsor and of value to the client.
4   Individual donors, sponsors, administrators, employees, and clients operate in their own best interests which may or may not be coincident with the organization's goals. Inappropriate incentives produce unintended consequences. Public good provision is constrained by constitutional considerations and "rules of the game" rather than strict economic efficiency.
5   Each managerial decision has a cost measured by the value of the foregone alternative; every choice, then, can either move an organization toward or away from furthering its purpose.

The best way to master these core economic concepts is through direct experience in the management of various NFP firms. But that would take a thousand lifetimes. By explaining and applying economic concepts to a variety of nonprofit situations, this text aspires to assist those in government and private NFP firms in the complex task of effectively providing social goods and services. The economic tools presented in this text do not require advanced mathematics, such as calculus. Nevertheless, understanding simple graphs and equations is essential, as is a calculator for solving end-of-chapter exercises. The Appendix to this chapter is a tutorial on regression, a statistical tool employed in many of the Applications presented in each chapter. Any statistical software program, such as Excel, is helpful but not required to understand the tutorial.

In this text, NFP issues and applications are fully incorporated with economic theory: indeed, the text follows the traditional microeconomic format as shown in the following parts:

I   Institutional Setting
II   Consumer Theory and Public Goods
III   Production Theory and Public Administration
IV   Input Markets and Cost–Benefit Analysis.

Gross Domestic Product (GDP) is the market value of all final goods and services produced within a country in the course of one year in all three sectors: government, private nonprofit, and profit-seeking. What share of GDP is produced in the two NFP sectors, the focus of this book? At present, we are unable to answer that

Table 1.1   Annual average total of persons, 16 years and over, employed as wage and salary workers in the United States, 2002 (thousands)

Industries	Total workers	Private sector	Government sector	% of total	Private sector	Government sector
Total employment, 16 years and over	126,438	106,750	19,689	100.0	100.0	100.0
Agriculture	1,282	1,229	53	1.0	1.2	0.3
Mining	490	488	1	0.4	0.5	0.0
Construction	8,367	7,899	469	6.6	7.4	2.4
Manufacturing	16,918	16,848	59	13.4	15.8	0.3
Wholesale and retail trade	18,625	18,536	89	14.7	17.4	0.5
Transportation and utilities	6,872	5,318	1,554	5.4	5.0	7.9
Information	3,545	3,386	159	2.8	3.2	0.8
Financial activities	8,881	8,699	182	7.0	8.1	0.9
Professional and business services	12,138	11,816	322	9.6	11.1	1.6
Education and health services	26,493	16,429	10,064	21.0	15.4	51.1
Educational services	11,541	3,125	8,415	9.1	2.9	42.7
Hospitals	5,321	4,661	660	4.2	4.4	3.4
Healthcare, non-hospital	7,357	6,830	527	5.8	6.4	2.7
Social assistance	2,274	1,812	462	1.8	1.7	2.3
Leisure and hospitality	10,907	10,519	388	8.6	9.9	2.0
Other services	5,613	4,827	30	4.4	4.5	0.2
Repair and maintenance	1,518	1,509	9	1.2	1.4	0.0
Personal and laundry	1,475	1,453	21	1.2	1.4	0.1
Membership associations and organizations	1,864	1,864	0	1.5	1.7	0.0
Private household	757	757	0	0.6	0.7	0.0
Public administration	6,307		6,307	5.0	0.0	32.0

Self-employed and unpaid family workers are excluded. Private nonprofit employment with respect to total nonagricultual private firm employment is 7.8 percent. A breakdown by industry for private nonprofit and for-profit employment is not available.
Source: Based on Current Population Survey.

question precisely. The amount of government spending, not used to purchase goods and services, is generally available and represents an approximate measure of the value of output produced by government employees. However, no similar figure exists for nonprofits in the United States.

Labor-force data, for those presently holding jobs or seeking work, is usually broken down by industry, but not by sector. We know, for example, the number of nurses working in various industries but not if the firm in which they are employed is a nonprofit or profit-seeking corporation. Therefore, we can merely estimate changes and the amount of workers in the NFP sectors. The Johns Hopkins Center for Civil Society and the United Nations Statistical Division have worked together to address this issue. Together they have issued the *Handbook on Non-profit Institutions in the System of National Accounts*.

The Urban Institute also collects data on the size and characteristics of the private nonprofit sector in the United States. The United States Department of Labor provides data on employment broken down into industries and into private versus government workers. As of now, the government does not survey private nonprofit employment by industries. Based on information provided in Table 1.1, we can make some generalizations about employment in both the private nonprofit and government sectors and the relative sizes of those sectors.

The United States government employs about 16 percent of the civilian labor force, and private nonprofits account for 7.8 percent of nonagricultural private employment. Thus, over 20 percent of all U.S. civilian employees work in either the government or in the private nonprofit sector. Half of all government workers are in education and health services and 32 percent in public administration. Another 4.3 percent of government workers are in social service or leisure/hospitality industries. Education, health services, and religious ministry dominate the private nonprofit sector, followed by social services.

In Europe, it is traditional to speak of the "social sector" including cooperative organizations, such as unions, buyer and seller co-ops, worker owned firms, and credit unions, as part of the private nonprofit sector. Cooperatives play a less significant role in the United States, because the distribution of net income (revenue minus costs) to those associated with tax exempt nonprofits is prohibited. In all economically advanced economies, the private nonprofit sector tends to be large and is increasingly regarded as a type of innovative public management. Therefore, this book focuses on private nonprofit as well as government management.

1.2   ECONOMIC THINKING IN
NOT-FOR-PROFIT ADMINISTRATION

Often students resist abstract graphical and mathematical models that stylize, compare, and generalize. What do drug treatment programs have in common with automobile production? Aren't differences between NFP and profit-seeking firms obvious and unique? What benefit does rigorous abstract analysis offer to practicing administrators? The simple answer is that rigorous theory counters generalizations about NFP firms that are wrong, misleading, and dangerous. Consider just a few of these generalizations:

- All large bureaucracies, profit-seeking or not, operate similarly.
- Certain goods and services, such as education or medicine, are best provided in NFP firms.
- NFP firms are under-financed.
- Medical care and education are basic necessities and human rights.
- NFP administrators cannot assess or measure effectiveness.

- NFP firms do not experience the highs and lows of the business cycle.
- NFP firms lack "bottom line" discipline and are therefore less efficient than profit-seeking firms.
- Competitive individuals go into business and humanitarians are drawn into the NFP sectors.
- NFP firms should treat clients like customers.
- Clients are always incapable of determining quality.

Some of the above generalizations are clearly wrong; most contain kernels of truth needing qualification. As you examine the nonprofit environment more carefully, you may come to find the following economic assumptions more useful:

- The institutional and legal structure of a firm matters.
- Public goods, such as safety, and quasi-public goods, such as education and medicine, are exchanged in a wide network of firms in all three sectors.
- Each NFP, given a fixed budget, can choose to maximize output and/or provide a better product.
- A profit-seeking firm is intended to maximize shareholder wealth. A non-profit firm is intended to further the goals of its sponsoring agency.
- Employees, regardless of the type of employer, are similarly motivated, responding to rewards and incentives.
- Administrators interpret NFP policy choosing what, how, and for whom to produce.
- NFP clients do not pay "out of pocket" full cost; they are subsidized.

A critical difference between profit-seeking and NFP firms is the ***non-distributional constraint***. If a firm claiming nonprofit tax status generates an amount of revenue exceeding costs, it may not distribute that surplus to individuals who own or control the organization. Clients are not entitled to rebates and administrators do not get bonuses based on financial performance. Budget surpluses in government are certainly not divided among employees and in most instances are forfeited to make up deficits elsewhere.

The term NFP refers to privately sponsored nonprofit firms as well as government agencies. We exclude all profit-seeking firms from our analysis including those operating in the education, healthcare, and social service industries. We exclude as well, all profit-seeking subsidiaries of nonprofit or government organizations. Included as NFP firms are all government units, nonprofit and state colleges and universities, healthcare organizations, voluntary health and welfare organizations, foundations, and other nonprofit professional, trade, scientific, and religious organizations. Whenever necessary, the term "private nonprofits" is used to distinguish these firms from government agencies.

1.3   ECONOMIC SCARCITY

Economics is the study of scarcity and choice because resources are limited. Every nonprofit firm, public or private, uses available scarce resources to create value.

Economic **resources** are the natural, physical, and human inputs used to produce goods and services; sometimes resources are referred to as inputs or factors of production. The amount of resources available for production is finite. Imagine if you will that the residents of a country decide that each person has a right to dental care. The goal is to provide dental care such that each permanent tooth of every resident is intact at death. All known cosmetic and orthodontic services are included. Estimate in thousands of dollars what this service would cost per household at current prices and compare this with the pre-tax salary of the average worker. However worthy the goal, the most affluent countries in the world could not provide this service without foregoing significant other services.

Economics and value

Economists are criticized as knowing the price of everything and the value of nothing. This is humorous but untrue. Value is at the heart of economics. The **opportunity cost** of anything equals the highest value of what one gives up in attaining that product. The opportunity cost of a 3-credit university class is, for example, $2,000 in tuition, $150 for textbooks, and $3,000 of foregone employment income missed through class and study time. The opportunity cost is $5,150 or $1,712 per credit hour. The expected stream of income or satisfaction is the best measure of benefits. The opportunity cost of a degree in public policy, for example, equals "out of pocket" tuition, books, and other fees *plus* any income given up in the process of attaining it. The benefits are the expected increases in income and/or satisfaction earned as a result of having the degree. Admittedly, individuals, firms, and societies often do not have clear information in assessing the net benefits (benefits minus costs) of what something is worth. You, at best, only have a general idea of the value of your time in taking this class and its future expected benefits.

Assume, however, that one does have a fairly accurate estimation of full costs and benefits. In certain situations, one does not have an incentive to reveal the net value (costs minus benefits) to anyone else. Consider, for example, that you know the extent to which a degree will increase your life-time earnings. You may wish to withhold this information. The financial aid officer, if he or she knew the value of your future earnings, is less likely to offer scholarship assistance, saving the taxpayer or donor the expense of subsidizing your education. Individuals at times have an incentive to be less than candid about costs and benefits; therefore, economists observe not what people say but what they do.

Economists study the market, a stage on which buyers and sellers meet, to provide information about the value that buyers and sellers place on a product. NFP administrators need to estimate client and sponsor willingness to spend for each level of service provided. In addition, he or she needs to calculate what the firm is capable of providing at different levels of support. Subsidized clients desire the highest level of educational and medical services available and, if they are able, subsidize that quality at personal expense. Parents, for example, supplement school-provided music training with privately paid lessons. Administrators may also wish to provide a high level of care, given best practices. Due to budget constraints, they compromise. Scarcity affects consumer choice studied in Part II and producer choice as presented in Part III.

Market prices do not always accurately reflect society's costs and benefits. For example, the costs to society of environmental pollution are underestimated, as are the benefits of childhood inoculations. Laws and regulations are needed to correct for this type of failure; policy development is not treated in detail in this text. However, when markets fail and profit-seeking firms fail to meet people's needs, NFP firms, public and private, come to the rescue. Decision-making within NFP firms is the focus of this text. Market failure is shown to be a primary justification for non-profit and government provision in Chapter 5.

Ordinary markets fail to measure the full value of public and quasi-public goods, such as security, safety, and park conservation. It is through voting, politics, and cooperative association that we express our desire for these types of goods. Chapter 3 outlines in detail the basic economic distinction between the demand for private and public goods. Because NFP firms specialize in providing these services, Chapter 5 analyzes collective provision of public and quasi-public goods.

1.4   ECONOMIC INSTITUTIONS

Macroeconomics (the forest) is concerned with the aggregate economic well-being of a particular region or country. It addresses such topics as GDP, unemployment, inflation, poverty, economic growth, government spending, and taxation. Macroeconomics assists decision-makers in formulating policy. *Microeconomics* (the trees) is concerned with individual firms rather than aggregates of firms, individual households rather than total populations, and specific industries rather than total output. Microeconomics assists decision-makers within economic institutions. This text is essentially microeconomics for those studying or working with NFP firms. The assumption is that public administrators do not make policy but rather implement it. Another assumption is that nonprofit administrators do not attempt to change society, but provide specific services which benefit recipients.

Consider the macro versus micro orientation of a nonprofit interest group, such as the American Association of Retired Persons (AARP) or the National Association for the Advancement of Colored People (NAACP), or the Sierra Club, the oldest American environmental organization, founded by John Muir. The expressed goal of these organizations is to affect national policy and hence they are macroeconomic in orientation. What we emphasize in this text, however, is that all administrators deal with the following microeconomic questions:

1   What combinations and how much of each service should they produce?
2   How should they allocate tax revenue, donations, fees, and other sources of income?
3   What technique should be used in producing these services?
4   How can they minimize costs for any given level of output?
5   To whom should benefits of this output be directed?

Economics, as a discipline, has developed a general theory of the firm, relevant to administrators wrestling with the above questions. Economics provides models and a standard vocabulary for discussing these issues. This framework can be abstract and generic, but, if correctly applied, it highlights the uniqueness and complexity of a particular task. The intention is to provide theoretical and practical assistance to those responsible for a firm's effectiveness.

Following Chapters 2's analysis of the role of the NFP sectors as a whole, subsequent chapters somewhat mirror or resemble a standard microeconomic managerial course. Supply and demand are introduced in Chapter 3. The optimization techniques, presented in Chapters 4 and 7, are microeconomic concepts. A framework for analyzing costs for a given output is provided in Chapter 6, and the optimal combination of labor and capital is addressed in Part IV.

1.5   ECONOMIC BEHAVIOR

Rational self-interest is the basic simplifying economic assumption of human behavior; individuals operate rationally in their own interest. This may seem overly cynical, especially when dealing with NFP firms. Yet, it is quite the opposite. Individuals are not assumed to be predatory; just aware of their alternatives. Therefore, they tend to make clear and consistent choices. Rational self-interest does *not* imply either of the following: (1) one's happiness increases as another's decreases; (2) individuals are fundamentally materialistic. Economists merely assume that individuals, including donors, sponsors, employees, and clients of all firms, define their particular preferences, including philanthropy, and act on them. However, even rational people make mistakes!

Self-interest does not preclude cooperation. Indeed, without cooperation government and nonprofit firms could not exist. Application 1.3 makes the case for *conditional cooperators*, individuals willing to initiate cooperative behavior anticipating that others will reciprocate.

APPLICATION 1.3
Fool Me Once, Shame on You; Fool Me Twice, Shame on Me!

Economists start with the following premise about human behavior. People are rational; they operate in their own self-interest and generally make clear and consistent choices. But suppose everyone were a pure forward-looking *rational egotist* making decisions based solely on individual benefits. Would NFP firms exist? Why should I donate or tolerate tax increases, if the benefits do not accrue to me personally? Indeed there is some support that certain rational individuals are not likely to cooperate in certain settings, even when such cooperation would be to their mutual benefit. What then are the circumstances that might induce one to contribute given the uncertainty of receiving anything in return?

After surveying the literature on cooperation in various experiments, Elinor Ostrom of Indiana University argues that along with self-interest some individuals bring with them a set of norms and values that support cooperation. In one study of a pool of 136 subjects, 40 percent ranked cooperative outcomes higher than other outcomes even when their individual payoff was lower. In games where one player divides a sum of money and the other player must accept the division, "nice players," who give away at least 30 percent of the funds, tend to choose cooperative strategies in subsequent games. Economists note, however, that cooperative behavior tends to decline in situations when individuals realize that they could win more by defecting. In subsequent rounds of experimental games in which players experience multiple instances of betrayal, cooperation and reciprocity diminish but are not completely eliminated.

Nonprofit firms are dependent on donations, and government agencies rely on general tax revenue. Therefore, certain individuals at times are required to or freely volunteer to behave in ways other than in rational self-interest. Ostrom makes the case for *conditional cooperators* as individuals willing to initiate cooperative behavior when they think others will reciprocate. These individuals continue to co-operate as long as a sufficient proportion of others reciprocates. You, for example, might be willing to initiate parties in your college dorm or apartment building and will continue to participate as long as you receive help and support from other residents. Ostrom identifies *willing punishers* who, if given the opportunity, will chastise or fine those who fail to cooperate. Their sense of fair play makes them willing to reward those who have contributed more than the minimal level. For example, *willing punishers* may argue that those who were willing to set up the party should at least be able to choose the music!

In any given society, *conditional cooperators* and *willing punishers* permit *rational egotists* to form institutions, such as nonprofits and government agencies, in order to provide goods and services that unsubsidized markets fail to deliver.

Source: Elinor Ostrom, "Collective Action and the Evolution of Social Norms," *Journal of Economic Perspectives*, summer, 2000, 37–158.

Psychologists and anthropologists have more sophisticated models of human behavior and preference formation, but economic methodology prefers to take individual preferences as given. Therefore, NFP clients, as analyzed in Chapter 3, seek the most service at minimal personal cost. Chapters 9 and 10 show how donors/volunteers and sponsors subsidizing a firm do so with certain goals in mind; they expect to attain the highest outcome for each hour volunteered or dollar donated.

Certain NFP administrators may be less competitive or more humanitarian than profit-seeking colleagues, but this stereotype does little to explain NFP behavior. Most employees work to provide for themselves and their families and to further their careers. Chapter 9 discusses conflicts between managerial behavior and firm mission. To prevent subversion by individuals of the NFP firm's primary purpose, Chapter 11 introduces a technique, called cost–benefit analysis. Cost–benefit analysis tests the extent to which proposed projects achieve appropriate outcomes.

1.6   ECONOMIC CHOICE AND OPPORTUNITY COSTS

Scarce natural resources, physical and mental labor, capital consisting of machinery and plant, and managerial know-how are combined to produce goods and services. NFP firms contract for resources in competitive markets in competition with profit-seeking firms. Government and nonprofit firms have to purchase their paper, computers, and computer programming services as all firms do by being willing and able to pay the going market price. The organization then decides how and for what these resources should be used. NFP administrators play an important role in allocating society's scarce resources.

No firm can survive in the long run if its expenses consistently exceed its revenue, and every worthwhile project involves costs that could be used to produce something else. In this text, we are concerned with choices made within NFP firms about what programs to introduce, to continue, to cut back, or to eliminate. The best way to approach this decision is to ask, "What is the highest value that could be obtained if the resources used in this program were shifted into producing something else?" The real or opportunity costs of a program are other programs forfeited, because the firm does not have sufficient resources to do everything. The real cost is what, for example, a university gives up in expanding student slots in one course of study by reducing slots in another.

Suppose the marginal or incremental opportunity cost of training one more dental hygienist is a reduction of two classical scholars. Assume that it takes the university twice as many resources to train a dental hygienist as it does a classical scholar. If it is less costly to produce classical scholars, why would a university train hygienists? Perhaps students, donors, and the state are willing to pay more than twice as much for hygienists as they are for classical scholars. The university, then, could be indifferent between the two programs. Note carefully that we are not saying that the university should be indifferent. The university may wish to subsidize classical studies. What we are suggesting is that resource allocation within a nonprofit firm reflects the desired outcomes of those making decisions. However, we wish to note that, like profit-seeking firms, the competitive external environment, discussed in Chapters 7 and 8 of this book, explains much of what we observe in NFP choice.

Production possibilities and scarcity

Figure 1.2 assumes a fixed annual budget for a university. This budget is allocated between thousands of undergraduate credit hours on the Y axis and thousands of graduate credit hours on the X axis. Along the linear production possibility frontier in Figure 1.2, if graduate credit hours are expanded, then fewer resources are

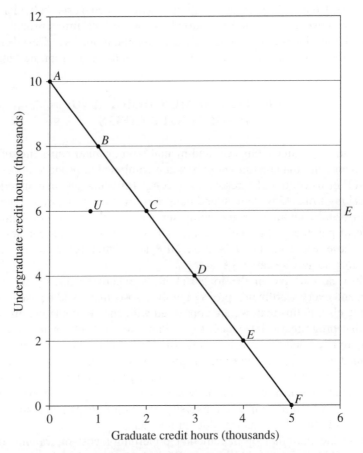

Figure 1.2   Possible combinations with a fixed budget: the production possibilities frontier. With a fixed budget, a university can provide a finite number of graduate and undergraduate credits. As graduate credits increase, undergraduate credits decline. The linear frontier in this figure assumes that the opportunity cost for each incremental increase in graduate credit is two undergraduate credits. For every graduate credit offered, the institution has an opportunity cost or forfeits providing two undergraduate credits.

allocated to undergraduates. Each incremental expansion of graduate credit hours by 1,000 reduces undergraduate credits by 2,000. The opportunity cost of each unit of X is two units of Y, suggesting that it costs the university twice as much to provide graduate credit as it does undergraduate credit.

In the linear production possibilities frontier presented in Figure 1.2, graduate credit is expanded one by one from 0 units of X to 5 units of X, until the budget is exhausted and 0 units of undergraduate education are supplied. This frontier demonstrates efficiency and cost. Productive efficiency is represented along the frontier as maximum possible production given present budgetary constraints. Costs are represented by the extent to which output of one program must be decreased to produce one more increment of the other program.

Productive and allocative efficiency

A firm achieves *productive efficiency* when maximum product is produced at least cost. Consider, for example, a firm operating at point U in Figure 1.2. It is producing 1 unit of X and 6 units of Y, yet it is capable of producing more output with its fixed budget. Each combination of X and Y along the frontier represents productive efficiency. All points, A through F, are equally efficient given existing technology. *Technology* is defined as knowledge about how best to produce a given product; an increase in technology reducing the cost of supplying undergraduate credit raises the intersection of the budget line along the Y axis. Application 1.4 discusses the controversial issue of the possibility of increasing productivity in service industries found in the NFP sectors. Assuming that the best available technology is in place and represented on the frontier, administrators maximize output somewhere along the possibility line for a given budget. An increase in the university's budget or technology pushes the frontier out to the right, and a budget decrease moves it inward.

APPLICATION 1.4
Can Government and Nonprofit Firms Become More Efficient in Providing Services?

NFP professionals are skeptical of increasing efficiency. They claim that economic models dealing with tangible products like refrigerators and automobiles are irrelevant in providing services, such as education and healthcare. Can a single first-grade teacher be expected to teach more than 25 students per year without decreasing quality? Can a single critical-care nurse tend to more than 6 patients per shift without decreasing quality? Perhaps, not. This does not, however, mean that services for existing clients cannot be improved.

Many profit-seeking firms, such as airlines and financial institutions, provide services. Yet, they have implemented technology to become more efficient and reduce costs. General Electric Co. and healthcare provider Intermountain Health Care have entered into an agreement to develop an internet computer package providing physicians access to clinical best practices at the moment of treatment.

Presently, it is very expensive to fully computerize the healthcare system to include newer best practice technology or even existing technology. Electronic medical records eliminate handwritten orders contributing to errors. Hospitals and physicians are reluctant to invest in technology as the best use of the scarce medical funding.

Do you believe that industries providing services can become more efficient? How would you go about determining if it is worthwhile for a healthcare facility to adopt computerized technology?

Source: Kathryn Kranhold, "GE, Nonprofit Plan Tool for Physicians," *Wall Street Journal*, February 17, 2005, D3.

Where on the production frontier should a firm produce? For example, how should a university decide between graduate and undergraduate programs? The answer varies and is normative, depending on the values of those involved. Some prefer all graduate programs, other all undergraduate, and still others some combination of X and Y. A firm achieves **allocative efficiency** if the budget is incrementally distributed to whatever program yields the highest sum of value for those sponsoring the project. If a nonprofit firm produces at C rather than B, allocative efficiency requires that the value to the firm's donors and clients of an additional unit of X be worth more than the loss of 2 units of Y. The real challenge in NFP provision is to estimate value when clients are not paying full cost.

Consider reasons why a private university might move from points B to C in Figure 1.2. First, a donor preferring X to Y may leverage a small or large donation to influence the move. Second, nonprofit administrators or senior faculty, depending on their interpretation of the university's mission, could shift resources to project X. Finally, students by their willingness to pay higher tuition for each unit of X can influence the change. Tuition is best understood as a fee rather than a price. User fees, paid by clients of NFP firms, generally fail to cover full cost. Similarly, any government-sponsored university, guaranteed a subsidy per credit hour from the state, has an incentive to direct more resources to graduate education if graduate students are willing to pay higher user fees than undergraduates.

Is there any objective way to determine if a move from B to C is "in the public interest"? In practice, net benefits are subjective and cannot be precisely measured. Economists attempt to frame the question theoretically by applying the **Pareto Criterion**. Pareto, a nineteenth-century Italian economist, suggested that a move from B to C is desirable if no one in society is worse off and at least one person is better off. Furthermore, the move should not take place, unless the benefits from an increase in X are sufficient to compensate those harmed by decreased Y. Because clients do not pay full cost, we cannot prove that present and future benefits of increased graduate credit hours shown in Figure 1.2 exceed the cost of reducing undergraduate hours. However, if we observe such a move, this is indeed what administrators intend to indicate.

There are five immediate advantages of adopting an economic approach to NFP administration.

1   It focuses on the differences between for-profit and NFP firms.
2   Budgetary constraints are made explicit. Choices must be made between alternative goals.
3   Optimization is stressed, meaning the practice of either (a) minimizing costs for a given level of output, or (b) increasing output with the same amount of resources.
4   Costly efforts to change human behavior are replaced with effective incentives.
5   NFP outcomes are viewed as a process whereby individuals filter their preferences through private markets as well as through collective and political choice. Parents, for example, provide schooling for their child by a combination of selecting to live in a certain school district, paying tuition, electing pro-education government officials, and participating in home-school associations.

Present and future administrators, regardless of their academic major and former resistance to economics, need a framework for analyzing various types of NFP firms and the industries in which they operate. Decision-makers in the NFP environment confront "what happens if?" type questions. The "if" may be a change in government tax policy, a shortfall in expected subsidies, or increased competition. Microeconomics tools assist managers in responding to "what happens if?" type questions. While the tools of microeconomics are more commonly applied in the profit-seeking sector, the economists' toolkit is useful as well to government and nonprofit administrators.

CONCLUDING NOTES

- Public and private not-for-profit (NFP) firms neither seek to profit nor intend to maximize profits. They are organized to produce a given outcome independently of income earned by the sale of their products.

- NFP firms are the dominant socializing institutions of all societies creating the environment and legal arrangements under which most transactions and all business take place.

- Private nonprofit firms and government agencies have institutional and legal structures affecting their behavior. They often engage in supplying services inadequately provided in profit-seeking markets.

- The non-distributional constraint stipulates that a NFP firm may not distribute any surplus to individuals who own or control the organization.

- Economics is the study of scarcity and choice given limited resources.

- Microeconomics, sometimes called managerial economics, provides nonprofit and government administrators with a framework for decision-making.

- Individuals, including donors, sponsors, employees, and clients of NFP firms define their preferences and act on those preferences.

- All NFP firms are constrained by revenue. Over time, they cannot spend more than clients, sponsors, taxpayers, and donors are willing to pay.

- The real or opportunity cost of a NFP firm producing a particular good or service is the value of the alternative products that could have been produced.

- Productive efficiency requires that society's scarce resources be used to produce at lowest possible cost. Allocative efficiency requires that society's resources be used to produce those goods and services most desired by persons contributing to or paying fees to obtain the product.

- Clients of public and nonprofit agencies generally do not pay full cost for the services received. Client fees do not cover all costs.

- Economists use the Pareto Criterion to examine if a move from situation B to situation A is beneficial. The move is considered desirable if no one in society is worse off as a result of the move and at least one person is better off.

KEY TERMS

Profit-seeking firm

Not-for-profit firm (NFP)

Nonprofit firm

Non-distributional constraint

Resources

Opportunity cost

Macroeconomics

Microeconomics

Rational self-interest

Conditional cooperators

Productive efficiency

Technology

Allocative efficiency

Pareto Criterion

SUGGESTED READINGS

McConnell, Campbell R., and Brue, Stanley L. 2002: *Microeconomics: Principles, Problems, and Policies*, New York: McGraw-Hill.

Silverman, Les and Taliento, Lynn 2006: "What Business Execs Don't Know – but Should – about Nonprofits," *Stanford Social Innovation Review*, summer, 37–43.

Young, Dennis R. and Steinberg, Richard 1995: *Economics for Nonprofit Managers*, New York: Foundations Center.

END OF CHAPTER EXERCISES

Exercise 1.1

Explain how the non-distributional constraint affects or does not affect the following organizations: the U.S. Department of Commerce, Hospital Corp. of America, the Teamsters, Sylvan Learning Centers, Indiana State Lottery, the National Football League, Main Street Cardiology Partnership, and your University bookstore.

Exercise 1.2

Discuss how the following individuals, with respect to each organization listed in Exercise 1.1, operate rationally in their own self-interest: owners/stockholders, donors, administrators/managers, employees, volunteers, customers, and clients. Does rational self-interest preclude cooperation?

Exercise 1.3

The following represents production possibilities of clients served in a hospital with a fixed amount of capacity, staff, and equipment:

Type of production (in thousands of clients billed in one year)	A	B	C	D	E
In-patients	0	2	4	6	8
Out-patients	30	27	21	12	0

a. Graph the information presented in the above table. (*Hint*: the production possibilities curve is curved because opportunity costs increase as the hospital becomes more specialized.)

b. What is the opportunity cost of the hospital serving 4,000 rather than 2,000 in-patients yearly?

c. What is the opportunity cost of the hospital serving 21,000 rather than 12,000 out-patients yearly?

Exercise 1.4
Refer to production possibilities information in Exercise 1.3.

a. Explain why and how the hospital is considered productively inefficient by serving 4,000 in-patients and 20,000 out-patients yearly?

b. Which alternative, B or C, is allocatively efficient? What type of information would help you determine this?

Exercise 1.5
How would you go about deciding if a move from B to C were Pareto Optimal? Assume that the production possibilities in Exercise 1.3 referred to the nation as a whole rather than a single hospital.

Exercise 1.6
Refer to the production possibilities information in Exercise 1.3.

a. If the hospital's capacity, staff, and equipment increased, how would this affect your graph?

b. Suppose a new technique is discovered that reduces the amount of resources needed to process registration and billing for both types of patients. How would this affect your graph?

Exercise 1.7
Two countries, Scandia and United, are capable of producing output at the alternatives given in the table.

Scandia's possibilities Value of output produced in the:	A	B	C	D	E	F
Government sector	100	80	60	40	20	0
Private sectors	0	20	40	60	80	100

United's possibilities Value of output produced in the:	G	H	I	J	K	L
Government sector	300	240	180	120	60	0
Private sectors	0	60	120	180	240	300

a. Scandia is currently producing at alternative B and United at alternative K. Are both countries achieving productive efficiency? Explain.

b.   Scandia is currently producing at alternative *B* and United at alternative *K*. Are both countries necessarily achieving allocative efficiency? What assumption are you making about preferences in answering yes or no?

Exercise 1.8

Refer to the table in Exercise 1.7. If United were producing goods in the government sector worth 50 and goods in the private sectors worth 230, is it possible to increase its production of public goods without reducing the amount of goods produced in the private sectors? Explain.

Exercise 1.9

"Redistributing national healthcare expenses from a few terminally ill elderly to improve the public health of children is economically efficient." Discuss this statement in terms of the Pareto Criterion.

Exercise 1.10

Clients, as compared with customers, can be viewed as submitting themselves to a process that may or may not achieve desired outcomes. Are students and patients more like clients than customers? Explain.

Exercise 1.11

Give an example of a NFP firm providing a service for which clients pay a fee. What information do you need to estimate the full cost of providing this service? Do you suppose that the full cost is less than or equal to the user fee? Explain.

CHAPTER 1 APPENDIX: REGRESSION TUTORIAL

In surveying this text, you find several Applications employing a statistical method called regression. Researchers and practitioners in public and nonprofit administration use regression to test and understand relationships. After reviewing the statistical tools underlying this research, you should be able to understand and test relationships in the increasing amounts of data presently available to public managers.

The simplest forms of regression analysis involve just one independent variable. The dependent variable is usually designated *Y*, and the independent variable is represented with an *X*. The relationship or model we seek to find could then be expressed as:

$$Y = a + bX$$

This is called simple or bivariate linear regression (BLR) model because there are just two variables: *Y* and *X*.

In this expression, *a* represents the intercept or constant term for the regression equation. The intercept is where the regression line crosses the vertical, or *Y*, axis. Conceptually it is the value that the dependent variable (*Y*) would have if the independent variable (*X*) had a value of zero. We will have more to say about the interpretation of the intercept later.

The value of *b* represents the slope of the regression line. The slope is the rate of change in the dependent variable for each unit change in the independent

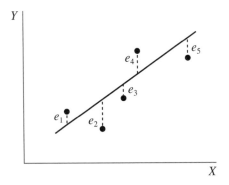

Figure A1.1   Ordinary least squares regression line for Y as a function of X.
Residuals, or deviations, between each point and the regression line are labeled e_i.

variable. Understanding that the slope term (b) is the rate of change in Y as X changes will be helpful to you in interpreting regression results. If b has a positive value, Y increases when X increases and decreases when X decreases. On the other hand, if b is negative, Y changes in the opposite direction of changes in X.

The most commonly used criterion for the "best" regression line is that the sum of the squared vertical differences between the observed values and the estimated regression line be as small as possible. To illustrate this concept, Figure A1.1 shows five observations of the relationship between some Y variable and some X variable. You can see from the scattering of points that no straight line would go through all of the points. We would like to find the one line that fits closest to all the points; the regression line meets this criterion. It minimizes the sum of the squared vertical deviations of the actual observed values from the best-fit regression line.

The vertical distance between each point and the regression line is called a deviation. We will represent these deviations with e_i (where the subscript i refers to the number of the observation). A regression line is drawn through the points in Figure A1.1, and the deviations between the actual data points and the estimates you would make from the regression line are identified as e_1, e_2, e_3, and so on. Note that some of the deviations are positive (e_1, and e_4), while the others are negative (e_2, e_3, and e_5). Some errors are fairly large (such as e_2), while others are small (such as e_3). By our criterion, the best regression line is that which minimizes the sum of the squares of these deviations. The deviations from the regression line are also frequently called residuals. You are likely to see the term residuals used in printouts from computer programs that perform regression analysis.

The method of finding the values of a and b (that is, the regression line) that minimizes the sum of these squared errors is called ordinary least squares regression (OLS). Using the method of ordinary least squares, we square each of the deviations and add them up. We square the deviations so that positive and negative deviations do not cancel each other out as we find their sum. The single line that gives us the smallest sum of the squared deviations from the line is the best line according to the method of ordinary least squares.

A1.1   Interpreting the Intercept and the Slope of a Regression Model

How should we interpret the regression equation? In particular, what do the estimated values of (a) and slope (b) mean? The value of the intercept (a) indicates, at least conceptually, that if we were to extend the regression line to its intersection with the vertical axis (the point where the X variable is zero), the value of the dependent variable would be a.

We must be cautious in making such interpretations. In many cases, it is erroneous to interpret the value of a as the expected value of the dependent variable when the independent variable is zero because often our data do not include zero. In most cases the size of a is best interpreted as a positioning parameter for the height of the function. We really do not know what the function looks like as we go beyond the boundaries of our data. Recall that b represents the slope of the regression function. That is, the value of b tells us the change in the dependent variable per unit change in the independent variable.

A1.2   Underlying Assumptions of the Ordinary Least Squares (OLS) Regression Model

Several assumptions underlie the ordinary least squares regression model. A general understanding of these assumptions is necessary to appreciate both the power and limitations of OLS regression:

1   For each value of X there is a conditional probability distribution Y. Figure A1.2 shows the conditional probability distributions of Y for two of the possible values of X (X_1 and X_2). Y is specified as the dependent variable and X as the independent variable. The means of the conditional probability distributions are assumed to lie on a straight line, according to the following equation: $Y = a + bX$. In other words, the mean value of the dependent variable is assumed to be a linear function of the independent variable (note that the regression line in Figure A1.2 is directly under the peaks of the conditional probability distributions for Y).

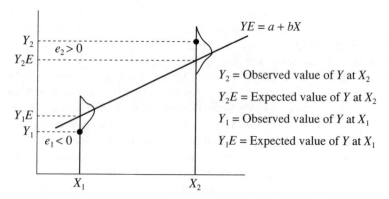

Figure A1.2   Distribution of Y values around the ordinary least squares regression line. For any X the possible values of Y are assumed to be distributed normally around the regression line. Further, the residuals (e) are assumed to be normally distributed with a mean of zero and a constant standard deviation.

2   OLS assumes that the standard deviation of each of the conditional probability distributions is the same for all values of the independent variable (such as X_1 and X_2). In Figure A1.2 the "spread" of both of the conditional probability distributions shown is the same (this characteristic of equal standard deviations is called homoscedasticity).

3   The values of the dependent variable (Y) are assumed to be independent of one another; so if one observation of Y lies below the mean of its conditional probability distribution, this does not imply that the next observation will also be below the mean (or anywhere else in particular).

4   All of the conditional probability distributions of the deviations or residuals are assumed to be normal. That is, the differences between the actual values of Y and the expected values (from the regression line) are normally distributed random variables with a mean of zero and a constant standard deviation.

These four assumptions may be viewed as the ideal to which we aspire in calculating a regression line; while these underlying assumptions of regression are sometimes violated in practice, they should be followed closely enough to ensure that estimated regression equations represent true relationships between variables. For the practitioner, it is important to note that if these four assumptions are not at least closely approximated, the resulting OLS regression analysis may be flawed. Summary statistics generally provided in most regression computer packages allow us to check compliance with these assumptions. These statistics are described below in this Appendix, together with the likely outcomes of violating these assumptions.

A1.3   Evaluation of OLS Regression Models

In this section we describe a relatively simple process that will help you evaluate OLS regression models. This process is summarized by a set of questions to ask when evaluating regression models, either those you developed or others. These questions are:

1   Does the model make sense? (That is, is the model consistent with a logical view of the situation being investigated?)

2   Is there a statistically significant relationship between the dependent and independent variables?

3   What percentage of the variation in the dependent variable does the regression model explain?

4   Is there a problem of serial correlation among the error terms in the model?

Let us now consider each of these questions and how they can be answered.

Step 1: evaluate whether the model makes sense
Never use a model that does not make sense. If the results are at odds with what logic suggests something must be wrong. For example, suppose you look at a regression of a hospital's admissions (S) as a function of the fees (P) charged per day and see the following result:

$$S = 240 + 1.22P.$$

What would you think? Would you go to management and suggest that if they want to increase admissions they should raise fees? And, if the initial price increase does not increase admissions enough they should keep increasing price because admissions are positively related to the price that is charged. Certainly not!

Clearly something is wrong with this model. Economic logic (as well as considerable empirical evidence) supports the notion that admissions and fees are inversely related in nearly all cases. Thus, we expect that the sign for the slope would be negative. When the sign of the slope term is not what logic suggests, the model does not make sense and should not be used.

The situation discussed above is not an uncommon finding when regressing sales of any good or service on price. What then is the problem that leads to such an illogical result? In this case the problem is that the model is probably *under specified*, meaning that there are additional factors that have not been included in the model that have caused sales to go up despite price increases rather than because of price increases. For example, perhaps incomes have also increased, or the size of the market has expanded due to the closing of other hospitals, or greater advertising has increased product demand. Later when we discuss multiple regression we will see how such other factors can be included in a larger regression model.

There is no statistical test to determine whether or not the model makes sense. You must do that yourself based on your understanding of the relationship being modeled. If you cannot make the correct judgment about the appropriate sign you probably do not know enough about the area of investigation to be working with the model.

Step 2: check for statistical significance
Suppose you ask 20 people to each give you the first number that comes to their mind. Then you split the 20 numbers into two sets of 10, calling one set Y and the other set X. After entering these data into a computer regression program, regress Y on X, i.e., Y as a function of X. The program churns out an intercept and slope. But does the regression equation have any useful meaning? Would you expect to find a real functional relationship between Y and X? With these two sets of numbers, the answer is no to both questions. That is, if the values for X and Y are arbitrarily selected, you would not expect to find a functional relationship between them.

If Y is not a function of X, the best estimate of Y is the mean of Y (Y_M), regardless of the value of X, since Y does not depend on X. If this is the case, the regression line would have a slope equal to zero ($b = 0$). The scattergram in Figure A1.3 illustrates such a case for the following data:

Y	14	19	10	14	9	18	20	13	8	19	14	16
X	5	6	7	10	13	13	13	15	18	18	21	21

Table A1.1 is the regression output produced from entering the above X and Y variables into data analysis under "Tools" in an Excel spreadsheet. The OLS regression

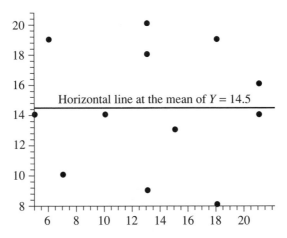

Figure A1.3   Scattergram when *Y* is not a function of *X*. Based on these 12 observations there does not appear to be a functional relationship between *X* and *Y*. When no such relationship exists, the best estimate of *Y* for any observed *X* is the mean of *Y* (Y_M).

equation for this set of points is: $Y = 14.66 - 0.012X$. The mean value of *Y* is 14.5. Note that the intercept value in the regression equation (14.66) is very close to the mean value of *Y*. In fact, if you draw the regression equation on Figure A1.3, you will find that it is very close to the horizontal line already drawn at the mean of *Y*.

Table A1.1   Regression results provided in the Excel spreadsheet

Summary output

Regression statistics	
Multiple *R*	0.016156
R square	0.000261
Adjusted *R* square	−0.09971
Standard error	4.253854
Observations	12

Anova

	df	SS	MS	F	Significance F
Regression	1	0.047244	0.047244	0.002611	0.960255
Residual	10	180.9528	18.09528		
Total	11	181			

	Coefficients	Standard error	t Stat	P-value	Lower 95%	Upper 95%	Lower 95.0%	Upper 95.0%
Intercept	14.65748	3.317646	4.418037	0.001298	7.265305	22.04966	7.265305	22.04966
X	−0.01181	0.231151	−0.0511	0.960255	−0.52685	0.503226	−0.52685	0.503226

Residual output

Observation	Predicted Y	Residuals
1	14.59843	−0.59843
2	14.58661	4.413386
3	14.5748	−4.5748
4	14.53937	−0.53937
5	14.50394	−5.50394
6	14.50394	3.496063
7	14.50394	5.496063
8	14.48031	−1.48031
9	14.44488	−6.44488
10	14.44488	4.555118
11	14.40945	−0.40945
12	14.40945	1.590551

We need some method of evaluating regression equations to see if there is a meaningful functional relationship between Y and X. This is done by using a t-test to see if the estimated slope (b_E) is statistically significantly different from zero. If it is, there is sufficient evidence in the data to support the existence of a functional relationship between Y and X.

However, if the value of b_E is not significantly different from zero, we would conclude that Y is not a linear function of X.

A t-test is used to test the null hypothesis that the slope of the true relationship between Y and X is equal to zero. You could write this null hypothesis as

$$H_0: \beta = 0$$

The t-statistic used for this t-test is calculated as follows:

$$t_c = (b_E - 0) \div (SE \text{ of } b_E)$$

Where SE of b_E is the standard error of b_E (the standard deviation of the probability distribution of the estimator). The standard error is included in the output of virtually all regression programs; it is derived from the residuals, or deviations, between each point and the regression line. The value of t_c indicates how many standard errors our estimate of β is from zero. The larger the absolute value of the t-ratio, the more confident you can be that the true value of β is not zero. Most regression programs provide the calculated t-statistic (t_c) as a standard part of regression output.

The statistical test of the significance for a regression coefficient can take any of the following three forms:

Case 1: $H_1: \beta \neq 0$
This form is appropriate when you are just testing for the existence of any linear functional relationship between Y and X. In this case, you have no reason to think that the slope will be either positive or negative.

Case 2: H_1: $\beta < 0$
This form is appropriate if you think that the relationship between Y and X is an inverse one. That is, you would use this form when you expect an increase (decrease) in X to cause a decrease (increase) in Y.

Case 3: H_1: $\beta > 0$
This form is appropriate if you think that the relationship between Y and X is a direct one. That is, you would use this form when you expect an increase (decrease) in X to cause an increase (decrease) in Y.

Situations such as described in case 1 imply the use of a two-tailed test. This means that if we want to have a 95 percent confidence level, we would have 2.5 percent of the total area under the t-distribution in the outer part of each tail of the t-distribution, as illustrated here in Figure A1.4.

A 95 percent confidence interval is the same as a 5 percent significance level. The confidence level and the significance level always sum to 1.0. The symbol α (alpha) is usually used to represent a significance level. Thus, in this example, $\alpha = 0.05$, and since we have a two-tailed test we split the significance level between the two tails of the distribution. That is, $\alpha/2$ is the area under each tail of the t-distribution.

In performing a t-test, we not only have to decide on a significance level, but we also have to correctly identify the number of degrees of freedom to use. In

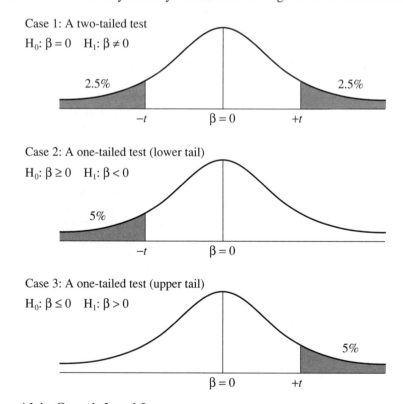

Case 1: A two-tailed test
H_0: $\beta = 0$ H_1: $\beta \neq 0$

2.5%   2.5%

$-t$ $\beta = 0$ $+t$

Case 2: A one-tailed test (lower tail)
H_0: $\beta \geq 0$ H_1: $\beta < 0$

5%

$-t$ $\beta = 0$

Case 3: A one-tailed test (upper tail)
H_0: $\beta \leq 0$ H_1: $\beta > 0$

5%

$\beta = 0$ $+t$

Figure A1.4   Cases 1, 2, and 3

bivariate linear regressions, the appropriate number of degrees of freedom (df) is: $df = n - 2$. Where n equals the number of observations used in determining the values of a and b and 2 is the number of parameters estimated.

For a two-tailed test we reject the null hypothesis if the absolute value of t_c is greater than the table value of t at the desired confidence level. As an example of using a two-tailed t-test, consider the data shown in the scattergram of Figure A1.3. In that case, you would have no reason to expect the slope to be either positive or negative. You would just be testing to see if the estimated value was indeed statistically significantly different from zero. Recall that the regression equation for that data is:

$$Y = 14.66 - 0.012X$$

Our null hypothesis is that the slope is equal to zero; that is, H_0: $\beta = 0$. The alternative hypothesis is that the slope is not equal to zero; that is, H_1: $\beta \neq 0$. The regression output on your calculator or computer should indicate that the standard error of b for this regression is 0.231, so we find t_c as follows:

$$t_c = (-0.012 - 0) \div (0.231) = -0.052$$

There were 12 observations, so the number of degrees of freedom is: $df = 12 - 2 = 10$. For a two-tailed test with a 0.05 significance level, the critical absolute value (ignoring the sign) for t would have to be greater than 2.228, based on t-tables available in most statistical textbooks. A rule of thumb is often used in evaluating t-ratios when a t-table is not handy. The rule is that the slope term is likely to be significantly different from zero if the absolute value of the calculated t-ratio is greater than 2. This is a handy rule to remember as you analyze regression studies presented in the Applications.

In this sample of 12 pairs of random numbers, the absolute value of the calculated t of -0.052 is not greater than 2, so we do not have enough evidence to reject the null hypothesis that the value of the coefficient is really 0. In fact, the P-value, provided in Table A1.1 indicates that if the true value of the coefficient were 0, the statistical deviation from 0 in our example of random numbers is expected in approximately 96 percent of similar tests. Therefore, we conclude that there is no statistically significant linear relationship between Y and X at a 5 percent significance level ($\alpha = 0.05$).

Situations such as those described in cases 2 and 3 call for the use of a one-tailed test because we are only concerned with being either below zero (case 2) or above zero (case 3). In these cases, if we want to be 95 percent confident, we would have the entire 5 percent significance level in the outer part of either the lower (case 2) or upper (case 3) tail of the distribution. The number of degrees of freedom is still equal to $n - 2$.

Step 3: determine the explanatory power of the model
The dependent variable (Y) used in a regression analysis varies with the value of the independent variable (X). Otherwise there would be no reason to try to model Y. Therefore, it is convenient to have a measure of how much of that variation in Y is explained by the regression model. That is just what the coefficient of determination (R^2) does for us.

The coefficient of determination (R^2) tells us the percentage of the variation in the dependent variable (Y) that is explained by the regression model. The worst possible explanatory power a model could have is to explain none of the variation in the dependent variable ($R^2 = 0$), and the best possible model would be one that explains all of the variation in the dependent variable ($R^2 = 1.0$).

The coefficient of determination (R^2) will always be a value between 0 and 1. The closer it is to 0 the lower the explanatory power of the model, while the closer R^2 is to 1 the greater is the explanatory power of the model. Suppose $R^2 = 0.67$ for a regression model. This would then mean that 67 percent of the variation in the dependent variable is explained by that model.

We rarely calculate the coefficient of determination by hand. Virtually all regression analyses are done using a computer. The coefficient of determination provided on a computer printout is generally identified as "R squared" or "R^2." In our example in Table A1.1 of made-up pairs, R squared is 0.0003 percent; variations in Y are not explained well by variations in X.

Step 4: check the distribution of the error terms
One assumption of OLS regression is that the error, or residual, terms are normally distributed random variables with a mean of zero and a constant variance. Therefore, we do not expect to find any regular pattern in the error terms. Whenever a significant time pattern is found in the error terms, serial correlation is indicated.

Figure A1.5 illustrates the two cases of serial correlation. In the left-hand graph, negative serial correlation is apparent. Negative serial correlation exists when a negative error is followed by a positive error, then another negative error, and so on. The error terms alternate in signs. Positive serial correlation is shown in the right-hand graph in Figure A1.5. In positive serial correlation, positive errors tend to be followed by other positive errors, while negative errors are followed by other negative errors.

With serial correlation, problems occur in using and interpreting the OLS regression function. Serial correlation does not bias the estimated coefficients, but it does make the standard errors smaller than the true standard errors. The *t*-ratios calculated for each coefficient will be overstated, which in turn leads to rejecting null hypotheses that should not have been rejected. That is, regression coefficients may be deemed statistically significant when indeed they are not. In addition, the existence of serial correlation causes the R^2 to be unreliable in evaluating the overall significance of the regression function.

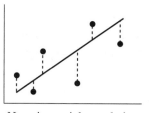
Negative serial correlation

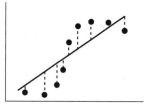
Positive serial correlation

Figure A1.5   Negative and positive serial correlation problems. Negative serial correlation is illustrated on the left, positive on the right. The residuals are indicated by dashed lines.

There are ways to test for serial correlation. The method most frequently used is the Durbin–Watson statistic (DW). It is calculated as follows:

$$DW = \Sigma(e_t - e_{t-1})^2 \div \Sigma e_t^2$$

where e_t is the residual for time period t and e_{t-1} is the residual for the preceding $(t - 1)$ time period. Regression analysis in statistical software generally includes the Durbin–Watson statistic, so you are not likely to ever have to calculate it directly. This statistic is not provided in Table A1.1. You may, however, check the residuals for any obvious patterns, although with merely 12 observations any observation or calculated DW (2.51 in this example) may be misleading.

The DW statistic will always be in the range of 0 to 4. As the value of the DW statistic approaches 4, the degree of negative serial correlation increases. As the value of DW approaches 0, positive serial correlation appears more severe. As a rule of thumb, a value close to 2 indicates that there is no serial correlation.

You might wonder what causes serial correlation. A primary cause of positive serial correlation, the most common form in business/economic analyses, is the existence of long-term cycles and trends in the data. Serial correlation can also result from a misspecification of the model.

If we find a problem with serial correlation we can try several relatively simple things to reduce the problem. One is to use first differences of the variables rather than the actual values when performing the regression analysis. That is, use the change in each variable from period to period in the regression. Other potential solutions involve adding additional variables and/or nonlinear terms to the model.

A1.4   Point and Interval Estimates

Regression equations are often used to make estimates of the value of the dependent variable for a given value of the independent variable. When such estimates are made, it is common to give both a point and an interval estimate. The point estimate is generated directly from the regression equation.

Point estimates are useful. Estimating a precise number is often preferred to a range, but it is generally not accurate. Thus, it is often preferable to make an interval estimate in such a way that we can say we are 95 percent (or some other percent) confident that the true value will be somewhere in the interval. A simple approximation for a 95 percent confidence interval for a general bivariate regression model can be given as:

$$Y = Y_E \pm 2(SEE)$$

where Y_E is the point estimate and SEE is the standard error of the estimate. The value for SEE is part of the output of nearly all regression programs.[1]

---

[1] However, it can also be easily calculated as follows:

$$SEE = [\Sigma(Y_i - Y_{iE})^2 \div (n - 2)]^{0.5}$$

where n is the number of observations used in the estimation of the regression equation. (The 0.5 power is the same as the square root.)

A1.5   Multiple Linear Regression

In many applications, the dependent variable is a function of more than one independent variable. In such cases, a form of OLS regression called multiple linear regression is appropriate. Applications in this text contain several multi-linear regressions. This technique is a straightforward extension of simple linear regression and is built on the same basic set of assumptions.

The general form of the multiple linear regression model is:

$$Y = f(X_1, X_2, \ldots, X_n)$$
$$Y = \alpha + \beta_1 X_1 + \beta_2 X_2 + \ldots + \beta_n X_n$$

where Y represents the dependent variable, and the X_i terms represent different independent variables. The intercept, or constant, term in the regression is α, and the β_i terms represent slope terms, or changes in the cefficients of the independent variables.

The addition of more independent variables to the basic regression model is helpful in developing better models. Doing so, however, adds to the four-step evaluation process discussed previously. You will recall that those four steps involved answering these questions:

1   Does the model make sense? (That is, is the model consistent with a logical view of the situation being investigated?)
2   Is there a statistically significant relationship between the dependent and independent variables?
3   What percentage of the variation in the dependent variable does the regression model explain?
4   Is there a problem of serial correlation among the error terms in the model?

For multiple regression we need to add a fifth question.

5   Does there appear to be multicolinearity among the independent variables?

Multicolinearity
Multicolinearity results when the independent variables are highly correlated with one another. Whenever multicolinearity exists, the regression may not be reliable. In particular, coefficients may be incorrect.

Two factors might indicate a multicolinearity problem. First, if the standard errors of the coefficients are large relative to the estimated coefficients (resulting in unacceptably low t-ratios) for variables that you expect to be significant, multicolinearity is likely. Second, if pairs of independent variables have high correlation coefficients, a multicolinearity problem may exist. It is therefore important to examine the correlation coefficients for all pairs of the independent variables included in the regression. If two or more independent variables move together, their relationship introduces bias in explaining the dependent variable. One should avoid using pairs of independent variables that have simple correlation coefficients much above 0.7. In practice, with the data that we have in economic analyses, this is sometimes a high standard to live with and we may end up using pairs of variables that have a higher correlation if everything else in the model is acceptable.

The existence of multicolinearity may explain why a coefficient's sign is contrary to expectations, such as including both SAT (Scholastic Aptitude Test) scores and high school grade point average to determine a student's university grade point average. These two measures have a very high correlation. One would expect a positive relationship between high school and university grade point average, but if SAT results were to be included in the model it is quite likely that one would have a negative coefficient causing us to reject the model in the first step of our evaluation. Using two highly correlated variables as independent variables is an example of *over specification* of a regression model. So you now see that either under specification or over specification of a model may lead to signs for coefficients that are counter intuitive and thus would lead to rejection of the model on the basis of economic logic.

When multicolinearity exists, it does not necessarily mean that the regression function cannot be useful. The individual coefficients may not be reliable, but as a group they are likely to contain compensating errors. One may be too high, but another is likely to be too low (even to the extreme of having signs which are the opposite of your expectations). As a result, if your *only* interest is in using the regression for prediction, the entire function may perform satisfactorily. However, you could not use the model to evaluate the influence of individual independent variables on the dependent variable. Thus, one would rarely, if ever, use a model for which multicolinearity was a problem. Some things can be done to reduce multicolinearity problems, such as removing all but one of the highly intercorrelated variables from the regression.

The adjusted $\bar{R}^2$

When working with multiple regression models the adjusted coefficient of determination is used rather than the simple R^2 because the unadjusted R^2 will always increase as *any* new independent variable is added to a model, whether the variable is relevant or not. The adjusted coefficient of determination is usually designated $\bar{R}^2$. It so happens that adding any additional independent variable will cause R^2 to go up but may or may not cause R^2 to rise. Thus, in interpreting multiple linear regression results one should always look at the adjusted coefficient of determination to evaluate the explanatory power of the model rather than the standard R^2.[2]

The diagrams in Figure A1.6 illustrate relatively high and low coefficients of determination for multiple linear regression functions. The graph at the top of the figure illustrates a regression plane with college applications as a function of tuition and a quality of education index. Six data points are shown to be not far from the

---

[2] The relationship between R^2 and $\bar{R}^2$ is:

$$\bar{R}^2 = 1 - (1 - R^2) \div [(n - 1)/\{n - (K + 1)\}]$$

where n represents the number of observations and K represents the number of independent variables. You can see that if n is large relative to K there will be little difference between R^2 and $\bar{R}^2$.

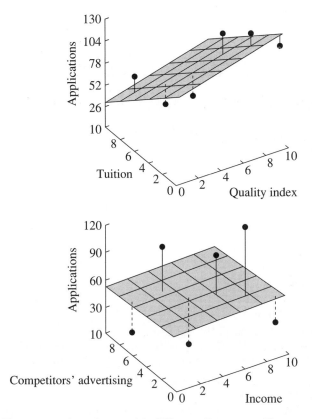

Figure A1.6   Two regression planes with different *R*-squares. The upper regression plane would have a higher coefficient of determination than would the lower one. Note that the six data points in the upper graph cluster closer to the plane than do the six data points in the lower graph.

regression plane and so the coefficient of determination would be relatively high. The lower graph shows a college's applications as a function of competitors' advertising and income revenue. Here you see that the data points are further from the regression plane and so the coefficient of determination would be lower. Therefore, a model using tuition charges and perceived quality better explains the number of applications than a model using a competitor's advertising and income.

2
Characteristics of the Government and Private Nonprofit Sectors

2.1   INTRODUCTION

The U.S. economy contains three sectors: the private for-profit business sector, the government sector, and the private nonprofit sector. Within all three sectors, firms produce goods and services, and each firm must earn or receive revenue equal to expenses in order to function and survive. Firms in the two NFP sectors are distinguished by missions that address public wellbeing or the non-pecuniary interests of a particular group; firms in the profit-seeking sector maximize profits and stockholder wealth.

Decision-makers in both NFP sectors, public and private, operate within the larger economy. They purchase market inputs and earn revenue from clients who purchase the NFPs' outputs directly or indirectly through contributions or taxes. NFPs are financed with user fees, donations of time and money, and government revenue. Private nonprofits receiving no direct government revenue may, nevertheless, be indirectly subsidized through tax laws, loans, and grants. The goal of this chapter is to understand the role nonprofit and government firms play within the whole economy.

Before tackling the finances of NFP firms, it is essential to differentiate stocks versus flows. A *flow* is output over a period of time; a *stock* is an accumulation. Your monthly paycheck and expenditures are flows; the size of your bank account on a particular date is a stock. The federal government yearly deficit or surplus, equal to taxes minus expenditures, is a flow. On the other hand, the national debt, the accumulation of past deficits, is a stock. A NFP firm's yearly output, donations, and budget deficits are flows that appear in its income or activity statements. Wealth, endowments, and total debt are stock concepts shown in its balance sheet on a particular date.

2.2   PROPERTY RIGHTS

The concept of property is essential to understanding how any family, business, or NFP operates. Early settlers in the American West cooperated in building schools across the land. Suppose that once built, anyone could strip them for firewood or claim them for whatever purpose. Then, there would have been little incentive to build them in the first place. Property rights determine the legal right to build, to decide on use, and to sell. Property rights are the most common and effective institution for providing incentives to create and care for assets and to use these assets for a given purpose.

Property rights do not make some people better off (i.e., communities with schools) while injuring others (i.e., communities lacking schools). Schools were initially built not at the expense of non-residents, but by residents who agreed to build and operate them. In areas lacking clearly established property rights, incentives to create worthwhile assets are virtually nonexistent, and living standards are low in general. NFP educational, medical, social, or religious institutions fail to thrive in the absence of clearly defined property rights. Legitimate accumulation is essential for any institution in the NFP sectors dependent on client fees, sponsorship, and donations.

Administrators plan and are more effective if the institutions with which they are associated have legal standing. The private and government NFP sectors are affected by property rights in three ways. First, each firm rests squarely on its legal standing and right to operate. Second, without property right protection, a firm is precluded from acquiring resources. Finally, NFP firms require autonomy in providing certain goods and services having unique characteristics.

2.3   PUBLIC GOODS

Private goods are different from public goods. A can of Coke is probably best described as a purely **private good** given two characteristics. First, consumption of a can of Coke is rival; if you drink it there is clearly less available for me. Second, if you own it, I do not have a right to the Coke and you may easily exclude me or anyone else from consuming it.

Not all goods and services by their very nature have clearly defined, secure, and assigned property rights. In these cases, economists say there is a **free rider problem** (sometimes called a *public goods problem*). Whenever more than one person has the right to a single shared resource, a free rider problem occurs and there is a propensity to overuse or misuse the product. Likewise, when more than one individual has the obligation to provide something, it will be under-supplied. Each person hopes that others will do the providing. You, for example, may have observed a free rider problem if one of your three roommates has an automobile and initially is expected to provide transportation for all four. Overuse and even damage to the car occurs because non-owners take unnecessary trips and/or haul heavy items in the owner's vehicle. An under-supply of transportation results because no one is willing to repair the present vehicle or purchase another. In this case, an arrangement acceptable to all three roommates concerning the use of private goods with clearly defined property rights needs to be worked out. It is even more difficult to avoid the free rider problem with goods having characteristics that make them truly public.

Public goods (and services) are jointly consumed by all members of society and are defined by two characteristics: non-rival consumption and non-exclusion. In **non-rival consumption**, one person's consumption does not limit consumption by others. The marginal or extra cost of providing one more unit of the good to an additional individual is essentially zero. National defense is non-rival; the next person entering the United States (by birth or immigration) receives the same amount of national defense as anyone else residing in the country. An extra person does not add to national defense costs nor does the presence of that person result in fewer defenses available for the rest of us. Hence, the marginal cost of providing service to an extra individual is zero.

Non-exclusion means that it would be prohibitively expensive or impossible to exclude anyone from consuming a good once provided. Again, national defense is a good example, although many services such as police and fire protection, highways, public libraries, and flood control projects are non-exclusionary to some degree. No practical way exists to exclude individuals from receiving benefits from an item already provided to others in the group.

Profit-seeking firms do not provide sufficient amounts of public goods. Economists call this market failure, a concept discussed at length further on in this text. The market mechanism does not work because there is no real market for, let's say, national defense.

NFP administrators are acutely aware of both the circumstances, legal or otherwise, in which they may exclude clients, and of their firm's capacity. Often they manage firms responsible for providing public goods as compared with purely private goods, and the measurement of individuals' demand for public goods is challenging. In Chapter 3, we present different techniques for determining private good versus public good demand; here we concentrate on merely distinguishing between types of goods.

Non-rival consumption and non-exclusion are not present in all public goods; some public goods have both characteristics (true public goods) while others have perhaps one of these characteristics to some degree. Technically, an emergency health facility can exclude clients from receiving care (that is rival), but legally it may be required to stabilize all who present themselves as patients.

It helps to think of all goods and services divided into four categories depending on *non-rival consumption* and *non-exclusion* characteristics. Each of the four clarifies the nature of a certain public good, but in practice the division is not so clear. Non-rival consumption and non-exclusion are not "yes or no" situations. They are a matter of degree, not absolutes.

Consider the upper left-hand corner of Figure 2.1, which includes purely private goods such as a can of Coke. The lower right-hand corner of Figure 2.1 presents the polar opposite of a purely private good: a purely *public good*. Police protection or national defense is enjoyed by everyone in the community without reducing the amount available for others; hence it is non-rivalrous. Police protection also is non-excludable because there is no practical way to exclude anyone from receiving the benefit.

Goods representing the two remaining portions of Figure 2.1 are more difficult to classify because they are neither essentially private goods nor purely public goods. A **collective good** is one that has non-rivalrous consumption but it can exclude.

| | Non-rivalrous consumption | |
	No	Yes
Non-excludability — No	Private goods (Can of Coke)	Collective goods (Theater)
Non-excludability — Yes	Commons (Ocean fishery)	Public goods (National defense)

Figure 2.1   All goods and services may be classified on the basis of two characteristics

Viewers together collectively enjoy a film in a movie theater. One extra person does not result in less enjoyment for any other viewer (up to the point of capacity or congestion); hence, theater attendance is considered non-rivalrous consumption. Theaters, however, exclude anyone without a ticket. Therefore, theaters produce a good which is neither purely private nor purely public.

Ocean fisheries or community grazing lands are examples of *commons*, as shown in the lower left-hand corner of Figure 2.1. A *commons* is non-excludable but rivalrous. Consider that part of an ocean in which a fishing fleet normally operates. To maintain the stock of fish, breeding must be ensured. Yet, any boat owner has the right to fish the area; the ocean is non-excludable. The catch of one boat rivals another and "over-fishing" may occur. Individual fishermen have an incentive to harvest as many fish as possible in a given season. Why would one boat owner economize on the number of fish taken now? If an individual boat owner does not harvest the fish, someone else will. Nothing is gained by a single boat owner economizing and saving breeding fish for the future. Such is the nature of any commons (sometimes referred to as the "tragedy of the commons").

The provisions of public and quasi-public goods

The nature of public goods has led to the development of unique types of firms providing them. Consider the following situation. An island economy wishes to build and maintain a lighthouse to warn ships of danger. The existence of the lighthouse will benefit each ship but no single ship owner is inclined to build a lighthouse. If one individual were to build and maintain a lighthouse there would be no way to recoup costs. How could this "lighthouse owner" charge other ship owners for lighthouse use?

Any captain can use the lighthouse for guidance without permission; there is no effective way to control usage and coerce ship owners into paying. If the lighthouse owner tried to sell "shares" in the lighthouse to potential users (thus treating the lighthouse as a private good), few would purchase shares because they can *free ride*, simply use the service without paying.

A lighthouse is clearly a public good, having the characteristic of non-excludability. A lighthouse has as well non-rivalrous consumption because any ship guided and protected by its light does not diminish the amount of light available to other captains. Without a lighthouse, all ships are in danger. Yet, no single ship owner has the monetary incentive to build one. A reasonable alternative is for an association of ship owners to build a lighthouse collectively. This association is essentially a private nonprofit firm because the collective effort is voluntary. The problem with this solution is that it will still give rise to free riding on the part of potential beneficiaries. To eliminate free riding, a political body, mandating the project, compels ship owners or citizens in general to "contribute" by assessing taxes, and a government firm is often established to provide the service.

Quasi-public goods have some public good characteristics or are perceived by nonprofit sponsors or voters to provide public benefits. Usually, but not always, NFP firms engage in services with public benefits. Nonprofits, at times, subsidize private services in order to further their primary mission, and governments often finance private goods for political reasons.

2.4   TYPES OF NOT-FOR-PROFIT (NFP) FIRM

NFP firms, at their best, are expected to be fundamentally socializing institutions. They operate in industries having public good characteristics. These industries include art, education and research, environmental and animal protection, health and human services, international development, public and social services, and religion. Each NFP firm, operating in a given industry, is unique in terms of its tradition, sponsor, donors, clients, and methods. NFP firms are expected to identify their goals and reason for being in mission statements. In jest, some observers suggest that the mission or original intent of the founders is already lost if a NFP needs to formalize it! However, a *mission statement* is a self-imposed duty intended to focus and direct the efforts of everyone employed by the firm. At a minimum, a mission statement contains a statement of purpose and identifies those served.

Government firms

Public or government agencies come into being by legal authorities that continue to fund and operate them. Residents of these political units own them collectively. U.S. citizens, therefore, are "shareholders" in the largest fiscal entity in the country: the federal government. The United States has adopted the Public Trust Doctrine, an ancient mandate, under which a sovereign holds unique natural resources in trust for the benefit of the general public. Yellowstone National Park, for example, is owned by the federal government. Although the federal government is the ultimate trustee of public resources, states in some instances interpret and administer the law in ways to maximize public benefit. All public firms obtain a portion of revenue by involuntary transfers, in other words, from taxes.

In section 2.3 we discussed "public" goods and now "public" institutions. Application 2.1 attempts to describe the various meanings of the word. In this text, we use the word "public" to imply government sponsorship.

APPLICATION 2.1
"Public or Private?" and "Going Public"

It may be, as one wag noted, that a common language separates Americans from the British. Consider the ways in which the word "public" can be used as an adjective and then realize that the same usage does not apply in different countries.

1   Concerning or affecting the community or the people: *the public good.*
2   Maintained for or used by the people or community: *a public park.*

3 Participated in or attended by the people or community: *public worship*.
4 Connected with or acting on behalf of the people, community, or government, rather than private matters or interests: *public office*.
5 Open to the knowledge or judgment of all; notorious: *a public scandal*.

In this text, we use the term "public not-for-profit enterprise" to refer to a government agency. Churches are considered "private nonprofits" even though most are open for public worship. On the other hand, the British use the word "public" to describe a school with open enrollment, such as Eton. Prep schools in the United States open to anyone qualifying and willing to pay tuition are called "private."

Increasingly in the literature, the term "public administration" refers to the study of and management of public and private firms that operate in the government and private nonprofit sector.

What does it mean when a profit-seeking firm "goes public"? In a privately held corporation, stock ownership formerly was issued to insiders: founders and employees. "Going public" indicates that shares will be sold to the general public.

Similarly, private nonprofits can "go public." Philadelphia's Pew Charitable Trusts, the 11th-largest foundation in the country, requested and was granted a change in status, from private to public charity. As a private charity set up by family members, Pew formerly funded programs operated by other nonprofits. It was not permitted to manage them. Pew depended on its endowment and could not lobby government. Since 2004, as a public foundation, it can petition for exemptions from various state taxes and from the 2 percent federal tax on its net investment income. It may use as much as 20 percent of its annual spending for lobbying purposes, and raise funds from other foundations for its causes. It is no longer a grant-giving foundation, but a public charity with its own programs.

What criteria does a private foundation have to meet in order to go public? Basically, its funding must come from a wider base of donors. For provisional approval, any single donor's gift may only account for 2 percent of yearly revenue with 10 percent coming from public support. A foundation qualifies for permanent public charity status on receiving more than one-third of its support from the public over a four-year period.

However, a "public" foundation is still a private nonprofit!

Source: John Anderson, "Will the Pew's Fine Print Determine the Fate of the Barnes Foundation?" *Wall Street Journal*, December 9, 2003, D12.

Private nonprofits

The private nonprofit sector is sometimes called the "voluntary" or "third" sector. According to those that sponsor or subsidize nonprofit firms, these non-governmental organizations (NGOs) are public-serving institutions. They are engaged in activities that are neither sufficiently provided nor addressed by the other two sectors. In some instances, government and/or the private market produce similar services. In heterogeneous societies, such as the United States, subgroups prefer differentiated services, tailored to their tastes. Nonprofit firms supplement government. For example, in a particular community, government may provide only half-day kindergarten for 5- and 6-year-old children. A private non-profit meets the needs of some parents by offering full-day programs, after school care, and/or specialized classes. Quasi-public goods, supplied by such nonprofit firms, have both private- and public-good components.

Economists make distinctions between types and levels of education based on their public good component. Basic literacy, civics, and hygiene are justified as public goods warranting full public support. Higher education is a quasi-public good, in that its consumption yields a large portion of private benefits, and individuals may be willing to purchase it privately. In some instances, such as university, when critical professionals are in short supply, third-level education is a public good. Developing countries often lack financial markets offering loans to those qualified for training in skills critical for national wellbeing. In addition, the return in the form of expected personal income must be sufficient for individuals to acquire educational debt. In developed economies, a good case can be made that upper-level education primarily benefits those who receive it and increases their future earnings potential. Application 2.2 describes how public universities are increasingly expected to expand tuition to cover operating expenses.

APPLICATION 2.2
Are State Universities Being Privatized?

From what sources does your university receive funding? Sources of revenue define a particular NFP firm. An article in the *Wall Street Journal* indicates that in the United States state universities with declining government revenue as a percentage of their total budgets are demanding more independence. State legislatures presently control everything from staff salaries and tuition to the size of a purchase requiring legislative approval.

University administrators have not initiated measures to reduce state financing and do not enjoy forfeiting funds for expanding classrooms and other infrastructure. However, state aid, 46 percent of university budgets nationwide in 1980, was down to 36 percent in 2000. At the same time, large public universities are attracting large numbers of out-of-state students and hold research contracts. Increasingly, they

desire independence from state government in order to seek alternative revenue sources.

Proposals to make up for declines in state financing include:

- Charging in-state and out-of-state students identical tuition
  and providing partial scholarships for in-state students.
- Permitting law and business schools to become self-
  supporting in return for some percentage of tuition and other
  revenue rebated to the university for overhead expenses.
- Charging more for degrees in high demand like business and
  less for programs like social work.
- Dropping yearly appropriations for state universities and
  offering vouchers to in-state students.
- Raising tuition for out-of-state students to the level of fees
  charged at similarly regarded private institutions.
- Having state legislatures match any private funds collected
  by universities.

Administrators are being required to compete with elite private
schools in number and quality of students, faculty, and facilities. State
legislatures are compelling state universities to compete for funds
as they feel the pressure to redirect funds to medical care, primary
education, infrastructure, etc. (see table).

State support as a share of university budgets, 2002–3 academic year

University	State aid % revenue	University	State aid % revenue
California, Berkeley[a]	39	Missouri	21[b]
Florida State	33	North Carolina,	
Illinois, Urbana–Champaign	22	Chapel Hill[a]	25
Iowa State	58	Ohio State	18
Miami–Ohio	22	Texas–System	22
Michigan	10	Virginia	13[b]
		Wisconsin, Madison	25

[a] 2001–2 academic year;
[b] excludes medical center.

Source: June Kronholz, "Schools Trim State Ties," *Wall Street Journal*, April
18, 2003, B1.

Quasi-public state universities in the United States, together with quasi-private
nonprofit universities, receive government grants, sponsor government funded
military training, and benefit from subsidized student aid.

Operating across a variety of industries, the United States has 1.6 million firms
operating in the private nonprofit sector. In other countries, the private nonprofit

sector is nonexistent or underdeveloped. Private nonprofit proliferation in the United States flows from a unique approach to charitable giving and volunteering. Communal self-help was initiated on a large continent settled without strong central government, without hereditary aristocracy, and without an established state religion. As early as 1831, de Tocqueville, a French scholar studying prison reform, noted a pattern of voluntary associations in the United States. Private associations were providing what members of the British aristocracy or the French government provided. During the nineteenth century, "communal self-help" evolved first to serve those less fortunate through "charity" and then to "philanthropy." The distinction may be made that charity is directed toward alleviating suffering and deprivation whereas philanthropy attempts to understand and enhance lives. In these terms, creating orphanages represents charity and creating libraries, philanthropy.

About 70 percent of U.S. households make charitable cash contributions each year and over half regularly contribute time to voluntary organizations. Application 2.3 summarizes the results of a 2007 study conducted by Indiana University's Center on Philanthropy on routine charitable giving by U.S. households. Government is a partner in this activity, because those itemizing deductions can deduct amounts donated from their taxable income. With a marginal tax rate of 35 percent, this can amount to $35 less in taxes for every $100 donated. Donations may be reduced if more households become subject to the Alternative Minimum Tax (AMT) and are thereby unable to adjust taxable income for donations.

In general, low-income families are less likely to itemize their deductions but nevertheless support many nonprofits, particularly religious organizations. In fact, the poor contribute a larger portion of their income to nonprofits than the middle class. However, because they tend not to itemize, the less affluent fail to receive tax benefits from charitable giving. Consequently, nonprofit firms preferred by the affluent have traditionally had a tax advantage over those supported by those with lower incomes.

APPLICATION 2.3
Philanthropy Panel Study on U.S. Household Contributions

About 6 in 10 U.S. households contribute to charity routinely, according to a study conducted by the Center on Philanthropy Panel Study (COPPS) and released by the Center on Philanthropy at Indiana University. Among households that gave in 2004, the average total amount given was $2,045.

The panel surveyed the same 8,000 families about charitable gifts made in 2000, 2002, and 2004. The total percentage of households that gave each year was about 70 percent but the same households did not consistently contribute. The study found that nearly one-third shifts between donating and not donating from year to year.

Eugene R. Tempel, executive director of the Center on Philanthropy at Indiana University, explained that the goal of COPPS in surveying the same families was to understand the factors that influence people's giving and the causes of change.

Center researchers found that 56 percent of households consistently donated in each of the three years. Persistent donors made total charitable gifts averaging $2,659 in 2004. Another 3 in 10 households (29 percent) contributed to charity in some but not all years studied. Occasional donors in 2004 (who gave in 1 or 2 of the 3 years) contributed an average of $820. Just under 15 percent of households did not contribute at all in any of the years studied.

Other key findings about giving in 2004 include:

- The largest percentage of households gave to religion, donating an average of $1,858.
- To meet others' basic needs, 28 percent gave $482 on average.
- Higher-income donor households, those with incomes of $100,000 or more, give a lower percentage of their income on average (2.2 percent of income) than do those with incomes under $50,000, who give 4.2 percent of their income.
- However, higher-income households are more likely to give: 93 percent of higher-income households reported charitable donations of $25 or more, compared to 56 percent of lower-income households.
- About 45 percent of households give to religious organizations, 60 percent give to secular organizations, and 37 percent give to both types.

COPPS is conducted every two years in conjunction with the University of Michigan's Institute for Social Research Panel Study of Income Dynamics (PSID). Analysis of COPPS data assists nonprofits to understand how and why people give and to strengthen their ability to raise funds. The data also allow policy-makers to evaluate the potential impact of tax law changes that could stimulate or hinder giving by changing tax rates, tax brackets, or types of tax deductible donations.

Source: Center on Philanthropy at Indiana University, December 4, 2007, http://www.philanthropy.iupui.edu/Research/giving_fundraising_research.aspx.

Countries, such as The Netherlands, have a relatively larger private nonprofit sector than the United States, but the sector is more directly subsidized by government. Quasi-public goods, such as education, are financed through taxes by but not necessarily as part of the public sector. For centuries, private nonprofit groups in Europe have provided humanitarian assistance abroad to Asia, Africa, Latin America, and the Middle East. At present, European governments co-finance and channel their overseas aid through private charitable organizations. Government can be thought of as an effective collector and provider of funds but not necessarily the most effective organization to deliver service to clients.

A flourishing nonprofit sector depends on property rights, which are residual rather than absolute and permit activities otherwise not proscribed by law or regulation. The right of individuals to associate freely enables nonprofit sponsors to establish corporations, own land and facilities, as well as contract for labor and supplies. They are free to provide certain public and quasi-public mission related goods and services in competition with government and profit-seeking firms.

Not-for-profit firms, both public and private, are multi-product organizations providing public or differentiated public goods, generally not available in profit-seeking markets. An art museum, for example, is formed to preserve art treasures for the general enjoyment of viewers and future generations. Art museums provide three distinct types of services: (1) art preservation, a public good, (2) opportunities to view the collection and attend classes, quasi-public goods, and (3) dining and gift shops, purely private goods. Quasi-public and private goods directly benefit individuals, and individual households pay partially or in full for these services in the form of user fees. Entrance fees and tuition for viewing the collection or attending class generally do not fully cover costs, but, nevertheless, contribute to revenue.

It is not unusual for nonprofits to engage in commercial activities unrelated or loosely related to their mission. These activities are called **unrelated business activities**. The intention of entering into unrelated business activities is to generate revenue to subsidize primary activities. A museum's restaurant or gift shop, when it works as intended, earns funds for the purchasing or conservation of masterpieces. At times, NFP firms, embarking on unrelated business activities, fail to consider all associated costs and end up redirecting scarce funds away from their missions. Unrelated business activities should subsidize or, at a minimum, complement mission.

As a **holding company**, a NFP can establish profit-seeking subsidiaries. The parent firm maintains control by appointing board members. A NFP *holding company* engages in three basic strategies. First, the parent NFP manages a subsidiary with the sole purpose of producing unrelated business income with which to cross-subsidize preferred activities. For example, a university could sponsor a subsidiary athletic facility and bookstore specifically to earn revenue. Second, a parent company attempts to lower its costs by delivering a specialized service to itself through a subsidiary, such as a university established subsidiary to provide residential services. Finally, a NFP firm, such as a university, could directly operate a subsidiary summer sports' camp, somewhat related to its mission, in order to generate revenue, to utilize excess capacity, and to provide off-season employment.

Profit-seeking firms use standard accounting practices to assess tax liability, to determine profit and net worth, and for decision-making. Some NFP firms employ standard accounting as well but not necessarily for the same reasons. All NFPs need some method for measuring accountability to donors/sponsors and for making decisions. Unfortunately, there are limitations on accurate NFP calculations of wealth. It is difficult and in some cases not worth the expense to place a precise value on a NFP's assets, such as single-purpose facilities, reputation, lists of donors, etc. Nevertheless, a NFP manager at a minimum must learn to prepare annual budgets and to interpret activity and balance statements.

Suppose that a private nonprofit firm ends up with a flow of ***net income***. Net income is the excess (or deficit) of total revenue coming into the firm in a given time period minus total costs. The general public sometimes comment with a knowing smile, "That nonprofit/government agency is just raking it in!" Where does this surplus go? Legally, it cannot be distributed to anyone associated with the firm, except in the special case of a cooperative. Any surplus (deficit) is, therefore, added to (subtracted from) the stock of the firm's assets, or, in the case of a government bureau, forfeited back (or absorbed) by its sponsoring agency. A more interesting question is "What happens to potential net income spent on unnecessary costs?" These funds, not calculated and hence unobserved, may be wasted on excessive compensation or other costs. Clients and sponsors lose.

Quasi-public firms

"Quango" is a euphemism for quasi-nongovernmental organizations. ***Quangos*** are privately managed firms but funded by a government or multinational organization. For example, a private health clinic providing hydration services to infants may be set up and receive virtually all of its funding from UNICEF. Several regional agencies and multinational organizations fall in a continuum between public and private. Quangos, however, do not hold the power to tax.

"Third-party government" is a term describing a pattern of relationships between government and the private nonprofit sector in delivering public services. Nonprofits become a partner with government rather than a substitute. How do these organizations behave economically? Are contracting organizations more like quasi-governmental bureaus than private nonprofits? Do they lack the inclusiveness of government and therefore cater to subgroups rather than to society as a whole? Do private nonprofit hospitals, funded primarily by government through Medicare and Medicaid, lose their altruism, their trustworthiness, and their ability to respond? Do government funded nonprofits arbitrarily withhold services from nontraditional clients or provide them with a lower quality? Such questions are part of the valuable research agenda of students in public administration.

Quasi-governmental provision stems from a nation's unique history and dynamic political changes. ***Privatization*** refers to the legal process whereby government agencies become private nonprofits or are sold off as profit-seeking firms. ***Nationalization*** is the process whereby private firms become government entities. ***Expropriation*** is a term describing nationalization of a private or international firm taking place without complete compensation to that institution's sponsor. On the other hand, an organization may decide to legally move from the nonprofit into the profit-seeking sector. Such was the case with certain Blue Cross and Blue Shield Insurance Associations in the United States. Other organizations may drop government sponsorship and change into private profit-seeking or nonprofit firms. Firms along with their institutional structures evolve due to regulations, competition, and challenges over time. Rational decision-making assumes that officials chose the appropriate legal structure of a particular institution based on cost, benefits, and mission. Application 2.4 discusses the evolving legal status of the British Broadcasting Corporation.

APPLICATION 2.4
The British Broadcasting Corporation as an Example of Nationalization and Potential Privatization

The British Broadcasting Corporation (BBC) was adversely affected when a story based on "an intelligence service source" dominated programming for several weeks. The story alleged that a dossier issued by the British government to help justify the Iraq War was "sexed up" by the Prime Minister's principal press advisor. It was subsequently determined that the BBC source, who committed suicide, was not, had never been, and had not claimed to be part of the security services. Critics now claim that the BBC tailors presentations to suit its bias. This is a serious situation for a government-funded agency whose traditional monopoly is being eroded by private firms with advertisers.

The British Broadcasting Company was founded in 1922 by private radio manufacturers but was funded by a compulsory tax on owners of radio receivers. In 1927, the BBC became a publicly owned (nationalized) corporation albeit with program content independent of government. The ownership tax continued after television was introduced and commercial (profit-seeking) independents began to broadcast. BBC audiences are diminishing in the face of cable and satellite services with hundreds of channels. People, buying advertised products and paying for satellite and cable directly, question why they have to pay license fees as well to fund the BBC.

The BBC's 10-year charter expired in 2006. A vocal minority advocated privatization. The political sentiment may be such that the BBC's traditional funding and independence will be subject to change.

Source: Gerald Kaufmann, "British Broadcasting Calamity," *Wall Street Journal*, July 24, 2003, A14.

In a *joint venture*, firms come together to create a formal legal alliance without changing their own organizational structures or mission. The intention of a joint venture may be to increase borrowing without compromising assets in the event of financial failure. Another motivation could be to ensure a steady flow of clients. Hospitals, for example, unite with some physicians in joint ventures to secure referrals. Joint ventures may also represent an additional source of revenue. The nonprofit National Trust for Historic Preservation in the United States has entered into an agreement with certain profit-seeking hotels deemed historic. Hotels donate 3 percent of the revenue booked through the trust's web site to the National Trust.

Special tax treatment and subsidies for nonprofits hinge on the provision of a type of public good, unavailable or preferred to services presently provided in the for-profit or government sectors. Local communities in the United States do charge nonprofits and government firms for utilities and certain government-provided services such as water, sewage, and trash collecting. However, these organizations at present do not pay property taxes, and thus are perceived as not contributing to road maintenance, education, emergency fire and medical services, etc. One proposal, under consideration by local counties is PILOT: "payment in lieu of taxes." PILOT varies from state to state but in general nonprofits are asked to voluntarily pay taxes up to the amount paid on homes and businesses. Some nonprofit utilities already pay PILOTs. Nonprofits paying these taxes will be forced to pass these expenses on to fee-paying clients, shut down, or transform themselves into profit-seeking institutions. The burden of these taxes and the subsequent loss of service will fall on those least able to pay.

The form that an organization takes depends on its mission, technology, market competition, and community support. Whatever their institutional structure, vigilance is required to ensure that government agencies, private nonprofits, and quasi-government organizations do not waste net income and continue working toward the vision that brought them into existence.

2.5   UNIQUENESS OF THE GOVERNMENT AND NONPROFIT SECTORS

Each firm is a unique bundle of relationships, but legal standing and the sector (profit-seeking, government, or nonprofit) in which it operates explains much of its behavior. Research shows that the type of industry (educational, medical, or beverage) in which a firm operates is less significant than its legal and organizational structure. Profit-seeking hospitals and schools, for example, follow for-profit commercial standards in their accounting statements. The sector of the economy in which a firm is placed matters and determines its legal, accounting, and managerial behavior.

A NFP firm involves a host of interests, including sponsors, auditors, board members, lenders, regulators, management/administration, taxpayers, donors/volunteers, employees, contractors, and clients. Conflict of interest is unavoidable. It is impossible to build a framework modeling all types of interactions between these constituencies. However, the study of public administration assumes that a NFP firm as a whole can act with a purpose and function effectively. It does this by focusing on specific goals.

NFP firm failure is due to either internal mismanagement or external environment factors beyond its control. Therefore, some well managed NFP firms may not be effective (allocatively inefficient) and others with very effective programs are not well managed (productively inefficient). Ideally, internal controls keep a school on track; thus its students perform well on state exams. What if students attending an adequately funded school do not perform well? In this case, we need to determine if the problem is due to administrative failure or factors over which the school has no control. To isolate management issues from overall effectiveness, it can be useful to separate external from internal firm characteristics.

2.6   EXTERNAL DIFFERENCES

NFP firms are fundamentally different from profit-seeking ones. They operate with severe limitations on how capital is raised and cannot distribute net income. NFP firms are prohibited from selling stock, limiting their ability to raise funds in capital markets. In addition, internal profit sharing and dividends to individual sponsors are prohibited. Churches, hospitals, and schools pre-date the existence of modern government, but external regulation and tax policy mold their behavior, limit expansion, and ban certain types of employee incentives.

Legal structure

The Governmental Accounting Standards Board (GASB) establishes procedures for governmental units. Government agencies derive much but not all their income from general tax revenue and answer to public authorities. GASB seeks firm accountability as a whole and for specific programs. Federal, state, county, and local government units and private nonprofits that report to government units use fund accounting. *Fund accounting* separates sources of revenue and expenditures restricted to specific programs. Agencies, public and private, contract with other agencies to provide specific services in return for per unit subsidies. A local school district receiving state funds per student cannot, for example, use these funds to build a municipal water plant.

Traditionally, government units ignored the value of their stocks of assets, including machinery, plant, tools, and equipment. At present, the value of capital assets, including infrastructure assets, is estimated and depreciated in government-wide financial statements. The financial values of bridges and highways, as well as city hall, are available for your hometown and made available to the general public.

Private nonprofits are generally formed as legal corporations subject to the now familiar nondistributional constraint. The unfortunate reductionist term, "nonprofit," used in the United States for the "third" or "voluntary" sector, evolved from the special tax treatment provided these firms in the tax code. Two separate issues concern U.S. federal nonprofit tax status: (1) certain but not all nonprofit firms are exempted from taxes on income, and (2) the U.S. Internal Revenue Service (IRS) permits taxpayers contributing to firms granted 501(c) (3) status to deduct some amount of that contribution from taxable income. IRS tax status depends on nonprofit firm type and on its funding sources. The tax preferences provided to private nonprofits are sometimes referred to as *tax expenditures* because they result in foregone revenue for the government.

Taxation and subsidies

It is the responsibility of the taxing authority to ensure that individuals do not construct pseudo-nonprofit firms. Regional offices of the Internal Revenue Service (IRS) have divisions responsible for determining the status of organizations defined in the IRS Code Section 501(c). Section 501(c) (3) includes organizations operated for religious, charitable, scientific, literary, or educational purposes; testing for public safety; fostering national or international sports competitions; or the prevention of cruelty to children or animals. A nonprofit may not devote a substantial part of its activities to influencing legislation and should not attempt to intervene in political campaigns or elections. In order to maintain nonprofit status as a 501(c) (3) organization, eligible for tax deductible contributions, a "public charity" must receive at least one-third of its total revenue from the general public. This includes direct donations, indirect contributions, and government funding. In other words, a small group of individuals cannot set up a nonprofit to avoid taxes or to achieve political or personal goals. For example, the spirit if not the letter of a NFP is violated if people fund foundation-like entities called supporting organizations, deduct donations from their federal tax liabilities, and then receive loans from the organization for personal use.

Certain nonprofit donations are ineligible for tax deductions. In the United States, nonprofits, not granted deductibility, include civic and fraternal units classified as 501(c) (4) organizations; cooperatives, as 501(c) (5); business leagues, as 501(c) (6), etc. Thus, a college fraternity, family foundation, farmers' coop, and athletic association have nonprofit status, but contributions are not tax deductible. Only 501(c) (3) organizations are eligible for tax deductible contributions.

All nonprofits pay specific types of taxes, such as federal payroll taxes (FICA), state unemployment taxes, and some excise taxes. Although nonprofits are generally exempted from local property and income taxes, they do pay for publicly provided utilities, as well as most sales taxes. Churches, schools, and hospitals, for example, are charged for local water, postage, sewage, and trash removal, and in some cases pay sales taxes on their purchases.

Tax exemption and donor tax deductions are implicit government subsidies with an opportunity cost equal to the tax revenue that would have been collected. These opportunity costs are substantial, and, therefore, the general public as well as stakeholders have an interest in assessing service quality and managerial accountability. GuideStar, a web site produced by Philanthropic Research, Inc., provides information about the operations and finances of thousands of U.S. private nonprofit firms. GuideStar information, which cannot be used for commercial purposes, is intended to assist donors in comparing 501(c) (3) nonprofits and in monitoring performance. It also serves to assure the general public that nonprofit tax benefits work as intended.

Is a particular nonprofit hoarding or squandering wealth rather than actively providing a quasi-public good? Patterns in the flow of resources in and out of an organization are used to answer this question. The Financial Accounting Standards Board (FASB) sets nonbinding reporting standards for private nonprofits. Nonprofit accounting does not focus on changes in net worth but, rather, monitors fiscal soundness in terms of its budget and separate funds. FASB requires that programs funded by government be audited separately from unrestricted general funds.

Small privately sponsored nonprofits are not required to use either government fund accounting or commercial standards. However, currently in the United States, all nonprofit firms accepting tax-deductible contributions with annual revenue exceeding $25,000 are required to file IRS Form 990. Form 990 and 990EZ requires reporting on financial position, activities, cash flows and compensation paid to board members, officers, and certain employees. As of May, 2007, any organization that does not file IRS Form 990 because its income is $25,000 or less will have to submit form 990-N, an electronic postcard. Churches continue to be excluded from this requirement.

Sponsors of large nonprofit firms generally purchase outside auditing services; smaller firms, not receiving government grants, are not required by law to engage independent auditors. Smaller nonprofits and churches often rely on staff and/or volunteers to prepare budgets and conduct internal audits.

Unrelated business tax

Massive change is occurring in the government and private nonprofit sectors as part of a pattern of growing commercialization in pursuit of additional revenue. Some activities are loosely related to firm mission and some not at all. NFP-unrelated business activities are justified as subsidiaries whose profits are designed to subsidize core activities.

Examples include:

- nonprofit hospitals operating exercise clubs;
- state universities sponsoring hotels and conference centers. In some cases, these activities are sponsored by alumni rather than directly by the university;
- nonprofit museums with shops selling jewelry, ties, and scarves in addition to art reproductions;
- nonprofit universities entering into research alliances with private firms.

Often, in these ventures, administrators' compensation is competitive with CEOs at comparable profit-seeking corporations. Profits from these activities are subject to an unrelated business income tax (UBIT) similar to the corporate income tax. The imposition of UBIT provides an incentive for NFP firms to focus on mission related activities. It is also intended to reduce a NFP firm's tax advantage in competing with taxed profit-seeking firms.

2.7   INTERNAL DIFFERENCES

Profit is a good indicator of efficiency and long-term potential in the profit-seeking sector. NFP firms lack a similar single overall economic measure of performance. Student credit hours, medical procedures, clients served, and church attendance may be monitored but are inadequate substitutes for measuring a firm's overall effectiveness. One cannot add apples and oranges, and a multi-product NFP firm cannot simply add up outputs. A foundation cannot, for example, add its "success" in environmental education to that in art conservation. Cost–benefit analysis, in Chapter 11, is a quantitative method placing a numeric value on each type of output. A public recreational facility, for example, can impute a dollar value on an hour of tennis, an hour of softball, and an hour of swimming and come up with a single measure of output. These proxies show increases or decreases in output, but, unlike markets driven by consumer choice, do not indicate productive or allocative efficiency.

Earnings reflect a competitive profit-seeking firm's efficiency, but not that of a NFP firm. Lacking a single overall measure of performance, NFPs rely on internal rules, regulations, and standard procedures. Professional standards and procedures are the hallmark of the NFP sectors, with economic tools assisting but not substituting for good practices. However, NFPs operate in a dynamic environment, and best practices change and require periodic consideration. Formal non-market controls and quality assessment information are needed. Industry standards, professional certification, and institutional accreditation each play a role in evaluating the quality of service provided by NFP firms. These controls are essential but suggest a legitimate question, having no clear answer, "Who monitors those that set the standards?"

Organizational framework

A NFP firm is characterized by its association with three groups: sponsor/donors who provide recurring appropriations or grants, suppliers of labor and other factors of production, and clients paying a per-unit rate for services. The sponsor relationship most strongly differentiates a particular NFP firm, because the structure of internal governance entails control and accountability. In the discussion that follows, we discuss the role of these three groups in terms of a generic NFP organizational chart presented in Figure 2.2.

Sponsor

Government bodies create and sponsor public agencies. Government schools and hospitals, like some private nonprofits, are monitored and accredited by government as well as private accrediting and professional associations. However, democracies rely to a large extent on criticism from opposing political parties to evaluate

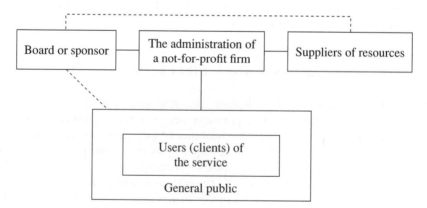

Figure 2.2   Organizational chart for a NFP firm. One critical difference in the organization of a NFP firm consists in those expected to benefit from its output. Clients directly utilize the services but a larger population benefits from the public goods provided and often subsidize production. A second difference is the role of various stakeholders. Dotted lines represent informal influences that employees, clients, and donors exert on a NFP board to affect policy.

government services. In cases where the user fee component of revenue is small or nonexistent, government agencies offer the public a package of promised activities in return for a budget. In contrast, a profit-seeking firm offers units of output at a price; for example, one can of pop for a dollar and two cans for two dollars. Unlike a merchant selling burglary alarms, a town's police department offers public safety in return for a portion of tax revenue.

In the private nonprofit sector, an agency's sponsor may be any religious, ethnic, professional, or like-minded group that coordinates contributions to subsidize a particular program. IRS form 990, required of many private nonprofits, is not a substitute for assessing program effectiveness or fraud. It provides some upward accountability to government and sponsors but lacks downward accountability to clients. Internal evaluations of successes and failures are needed in addition to formal accounting to shape goals into effective programs. The danger, of course, is that the demand for greater efficiency and accountability in the expenditure of public funds will lead to a nightmare of over-regulation, whereby administrators become more absorbed with paperwork than in serving clients.

Boards

Boards are entrusted with the rights and responsibility to control nonprofit and government agencies; they are considered the legal owners of NFP corporations. Board members of a government firm are sometimes elected by the public. Other boards are composed of donors, citizens, members of the sponsoring agency, and appointed officials. Unlike profit-seeking firms, board members, sometimes called trustees, are not directly accountable to shareholders and are not subject to outside takeovers. Board members are often nominated by top administrators or by existing board members. As such, nonprofit boards can be self-perpetuating, creating a conflict of interest. Board members are legally required to act conscientiously and responsibly, to avoid or disclose any conflict of interest in decision-making, and to keep the organization operating within the law. One of the board's important roles is hiring, firing, and setting compensation for top administrators.

Unnecessary travel expense and/or loans to board members or top administrators raise questions about insider benefits. The Independent Sector and Board Source, in Washington, DC, is designed to improve the effectiveness of nonprofit boards. For example, this organization has pressured charities to ban loans to insiders. Such loans are legal in most states; fortunately, the practice is not widespread.

Board responsibilities include the development of firm strategy. However, when technical expertise is needed, top administrators initiate most new proposals. There is no law requiring boards to act specifically in the interest of donors, clients, or sponsors. It is, however, legally required to advance firm mission. The role of board chairperson is critical. He or she sets board agendas, manages meetings, and controls the flow of information to other board members.

Those appointed to boards in nonprofit and government agencies should be very clear about the type of board to which they are called. There are official "boards of trustees" and there are "advisory boards." Members of advisory boards have no power to interpret mission, create policy, and hire chief administrators. They also have no legal responsibility and their positions reflect the perceived expertise they bring in making suggestions to those who do have authority.

Official boards of trustees, based on their behavior, can be classified as either a "guidance board" or a "compliance" board. In a firm run by a "guidance" board the roles of the head administrator and board chair are separated. A NFP "guidance" board engages intensively in strategy, tactics, hiring, firing, and defining core services. Initially, this type of board is small, takes responsibility for decisions, and is involved in every decision made by management. Over time, as both the organization and board become larger, the board may concern itself more with social responsibility, inclusivity, and accounting standards. The emphasis shifts to being a "compliance" board concerned with laws pertaining to NFP organizations. Compliance is necessary because the board is legally responsible. However, the ideal board integrates "guidance" and "compliance" in ways that do not isolate each task. Trustees, who understand the fundamental nature of their particular NFP and its mission, are more likely to determine when an organization is going off course (Perkins, 2001).

Administrators

NFP leaders are referred to as "administrators," rather than "executives" as in profit-seeking firms. Some NFP firms use alternate terms such as head, chancellor, chief, or director. Whatever title used, the executive director is the immediate authority on every program. Generally, provisions in a firm's bylaws describe this position, outline its responsibility, and designate if the person sits on the board or has voting rights. We use the term "public manager" in this text to denote a person who has the responsibility of administrating an identifiable budget in a NFP firm, public or private.

Head administrators are appointed by the board. In turn, the board does not appoint but approves the hiring of lower-level administrators. How does a board select benchmarks for administrative performance? Mission statements are vague and productivity is difficult to measure. How does a board challenge NFP managers with appropriate incentives? Obviously, it cannot offer stock options! In addition, it is even prohibited from offering bonus-type incentives. Recall the nondistributional constraint. To compensate for financial incentives, managers in NFP firms generally receive a degree of autonomy, which service professionals tend to prefer.

The characteristics of a firm's board or sponsor determine how the chief administrator directs time and effort. The president of a private university, for example, allocates efforts toward donors, parents, alumni, and the board of trustees. The president of a state university allocates less time to these groups and focuses more on the state legislature. An effective administrator in either sector is one who handles these relationships well.

Donors/volunteers

Economists study donations intently because they contradict the tendencies toward free riding and self-maximizing behavior. Individuals may contribute publicly to win others' approval. In fact, experiments suggest that people associate donating behavior with leadership characteristics (Brooks, 2006). Although altruistic behavior is not fully understood, donations provide public goods. A tradition of voluntary donations in some countries exists whereby large groups desire certain quasi-public goods and/or wish to subsidize access to these goods. Apparently, individuals "buy into" feeling good about charity, desire to do their fair share, or feel social pressure to contribute "voluntary taxes" to their communities. Whatever the motivation, observed giving by some provokes others to contribute.

Individuals rarely contribute to profit-seeking corporations, and government taxes are not voluntary. Private nonprofits, on the other hand, cannot exist without the potential for voluntary donations of time and money. The influence of donors/volunteers in formulating policy varies from institution to institution, but, surprisingly, is generally insignificant. Discontented volunteers take their services and donations elsewhere. Donors selecting from a variety of institutions increase the inflow of revenue into certain organizations and in return receive personal compensation in the form of tax deductions, peer prestige, and networking advantages as active community participants. Volunteers, ideally, reduce a NFP's costs. Both donors and volunteers receive, in addition, a deep sense of personal satisfaction; otherwise, they would not contribute.

Although in practice they have little direct influence on policy, it is not uncommon for donors and volunteers to have personal agendas and a desire to shift the focus of the firm. Boards and administrators, charged with keeping an organization on track, can and do refuse restricted donations and screen volunteers.

Clients

A client is usually defined either as one for whom professional services are rendered or as one dependent on the patronage of another. We differentiate clients from customers in that a client does not pay full price and receives some form of direct or indirect subsidy from donors, sponsors, or taxpayers. Client choice is therefore more limited than that of market customers. Clients, either through taxes or membership fees, have already indirectly financed production in particular NFP firms. He or she is locked in and cannot switch providers without increased personal costs. Furthermore, NFP firms dominate in services to which the user submits over time. For example, a student half way through a two-year program in public administration may not easily transfer credit to another institution. Clients commit themselves to procedures with indefinite outcomes. Attendance does not guarantee attainment of a degree, and not all root canals are successful!

It is easy to define customers in a for-profit firm. On the other hand, who exactly is the client of a NFP firm? Is a university student on full scholarship a client? Do alumni making yearly donations to enhance the school's academic reputation constitute the client base? User fees constitute at times a relatively small percentage of most NFP income, and therefore users may not be clients. Unlike a customer, those receiving NFP services pay fees equal to less than cost, and those providing funds are not necessarily users of the service.

Some individuals wear several hats, functioning as board member, donor/volunteer, and client. Consider opera companies and museums where most of the audience consists of donors, volunteers, or board members. In these situations, volunteers serve a useful role in monitoring the output of the organization and provide a measure of client control. Rights and responsibilities with respect to any firm depend, however, on function not the individual. Ideally, a board member, who happens to be a client or donor, makes policy decisions in terms of mission independent of his or her needs and preferences.

NFP firms represent a network of relationships between sponsors, board, donors, employees, and clients. Derek Bok, the former president of Harvard University, warns that NFP firms answering to so many constituencies and expected to service so many ends need to agree on a few common goals. Otherwise, they become ineffective and complacent. Economic theory of a firm offers insight into each transaction between different stakeholders. In place of threats and political games, market discipline and free choice, under the rubric of defined rules, policies, and procedures, point the organization toward more and higher-quality output at lower cost.

2.8 SOURCES OF REVENUE

NFP firms develop yearly budgets and engage in long-range planning. The process begins with guidelines sent to subunits authorized to make expenditures. Invariably, units submit larger proposed budgets than those desired by higher-level administrators. Sometimes this stalls the approval process; in the meantime, commitments are made for the following year. Staff is hired and catalogs published prior to budget approval. In the absence of a comprehensive set of goals and priorities, resources are allocated internally by tradition or by some sort of political or authoritarian process. It may be legally and technically possible to develop performance measures for NFP organizations in order to allocate resources on a more rational basis. One step in this direction is to begin the budget process from the revenue side and build contingencies into the budget for uncertainties.

Clients naturally prefer that all professionals engaged in their treatment ignore costs, discount revenue, and concentrate on client needs. Unfortunately, a public administrator has to be acutely aware of revenue sources and how funds are allocated. A NFP firm is one in which clients do not pay full cost for the services received. How many opportunities should a student have to fail out at taxpayer expense? When is another liver transplant not cost effective in terms of payment received? An organization permitted to screen and select clients does not preclude or prohibit similar services made available elsewhere.

Revenue linkage between different government levels in a federal system complicates decision-making and is an example of contingent funding. Contingent funding is often referred to as matching funds because it is based on units of a service provided or funds expended. Consider some examples financed by different tax authorities: (1) local highway construction supplemented with state and federal funds, (2) a healthcare program such as Medicaid administered by a state but financed by state and federal government, (3) city operated schools financed with county property and state taxes as well as federal government grants, and (4) charter schools sponsored by local, state, or private agencies with state funds and federal grants.

Contingent funding operates in the private nonprofit sector, when government units offer tax credits for donated funds. Some corporations as well match employee nonprofit donations for specific projects. The rationale is that NFPs create public benefits so much valued by some that they are willing to get the ball rolling by providing initial funding. Another positive aspect of matched funds is the oversight provided by large donors. The larger donors sift through NFP applicants and determine effective providers; this assures small donors that their funds will be spent wisely.

Although matched funding has the potential of providing a firm with needed revenue, there are unintended consequences. Projects with matching funds become more attractive to an organization than projects more in keeping with mission. There are costs associated with becoming eligible for matched funds. Is it worthwhile spending $99 on fundraising to receive $50 in individual donations and $50 in matching funds? Most likely, no. Is it efficient to spend $99 on fundraising in order to receive $100 in individual donations and thereby collect $100 in matching restricted funds from a sponsoring agency? It may or may not be. Application 2.5 provides an example of local mental health agencies reacting to incentives provided by state funding.

APPLICATION 2.5
Intergovernmental Mental Health Funding Affects Who Is Treated and How

Intergovernmental transfers is a method by which out-of-tax revenue at one level of government is used to influence the production of public goods on another level. In the United States, it is increasingly the case that intergovernmental transfers affect job training, schools, medical care for the elderly, etc. For example, some local school districts receive over 50 percent of funding from state and federal government combined. NFP managers consciously or unconsciously respond to funding sources, sometimes in unexpected ways contrary to the intention of those providing funding. Frank and Gaynor estimate the reactions of local mental health agencies in Ohio to incentives embodied in how the state transfers funds.

Mental health agencies generally finance and operate state mental hospitals and finance community mental health services, delivered at the local level. State mental hospital capacity has decreased by approximately 75 percent, but hospitals' share of state mental health funds has remained relatively constant at around 65 percent of the total. Remaining state funds are allocated to local mental health boards. Local agencies transfer seriously ill patients to state hospitals subject to capacity limitations.

Local boards do not directly provide mental healthcare but contract with nonprofit providers and serve as regulators. Mental health boards, appointed by the governor or county commissioners, levy property taxes in addition to receiving state funds. Thus, communities have a strong incentive to either not service or transfer high-cost clients to state hospitals.

In the mid-1980s the Ohio Department of Mental Health changed its method of intergovernmental transfers. It agreed to pay a bonus to local boards for each person certified as severely mentally disabled. The goal was to address the under-treatment of severely mentally ill individuals. This created an incentive to enroll individuals but not necessarily provide extended treatment. In addition, under the Ohio Mental Health Act of 1988, local boards were required to pay the average per day cost of its clients confined to state hospitals. The "effective price" of state hospital days paid by the local mental health boards increased as the policy was phased in over a six-year period.

From 1989 to 1990, the first operative year of the Mental Health Act, local boards participating in the program reduced state metal hospital stays by 17.5 percent. Initially, local enrollment of the mentally ill increased in order to accept state bonuses. Unfortunately, enrollment tapered off reflecting costs in excess of the state bonus for treating severely ill clients.

Local Mental Health Boards respond to financial incentives incorporated into intergovernmental transfers.

Source: Richard G. Frank and Martin Gaynor, "Organizational Failure and Transfers in the Public Sector," *Journal of Human Resources*, 29 (1), 2004, 108–25.

Tables 2.1 and 2.2 provide revenue and expenditures data for two NFP firms with multiple revenue sources and matched funding. These firms, one government and one private nonprofit, provide social services. Table 2.1 is the partial budget for the Department of Human Services of Arlington County, Virginia. Table 2.2 is an income statement for Catholic Charities of the Diocese of Joliet, Illinois.

Note that federal and state revenue received by Arlington County, in Table 2.1, is restricted to specific programs and contingent on local funds. Other programs are fully funded locally. The Arlington County budget is a good example of *fiscal federalism*, a system of transfers or grants by which revenue, collected in federal taxes, is allocated to state and local governments for specific programs.

You will observe in Table 2.1, under general relief in Part B, that the federal government pays 60 cents to Arlington County for every 40 cents allocated locally. In fact, some services, such as those for refugees, are fully funded by the federal government, with the county administrating programs according to federal guidelines. Fiscal federalism is based on the assumption that local agencies respond better and more quickly, although the federal government collects revenue efficiently. In some instances, the programs are federally mandated by the U.S. Congress and financed locally with some reluctance.

Catholic Charities of the Diocese of Joliet is a nonprofit providing social services to seven local Illinois counties. Note that the organization represented in

Table 2.1 Funding a county government social service agency. In part A, note that most revenue is derived from state and federal grants. In part B, note that some local spending is matched on a percentage basis with state and federal funds.

Part A: Revenue and expenses, Department of Human Services, Arlington County, Virginia (dollars)

Revenue: fiscal year 2000	Expenditures: fiscal year 2000
Federal government 3,816,026	Economic Independence Div. 3,706,092
State government 2,038,088	Aging and disability services 1,022,633
Arlington County 3,772,156	Child and family services 4,898,091
Other 546	
Total revenue 9,626,816	Total expenditures 9,626,816

Part B: Sub-total of Public Assistance Fund of Arlington County, Virginia, fiscal year 2001 (dollars)

Program	Total	Federal (F)/ state (S) match	Local (L) match	Unmatched local funds	Local total
Auxiliary grants	260,429	208,343	52,086	0	52,086
General relief	718,579	440,682	254,410	13,487	277,897
Refugee assistance	60,000	60,000	0	0	0
Energy assistance	500	500	0	0	0
Food stamp cash out	438,696	438,696	0	0	0
State/local hospitalization	27,543		27,543	0	27,543
Sub-total	1,505,747	1,148,221	344,039	13,487	357,526

Source: Based on Arlington County FY 2002 Approved Budget, Department of Human Services, September 2003.

Table 2.2 is not the religious diocese of Joliet and, therefore, has a board independent of the diocese. As such, Catholic Charities of Joliet, Inc., applies for and receives funding from county, state, and federal government for specific programs. A public accounting firm, in compliance with government guidelines, audits each program receiving government-restricted funds.

User fees

User fees, regardless of size, guarantee a minimum level of service to clients who freely pay for the service. Observe that fees paid by clients, in Tables 2.1 and 2.2, account for less than 3 percent of total revenue. Clients pay out-of-pocket fees for some services such as counseling. Otherwise, general taxpayers and donors pay for services that they are unlikely to use personally. Other types of NFP firms, receiving most of their revenue from user fees, market directly to clients. Government

Table 2.2   Funding a private nonprofit social service agency. Private nonprofit firms, in this case Catholic Charities of the Diocese of Joliet, Inc., contract with the government for funding restricted to particular programs. Each large program operated by the private nonprofit firm requires a separate audit.

Catholic Charities of the Diocese of Joliet, Inc.

Public support and revenue, 2006 (dollars)		*Expenses, 2006 (dollars)*	
Federal government	9,343,861	*Program services*	
State and regional government	4,994,659	Children's services	3,189
Townships	57,093	Community services	4,758,308
In-kind contributions	1,054,692	Counseling services	429,160
Diocese of Joliet	1,120,824	Early childhood services	7,595,071
Bequests	269,874	Senior services	1,957,887
United way	614,042		
Program fees	816,081	*Supporting services*	
Special events	415,943	General administration	1,430,245
Individual and organizational		Rental properties	68,869
contributions	694,676		
Foundation contributions	256,058	Fundraising	386,719
U.S. Catholic Bishops' Conference	49,374		
Rental income and parking	47,686		
Interest	36,640		
Miscellaneous	97,735		
Total support and revenue	19,869,238	Total expenses	19,816,165
Excess of support and revenue			
over expenses	53,073		

Source: Based on Statement of Support, Revenue and Expenses for the Year Ending June 30, 2006, administrative offices of Catholic Charities of the Diocese of Joliet, Inc.

firms in this group include municipally owned water and electric departments, toll bridges, and controlled access highways. These firms charge and receive virtually full cost from their clients.

Private nonprofits, such as hospitals, nursing homes, and some educational institutions, receive as well most but not all of their revenue from fees. Most nonprofit services contain a partial subsidy. Ice skating for a few dollars at the city rink, overnight camping fees in a state park, and subsidized care at religiously sponsored retirement facilities are bargains, compared with market prices for similar services. Therefore, clients do not hesitate to take advantage of low-cost NFP alternatives pre-paid in the form of taxes or contributions.

User fees are a serious drawback in allocating scarce services among potential clients. They often exclude those whom NFP firms are designed to serve. In some instances it is virtually impossible for NFP firms to assess user fees for services, such as charging prisoners for room and board. User fees represent an insurmountable barrier for low-income households. They are thereby excluded from access to public facilities, such as golf courses and universities, which they subsidize involuntarily through taxes. General tax revenue, paid by all, subsidizes the affluent.

In general, however, user fees offer economic advantages and operate effectively. User fees provide an incentive for NFP firms to be responsive to clients, one of the most desirable characteristics of the profit-seeking sector. It should be stressed, however, that responsiveness to clients is different from permitting clients to determine policy. McDonald's does not serve pizza even when requested by its best customers, but it would if it were in stockholders' best interests. The responsiveness that we observe in the profit-seeking sector is merely a means for increasing shareholder profits. It is inappropriate for the NFP firm as well to equate responsiveness to clients with firm effectiveness. NFP clients have the right to be well served but not to make administrative policy or interpret firm mission.

Given finite resources, user fees ration scarce goods. They provide an efficient means of determining who will obtain campgrounds in national parks and seats in state universities. In this way, user fees direct the goods to those who value them the most and are willing and able to pay. However, they do not necessarily direct them to those who need them or will benefit the most.

Fees alone do not guarantee an organization's responsiveness to clients. In Chapter 8, we shall see that any provider, profit-seeking or NFP, protected from competition has little incentive to focus on the consumer, even for customers paying full cost. We observe, however, that the larger the percentage of total revenue derived from user fees the more responsive a NFP is toward its clients.

A *voucher*, funded by taxpayers or others and paid directly to clients, completely or partially finances services from designated providers. In this way, government can provide goods and services without actually producing them. Vouchers permit limited client choice, and like user fees provide incentives for firms to be more client-directed.

Sponsor subsidies

Every NFP firm generally has a sponsor providing at least a portion of its revenue. Firms financed mainly by user fees, such as hospitals and public utilities, receive relatively little financial support from their sponsors. Credit unions, public radio and public television in the United States are examples of NFP firms that receive no operating expenses but may share facilities and space with sponsoring organizations. For example, Arlington County (Table 2.1) is the primary sponsor of the Department of Social Services, providing it with approximately 39 percent of its revenue. Catholic Charities' traditional sponsor, the Diocese of Joliet (Table 2.2) continues to provide 6 percent of its total revenue.

Contributions

In the United States, private donations account for approximately 25 percent of the nonprofit sector's revenue, but this figure varies widely between organizations. Many NFPs dedicate staff, sometimes called development officers, to maintaining this important source of revenue. The development office is charged with interpreting the mission of the institution to donors and channeling their concerns back to policy-makers within the organization. Donors, unlike the sponsor or board, are not legally responsible and therefore do not determine policy. Private nonprofit firms, however, owe their existence to voluntary contributions. As indicated previously in Application 2.3, the average contributing household provides an average yearly amount of over $2,000 mainly to private nonprofits.

All NFP organizations are dependent on government appropriations and/or voluntary donations, and these funds are likely to vary from year to year. Donations and continued government support are not entitlements and can have a destabilizing effect on an organization's budget. Application 2.6 indicates how any NFP, depending on private donations, needs to factor into its budget the risk of unfulfilled pledges.

APPLICATION 2.6
Budgeting When Pledges Don't Show Up or Are Delayed

Fundraising is costly and risky. Like other universities, Haverford College in Pennsylvania establishes scholarships, professorships, and buildings dedicated to the memory of certain large contributors. The case of J. Howard Marshall II, a reluctant donor, and Haverford, a prominent institution, provides a lesson for nonprofit firms on the hazards of miscalculating the expected return of a given pledge.

Marshall, who made money in Texas oil, was one of the college's wealthiest alumni, a longtime board member, and honorary degree recipient. In 1976, Mr. Marshall agreed, after some cajoling, to what was then the largest pledge in Haverford's history. Hoping to receive over 12 times that amount, the administration and other alumni showered much attention on the donor over the following 20 years. By his death in 1996, Marshall had actually contributed only half his initial pledge. Funds paid to Haverford from the estate will not exceed the original pledge expected to pay for a fine arts building. Meanwhile, the college endowment, considered a separate entity from the college itself, will have to write off a $1 million loan to help build Haverford's Fine Arts Center and $1.2 million in interest income.

When donors and their heirs fail to honor non-binding pledges, colleges rarely resort to legal means. They do not sue for damages due to the expense involved, the negative effect on potential donors, and the uncertainty of enforcing oral commitments.

Pledged donations are the lifeblood of most nonprofits. However, institutions need to adjust for risk and lapsed time between pledge and payment. The mathematics of discounting are discussed in a later chapter, but a simple case demonstrates its importance. If, for example, an institution's best estimate of the percentage of pledges actually received is 90 percent, then any expected $1,000 pledge must be adjusted downward to $900. If the interest rate on its endowment is currently 5 percent and the pledge is to be paid at the end of one year, its present value is $857.14. If the institution has to wait 5 years to receive the pledge, the present value of a $1,000 pledge is $703.13. It is only prudent not to spend or allocate funds based on "a bird in the bush" or to permit fundraising costs to approach the expected value of pledges.

Source: Daniel Golden, "College Finally Got Alumnus to Pledge; Next Job: Collecting," *The Wall Street Journal*, July 24, 2003, A1.

Are firms in the private nonprofit sector relegated to areas of the economy heavily dependent on donations? Not necessarily. Donations play a relatively small role in the healthcare industry where private nonprofits thrive. We should not assume that all donations originate in households. An increasingly important source of NFP revenue comes through grants provided by large private foundations. In addition, government sponsored community foundations hold assets bequeathed to them in order to fund scholarships, specified programs, and institutions. In general, however, private contributions of time and money are an important source of revenue for private nonprofit firms.

Endowment income

NFP firms accumulate endowments from donated funds and from net income (revenue minus costs). An endowment is a stock, equal at any point in time to a particular amount. Income earned on the endowment in the course of a year is a flow. Revenue income from an endowment, unlike loans, does not require the NFP to make payments, and in fact the organization can plough the earning back to borrowers to earn even more income in the long term. Endowment income is different, as well, from equity capital, raised by profit-seeking firms, to purchase new machinery, plant, tools, and equipment in the near future. Endowments, in NFPs, are not viewed merely as reserves for unanticipated expenses but, rather, to provide income over time and/or maintain property assets. To prevent nonprofit foundations from accumulating excessive wealth, they are required to spend at least 5 percent of their invested assets each year in charitable activities.

Most stakeholders are aware of administrative costs associated with small donations. Combined or federated campaigns, such as the United Way, represent an attempt to lower fundraising expenses. Umbrella collectors of donations are a means of outsourcing fundraising specialization eliminating intra-firm development offices. From the donor's point of view, united campaigns monitor administrative and fundraising expense ratios and see to it that these expenses are not shifted into program expenses. Warren Buffett admits that he decided to turn his considerable fortune over to the Bill and Melinda Gates Foundation for efficiency reasons. Buffett knows that his comparative advantage in evaluating profit-seeking firms does not extend to evaluating individual charities.

In summary, the three legs of NFP financing are government funding, present and past charitable contributions of time and money, and earned income from user fees. The relative sizes of these revenue sources determine to a large extent how NFP administrators, public or private, focus their attention.

2.9   GRANTS VERSUS PURCHASE OF
SERVICE CONTRACTING

Tax revenue provides the bulk of financial support for personal social services in the United States. Government provides these services through public agencies or in partnership with private nonprofits in the form of grants or contracts. Grants are awarded to nonprofits for facilities, infrastructure and program development. A *purchase of service contract (POSC)* provides government payment to a nonprofit firm for a specific level of output. Grants, as compared with contracts, encourage innovation and program independence. Contracts, as compared with grants, result in a high level of service delivery.

Government funding of nonprofits poses two potential problems. First, public money should not be used to subsidize a mission objective different from that of the public interest. Second, a private nonprofit runs the risk of becoming an instrument of the general public rather than serving the constituency defined in its mission statement. Indeed, there may be an imaginary line in terms of support over which a nonprofit firm, regardless of its private legal status, crosses into becoming a bureau of its funding organization. Technically, a nonprofit enterprise retains its independence if it is not required to turn over any net income to another agency. Consider in a given year, for example, a religiously sponsored firm contracting to provide services to released prisoners. Suppose at the end of the year the firm shows positive net income (revenue minus costs). The private nonprofit firm needs to be able to retain control over these funds to be considered technic-ally independent.

Adelaide Madera, from the University of Messina, argued at a recent conference that a core of non-negotiable values should dictate the relationship between private nonprofits and the government. The government/nonprofit relationship varies from country to country with a tendency toward convergence. For example, in the United States, healthcare is client and private insurance based with Medicare and Medicaid providing funds for certain lower-income groups and the elderly. In Italy, the duty to provide all healthcare is entrusted to public enterprises that do not provide the actual service. In both countries, increased emphasis on productivity could harm the traditional healthcare provider–patient relationship and lead to a deterioration of trust. Also, third-party funding may induce private nonprofits to marginalize the mission focus of their religious founders for greater remuneration. Ideally, the sponsoring organization should be able to remain faithful to mission and, at the same time, enter into a contract with government to provide X units of output at Y number of dollars per unit.

Government contracts with profit-seeking firms need to be carefully specified. Unless quality is monitored, profit-seeking firms may provide inferior weapons to the military, meals to pensioners, and care to the elderly. In addition, contracts with fixed prices lead to renegotiation and/or work stoppages. The goal is to anticipate hazards increasing cost and causing delays. Cost-plus contracts are one solution, assigning specific responsibilities to government and corporations for unexpected events.

Why would the government finance but not produce services directly? A nonprofit firm augments government funding with donations and volunteer labor. By allocating funds through private nonprofit organizations, governments avoid raising taxes, reduce labor costs, and benefit from private contributions. Note how Catholic charities in Joliet (Table 2.2) receives substantial private donations and volunteer services. In addition, nonprofit contracting frees the government to initiate, eliminate, and change output specifications without maintaining facilities and staff. The government can shift funding from grants to contract and from one provider to another in order to achieve the desired quality of service. In other words, government is free to reduce, redirect, or eliminate funds awarded to a specific private nonprofit at the end of the prevailing contract.

2.10   TYPES OF EXPENDITURES

Economists refer to the stream of funds into a firm as revenue and the flow out as costs. Accountants use the terms "income" rather than revenue and "expenses" rather than costs. The economic theory of cost minimization theory is presented in detail in Chapter 6. Here, we discuss an overview based on income statements of the typical NFP firm's allocation of funds received.

A snapshot, so to speak, of expenditures and the proportion of funds allocated to specific activities is closely examined by regulators, potential donors, and clients in evaluating a particular NFP firm. The emphasis on the proportion of funds allocated to specific programs compensates somewhat for a NFP's lack of a single measure of effectiveness, like profit. In addition, those providing NFPs with revenue realize that clients do not pay full cost and are less inclined or lack the knowledge to evaluate service quality. Donors, in particular, are interested in what portion of their contribution will be expended on administration and fundraising. Taxpayers aspire to repair "leaky buckets," a term referring to funds lost in the bureaucratic process of delivering transfers to targeted clients. In all cases, it is desirable that a large percentage of every dollar donated or collected in taxes reach needy clients.

Refer once more to Tables 2.1 and 2.2 to observe the pass-through rate of funds to clients. Table 2.1 for Arlington County indicates specific program expenditures. This information is relevant because one set of taxpayers is financing another set for a specific purpose. Federal taxes, so to speak, are being transferred from someone in Montana to provide refugee services in Virginia. Government accountants show exactly how these funds are directed, and all realize that a certain percentage must be allocated to reasonable administrative expenses. In Table 2.2, in the case of a private nonprofit, we are given the amount of funds spent on various programs. Virtually all private nonprofits, such as Social Services for the Diocese of Joliet, separate program expenses from supporting services. General administration and fundraising expenditures are explicitly given and the percentages of total expenditures are easily calculated. Unfortunately, we cannot determine from this limited data the percentages spent on salaries and administrative costs for each program and if these costs are excessive. To compensate for this lack of information, private nonprofits are required to list the names and salaries of top employees on reports to the Internal Revenue Service. In all public NFPs, compensation is a matter of public record.

Suppose the distorted goal of a particular NFP administration were to maximize the difference between firm income and expenses (net income). Doing this may enrich the nonprofit firm, but is incompatible with firm mission, donor intent, and its tax exemption status. Profit-seeking is not an appropriate NFP economic goal. However, firms, in all sectors, have one common general objective. That is, for any given level of quality and output, they seek to minimize expenses. How do we know this is being done? Transparent accounting helps but, at least in the NFP sector, it is not a substitute for oversight and/or client choice.

2.11   INTERACTION BETWEEN SECTORS

Suppose you talked with government and nonprofit administrators across the world. Your conversations could include the head of a Chilean university, a London subway supervisor, a healthcare administrator in Grand Forks, North Dakota, the proprietor of a credit union in Mule Shoe, Texas, the superintendent of schools on Prince Edward Island, Canada, or a police officer in Shanghai. You would discover a remarkable similarity in their concerns. In addition to management concerns, each would likely express a general interest in the overall health of their country's economy, in other words macroeconomics. Interest rates, inflation, unemployment, and economic growth, and even exchange rates impact NFP firms. These issues are beyond the control of an individual, but all administrators are put in a position of responding to macroeconomic events.

The circular flow diagram in Figure 2.3 provides a visual way of understanding flows between sectors. It identifies transactions between households and the three producing sectors. This macroeconomic tool shows how flows of income and expenses interact. Figure 2.3 lacks detail, but nonetheless provides an important reference framework for a public administrator. It visualizes how general macroeconomic conditions impinge on a particular NFP firm.

Note the flows of income into households at the bottom of Figure 2.3 from all three producing sectors. This income is predominately in the form of wages, but includes interest, rent, profit, and government transfer payments, such as social security, unemployment compensation, veterans' benefits, and welfare. Households allocate income by purchasing services from all three sectors, pay taxes to government and donate to private nonprofits. In addition, households save. Not represented in Figure 2.3 is the flow of household savings into a variety of financial intermediaries such as banks, credit unions, and insurance companies. Firms, government, and households, in turn, borrow these funds and in return pay interest.

The profit-seeking sector, on the left side of Figure 2.3, provides products for those willing to pay full price. This sector includes corporations (about 20 percent of the total in the United States accounting for about 90 percent of the dollar volume), partnerships (about 10 percent, doing about 4 percent of the dollar volume), and proprietorships (about 70 percent, doing about 6 percent of the dollar volume).

What about intra-sector sales, not represented in Figure 2.3? Flows within firms represent business to business sales. The value of business to business sales is generally included in the total price of final goods and services sold to consumers. The price of paper on which exams are copied is considered a business to business sale and is included in tuition expenses. To include the value of intermediate good sales between firms in the flow of payments between sectors would introduce double counting into attempts to measure the total value of goods and services produced.

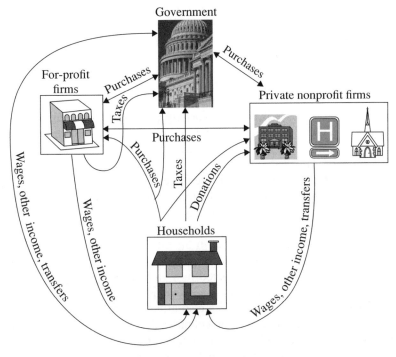

Figure 2.3   The circular flow of payments between sectors. Households receive income from the for-profit, nonprofit, and government sectors. They purchase goods and services from for-profit, nonprofit, and government firms. In addition, households pay taxes to government and donate to nonprofits. For-profit firms receive revenue from goods and services provided to households, government, and nonprofits. Profit-seeking firms pay taxes to government and provide income to households. Government receives revenue in the form of taxes from for-profit firms and households and in the form of payments for government produced goods and services. Government pays wages and distributes transfer payments to households and purchases goods and services from for-profit and nonprofit firms. Private nonprofit firms in providing quasi-public goods earn revenue from households, government contracts, and for-profit firms. They purchase goods and services from for-profit firms and government. In addition, they provide households with wage income and transfer income in kind to clients.

At the top of the circular flow diagram in Figure 2.3 is the government sector. Government receives revenue both from business and household taxes and from user fees charged by government. In return for taxes, businesses and households expect to receive public goods and services (such as defense, a legal system enforcing contracts, a network of highways over which goods may be transported, etc.).

Taxes are used to pay government employees' wages and to distribute transfer payments to households. In addition, government units provide grants and purchase goods and services from the two private sectors. Corporations and nonprofits in the private sector trade with the government sector in exchange for payment. Examples include: the manufacture of military equipment, highway and public construction, and social service contracts.

Some suggest that the private nonprofit sector be included within the household sector. Others suggest it is part of the corporate sector. There are two good reasons for placing nonprofits in the household sector: first, nonprofit firms act as transfer agents between households, and, second, donating households do not receive direct benefits and beneficiary households do not make full payment. Thus, transactions between households cancel out. In addition, there are two good reasons as well for placing nonprofits in the profit-seeking sector: first, they charge fees and sell services to households and government, and, second, nonprofit institutions accumulate surpluses and invest them in order to earn income. Nevertheless, in this text the private nonprofit sector is treated separately and placed on the right in Figure 2.3. We do this to clarify relationships and contracts between all three sectors, and as a reminder that not all nonprofit organizations are exempt from federal income taxes and/or permit tax deductible donations. Note: nonprofits receive revenue from both the household and government sectors and transfer income to employees in the household sector. In addition, a nonprofit firm is generally required and can be held liable for withholding income, Social Security, and Medicare taxes for its employees. Thus, it is imperative that nonprofit employee contracts be distinguished from independent service contractors in the other sectors.

Not represented, in Figure 2.3, is the global economy, although most nonprofits and government agencies are impacted in a variety of ways by global economic events. Interest rates, for example, for new bonds can vary with currency values in international markets. Exchange rates also affect the cost of imported medicines. Donations to nonprofits in developing countries decline during recessions. Currency fluctuations and inflation affect international enrollments at domestic universities.

The general level of economic activity in a given year is a flow concept, called gross domestic product (GDP), represented by lines drawn between sectors in Figure 2.3. If aggregate spending flows slow down, an economy falls into recession. A recession is a highly variable cyclical downturn in the economy that on average lasts eighteen months from start to finish. Recessions reduce the circular flow of products and funds between sectors aggravating social problems. Nonprofits' donations fall in recessions at the very time that their expenses increase due to economic and social distress. Similarly in government firms, tax revenue as a percentage of income declines as those qualifying for social services increase. During boom periods when the economy is in overdrive, NFP firms experience increased prices, wages, interest rates, and construction costs.

CONCLUDING NOTES

- Four sectors characterize the macro economy. Households represent the basic units of any society. The remaining three sectors including profit-seeking, private nonprofit, and government firms produce goods and services that the household sector consumes.

- Public goods are jointly consumed by all members of society and are characterized by both non-rival consumption and non-exclusion. As such they are subject to the free rider problem.

- Government and nonprofit firms operate in industries producing goods and services with public good characteristics. Mission statements contain the self-imposed or chartered duties of these firms.

- NFPs engage in activities related or closely related to their core mission. In some cases, NFPs or their subsidiaries engage in profit-seeking activities unrelated or loosely related to their mission. Unrelated business activities are taxed and any net income subsidizes mission-related activities.

- Not all well-managed NFP firms are effective and others whose programs are very effective are not well-managed. Unlike profit-seeking firms, NFPs cannot raise funds by issuing stock. The non-distributional constraint limits their ability to provide employee incentives.

- If granted 501 (c) (3) status by the U.S. Internal Revenue Service (IRS), a private nonprofit firm is exempted from taxes. In addition, its donors can deduct parts of their contributions from taxable income.

- In both the government and nonprofit sectors, no single overall measure of performance exists. Beyond mission, a particular NFP firm is defined by relationships, including its donor/sponsor, board, administration/staff, and clients. The economic goal is to direct resources toward producing more of the intended good or service at the lowest cost maintaining a certain level of quality.

- In the NFP sectors, internal rules, regulations, standard procedures, public and private accreditation, and independent auditing substitute for market measures of success. Sponsor oversight and some degree of client choice are essential.

- NFP firms are not isolated from the national and world economy. Public and nonprofit decision-making involves industry competition, interest rates, inflation, unemployment, and global issues.

KEY TERMS

Flow	Holding company
Stock	Net income
Private good	Quangos
Free rider problem	Privatization
Public goods	Nationalization
Non-rival consumption	Expropriation
Non-exclusion	Joint venture
Collective good	Fund accounting
Commons	Tax expenditure
Free ride	Fiscal federalism
Quasi-public goods	Voucher
Mission statement	Purchase of service contract
Unrelated business activities	(POSC)

SUGGESTED READINGS

Arrow, Kenneth J. 1998: "Foreword," *To Profit or Not to Profit: The Commercial Transformation of the Nonprofit Sector*, ed. Burton A. Weisbrod, Cambridge, UK: Cambridge University Press.

Brooks, Arthur C. 2006: *Who Really Cares: The Surprising Truth about Compassionate Conservatism*, New York: Basic Books.

Croteau, John T. 1963: *The Economics of the Credit Union*, Detroit, MI: Wayne State University Press.

Gassler, Robert Scott 1986: *The Economics of Nonprofit Enterprise: A Study in Applied Economic Theory*, Lanham, MD: University Press of America.

Kramer, Ralph M. 2001: "Voluntary Agencies and the Contract Culture: Dream or Nightmare?" *The Nature of the Nonprofit Sector*, 369–79, ed. J. Steven Ott, Boulder, CO: Westview Press.

Mayer, Lloyd Hitochi 2004: "Political Activities of Tax-exempt Organizations: Useful Guidance in Revenue Ruling 2004–6," *Journal of Taxation*, 181 (3), 181–9.

Organization for Economic Co-operation and Development 2003: *The Non-profit Sector in a Changing Economy*, Paris: OECD.

Perkins, Tom 2001: "The Compliance Board," *Wall Street Journal*, Friday, March 2, A11.

Rose, Daniel 2003: "The American Philanthropic Tradition: Spending Our Wealth with Energy and Imagination," Address delivered to the International Fellows Program, Center for the Study of Philanthropy, Graduate Center, CUNY, April 2.

Rudney, Gabriel and Young, Paula 1989: "The Nonprofit Sector of the U.S. Economy: A Methodological Statement," *Review of Income and Wealth*, 35 (1), 57–80.

Tropman, John E. and Tropman, Elmer J. 1999: *Nonprofit Boards: What to Do and How to Do It*, Child Welfare League of America.

Tuckman, Howard P. 1998: "Competition, Commercialization, and the Evolution of Nonprofit Organizational Structures," *To Profit or Not to Profit: The Commercial Transformation of the Nonprofit Sector*, 25–46, ed. Burton A. Weisbrod, Cambridge, UK: Cambridge University Press.

END OF CHAPTER EXERCISES

Exercise 2.1

Place each of the following goods and services into one of the four categories shown in Figure 2.1: public art such as fountains and statues, urban freeways, clothing, symphonies, open highways, tornado warning sirens, tennis courts, food, and underground oil deposits. Explain your selection for each product in terms of non-rival and non-exclusionary characteristics.

Exercise 2.2

Consider types of healthcare along a continuum of public to private interest. Include healthcare information, various types of pharmaceuticals and procedures, cosmetic surgery, diagnoses, as well as critical and long-term nursing care. Differentiate healthcare services as purely public, quasi-public, and private. How does this differ from viewing healthcare as a necessity or right? Discuss.

Exercise 2.3

Select two mission statements, one from an autonomous public enterprise and one from a private nonprofit.

    a.   Evaluate the statements in terms of length, statement of duties, and targeted clients. Outline the responsibilities of their respective boards in terms of these statements.

b.   Obtain an income statement for each of these firms.
c.   Generalize the sources and uses of funds for both firms.

Exercise 2.4

Compare and contrast two nonprofit agencies of your choice providing similar social service.

a.   Determine approximately what percentage of revenue is derived from sources other than client services?
b.   Do government agencies provide a similar service? Do for-profit firms provide a similar service?
c   Are production costs higher or lower in the nonprofit firm you selected than they would be if the firms operated in another sector of the economy? Explain.
d.   Check out and summarize available information, including recent annual returns to the Internal Revenue Service, posted on the following web sites: www.guidestar.org, www.charitywatch.org, www.give.org.

Exercise 2.5

Provide real-world examples of:

a.   A NFP firm and one of its unrelated business activities.
b.   A nonprofit firm and its collaboration with a government agency.
c.   A nonprofit firm and its collaboration with a for-profit firm.
d.   A nonprofit firm holding a purchase-of-service contract with the government.

What are the risks of such relationships? What are the benefits?

Exercise 2.6

In Figure 2.3, there are arrows showing revenue and income flows between house-holds and the three producing sectors of the economy. List and explain how at least five of these flows are affected by a recession defined as a general downturn in business activity.

Exercise 2.7

Research the legal requirements for nonprofit solicitation of funds from the following list of government and private sources:

Internal Revenue Service: www.irs.gov. Click on the "Charities & Non-profits" tab.
National Association of State Charity Officials: www.nasconet.org.
American Society of Association Executives: www.asaecenter.org.
BoardSource: www.boardsource.org.
Council on Foundations: www.cof.org.
Independent Sector: www.independentsector.org.
National Council of Nonprofit Associations: www.ncna.org.

Exercise 2.8

If individuals are able to "free ride" will the activity tend toward using too many or too few scarce resources? Explain.

Exercise 2.9

Carefully describe two characteristics of private goods as compared with public goods? Explain how these characteristics of private goods eliminate free riders?

Exercise 2.10

Provide two examples of services publicly provided and produced that are actually rival in consumption and therefore quasi-public.

Exercise 2.11

Most agree that fireworks displays are non-rival in consumption. Would you classify them as a collective good or a public good? Explain.

Exercise 2.12

As a board member of a private nonprofit organization, how would you determine if a particular unrelated business activity is contrary to mission.

Exercise 2.13

NFP firms do not earn net income due to the nondistributional constraint. True or false? Explain.

Exercise 2.14

Explain why a for-profit corporation is less concerned than NFPs with fund accounting for different product lines.

Exercise 2.15

In responding to military or civic disturbances, a nation can requisition dorms, classrooms, and other facilities of private universities. Carefully differentiate between exprepriation and nationalization.

Exercise 2.16

Provide an example, hypothetical or real, of a federal unfunded mandate. How does this compare with fiscal federalism?

Exercise 2.17

Explain how government-provided vouchers for elementary school students, for example, are not government grants but purchase for service contracts. Demonstrate how these contracts potentially conflict with a private school's mission. What mechanism could be built-in to constrain budget maximizing administrators from seeking funds inappropriate in terms of mission contracts?

Exercise 2.18

Describe how the net income of a NFP service provider, such as a food bank, is cyclically related to the business cycle.

Exercise 2.19

Suppose a private nonprofit golf club uses retirees to clean, garden, and perform other functions. Legally, are they able to treat these workers as volunteers and/or offer them a small mutually negotiated token payment for their services? Explain.

Exercise 2.20

Social services fully financed from user fees and donations to private nonprofits are provided at no cost to taxpayers. True or false? Explain.

Part II

Consumer Theory and Public Goods

3
Demand and Supply

3.1   INTRODUCTION

User fees, similar but not identical to prices, provide revenue for government and nonprofit agencies. Tuition, patient hospital bills, and counseling fees do not account for an organization's full cost in providing services, but they represent a substantial percentage of total revenue. Administrators, influenced by what the market will bear, set these fees. What the market will bear is just another way of referring to the two most fundamental concepts of economics, namely demand and supply. In this chapter, we will build the supply and demand framework for determining market price and analyze the distortions created when administered prices deviate from market. This chapter includes not only the demands for private goods but for public and quasi-public goods as well.

3.2   CONSUMER DEMAND

Recall the last time that you made a major purchase. It could have been a car, admission to a state park, tuition, a new tennis racquet, dental care, or a ticket to a concert. Whatever decision you made, you bought the good or service because it pleased you. You were not forced to make the purchase. You did so in anticipation of increasing your personal satisfaction. NFP administrators do not determine what clients are willing to pay for their services, individuals do.

If these goods and services provide us with satisfaction, we say that they have value to us. Used in this way, value implies value in use. Air has a value in use because we benefit from breathing air. But air is free. If air has value to us, why is it free? We certainly would be willing to pay for air rather than do without it. But air is available in such abundance that we treat it as a free good.

We also get satisfaction from using gasoline. Gas has value in use. But unlike air, we must pay for the gas we use. That is, gasoline has value in exchange as well as value in use. We are willing to exchange something – usually money – for the use of some gas.

Why is air free, but gasoline costly? Gas is scarce while air is abundant. This illustrates the economic role of scarcity. But be careful in attributing price with scarcity alone. Just because something is scarce does not necessarily mean it will have value in exchange. You may be the best classical ukulele player in the world, but few symphonies are willing to offer you a chair with salary. Also, something may have no exchange value because it is not useful. That is, people do not get any satisfaction from possessing or using it.

Clients have a limited income to exchange for goods and services. They will not freely pay for abundant public goods, even if they value them highly. Clients will not pay for private goods they do not value. Finally, clients often cannot afford to purchase services even when they desire or need them. For some, that limit is severe. A public school teacher typically has less to spend than a Wall Street investment banker. A family on public assistance has less to exchange for goods and services than a skilled laborer. However, everyone (even the richest) has limited funds. Because of this limit, we must make decisions about how we will spend, save, and/or borrow money. How individuals allocate their income determines the demand for various goods and services in the economy.

Demand refers to the quantities of a good that consumers are *willing and able* to purchase at various prices during a given period of time. For your demand to be meaningful in the marketplace you must be *able* to make a purchase; that is, you must have enough money to make the purchase. There are, no doubt, many items for which you have a willingness to purchase but you may not have an effective demand for them because you don't have the money to actually make the purchase. For example, you might like to have a 3,600-square-foot ski lodge in Vermont, an equally large beach house on the Carolina coast, and a private jet to travel between these places on weekends and between seasons. In addition, you might like the latest in cosmetic surgery and private tutors. But, it is likely that you have a budget constraint that prevents you from having all these items.

For product demand to be effective a consumer must also be willing to make the purchase. There are many products that you could afford (that is, you have the ability to buy them) but for which you may not be willing to spend your income. Each of us has a unique perspective on our own personal satisfaction and the things that may enhance that satisfaction. The important point is that if you do not expect the consumption of something to bring you added satisfaction you will not be willing to purchase that good or service. Therefore, you do not have a demand for such things despite the fact that you might be able to afford them.

When we discuss demand, we are always referring to purchases made during a *given period of time*. For example, you might have a weekly demand for candy bars. If you are willing and able to buy four candy bars at a price of 50 cents each, your demand is four candy bars a week. But your demand for shoes may be better described on a yearly basis such that, at an average price of $65 a pair, you might buy three pairs of shoes per year. The important point here is that when we refer to a person's demand for a product we usually mean the demand over some appropriate time period, not necessarily over the rest of the person's life.

For most goods, consumers are willing to purchase more units at a lower price than at a higher price. The inverse relationship between price and the quantity consumers will buy is so widely observed that it is called the *law of demand*. The law of demand is the rule that people will buy more at lower prices than at higher prices, if all other factors are constant. This concept of the law of demand is a logical and accurate description of the behavior we would all expect to observe. This law operates in the NFP sectors as well. For example, increased tuition generally lowers applications, and reduced entrance fees raise state park entries.

The reason individuals purchase more of a given product when price decreases is due to income and substitution effects.

- *Income effect*. The **income effect** is a term used in demand analysis to indicate the increase or decrease in the amount purchased because of a price-induced change in purchasing power. If the price of a product increases (decreases) then I must pay more (less) of my money income to purchase it. This reduces (increases) the amount of income available to me, and therefore I am likely to reduce (increase) the quantity demanded of the product due to affordability. Reduced park entrance fees means that I can afford to enter the park more frequently.
- *Substitution effect*. The **substitution effect** is a term used in demand analysis to indicate the increase or decrease in the amount purchased because of a price-induced change in the relative attractiveness of a good. If the price of a product increases (decreases), even though my preference for the product remains the same, other goods whose prices remain the same appear to me to be a better (worse) value. If tuition at my preferred school increases, a less preferred school may seem more attractive.

If the price of a product increases, income and substitution effects operate to affect decreases in the quantity of that product purchased. Conversely, if the price of a product declines, income and substitution effects operate to affect increases in the quantity of the good purchased.

3.3   INDIVIDUAL AND MARKET DEMAND

A *demand curve* is a graphic illustration of the relationship between *price* and the *quantity purchased* by willing and able consumers at each price. When graphing a demand curve, price is measured along the vertical axis and quantities purchased at various prices are measured along the horizontal axis. Eight hypothetical price-quantity combinations for a consumer's demand for state park entries are shown in Figure 3.1. Consider, for example, a fee of $18.00. At $18.00 the consumer would be willing and able to buy two entries per month, other things being held constant. This point is labeled A in Figure 3.1.

A market demand curve is the horizontal sum of the quantities that all consumers in a particular market are willing and able to purchase at each price. If we plotted the quantity that all consumers in this market would buy at each price, we might have a market demand curve such as the one shown in Figure 3.2. The market demand curve in Figure 3.2 shows that at a price of $13.00, the market demand is 7,000 park entries. This is the point marked C* along the market demand curve.

The market demand curve shows that the quantity purchased goes up from 2,000 to 12,000 as price falls from $18.00 to $8.00. This is called a *change in quantity demanded* or a movement along the demand curve. As price falls, a greater quantity is demanded. As the price goes up, a smaller quantity is demanded. A change in quantity demanded is caused by a change in the price of the product for

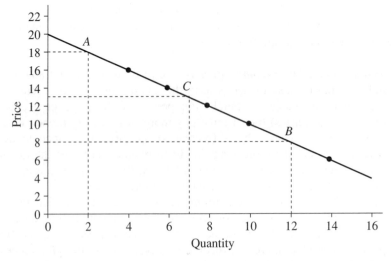

Figure 3.1   A consumer's demand for state park entry tickets. At lower prices, the consumer will purchase more tickets per month than at higher prices. Thus, the demand curve slopes downward to the right, which illustrates the law of demand.

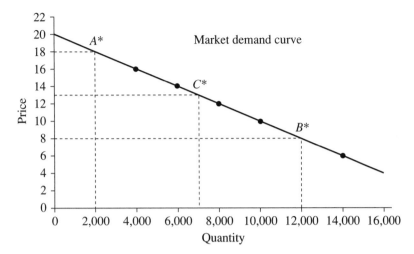

Figure 3.2   The market demand curve for state park entry tickets. Adding together all consumers' demand curves gives the market demand curve. The market demand curve also follows the law of demand and has a negative slope.

any given demand curve. This is true of individual consumers' demand as well as for the market demand.

But what determines how much will be bought at each price? Why are more wood-burning stoves bought now than ten years ago despite higher wood-burning stove prices? Why are more health services bought today than in previous years, even though the price of health services has increased? Questions such as these are answered by looking at the determinants of demand. Figures 3.1 and 3.2 assume that these determinants are held constant (*ceteris paribus*).

3.4   DETERMINANTS OF DEMAND

Demand and the position of the demand curve is determined by consumers' incomes, their attitudes or feelings about products, the prices of related goods, their expectations, and by the number of consumers in the market. These factors are referred to as the determinants of demand. As these underlying determinants change over time, the overall level of demand may change. More or less of a product may be purchased at any one price because of changes in factors that are usually assumed to remain constant.

Changes in determinants are shown by a shift of the entire demand curve. If the demand curve shifts to the right, we say that there has been an *increase in demand*. This is shown as a move from the demand curve labeled "Original demand" to the demand curve labeled "Higher Demand" in Figure 3.3. The original demand curve can be thought of as being the market demand curve for park entries shown in Figure 3.2. As shown in Figure 3.3, at a price of $13.00, given the initial level of demand, consumers purchase 7,000 entries. If demand increased to the higher demand, consumers purchase 9,000 entries at a price of $13.00 rather than the 7,000

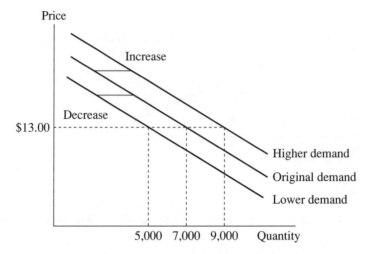

Figure 3.3   Shifts in the market demand for state park entry tickets. An increase in demand can be represented by a shift to the right, such as from the "Original demand" to "Higher demand." A decrease is shown by a shift to the left such as from "Original demand" to "Lower demand." Higher household incomes, for example, may shift the demand curve to the right. Fear of insect bites depending on season may shift the curve left.

along the original demand curve. A change in demand due to a change in determinants shifts the whole curve; a change in quantity demanded due to a price change moves along the original demand curve.

A *decrease in demand* can be illustrated by a shift of the whole demand curve to the left. In Figure 3.3 this is represented by a move from the original demand to the lower demand. Given the lower level of demand, just 5,000 entries would be purchased at $13.00 each.

It is important to see that these changes in demand are different from changes in quantity demanded. We discussed how changes in price cause a change in quantity demanded. As price changes, people buy more or less along a given demand curve. Movement from *A** to *B** or to *C** in Figure 3.2 shows the change in quantity demanded as price changes. It is not a shift in the whole demand curve, such as that shown in Figure 3.3. When the whole demand curve changes, there is a *change in demand*. Some factors causing a change (shift) in demand are changing incomes, changing tastes of consumers, changes in the price of complementary and substitute goods, changes in consumer expectations, and changes in the number of consumers in the market.

There is an alternative way of noting this relationship that is widely used and versatile. A letter such as f is chosen to stand for the function or relationship itself. The symbol $f(x)$ is read "f of x." Using this functional notation, you can express the demand function as follows:

Quantity demanded $= f$ (price of the product, income, tastes, prices of
substitutes and complements, expectations, and
the number of consumers).

Figures 3.1 and 3.2 are two-dimensional and show the relationship between quantity demanded and price. It is possible to do this because income, tastes, the prices of related goods, expectations, and the number of consumers remain the same (ceteris paribus). Figure 3.3 shifts the whole demand curve to indicate that a determinate, other than the price of the product itself, has changed. Increases in income or preference for a good will shift the demand curve to the right.

Substitute goods and services are ones such that if the price of one changes, the demand for the other good shifts to the left or right. Assume that digital and film cameras are substitutes. If the price of one product, such as digital cameras, decreases, the demand for digital cameras stays the same but the quantity demanded of digital cameras increases. This is represented as a movement along the demand curve. However, the change in a product's price actually shifts the demand curve for its substitute. Thus, a decline in the price of *digital* cameras shifts the whole demand curve for *film* cameras to the left. Similarly, if fees charged at state schools increase, the quantity demanded will decrease. This could increase demand at private nonprofit schools, shifting the demand curve for private schools to the right.

Services provided in the private nonprofit sector are substitutes for those provided in the government sector and vice versa. Economists argue that culturally, ethnically, and religiously homogeneous societies have more uniform tastes in public goods. In these societies, the size of the private nonprofit sector may be smaller. Citizens do not insist on differentiated services, and are willing to accept the goods provided in the government sector. In countries that traditionally have had relatively homogeneous populations, such as Scandinavia, government meets most people's need for collective-type services. Pluralism and diversity in the United States explain why the nonprofit sector is large. The government and nonprofit sectors provide substitutes but both are responding to the same demand for quasi-public goods. Demand for services, between the government and nonprofit sectors, is therefore interrelated. Reduced out of pocket user fees or perceived quality increases in one sector decreases demand in the other sector. Clients benefit with a choice between substitutes.

Consider goods that are complementary. *Complementary goods* and services are ones that are used together. If the price on one good changes, the demand for its complement shifts to the right or left. A decrease in the price of computers results in more computers being purchased. This is a change in quantity demanded represented by a movement along the demand curve for computers. However, the lower price and increased quantity demanded of computers causes the demand for complementary software to increase. This is represented by a shift in the total software demand curve to the right.

Weisbrod (1977) suggests that demand in the two NFP sectors is complementary. Government introduces an activity, such as universal education, and people decide to supplement it in the nonprofit sector. Nonprofit religious organizations initiate homeless shelters and government steps in with similar shelters. In fact, nonprofits flourish in industries where government accepts some financial responsibility. For example, if a state school has a good music program, households supplement with private lessons at a local nonprofit conservatory. The two NFP sectors are symbiotic and complementary and together increase the quality of life.

3.5   SUPPLY

Supply represents the quantities of a product or service that a firm is willing and able to make available for sale at different prices. We expect that firms need to earn higher prices for the products they sell if they are to increase the quantity they supply. In other words, higher prices induce firms to increase their output. A NFP firm producing educational, medical, or social services is offering a product to both clients paying user fees and sponsors willing to subsidize their production. Higher per unit compensation in a given NFP industry enables each firm to increase its quantity supplied while still covering costs.

3.6   FIRM AND MARKET SUPPLY

A *supply curve* is a graphic representation of quantities supplied at each price. A supply curve demonstrates the positive relationship between price and quantity supplied. The explanation for this positive relationship between price and the quantity supplied lies in the principle of diminishing marginal productivity and how it affects costs. This is discussed in detail in Chapter 6. It is more costly to increase output with a fixed-sized plant. To produce more, firms must receive a higher price. Thus, the supply curve is determined by the level of cost and the level of cost is in turn influenced by diminishing marginal productivity of additional inputs. The supply curve for a hypothetical college that sells pizza in the campus snack shop is shown in Figure 3.4.

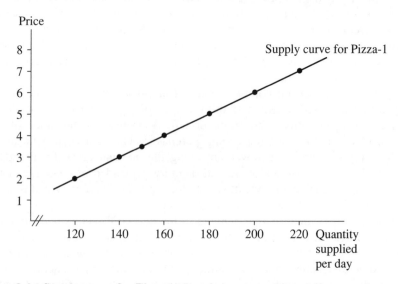

Figure 3.4   Supply curve for Pizza-1. As price goes up, Pizza-1 increases the number of pizzas supplied per day. At a price of $2, they will supply 120 pizzas, at a price of $4, they will supply 160, and at a price of $7, they will supply 220 per day. Note that the double slash (//) on the horizontal axis indicates the scale is broken at that point.

Table 3.1   Firm and market supply of pizza

Individual firms' supply schedules, quantity supplied per day by:

Price ($)	Campus	Firm W	Firm X	Firm Y	Firm Z	Market supply = total of the five firms
2	120	90	115	140	135	600
3	140	100	120	150	140	650
4	160	110	125	160	145	700
5	180	120	130	170	150	750
6	200	130	135	180	155	800
7	220	140	140	190	160	850

Market supply combines quantities that all firms make available for sale at various prices. Thus, to get the market supply, we add up all the quantities each firm supplies at every price.

Suppose Campus Snack Shop serves a market in which there are four other firms. We will use a small number of firms for illustration, even though there would prob- ably be many more in real life. We will call these firm *W*, firm *X*, firm *Y*, and firm *Z*. The supply schedule for these four firms is given in Table 3.1, along with Campus Snack Shop's supply schedule. In the last column of Table 3.1, the market supply schedule is given. It is simply the sum of columns two through six. That is, the market supply is the sum of the amount supplied by all of the firms in the market at each price.

The market supply schedule is used to draw market supply on a graph. The mar- ket supply curve for pizzas is illustrated in Figure 3.5. You see in Figure 3.5 that the market supply curve has a positive slope, like that of an individual firm. As price goes up, each firm, and thus all firms combined, supply a greater quantity. At higher prices, firms are able to supply larger quantities even though their extra costs per unit are rising.

As price changes the amount supplied changes along the supply curve. This is true for the individual firm and for the market as a whole. If price goes up, more units are made available for sale. If price goes down, fewer units are made available.

This change in the number of units made available due to a price change is called a *change in the quantity supplied*. For the market supply curve in Figure 3.5, move- ment from Point *J* to Point *K* is an example of a change in quantity supplied. When price goes from $3 to $5, the quantity supplied goes up from 650 to 750 per day. If the price falls from $5 to $3, the quantity supplied decreases from a total of 750 to 650 per day. A change in the quantity supplied is shown as a change along a given supply curve. The quantity supplied of hospital beds or pre-school openings increases if compensation for these services increases and decreases if compensa- tion decreases (ceteris paribus).

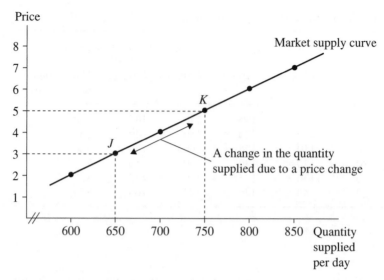

Figure 3.5   Market supply curve for pizza. The market supply curve for pizza is the sum of the quantities supplied by all firms in the market at each price. At a price of $3, there would be 650 pizzas supplied in the entire market. At a price of $5, the quantity supplied would increase to 750 per day.

3.7   DETERMINANTS OF SUPPLY

A *change in supply* indicates a shift of the whole supply schedule or curve. An increase in supply means more units are supplied at each price. A decrease in supply means fewer units are supplied at each price.

Representative changes in supply are illustrated in Figure 3.6. The curve labeled "Original market supply" is the original supply curve (it is the same as the market supply in Figure 3.5). The curve labeled "Decreased market supply" represents a decrease in supply. Less is supplied at each price along this lower supply curve than along the original supply curve. For example, at a price of $4, the original supply was 700 units. After the decrease in supply, only 650 units are supplied at that same price.

An increase in supply is shown by shifting to the curve labeled "Increased market supply," in Figure 3.6. More is supplied at each price along this higher (i.e., further to the right) supply curve than along the original supply. At $4 along the original supply, 700 units are supplied. After the supply shift, 750 units are supplied at $4.

What causes the supply curve to shift (i.e., a change in supply)? The most common causes are technological change, a change in the cost of inputs, prices of other goods, expectations, and a change in number of firms in the industry.

Using functional notation, the quantity supplied is as follows:

Quantity supplied $= f$ (price of the product, technology, cost of inputs, prices of related goods, expectations, and the number of producers).

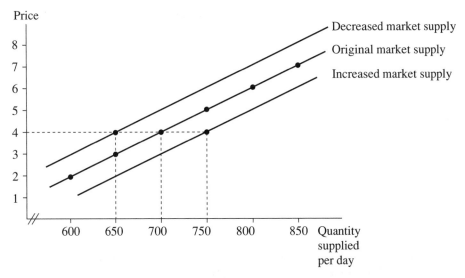

Figure 3.6   Changes in supply represented by shifts in the supply curve. An increase in supply is shown as movement from the original supply curve to the supply curve labeled "Increased market supply," which is to the right of the original curve. A decrease in supply is shown by the shift to the lower supply labeled "Decreased market supply," which is to the left of the original supply. Higher costs for ingredients used in pizza shift the supply curve to the left. Better baking technology shifts the supply curve to the right.

Figures 3.4 and 3.5 are two-dimensional and show the relationship between quantity supplied and price. It is possible to do this because technology, input costs, etc. remain the same. Figure 3.6 shifts the whole supply curve to indicate that a determinate, other than the price of the product itself, has changed. Suppose that administrators of homeless shelters anticipate an increase in clients with children. They may shift resources from single clients to families in order to meet this need, even if their compensation from government and donors did not increase. In other words, the supply schedule would shift to the right due to one of the determinants, i.e. expectations, changing. Similarly, if the cost of providing services increased, administrators are forced to reduce services, shifting the supply curve to the left. Changes in government or donor compensation to the firm for different types of services will also shift the supply curve.

3.8   EQUILIBRIUM OF DEMAND AND SUPPLY

At this point, we combine supply and demand to determine market price. In a market economy, natural economic forces lead to an equilibrium, or balance. In Table 3.2, you see hypothetical demand and supply schedules for one serving of pizza. At prices higher than $3.60, the quantity supplied is greater than the quantity demanded. As such, there is downward pressure on price because suppliers will be willing to lower price in order to sell more. At prices below $3.60, the

Table 3.2   Hypothetical demand and supply schedules for pizza

Price ($)	Quantity demanded	Quantity supplied
2.80	2,400	1,600
3.00	2,300	1,700
3.20	2,200	1,800
3.40	2,100	1,900
3.60	*2,000*	*2,000*
3.80	1,900	2,100
4.00	1,800	2,200
4.20	1,700	2,300
4.40	1,600	2,400

quantity demanded is greater than the quantity supplied. When the quantity demanded is greater than the quantity supplied, there is upward pressure on price.

Only at equilibrium of $3.60 is there no pressure for a price change. The ***equilibrium price*** is the price at which the quantity demanded equals the quantity supplied. At the $3.60 price, the quantity demanded is 2,000 units, as is the quantity supplied. Thus, 2,000 units represent the equilibrium quantity. The equilibrium quantity is the quantity that is both demanded and supplied at the equilibrium price.

This equilibrium is shown graphically in Figure 3.7, where the equilibrium price and quantity are enclosed in boxes. The equilibrium point, or the intersection of

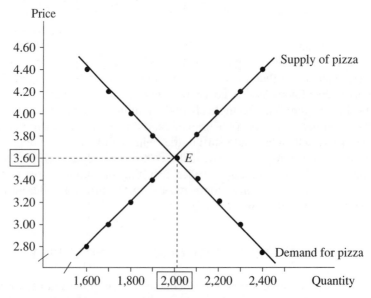

Figure 3.7   Balance between demand and supply. When the price is at a level where the quantity demanded equals the quantity supplied, the market is in equilibrium. In this graph, at a price of $3.60, both the quantity demanded and the quantity supplied would number 2,000 units. Thus, there is no incentive for the price to change.

demand and supply, is labeled E in Figure 3.7. Only at this point does the quantity demanded by potential purchasers equal the quantity supplied by potential producers. At any price above $3.60, the quantity supplied is greater than the quantity demanded. At such prices, economic forces push prices downward. The quantity demanded then increases while the quantity supplied decreases until Point E is reached.

For any price below $3.60, the quantity demanded is greater than the quantity supplied, which puts upward pressure on price. The quantity supplied rises, and the quantity demanded falls until Point E is reached.

3.9   PRICE AS A RATIONING DEVICE

Both demand and supply depend on price. Consumers and clients (demanders) observe prices in deciding how to spend their money and producers (suppliers) observe prices in deciding what goods or services to produce. Prices act as signals. As such, *prices help to ration both finished goods and raw materials among competing uses.* Some universities title their microeconomics course "Price Theory," because allocative and productive efficiency are realized through prices in market competition.

Shortages

What does it mean to say there is a shortage of some product? What does it mean when a newscaster announces that there is likely to be a shortage of flu vaccine? What exactly does this mean? A shortage exists when people are willing to buy more than producers have for sale at a particular price. That is, there is a **shortage** when the quantity demanded at a certain price is greater than the quantity supplied. A shortage of vaccine means that clients wish to purchase more at the present price than is currently available.

Figure 3.8 helps explain a shortage of pizza servings at a given price. At a price of $3.20, the quantity supplied is 1,800 units. What is the quantity demanded at that price? From the demand curve you can see that it is 2,200 units. Therefore, at $3.20, there is a shortage. Consumers express demand for 2,200 units, but suppliers are only willing to supply 1,800 units. Not everyone who wishes to buy pizza at that price is able to do so. There is a shortage of 400 units. This gap equals the distance between A and B.

Some are willing to pay more than $3.20 per serving, as shown on the demand curve in Figure 3.8. Consumers are willing to pay $4.20 for 1,700 units, and pay even more, rather than do without their favorite lunch.

Suppliers know that the quantity demanded is greater than the quantity supplied and that some will pay a higher price. Suppliers raise price. A shortage causes upward pressure on the price, shown by the arrow in Figure 3.8. Upward pressure is due to spontaneous economic forces on both the demand and supply side of the marketplace.

As price rises, quantity demanded decreases. Some consumers drop out of the market while others cut back on their use of the product. As price rises, producers increase the quantity they supply. As the quantity demanded decreases and the

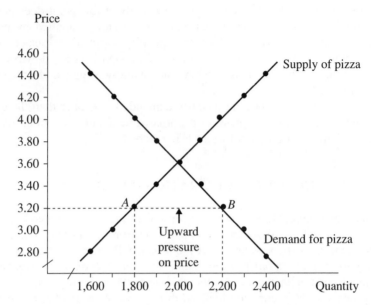

Figure 3.8   A shortage. A shortage results when demand is greater than supply at a certain price. In this case, at a price of $3.20, the quantity demanded is 2,200 units while only 1,800 units are supplied. This distance between A and B (400 units) is a measure of the quantity of the shortage.

quantity supplied increases the shortage is reduced. As long as quantity demanded is greater than the quantity supplied, the process continues until the upward pressure on price eliminates the shortage.

Surpluses

A *surplus* implies that the quantity supplied is greater than the quantity demanded at a certain price. People are not willing to buy as much as is produced at a given price. At a certain price, pizza shops may produce more than consumers wish, resulting in a surplus.

A surplus is illustrated in Figure 3.9. At a price of $4.20, the quantity demanded is 1,700 units, at the point labeled C along the demand curve. As indicated by Point D along the supply curve, 2,300 units are supplied. There is a surplus of 600 units. This surplus is shown by the distance between C and D in Figure 3.9. Suppliers have more of the product than they can sell at this high price. They are likely to reduce price to try to increase sales. Consumers recognize that they have greater bargaining power and may offer to buy the product, but only at a reduced price. Thus, when there is a surplus, there will be downward pressure on price, shown by the arrow in Figure 3.9.

Administrators' response to unfilled hospital beds or university dorm rooms may be to close off facilities or lament clients' ability to pay. As supply and demand analysis suggests, when quantity supplied exceeds quantity demanded, we would expect tuition and hospital charges to adjust. At times, NFP firms offer rebates to

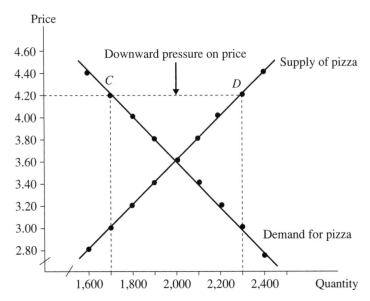

Figure 3.9   A surplus. Surplus results when the quantity supplied is greater than the quantity demanded. In this case, at a price of $4.20, the quantity supplied is 2,300 units, but consumers would only purchase 1,700 units at that price. The distance between *C* and *D* (600 units) is a measure of the quantity of the surplus.

reduce excess capacity. A rebate is a way of lowering the effective price to consumers. If you are awarded a tuition reduction of $1,500, that is really a price reduction of $1,500. In fact, some colleges, to increase applications, guarantee tuition reductions before students are formally admitted.

Both demand and supply sides of the market react with downward pressure on price whenever there is a surplus. As price comes down, the quantity demanded increases. This helps reduce the surplus. Also, as price falls, the quantity supplied decreases as firms reduce production. This also acts to reduce the surplus.

As long as the quantity demanded is less than the quantity supplied, price will continue to fall. As price falls, the quantity demanded increases and the quantity supplied decreases, until the surplus is eliminated and there is no longer downward pressure on price.

3.10   CHANGES IN SUPPLY AND/OR DEMAND

Why should public administrators do supply and demand analysis? They need to accurately deduce what will happen to equilibrium price and quantity when demand, supply, or both shifts. You recall that a change in supply and/or demand shifts the curves to the right or left.

When the demand for a product goes up, the equilibrium price and quantity are affected. An *increase in demand* means that consumers are willing to buy more at each price than they would have before the rise in demand. If the quantity supplied did not change, price would surely rise. The original quantity supplied would no longer satisfy demand at the original price. There would be a shortage at the original price. As you have seen, price will be pushed up when there is a shortage. But remember that if price goes up, the quantity supplied will go up also as producers respond to the higher price. A new equilibrium price is reached where the new higher demand intersects the supply curve. Supply and demand indicates that an increase in the demand for nursing home spaces in a particular community results in a temporary shortage. If the market is permitted to operate, the price of care will increase and suppliers will produce more spaces at the higher rate.

When the demand for a product falls, consumers are willing to buy fewer units at each price. This will also affect both equilibrium price and equilibrium quantity. With a lower level of demand, there would be a surplus if the quantity supplied did not change. A surplus would put downward pressure on price. As price falls, the quantity supplied by producers would also fall. This process would go on until the quantity supplied and the quantity demanded were once more in balance.

A shift of the supply curve can also upset the balance between the quantity demanded and the quantity supplied. An *increase in supply* means that producers are willing to supply more at each price. If there is an increase in the supply of nursing home spaces, the supply curve would shift to the right. If demand stays the same a surplus will result. A surplus indicates downward pressure on price. As the price begins to fall, quantity demanded increases, following along down the demand curve. Clients will be willing and able to purchase more at lower prices than at higher prices. As the quantity demanded increases, surplus is reduced. At the same time, producers cut back on quantity supplied due to the fall in price. This further lowers the amount of the surplus. After all changes take place, the price will have fallen just enough that the quantity demanded and the quantity supplied are again balanced.

Supply shifts to the left (decreases) if the costs of production rise. Cost increases are often due to a rise in the costs of inputs. Increased regulations also increase costs. An increase in cost per unit of output gives suppliers two choices: either offer fewer units for sale at each price or charge more for any given rate of output.

Consider the case of a decrease in the supply of nursing home spaces, due to increased regulations or increased labor costs. The immediate effect of decreased supply is a shortage. We know that when there is a shortage there will be upward pressure on price. As price rises, clients, paying out of savings or family income, reduce the quantity of nursing home care that they are willing and able to purchase. This does not solve the problem but it does alleviate the shortage. As price goes up, nursing home providers expand places along the new lower supply curve. The process continues until the quantity demanded and the quantity supplied are again in balance.

The market is dynamic; supply and demand are continually shifting. The net effect of these shifts will determine if price goes up or down. Calculating the precise effect on an individual firm may be difficult, but administrators use supply and demand analysis to assess general changes in their respective industries. Application 3.1 indicates how tuition increases are related to supply and demand changes.

APPLICATION 3.1
Supply, Demand, and University Tuition

In 1980, tuition charges in the United States as well as the total of tuition, fees, room, and board began a steady climb increasing substantially more than inflation. Between 1980–1 and 1990–1, tuition charges increased in both sectors, but the tuition gap between public and private colleges grew substantially.

Tuition prices are influenced by a variety of demand and supply factors each of which must be analyzed:

1 Subsidies, in the form of state appropriations and endowment income, reduce upward pressure on price by increasing supply and thus shift the supply curve to the right.

2 Increases in institutional costs or expenditures, such as new computer technology, decrease supply, shift the supply curve to the left, and put upward pressure on tuition.

3 Increases in productivity, such as a higher student–faculty ratio, reduce the unit costs per student, increase supply, shift the supply curve to the right, and tend to lower prices, often at the unmeasured expense of reduced quality.

4 An increase in the benefits consumers expect from the purchase of the product, such as higher future incomes, increases the demand, shifts the demand curve to the right, and raises price.

5 Increases in the number of applicants, such as rises in international and college-aged students, increase demand, shift the demand curve to the right, and raise prices.

6 Increases in student grants and loans will increase demand, shift the demand curve to the right, and put upward pressure on tuition.

7 The prices of substitutes, such as tuition abroad, and the prices of complements, such as books and living expenses, affect the position of the demand curve.

Complex sets of government policies and market forces influence the way tuition is set by institutions.

Source: Edward P. St. John, *Refinancing the College Dream*, Baltimore, MD: Johns Hopkins University Press, 2003.

3.11   CONSUMER AND PRODUCER SURPLUS

In competitive markets, consumers and producers buy and sell at market deter-mined prices. Sometimes, as demanders, we strike it lucky and pay a price lower than what we would have been willing to pay. Sometimes, as suppliers, we are actually paid more than what we would be willing to accept. The subjective value of a product to a particular buyer or seller is *not* the market price of the item.

Consumer surplus is the difference between what a consumer is *willing to pay* for an additional unit of a product and its market price. Think of surplus as extra value to the consumer, not excess quantity. For example, the subjective value of daycare services for children is probably higher for a couple earning $250,000 a year than for a couple earning $50,000 a year. Yet, in a competitive market, both couples pay the market price of approximately $120 per child per week. The higher-earning couple receives consumer surplus from this transaction. The lower-income couple is paying the maximum that they willing to pay rather than do without the service. At a higher price, one of the partners quits his or her job and cares for the child at home.

Figure 3.10 describes two situations. In one case, it shows a demand curve that declines in steps as an individual is willing to buy an extra unit for every two

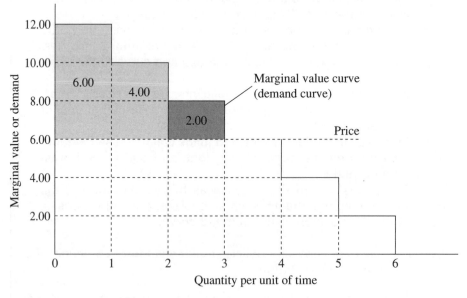

Figure 3.10   The marginal value (demand) curve and consumer surplus for individually purchased units. The consumer surplus is the area under the marginal value (demand) curve and above the market price which you pay for that quantity. If the market price is $6.00 and you purchase one unit, your consumer surplus is $6.00. If you purchase two units at the $6.00 price, your consumer surplus is $10.00; $6.00 from the first unit purchased and $4.00 from the second unit purchased. The consumer will purchase the fourth unit, even though it does not add to consumer surplus, because the price paid is at least equal to its marginal value to the consumer.

dollar decrease in price. Figure 3.10 could also represent one person paying $12, and other $10, and yet another $8 for one unit each. In both cases, price represents the marginal value that a consumer places on a unit of the product at a given time.

The value of an extra item (say, one more t-shirt) to a single individual is shown on the vertical axis and is labeled "marginal value"; these values in Figure 3.10 form a demand curve. If the market price for similar t-shirts is $6 and the consumer purchases one t-shirt, the marginal value to the individual of this first shirt is $12.00. The price paid (that is, the marginal value given up), however, is only $6.00; thus the individual is $6.00 better off than before the transaction. If the consumer purchases a second t-shirt, the marginal value received is $10.00 while the price paid is again only $6.00; the individual is better off by an additional $4.00. Thus buying two t-shirts instead of one makes the consumer better off by a total of $10.00 ($6.00 + $4.00), which represents consumer surplus. The consumer will earn consumer surplus on the third unit and will go on to purchase a fourth unit providing her with value equal to or greater than price.

Notice that by purchasing the second unit the consumer does not now have $10.00 more than before the first t-shirt purchase; he has $12.00 less ($12.00 is the amount paid for the two t-shirts). What then do we mean when we say the consumer is better off by $10.00? We mean that the consumer owns two shirts, worth $22 to him or her, but paid only $12.00. The consumer is indifferent between the following two choices:

1   having his present income *and* buying two t-shirts;
2   having an income of $10.00 more *but* not being able to purchase any t-shirt.

Some consumers then are receiving more value than the market price they are paying; these consumers would pay more for the good or service if they had to. Economists call the extra value consumers receive beyond the amount they pay, consumer surplus.

Now, consider the supply curve. **Producer surplus** is the difference between what a firm receives on the market and what it costs the firm to supply the product. The concept is similar to consumer surplus. Think of this surplus as extra benefit or profit to the producer. Suppose the price paid on the open market for t-shirts is $10 as shown in Figure 3.11. Given a price of $10.00 per unit, the curve labeled "marginal value" shows the cost to the firm of producing one more t-shirt (it is, of course, also the supply curve of the firm). In our daycare example, providers may be willing to care for children at less than the community's market price of $120 per week. Of course, the provider will charge the full price if clients are willing to pay $120.

Figure 3.11 is drawn as a smooth curve, but the quantity supplied could just as well be shown as a step curve. If a nonprofit with a t-shirt promotion is willing to produce the first t-shirt for about $1.50 but receives the market price of $10.00 for it; the net gain is $8.50. The second t-shirt is worth about $1.75 to the nonprofit (because the company must give up resources worth about $1.75 to purchase and have its logo stamped on that unit), but again the second t-shirt is sold for $10.00 and so the nonprofit receives a net gain on the second t-shirt of $8.25. This process continues until the tenth t-shirt is sold. The sum of the net gains is shown

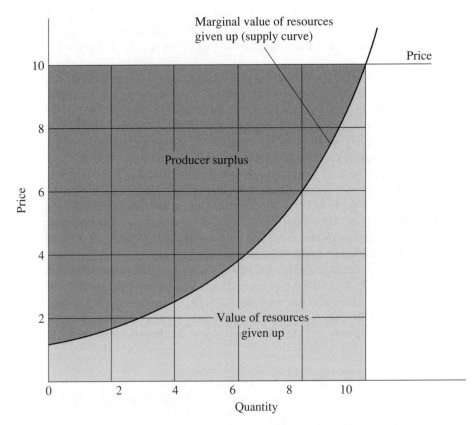

Figure 3.11   The producer surplus and the marginal value of resources given up.
The area above the marginal value function represents the producer surplus, while the
area below the curve represents the value of resources foregone at a price of $10.

in Figure 3.11 as producer surplus. The total area above the marginal value or
supply curve and beneath the market price is producer surplus, the amount the
firm is better off by producing and selling ten units at $10.00 each.

Consumer and producer surplus are both clearly indicated in Figure 3.12.
Consumers purchase goods having a personal value to them greater or equal to
price as shown by the triangular area under the demand function above price; this
represents consumer surplus. Total revenue paid equals the rectangle of market price
times quantity purchased. The producer, on the other hand, values the product by
its marginal value along the supply curve. Therefore, producer surplus is the difference between total cost and what the firm gives up to produce the product. This
is the area below market price and above the supply curve.

Experimental economics

Beginning in the early 1960s, a small group of economists began conducting
laboratorylike experiments of economic phenomena. They believed that the study
of economics is not much different from lab sciences like chemistry and physics.

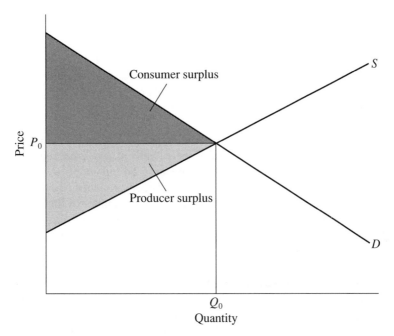

Figure 3.12   A market without price controls. Producer surplus measures the net
benefit to producers; it is the area above the supply curve but under the market price.
Consumer surplus measures the net benefit to consumers; it is the area below the
demand curve but above the market price. The sum of both producer surplus and
consumer surplus measures the net benefit to society of a competitive market.

Laboratory experiments could be run under controlled conditions to test various
economic hypotheses. Early experiments dealt with supply, demand, and market
characteristics.

Nobel Prize Winner, Vernon L. Smith, created artificially constructed markets
with large numbers of individuals. Smith studied how quickly convergence to equilibrium took place under certain conditions. For example, if consumers in one
market were able to earn very large consumer surpluses, while consumers in another
were only able to earn much smaller amounts, would the two markets converge
to equilibrium at different rates? Would the convergence to equilibrium also be
affected if producer surpluses varied among markets? What characteristics would
bring about rapid convergence to equilibrium?

In a typical experiment conducted by Smith, participants are divided at random
into two subgroups, a group of consumers and a group of producers. Consumers
each receive a card containing a number, known only to that consumer, which represents the maximum price each consumer is permitted to pay for one unit of the
imaginary good. Consumers are told they cannot purchase above that price, but
that they should be quite happy to purchase a unit below that price. The lower the
price the better, but participants are permitted to pay the price on the card rather
than pass up a deal. The difference between the price on the card and the price
paid is consumer surplus. In some versions, Smith pays participants real money

related to any earned consumer surplus during the experiment (plus a flat amount for making a purchase).

Participants representing producers also received a card with a number, known only by that producer. This is the minimum price at which they would be willing to sell one unit of commodity. Producers are told that they are able to earn producer surplus in proportion to the excess of prices received over the price assigned to them. They are, of course, prohibited from selling below this price. Producers earn money equal to producer surplus.

Each experiment is conducted over a trading period lasting between five and ten minutes. Consumers and producers raise their hands at any time and orally make a verbal offer to purchase or sell one unit. Because all bids are oral, the process is public, and participants know the price of all deals consummated. Buyers and sellers consummating deals drop out of the market for the remainder of that period. After calls for final bids are given, the market closes and the first trading period ends.

Then, the market opens for a second "day" of trade assuming that consumers now have a renewed urge to buy (even though they may have purchased the previous day) and producers have overnight acquired one new unit. The range of reservation prices hold day after day representing demand and supply per unit of time.

These experiments conform to real markets in a number of ways. Participants are unaware of the reservation prices of other consumers and producers. They can observe the offers and bids and whether or not they are accepted; the markets are transparent.

The striking characteristic of these experiments is the tendency for exchange prices to approach predicted equilibrium. It is also clear that the shapes of the demand and supply curves matter. Whenever large amounts of consumer or producer surplus exist, competitive markets approach competitive equilibrium quickly, making the "invisible hand" of Adam Smith distinctly more visible.

Participation in these experiments requires no economic knowledge; the experiments work in the same manner with engineering students or optometrists. The fundamental lessons to be learned from these experiments are:

- the meaning of a demand and supply curve;
- the meaning of the concepts of consumer and producer surplus;
- markets tend to move toward equilibrium;
- not all markets move toward equilibrium at the same speed;
- not all markets move toward equilibrium in the same manner.

3.12   DEADWEIGHT LOSS AND ECONOMIC WELFARE

Using consumer surplus and producer surplus, we can estimate gains and losses in price-controlled markets. Consider a competitive daycare market for children charging $120 per week per child. Then, suppose that local government mandates that charges not exceed $100 a week. Let us see how this changes the consumer and surplus represented in Figure 3.12.

A government imposed price control is shown in Figure 3.13. P_0 and Q_0 represent market price and quantity in the absence of government intervention.

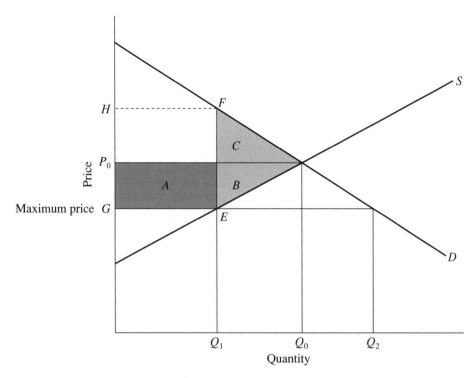

Figure 3.13   A market with price controls. The highest price which can be paid for the item is labeled "maximum price," which is below the competitive market price of P_0. The gain that consumers receive is equal to the difference between rectangle A and triangle C. The loss to producers is equal to the sum of rectangle A and triangle B. The sum of triangles B and C equals the deadweight loss to society from price controls.

Because government has fixed price below equilibrium, the quantity of the good provided falls to Q_1 and some potential purchasers are rationed out of the market.

Notice carefully, however, that the consumers who get to purchase the good at the lower price are better off. Clearly, some consumers are worse off (because they can no longer purchase the good). The shaded area labeled A shows the increase in consumer surplus for those consumers still able to make purchases. The shaded area labeled C is the loss in consumer surplus for those now not able to make purchases. Looking at potential consumers as a group, the net change in consumer surplus is given by subtracting the loss of triangle C from the gain of the rectangle A. That is, consumers are generally better off, depending on the relative sizes of A and C.

Suppliers also will face a change in their surplus condition. Fewer products are being supplied after the price control than before, and those still supplying the product are doing so at a lower price than previously. Producers still supplying the product have lost producer surplus in the amount shown by the area of A. But some suppliers are not selling any product because total sales have fallen; their producer surplus loss is shown by the area of B. Thus, total producer surplus decline is given by the sum of areas A and B ($A + B$).

It seems that consumers have gained on net while suppliers have clearly lost on net. Can the losses of suppliers be compared to the gains by consumers to get a picture of how society, in total, has fared? Yes, we can compare the size of the gain to consumers written as $A - C$ to the losses to suppliers written as $A + B$:

Net gain or loss $= (A - C) - (A + B)$

Net gain or loss $= -B - C$

Clearly the net loss to society equals the sum of the triangles labeled B and C. These losses are called ***deadweight loss*** and represent the net loss of total surplus to consumers, producers, or society as a whole. In the daycare example, a lower fee benefits some consumers at a cost to providers but the net loss to society is the value of daycare that ceases to be provided at the mandated lower price. These deadweight losses are inefficiencies caused by the government price fixing scheme. An additional consideration is the arbitrary shifting of surplus from one group to another. In our daycare example, some couples benefit by paying less but the earnings of low-paid childcare workers are reduced. However, the deadweight loss and income redistribution are not the only effects of mandated prices.

The economist David Friedman outlines other ***non-pecuniary costs***. These costs might include, for instance, time spent on a waiting list to access price-controlled daycare. With price set at the maximum legal level, waiting lines form until the costs of standing in those lines reduces the quantity demanded to quantity supplied. Additionally, costs are incurred by the government in setting up and enforcing the controls.

You should begin to see clearly now why many economists believe that the competitive market should be left alone. By leaving the market to operate freely, the inefficiencies of deadweight losses are eliminated, and leaving the market to operate freely maximizes the total welfare of consumers and producers. There are situations, however, that would mandate government intervention into a free market. All of these situations involve *externalities*, that is, effects on third parties to a transaction. Externalities, discussed in Chapter 5, are particularly relevant to nonprofit and public agencies.

3.13   PRICE CONTROLS

The free market eliminates deadweight losses and arbitrary transfers of surplus from consumers to producers and vice versa. However, elected officials are influenced by political and economic forces. Sometimes, they submit to pressure from special interest groups who believe the market price is either too high or too low. Governmental actions take many forms: import quotas, agricultural price supports, rent controls, and minimum wages. Two government programs illustrate the effects: (1) regulations maintaining price above equilibrium, and (2) regulations maintaining price below equilibrium.

Price floors

A ***price floor*** is a minimum price set by government above market equilibrium price. A price floor is illustrated in Figure 3.14. Consider an example in which, the equilibrium hourly wage rate for laundry workers is $6.60. Note that the

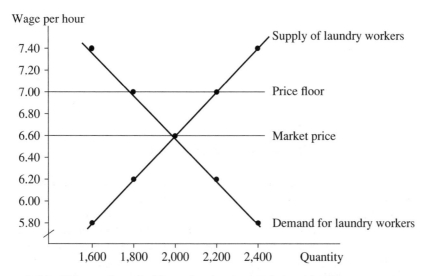

Wage per hour

Figure 3.14   Effects of a price floor. A price (wage) floor of $7.00 prevents the market from working and balancing the quantity demanded and the quantity supplied at $6.60. At $7.00, employers pay a higher price, but they purchase less. The floor creates a surplus of 400 unemployed laundry workers.

suppliers in this case are laundry workers and the demanders are the firms that hire them. But suppose government is convinced that $6.60 is too low an hourly wage? If $7 per hour is approved, a price floor is set. Now, laundry workers cannot be hired legally for less than $7 an hour.

Why do we use the term *price floor*? If you were on the second floor of a building and dropped your pencil, where would it stop? On the floor. The floor would keep your pencil from falling farther. Similarly, *a price floor keeps price from falling below a certain level.* To be effective, a price floor must be above the equilibrium price.

With a price floor of $7 per hour, how is the quantity supplied compared to the quantity demanded? From Figure 3.15, you see that at $7 the quantity supplied is 2,200 units. But the quantity demanded at $7 is 1,800 units. The quantity supplied would be greater than the quantity demanded by 400 units. This 400-unit surplus is shown as the distance from A to B in Figure 3.14.

Normally a surplus in the quantity supplied pushes wages down, increasing the quantity demanded and decreasing the quantity supplied. This process continues until price falls enough to balance the quantity demanded with the quantity supplied. But with a price floor, a free market adjustment is blocked.

Consider the effect of a wage floor on firms and clients. At the free market equilibrium, wages are $6.60, and firms hire 2,000 workers. With the price floor at $8, firms purchase less (1,800 workers), but pay a higher wage ($7). More workers are attracted into the market by the higher wage but fewer workers are demanded. Laundry workers that have jobs at $7.00 per hour are benefited but others are displaced. For example, hospitals, hiring laundry workers, mechanize or contract out these services, and former employees enter the ranks of the unemployed. The higher wage rate paid to retained laundry workers is likely passed on to clients in the form of higher prices. The intention of raising per-hour wages of laundry workers is good, but economists must consider the effects.

Application 3.2 indicates that the United States' minimum wage is an example of a price floor. The minimum wage is the legal requirement that employers pay all workers a specified wage. In some industries, this minimum wage is above equilibrium.

APPLICATION 3.2
The Minimum Wage as a Price Floor

The minimum wage is an example of a price floor, where the wage is the price paid for labor services. The theoretical effects of a minimum wage can be seen with the help of a supply and demand diagram.

The minimum wage was first instituted in the United States in 1938 when it was $0.25 per hour. Since that time it has been increased from time to time and always with considerable public debate. At the start of 1995, about 2.5 million Americans were earning the minimum wage. Would raising the minimum wage help the poor of the country? That is the issue of much economic and political debate.

Raising the minimum wage reduces employment, unless the demand for labor is a perfectly vertical line, which is quite unlikely. The decrease in employment is shown as the drop from E_2 to E_1 in the figure. You can see that at the minimum wage the actual unemployment gets worse because E_3 units of labor would be offered while only E_1 units would be employed.

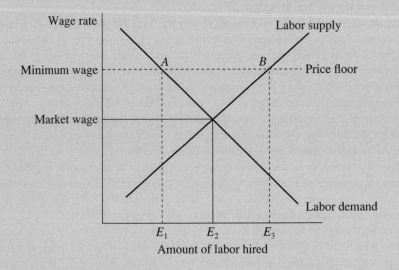

Source: Mike McNamee, "A Minimum-wage Hike Spells Maximum Damage," *Business Week*, January 3, 1995, 36; Michael Kramer, "Minimum Wage, Minimum Sense," *Time*, February 6, 1995, 27.

Price ceilings

A *price ceiling* is a maximum price set by government below market equilibrium price. A price ceiling is the opposite of a price floor. It keeps price from going above some upper limit. If you threw your pencil up in the air as hard as you could, it would hit the ceiling. The pencil would not go any higher because the ceiling would limit how high it could go. A price ceiling keeps price down to the level the government thinks is right. To be effective, *a price ceiling must be below the equilibrium price.*

Suppose it is generally suspected that landlords are making too much money at the expense of renters. Government might set a ceiling flat rental price of $1.00 per square foot of living space. The horizontal line at $1.00 in Figure 3.15 shows this.

At a price of $1.00, consumers demand 4.2 million square feet of apartment space. Landlords, on the other hand, are only willing to supply 3.8 million. A 0.4 million square foot shortage results. This shortage is shown as the distance from A to B in Figure 3.15. A shortage normally results in upward pressure on price. In a free market, price would rise, increasing the quantity supplied and decreasing the quantity demanded. When price rises to $1.40, the shortage is eliminated. The quantity demanded and the quantity supplied both equal 4.0 million square feet.

But this cannot happen because of the price ceiling. If the $1.00 price is enforced, the quantity supplied is less than the quantity demanded. We must find some artificial way of allocating 3.8 million square feet among consumers who want 4.2 million square feet at that price. A costly bureaucracy can allocate rationing coupons when households purchase multiple units of a product, like coffee or sugar, but this does not work as well with housing.

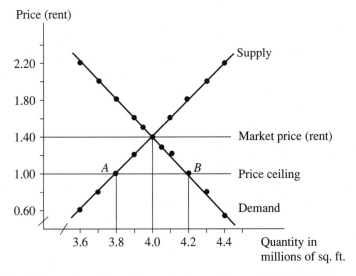

Figure 3.15   Effects of a price ceiling. A price ceiling at $1.00 blocks the market from working and balancing the quantity demanded and the quantity supplied at a price of $1.40. A shortage results. Consumers pay less but cannot satisfy their demand.

Given housing shortages due to price ceilings, government may be forced to provide public housing. Consumers may bribe private suppliers with illegal payments to position themselves higher on the waiting lists. The intention of voters and politicians to keep rents low is good, but again economists cannot ignore the transfers, the deadweight loss, taxpayer costs, and corruption. Rent control, whereby government freezes amounts landlords may charge, is an example of a price ceiling discussed further in Application 3.3.

APPLICATION 3.3
Santa Monica Rent Control

Santa Monica is famous for its beachfront and pier but it is also infamous for its rent-control laws. The city initiated rent control (some would call it a "renters' rights" regime) in the early 1980s. Ten California cities adopted similar regulations, placing more than half the state's renters under rent-control laws.

Once in place, rent controls are politically difficult to undo. Rent controls persist in London and Paris based on temporary measures taken in World War I. Price ceilings of any type result in several foreseeable and unfortunate consequences.

Santa Monica is a pleasant community of 86,000 people, "tree-lined avenues," and a sort of 1950s look. It looks like the 1950s because little in the way of development took place in the two decades following rent controls. After all, why would a landlord erect a new apartment building or improve an old one if the rents to be collected could not increase to cover the costs? Apartments rent for about half their potential if landlords had the possibility of charging more.

There is little incentive for current renters to downsize to smaller apartments. Why try moving to a smaller apartment outside Santa Monica renting for more than your current large apartment? There are no small apartments to rent within the city. Therefore, the quantity demanded for rent-controlled apartments outstrips the quantity supplied.

When landlords start losing money they seek lower property assessments which in turn leads to less government revenue. Then, we observe shortages in rental units side by side with an unregulated "shadow market." Rents in the unregulated portion of regulated markets become dramatically higher than those paid for available apartments in cities without rent control.

On January 17, 1994, the California earthquake left 2,000 units in Santa Monica unoccupied because of damage. The earthquake accelerated what would have taken place naturally over a much longer time to buildings not being maintained. However, there was no haste in repairing earthquake damage. Landlords were unwilling to incur extra expenses just in order to be able to charge the same controlled rent as before. Meanwhile the city is famous for its home-less population and urban professionals oppose construction of high-rise beachfront apartments.

Fully 80 percent of the residents in Santa Monica are renters and hence there is a strong lobby for keeping the controls in place. As of April, 2007, Commissioners of the Rent Control Board in Santa Monica continue to advise on how much rent may be collected for any specified rent controlled unit.

Sources: "In the Eye of Another Rent Control Storm," *Wall Street Journal*, June 21, 1994, A15; William Tucker, "How Rent Control Drives Out Afford-able Housing," *Cato Policy Analysis*, no. 274, May, 2007, www.cato.org.

3.14   THE UNIQUENESS OF DEMAND FOR PUBLIC GOODS

Recall that *nonrival consumption* means that one person's consumption of a par-ticular good does not limit consumption by others. *Non-exclusion* refers to the fact that it would be impossible, or prohibitively expensive, to exclude any one person from consuming the good. These are two characteristics of pure public goods (and services). The best example of a public good is probably national defense, although such things as police and fire protection, highways, public libraries, and flood control projects are also illustrative.

An individual cannot purchase public goods in markets like bikes, haircuts, magazines, or other private goods. Dollar voting in the profit-seeking sector does not work for public goods. They must be provided through communal decisions. Of course, we pay for public goods, albeit indirectly, through donations, assess-ments, or taxes. Most NFP firms provide quasi-public goods paid for with user fees plus a variety of indirect revenue sources.

We do not express our demand for public goods directly, yet public goods yield satisfaction like private goods. Consider, for example, police protection. If asked to think about it, most people would say that they would rather have police pro-tection than live without it and suffer the greater risk of being a crime victim. Thus, we can conclude that people get some benefit from police protection. It also seems reasonable to assume that total benefits from more of a public good such as police protection continue to expand, but, at some point, the extra benefits received from additional protection diminish.

The marginal benefit received from having a particular unit of a public good avail-able for "consumption" is taken as a measure of its worth to the consumer. An indi-vidual would not be willing to pay more for more of a particular public good if the price is higher than the marginal benefit of the last unit made available. Thus, the diminishing marginal benefit function is considered to be the individual's demand curve for a public good. This is illustrated in Figure 3.16, in which price is considered to measure the value, or marginal benefit, of successive units of the public good.

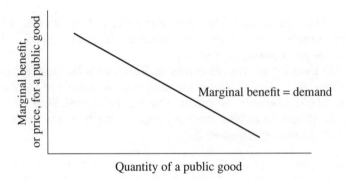

Figure 3.16   Individual demand curve for a public good. Individual demand for public goods is usually related to the marginal (extra) benefit the individual gets from the good. Since marginal benefits generally decline as quantity increases, the demand for public goods is negatively sloped.

Now, let's consider how we might construct the total demand for a public good. You will recall that for private goods, we added all of the individual consumers' demand functions *horizontally* to get a market demand function. That is, we added the quantities consumers are willing and able to purchase at various prices. This does not work for public goods. Once a decision is made about how much police protection, national defense, or any other public good is to be made available, that fixed amount is available for each person in the community. We need to find the total value society places on each possible level of provision of the public good in question. This implies a *vertical* summation of the demand curves for all individual consumers.

To illustrate this process and to facilitate comparison with a private good, we use three individual demand functions. Here, we assume that these functions represent the individual's demand functions for a public good rather than a private good. The demand functions are

Consumer 1: $P = 12 - Q$

Consumer 2: $P = 10 - 2Q$

Consumer 3: $P = 10 - Q$

For a public good, these functions are added vertically for a given quantity, as shown in Figure 3.17. Compare this figure to Figure 3.2, which illustrates the horizontal addition for individual demand curves (Figure 3.1). D_1, D_2, and D_3 in Figure 3.17 are functions showing the marginal benefit for individuals for various levels of a public good. In determining the total demand for, let us say, 4 units, we add up the marginal benefits in the bottom part of Figure 3.17 and find that the sum equals approximately a total of 16 marginal benefits/price on the upper part.

Individuals responding to price decide how many units of private goods they wish to purchase. A **community demand curve** for a public product is the sum of what each person is willing to pay (in terms of taxes or membership dues) to purchase a pre-determined level of the output. If my neighbor is willing to pay $1,000,

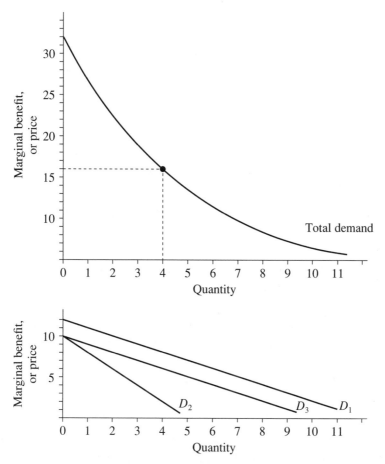

Figure 3.17 Determining demand for a public good. In determining the demand for a public good, the individual marginal benefit functions are summed vertically.

the cost of repairing the public road in front of our houses, I am willing to free ride knowing that I cannot be excluded from using it. Consequently, it is difficult to get individuals to reveal precisely how much he or she would be willing to pay for a particular public good. Collective decision-making involves considerable give and take.

CONCLUDING NOTES

• Households have a limited amount of income to exchange for goods and services. Demand refers to the quantities of a good that consumers are willing and able to purchase at various prices during a given period of time.

• The inverse relationship between price and quantity purchased is called the law of demand and is due to income and substitution effects. Demand changes cause the demand curve to shift whenever tastes, income, the prices of complements and substitutes, expectations, and the number of consumers change.

- Services provided in the private nonprofit sector are substitutes for those provided in the government sector. Homogeneous societies have more uniform tastes in the types of public goods preferred. In both homogeneous and heterogeneous societies any change in out of pocket user fees or quality in one sector affects demand in the other NFP sector.

- A supply curve shows a positive relationship between price and quantity supplied. The position of the supply curve is affected by technology, the cost of inputs, other products the firm is capable of producing, expectations, and the number of suppliers in the market.

- Markets tend to move toward an equilibrium price where the quantity demanded is equal to the quantity supplied.

- A shortage occurs when actual price is below equilibrium price and causes upward pressure on price. A surplus occurs when actual price is above equilibrium price and causes downward pressure on price.

- Consumer surplus is the difference between what a consumer is willing to pay for an additional unit of a product and its market price. Producer surplus is the difference between what a firm receives on the market and what it costs the firm to supply the product.

- When administered price floors and ceilings are imposed, surpluses and shortages occur. These prices transfer benefits to some individuals at a cost to others. Overall efficiency is reduced by a deadweight loss.

- Public goods are financed through taxes. Quasi-public good are financed partially through user fees that typically do not cover full costs. One way of calculating the demand for public goods is to start with various levels of provision and determine the total price each person is willing to pay, directly or indirectly, for a pre-determined level of output.

KEY TERMS

Income effect	Shortage
Substitution effect	Surplus
Demand curve	Consumer surplus
Change in quantity demanded	Producer surplus
Change in demand	Deadweight loss
Ceteris paribus	Non-pecuniary costs
Substitute goods	Price floor
Complementary goods	Price ceiling
Supply curve	Nonrival
Change in quantity supplied	Non-exclusion
Change in supply	Community demand curve
Equilibrium price	

SUGGESTED READINGS

Beam an, Jay, Hegmann, Sylvanna, and DuWors, Richard 1991: "Price Elasticity of Demand: A Campground Example," *Journal of Travel Research*, 30 (summer), 22.

Braley, George A. and Nelson, Paul E., Jr. 1975: "Pricing the School Lunch: A Consumer Problem," *Journal of Consumer Affairs*, 9 (2), 139–47.

Friedman, David 1986: *Price Theory*, Cincinnati, OH: South-Western.

Kinnucan, Henry and Forker, Olan D. 1986: "Seasonality in the Consumer Response to Milk Advertising with Implications for Milk Promotion Policy," *American Journal of Agricultural Economics*, August, 562–71.

Smith, Vernon 1964: "Effect of Market Organization on Competitive Equilibrium," *Quarterly Journal of Economics*, 78 (May), 181–201.

Smith, Vernon 1965: "Experimental Auction Markets and the Walrasian Hypothesis," *Journal of Political Economy*, 73 (August), 387–94.

Weisbrod, Burton A. 1977: *The Voluntary Nonprofit Sector*, Lexington, MA: D. C. Heath.

END OF CHAPTER EXERCISES

Exercise 3.1

Suppose that you are the vice-president of a:

a. Local hospital.
b. Profit-seeking financial institution issuing student loans.
c. Private nonprofit university.
d. Local Girl Scout Council.
e. Credit union.

On the way to the office you hear on the radio that the Federal Reserve Chairman has cut the discount rate by a full percentage point (a very substantial reduction) that will have the effect of lowering interest rates in general. How do you expect the change to affect your organization? Discuss and use supply and demand analysis to determine the effect on each institution.

Exercise 3.2

Technological advances shift the supply function for an industry to the right. Use a graph of supply and demand to illustrate what would be expected to happen to the price level and the level of equilibrium output assuming that demand remains constant.

Exercise 3.3

Given that an individual consumer's demand curve is $P = 200 - 4Q$:

a. Find the quantity this consumer would purchase at a price of $20.
b. If the price increased to $60, how much would the consumer now purchase? Would this represent a change in demand or a change in quantity demanded? Explain?

Exercise 3.4

Draw five supply and demand diagrams representing the demand and supply for influenza inoculations in a medium sized town. Label the axes, and indicate the initial equilibrium price and quantity. On each diagram, illustrate the effect of one of the following:

    a.   Development of an inhaler or pill for ensuring immunity.
    b.   Increases in the amount of influenza vaccine available.
    c.   Availability of pneumonia inoculation at each distribution site.
    d.   Media reports last year of influenza-related deaths.
    e.   Media reports of negative side effects from influenza inoculations.

Exercise 3.5

    a.   Draw a graph with linear supply and demand curves representing per day hospitalization charges in an area. Label the equilibrium price and quantity. Indicate consumer and producer surplus and explain what they mean.
    b.   Draw a line across your graph at a charge lower than equilibrium charges to represent a price ceiling. Identify the areas on your graph representing consumer surplus gain, producer surplus loss, and deadweight loss.

Exercise 3.6

    a.   Repeat part a. of question 1.5.
    b.   Draw a line across your graph at a charge higher than equilibrium charges to represent a price floor. Identify the areas on your graph representing producer surplus gain and consumer surplus loss if the quantity demanded actually decreases. Do you think that hospital beds in the area will increase or decrease? Discuss.

Exercise 3.7

Use income and substitution effects to explain why individuals use alternate routes whenever tolls are increased on highways, bridges, and tunnels.

Exercise 3.8

Tolls on a particular highway increase, and automobile traffic declines. A new public transportation system is initiated, and traffic on highways declines. Use these examples to explain a change in quantity demanded along an existing demand curve and a change or shift in demand. What is the effect on a demand curve when the price of a substitute declines?

Exercise 3.9

Homemakers, trained as nurses, enter the labor force as wages for nursing increase. More nurses are supplied as hospitals offer to pay off student loans for new nurses. Use the above example to explain a change in the quantity of labor supplied along an existing supply curve and a change in labor supply. What happens to any supply curve when the cost of supplying the product decreases?

Exercise 3.10

Numbers of office visits requested	Fee per visit with a primary care physician ($)	Number of appointments offered	Surplus (+) or deficit (−) of appointments offered
85	34.00	72	
80	37.00	73	
75	40.00	75	
70	43.00	77	
65	46.00	79	
60	49.00	81	

Suppose total demand for office visits with a primary care physician and total supply of available appointments per day in a community are as shown in the table.

a. What is the equilibrium price? What is the equilibrium quantity? Fill in the surplus/deficit amounts.
b. Graph the demand and supply and label the axes. Indicate equilibrium price and quantity.
c. Given a surplus of quantity supplied, is price above or below equilibrium? Given a shortage, is price above or below equilibrium? How is equilibrium restored given a surplus? A shortage?

Exercise 3.11
Refer to the table provided in Exercise 3.10:

a. Suppose that government legalizes a maximum fee ceiling of $37.00 per office visit. Explain probable intentions in setting a price ceiling and discuss consequences.
b. Suppose that government legalizes a minimum fee floor of $46.00 per office visit. Explain probable intentions in setting a price floor and discuss consequences.

Exercise 3.12
How does a market respond to a shortage? Would this work for a shortage of professionals? For a shortage of hospital beds? For a shortage in openings at a university for a particular course of studies? Explain.

Exercise 3.13
How does a market respond to a surplus? Would this work for an area where the number of trained teachers in elementary education exceeds the quantity demanded? For under-enrollment in a particular major? Explain.

Exercise 3.14
A couple's educational fund is sufficient to pay tuition and expenses for each of their children at any university. The best program for one of their children is offered at the local community college with relatively low tuition for in-state residents. Explain consumer surplus in terms of this example.

Exercise 3.15
Band parents form a Boosters' Club to donate a tuba for each student enrolled in the musical program at a secondary school. Explain the effect on producer surplus in terms of the providers of the musical program financed on a per capita rate out of general revenue.

Exercise 3.16
Draw a normal supply and demand diagram, label the axes, and identify equilibrium price and quantity. Suppose this represents the market for professional teeth cleaning. If the government set a price ceiling for this service, identify the change in producer surplus, consumer surplus, and deadweight loss. On another diagram, identify the change in producer surplus, consumer surplus and deadweight loss if the government sets a price floor. Explain what deadweight loss means in terms of dental care.

Exercise 3.17
Two band boosters are willing to donate funds to replace old trombones in order to increase sound volume at football and basketball games. Trevor Smith is willing to donate $1,000 for 5 new trombones and a total of $1,500 for 10. Mary Lee is willing to donate $3,000 for 5 new trombones and $3,300 for 10. Draw a community demand curve for replacement trombones based on this information. Approximately what amount may the purchasing agent offer to pay for each of 7 new trombones requested by the band director?

4
Estimating Client Choice

4.1   INTRODUCTION

In many instances, households are expected to pay part of the costs associated with government and nonprofit services. After budgeting basic necessities for a given year, a family is left with some funds for supplementing basic healthcare or education services. Will they purchase orthodontic services to improve smiles, have their kids tutored in math, or perhaps increase their donations? In this chapter, we will see how economists analyze and estimate this type of decision-making.

An administrator, setting user fees for particular services, needs to be aware of client response to changes in fees. If clients are very responsive to fee changes, we say that demand is elastic. In this case, even a small increase in a fee results in less revenue coming into the firm as clients reduce their purchases. Professionals and administrators often treat their client base as fixed. This is incorrect; clients respond to fee changes. The concept of elasticity is, therefore, an essential economic tool for any firm dependent on fees as a partial source of revenue.

On completing this chapter, you will understand how to interpret and evaluate client demand in NFP firms. You may actually be able to build basic statistical models and forecast economic relationships. An economic *model* is a tentative identification of relevant variables used to hypothesize about economic relationships. Even if you never create models, it is likely that you will, at some point in your career, be expected to understand theoretical and statistical models of client demand.

4.2   INDIFFERENCE CURVES AND BUDGET CONSTRAINTS

The demand for any good or service is based on the desire of consumers to provide themselves with the greatest possible satisfaction given limited income. *Utility* is the capacity of a good or service to provide satisfaction. It is not synonymous with usefulness; concerts and food as well as bridges provide utility. Utility is subjective and difficult to quantify. There is no such thing, for example, as a "utility meter" registering enjoyment from attending 1, 2, or 3 concerts.

However, if a "utility meter" existed, economists agree that in a given time period total utility derived from attending concerts or consuming additional units of any product would increase up to a certain amount. However, the extra or marginal utility you receive from each additional unit begins to decrease at some point. Total utility is the satisfaction derived from consuming some specific quantity – let's say a total of six concerts. Marginal utility is the extra satisfaction from consuming one more unit – let's say the fifth concert as compared with the fourth.

The *law of diminishing marginal utility* indicates that additional units provide less satisfaction sooner or later. This explains why a lower price is needed to induce a consumer to purchase additional units of the same good in a given time period. With a fixed budget, if you currently attend four university art or athletic events a year, you are likely to attend five if the prices of one or both decrease.

In any given time period, a consumer has little control over income, which is fixed at some money amount. The consumer faces a range of prices for products which are also fixed. A ***budget constraint*** is the limited money available to an individual. Products can only be had at set prices, and one is able to purchase a limited amount. We assume that any individual contributing to NFP organizations gains utility from this activity, but even the wealthiest is limited in her capacity to donate. A wealthy philanthropist earning $1,000,000 a year and allocating $100,000 for personal needs is limited to 18 major donations at $50,000 each. The rest of us similarly allocate scarce income knowing that one more unit of X means less of other things, including charitable donations.

Figure 4.1 shows a budget constraint graphically. The budget line shows various combinations of two products a consumer can purchase with a specific money income: $24 in this example. If the price of product Y is $1.50 and the price of product X is $1.00, then at the extremes the consumer could purchase 16 units of Y or 24 units of X. Allowing partial units, the consumer can purchase all combinations represented on the budget line in Figure 4.1.

Note carefully how a change in the price of one or the other product shifts or rotates the budget line. Suppose the price of Y in Figure 4.1 were to decrease from $1.50 to $1.00. This rotates the budget line up to 24 units of Y while the X intercept remains the same at 24 units. Lowering the price of even one product increases purchasing power and real income. An increase in money income does not change the slope of the line, but instead it shifts the budget curve to the right in parallel fashion.

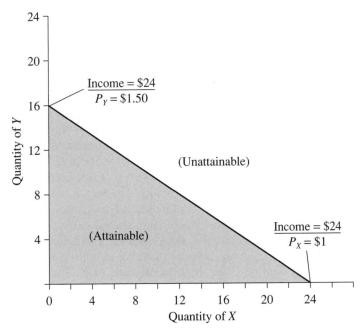

Figure 4.1   A budget constraint. A consumer with an income of $24 can purchase 16 units of Y if the price of Y is $1.50 *or* 24 units of X if the price of X is $1. The budget line shows the combination of X and Y that the consumer purchases with a given amount of money income.

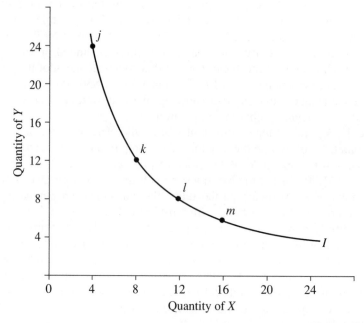

Figure 4.2   Indifference curves. A consumer by changing the composition of products X and Y can stay on the same indifference curve along which satisfaction is constant.

An *indifference curve* represents the combinations of two products X and Y that provide the same amount of total satisfaction. For example, if X is the quantity of musical or athletic events and Y is the quantity of donations, then events could be substituted for donations with the consumer maintaining the same level of enjoyment or utility. Needless to say, indifference curves are subjective. They are virtually impossible to quantify but useful theoretically in estimating the direction of consumer behavioral response to relative prices, income, and tax changes.

Figure 4.2 shows that indifference curves are downward sloping and bowed inward (convex) to the origin. The slope of indifference curves is consistent with and caused by the assumption of decreasing marginal utility. The rate at which a consumer is willing to substitute X for Y along an indifference curve is called the *marginal rate of substitution* (MRS). The marginal rate of substitution is the slope of the indifference curve. At point j, in Figure 4.2, the consumer is willing to give up a large amount of Y in return for a certain amount of X, but at point k, the consumer will give up a smaller amount of Y for the same amount of X. The marginal rate of substitution declines as one moves down along an indifference curve.

Indifference curves avoid the measurement problem of subjective utility. It is possible to create an indifference curve by having a consumer reveal his or her preferences for combinations of goods that maintain the same level of satisfaction. Note that an indifference curve to the right of I in Figure 4.2 would represent a higher level of total consumer satisfaction. Indifference curves by definition and logic cannot intersect.

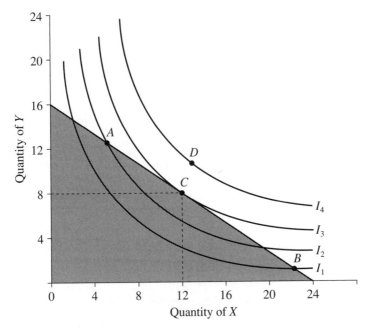

Figure 4.3   Consumer equilibrium. Given a budget constraint, the consumer will maximize satisfaction at that point (C) where the slope of the indifference curve is tangent to the present budget constraint. I_2 and I_3 represent higher levels of satisfaction.

4.3   MAXIMIZING UTILITY

The consumer's goal can be stated in mathematical terms as follows:

Maximize utility: $U = f(X_1, X_s \ldots X_n)$ where each X is a different product.

Subject to the budget constraint:

$M = P_1 X_1 + P_2 X_2 + \ldots + P_n X_n$ where M is money income and P is price.

Utility increases if one unit of a product in a bundle of products increases. The budget constraint places a limitation on spending whereby the sum of each product (X) times its price (P) equals money income (M). Figure 4.3 represents the mathematical solution for a consumer maximizing utility subject to a money income of $24 divided between two products (X and Y) selling at $1.00 and $1.50 ($P_x$ and P_y). Alternate indifference curves, moving to the right, represent a third dimension of increasing utility levels. The goal is to reach the highest attainable indifference curve with a given income. This is represented at point C in Figure 4.3. At tangency (C), the slope of the indifference curve (marginal rate of substitution) is equal to the slope of the budget line ($-P_x/P_y$).

A consumer achieves **maximum utility** when money income is allocated so that the last dollar spent on each product yields the same amount of extra utility. This condition is met when:

(*MU* of product *X*/Price of product *X*) = (*MU* of product *Y*/Price of product *Y*)

If the slope of the indifference curve and the slope of the budget curve are not tangent, the above condition is not met. The consumer could then increase his or her utility by changing the quantities of *X* and *Y* purchased. If the last dollar spent on education yields more satisfaction than the last dollar spent on healthcare, then utility will be maximized if the client redirects income. Spending more on education will decrease the marginal utility of the last unit of education. Spending less on healthcare will increase the marginal utility of the last unit of healthcare.

A price reduction for either *X* or *Y* or an increase in money income permits the consumer to climb up to a higher indifference curve. For example, suppose the quantities of *X* and *Y* purchased meet the condition above in which the ratios of the marginal utilities over price are equal for *X* and *Y*. Then, a decrease in the price of either *X* or *Y* in Figure 4.3 rotates the budget line so that it becomes tangent to a higher indifference curve, yielding higher utility. If the price of one or both goods decreases or money income increases, the budget line shifts to the right and the tangency takes place on a higher indifference curve.

Demand for medical care

Consider a NFP healthcare firm estimating the effect on demand of a policy change, affecting out-of-pocket client fees. Figure 4.4 illustrates this.

In Figure 4.4, product *Y* represents all goods and services purchased by households out of money income (*M*) other than medical care (*X*). Initially, consumers are in equilibrium at point *C* in part (a) of Figure 4.4. At this point, the satisfaction received from the last unit of healthcare over its price equals the satisfaction from the last unit of other goods over their average price. Part (b) of Figure 4.4 shows client demand curve for services. Presently, clients demand 6 units at a price of $11.50 each.

Now consider healthcare demand when client price declines. The price decline could be due to policy changes such as increased third-party insurance payments. Or, perhaps, certain health expenditures are exempted from taxes. Any measure that effectively reduces price to clients has the effect of rotating the budget line in part (a) of Figure 4.4. More healthcare can be purchased at the same level of money income (*M*). Clients in Figure 4.4 move to point *C'*, purchase more healthcare, and achieve higher levels of satisfaction.

In part (b) of Figure 4.4, we see an increase in the quantity demanded. The client is purchasing more healthcare moving from *C* to *C'*. A client fee reduction results in an income effect increasing client real income and a substitution effect that makes healthcare more attractive relative to other goods.

Certainly, an increase in real income could be channeled away from a good experiencing a price decline toward the purchase of other goods. However, for all normal goods such as healthcare, a price decrease or increased subsidy increases quantity demanded. For example, if government or private health insurance offers lower-priced optical services, most of us avail ourselves of extra pairs of glasses, prescription sun glasses, or possibly contact lenses in a variety of colors.

Indifference curve analysis is theoretical, but demonstrates why consumers are willing to purchase more of a good at lower prices; it justifies the negative slope

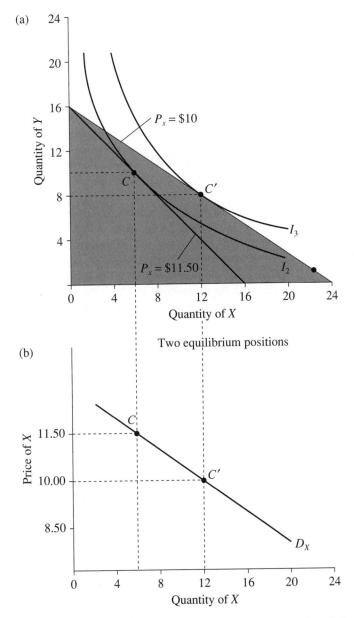

Figure 4.4 Deriving the demand curve. (a) when the price of product X (healthcare) decreases from $11.50 to $10.00 the equilibrium position moves from C to C′, increasing the quantity of product X demanded from 6 to 12 units; (b) the demand curve for product X is determined by plotting $11.50 (6 unit price quantity combination) and $10.00 (12 unit price quantity combination) for product X.

of the normal demand curve. In addition, indifference curves indicate how changes in income shift the budget constraint, increasing or decreasing purchases or non-profit donations. Every NFP firm, dependent on client fees, needs to recognize that its clients are in the process of allocating scarce income between various goods and services. The decision of a NFP firm to raise or lower client fees affects revenue in ways that are not immediately apparent. To master the relationship between fees and NFP revenue, we turn to the economic concept of elasticity.

4.4   SENSITIVITY OF DEMAND: ELASTICITY CONCEPTS

A NFP manager might wish to measure the sensitivity of client demand to price. How does a tuition increase affect enrollment? If we subsidize inoculations will the percentage of children immunized increase? It is possible, as well, to measure sensitivity to changes in a non-price determinant of demand, such as income. How do national recessions affect donations to a particular nonprofit firm? Elasticity is a general concept assisting both profit-seeking and NFP managers. *Elasticity* is the ratio of the percentage change in quantity demanded to the percentage change in some factor provoking the change, such as price or income.

4.5   PRICE ELASTICITY OF DEMAND

The most commonly discussed elasticity is price elasticity of demand. *Price elasticity of demand* is the ratio of the percentage change in quantity demanded to the percentage change in price. It measures the relative responsiveness of quantity demanded to a change in the product's price. The way in which the price elasticity of demand is calculated is shown below.[1]

$$\text{Price elasticity of demand} = \frac{\text{Percentage change in quantity demanded}}{\text{Percentage change in price}}$$

From the law of demand, we know that price and the quantity demanded move in opposite directions. As a result, price elasticity is always negative, reflecting the inverse relationship between price and sales. However, it is common to use the absolute value (the numeric value ignoring the negative sign) when discussing price elasticities. So when you read about a price elasticity being 0.4 you know the actual calculation gave a value of -0.4.

---

[1] Price elasticity using the midpoint formula can be calculated for specific change in price as follows (let E_p represent the price elasticity):

$$E_p = [(Q_1 - Q_2) / (Q_1 + Q_2)/2] / [(P_1 - P_2) / (P_1 + P_2)/2]$$

Where the 1 and 2 subscripts refer to the two price and quantity observations used in the calculation.

Elastic demand with respect to price

Suppose, for example, that a 5 percent decrease in price stimulates a 10 percent increase in the quantity demanded. The price elasticity of demand would be 2.

$$\text{Price elasticity of demand} = \frac{10 \text{ percent change in quantity demanded}}{-5 \text{ percent change in price}}$$

$$= -2$$

For a given product, we would say that the quantity demanded is quite responsive to changes in price. A 5 percent reduction in price results in a percentage increase in sales that is two times the percentage reduction in price. In this case, demand is elastic with respect to price. The term *elastic* implies responsiveness. If something is elastic, it is responsive. Any time the calculated value of price elasticity is greater than one, we say demand is *price elastic*. Thus, when economists say that a product is price elastic, they mean that the quantity demanded is quite responsive to a change in price. In such cases, the percentage change in quantity is greater in absolute terms than the percentage change in price, as in the above example. Sales of a particular breakfast cereal are a good example of elastic demand. Because there are many substitutes (other cereals as well as other breakfast foods), consumer demand for any particular cereal is elastic. The relative percentage quantity decline (increase) exceeds a percentage increase (decrease) in price.

Inelastic demand with respect to price

Now suppose that a 4 percent increase in price for a product causes the quantity demanded to fall by just 1 percent. The quantity demanded in this case is not very responsive to a price change. The numeric value of the price elasticity of demand is 0.25.

$$\text{Price elasticity of demand} = \frac{-1 \text{ percent change in quantity demanded}}{+4 \text{ percent change in price}}$$

$$= -0.25$$

In this case the percentage change in quantity demanded is just one-fourth as large as the percentage change in price.

When the quantity demanded is not very sensitive to a change in price, we say that demand is *price inelastic*. This is true in cases where the percentage change in quantity is less than the percentage change in price and the absolute calculated value of price elasticity is less than one. Thus, in the present example, demand is considered price inelastic because the calculated value is just 0.25. School lunches are an example of a product which has an inelastic demand. There are few good substitutes and thus the price elasticity for school lunches is about 0.47.

Given this information, we would expect that a small increase in school lunch prices will not have much effect on the quantity sold. Due to the inelastic demand, user fee revenue is expected to increase.

Unitary price elasticity of demand

The percentage change in quantity demanded can exactly equal the percentage change in price. In such a case, price elasticity equals one. For example, suppose that a 3 percent decrease in price caused a 3 percent increase in the quantity demanded. The price elasticity of demand would be:

$$\text{Price elasticity of demand} = \frac{+3 \text{ percent change in quantity demanded}}{-3 \text{ percent change in price}}$$

$$= -1$$

This is unitary *price elasticity* because the calculated value is equal to one (or unity). The price elasticity of demand for hard liquor in the United States is very close to one. In other words, a price increase of 1 percent results in a 1 percent decrease in quantity demanded.

Elasticity generally measures responsiveness between two points on a demand curve. Other techniques may be used to measure general responsiveness to price. Consider the case of a school trying to determine if donation amounts needed to gain priority seating affect capacity attendance at athletic events. Application 4.1 uses regression analysis to study this and other factors affecting ticket purchasing. Note that increases in donations required to get better seats reduces attendance.

APPLICATION 4.1
Can Regression Analysis Help Fill the Football Stadium?

Some colleges and universities with football programs get substantial revenue from the sale of football tickets and so are concerned with filling their stadiums for home games. This can be seen as a business problem and can be analyzed within the framework of the "4Ps of marketing" – product, price, promotion, and place. The extent to which a stadium is filled can be measured as a market response rate (MRR):

MRR = (Actual attendance at home games ÷ Potential attendance at home games)

In one study a large number of possible independent variables which could influence MRR for a particular school were originally identified, only 4 turned out to be statistically significant at a 95 percent confidence level, based on data from 73 NCAA Division 1-A schools. Interestingly, 1 of these 4 variables was associated with each of the 4Ps. The regression model for MRR is:

MRR = 549.618 + 9.436 Product – 0.207 Price + 2.96 Promotion + 86.44 Place

The independent variables used to explain attendance are as follows:

- *Product.* Total games won in the past two seasons.
- *Price.* Mean donation levels for priority seating.
- *Promotion.* Number of stations in radio network.
- *Place.* Ticket sale locations.

Note that the sign of the coefficient for price is negative. This indicates that, when the price of priority seating increases, the ratio of the number of people attending relative to potential attendees declines. Regression analysis provides evidence that attendance at university football games declines when required donations for priority seating tickets increase.

Source: Thomas G. Ponzurick, G. Louis, C. L. Abercrombie, and Robert L. Berl, "Managing the Marketing Mix for a Nonprofit Service," *Journal of Marketing Management*, spring/summer, 1992, 1–12.

4.6   DEMAND, PRICE ELASTICITY, AND TOTAL REVENUE

Money a company receives from sales is called total revenue, mathematically equal to:

Total revenue = (Price) * (Quantity sold)

You might expect, then, that a firm's total revenue varies, depending on price and price elasticity of demand. To illustrate this, we will use the special case of a linear demand curve for entry tickets at Hungry Rock state park. Note that elasticity varies along a linear demand curve. In Table 4.1, we calculate the total revenue for several potential ticket prices.

Table 4.1   Demand schedule for Hungry Rock state park and the corresponding total revenue

Price (P) ($)	Quantity sold per week (Q)	Total revenue ($) per week $TR = P \times Q$
$20.00	0	0.00
18.00	400	7,200.00
16.00	800	12,800.00
14.00	1,200	16,800.00
12.00	1,600	19,200.00
10.00	2,000	20,000.00
8.00	2,400	19,200.00
6.00	2,800	16,800.00

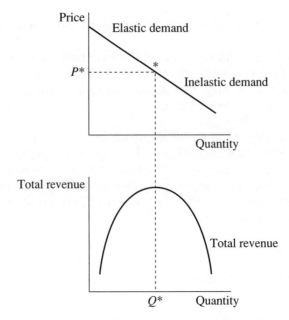

Figure 4.5   The relationship between price elasticity and total revenue. In the region where demand is price elastic, price and total revenue move in opposite directions. When demand is price inelastic, price and total revenue move in the same direction.

Table 4.1 shows some interesting relationships. At first, price cuts stimulate new sales such that total revenue increases. But this is not true for all price reductions. From $20.00 to $10.00 per entry, total revenue increases as price falls. However, if price is reduced below $10.00, additional sales do not compensate for the lower price per unit, resulting in lower total revenue.

This relationship depends on the price elasticity of demand. *When demand is price elastic lowering price increases total revenue, and when demand is inelastic lowering price decreases total revenue. The reverse is true for price increases. When demand is price elastic increasing price decreases total revenue, and when demand is inelastic increasing price increases total revenue.*

Figure 4.5 illustrates the relationship between total revenue and price. Above and to the left of the * along the demand curve (which corresponds to a price $P*$ and quantity $Q*$) demand is elastic. The total revenue curve, associated with this portion of the demand curve, indicates that additional sales increase revenue as price decreases. This corresponds in Table 4.1 to total revenue increasing from $7,200 to $20,000, when price declines from $18.00 to $10.00. The price elasticity in this range turns out to be about 1.65, which represents elastic demand (elastic because the price elasticity is greater than one). You can also see that in this elastic portion of the demand curve an increase in price, and the corresponding decrease in the quantity demanded, results in a reduction in total revenue.

Now let's consider the portion of the demand curve that lies below and to the right of the * in Figure 4.5. In this part of the demand curve, a price decrease increases sales but total revenue falls. In Table 4.1, a price reduction from $10.00 to $6.00 corresponds with sales increasing from 2,000 to 2,800, and revenue decreasing from $20,000 to $16,800. Over this interval the price elasticity of demand is about 0.37 (demand in this region is inelastic because the price elasticity is less than one). In this region an increase in price reduces sales, but total revenue rises. *Marginal revenue*, the change in total revenue divided by the change in quantity, is zero at Q^* in Figure 4.5.

Elasticities of demand have been estimated for some products associated with the NFP sectors. Legal services and physician services in the short run tend to be inelastic. Revenue increases when fees increase. Private school education in the United States is approximately unitary, increased fees reduce enrollment but revenue stays the same. Because a substitute for private education (public schools) exists, the quantity demanded of private education responds to increases in tuition fees. With an elasticity coefficient close to one, a 10 percent increase in private school tuition decreases private education enrollment by approximately 10 percent.

4.7   A NOTE ON PRICE ELASTICITY OF SUPPLY

Price elasticity of supply measures responsiveness of the quantity supplied to changes in product price. This concept is similar to the price elasticity of demand, but refers to the response of firms not clients. Because a supply curve slopes upward the elasticity of supply coefficient is positive. *Price elasticity of supply* is the ratio of the percentage change in the quantity supplied to the percentage change in product price. E_S represents the price elasticity of supply; the formula for price elasticity of supply is:

$$E_S = \frac{\text{Percentage change in quantity supplied}}{\text{Percentage change in price}}$$

When E_S is greater than one, supply is price elastic. That is, the quantity supplied is very responsive to price changes. If E_S is less than one, supply is price inelastic. Inelastic supply does not respond very much to price changes; firms, in this case, do not greatly increase the quantity supplied when price increases. When E_S equals one, supply is said to be unitary. Here, the percentage change in quantity supplied exactly equals the percentage change in price. Supply elasticities are useful in determining the supply responsiveness of NFP firms when client fees change. For example, if Medicare increases permissible charges for overnight hospital stays by X percent, by what percent will hospitals expand the supply of beds available?

4.8   INCOME ELASTICITY OF DEMAND

How do clients change their purchases when their income increases or decreases? To measure this, economists use income elasticity of demand, where the negative or positive value of the coefficient is meaningful. *Income elasticity of demand* is the percentage change in quantity divided by the percentage change in income. This is calculated in the following manner:

$$\text{Income elasticity of demand} = \frac{\text{Percentage change in quantity}}{\text{Percentage change in income}}$$

This ratio measures the relative responsiveness of demand to changes in consumers' incomes.

- *Income elastic demand.* If demand is very responsive to changes in income, then demand is *income elastic*. When demand is *income elastic*, the percentage change in quantity is greater than the percentage change in income. Therefore, the calculated value of the income elasticity is positive and greater than one.
- *Income inelastic demand.* When demand is not very responsive to a change in income, the income elasticity is positive and less than one. In these cases, the product is *income inelastic*. This means that the percentage change in quantity is less than the percentage change in income that caused demand to change.
- *Unitary income elasticity of demand.* If the value of income elasticity equals one, the good has unitary income elasticity. The percentage changes in quantity and income are the same. For example, if a 5 percent increase in income stimulates a 5 percent sales increase.

A *normal good* is defined as a good or service in which consumption increases when income increases. An *inferior good* is one whose consumption declines as income rises. Regression elasticity coefficients assist in measuring this relationship; the positive/negative sign of the coefficient suggests whether the product is normal or inferior. A positive income elasticity coefficient indicates that clients not only purchase more as income increases but increase the percentage of income spent on that good or service. A negative income elasticity coefficient suggests an inferior good; clients with increasing incomes allocate a smaller percentage of income to that product. Within a certain range of income, public or shared transportation is an inferior good as households allocate more income to private transportation as income rises. A statistical study, presented later in this chapter, on attendance at zoos indicates that the income elasticity coefficient is positive. This means that the percentage change in attendance at zoos increases by more than the percentage increase in income. For households, in general, a zoo outing is not only a normal good, increasing as income rises, but zoo attendance increases at a higher percentage than the change in income.

4.9 CROSS-ELASTICITY OF DEMAND

Consider how the demand for one product is affected by a change in another product's price. Braley and Nelson (1973) estimated the demand for needs-based school lunches due to the effect of a price change on paid lunches. One would expect total revenue to increase as the price on paid lunches increases because students have no other hot-lunch options. The researchers found, however, that the number of free lunches served increased due to a price increase on paid lunches, potentially reducing revenue. At a higher price, it became more worthwhile for households to seek eligibility for free school lunches.

Cross-elasticity is calculated in the following manner:

$$\text{Cross-elasticity of demand} = \frac{\text{Percentage change in quantity of } X}{\text{Percentage change in price of } Y}$$

If goods are substitutes, as in the example of free or paid lunches, then the calculated cross-elasticity of demand will be positive. If X and Y are complementary goods, then a percentage price increase (decrease) in Y will decrease (increase) the percentage of X purchased. With complementary goods, the calculated cross-elasticity has a negative sign. If the calculated cross-elasticity of demand is zero, then the goods are independent and do not respond to each other's price changes.

4.10   THREE ELASTICITY APPLICATIONS IN THE NFP SECTORS

(1) Suppose the president of a nonprofit club with declining membership and declining revenues proposes raising annual dues from $15 to $20 to meet expenses. The expectation is that total revenue will increase from $1,500 to $2,000 a year, given the present 100 members. If, however, membership, due to the fee increase, declines by 25 over the next two years, there will be no increase in revenue. Most likely, membership will somewhat decline but not by 25 percent. However, anticipated revenue increases will not be achieved and fall below the expected $500 increase. The club could actually collect more revenue by decreasing fees in order to attract new members. If membership is responsive to price, decreasing dues will increase revenue.

(2) Most large cities in the United States have some form of mass transit system operated or closely regulated by government. Commonly, the managing board of a mass transit system seeks permission from its regulatory agency to increase fares to cover costs. A fare increase may seem logical, but will most certainly aggravate the problem.

If demand is price elastic then increasing the fare results in a decline in revenues. There is strong evidence that the demand for mass transit, at current fares, may indeed be elastic. This is particularly likely for young and elderly riders. Thus, officials making decisions about the structure of fares need to consider elasticity of demand. Fare elasticity is also dependent on time of day. Higher fares increase revenue during hours when demand is known to be inelastic. Lower fares on elastic demand between rush hours increase revenue; lower fares on inelastic demand during rush hours decrease revenue.

(3) A sales tax is a broad based tax on the sales of a product or service and applies to all items except for those explicitly excluded. This is a popular way for states to raise revenue and most states exclude some items such as prescription medicines, food, etc. An excise tax is like a sales tax except that an excise tax

only applies to a specific product. Examples of excise taxes include gasoline, cigarettes, and tire taxes.

Consider client response to sales and excise taxes. Such taxes are generally levied to generate government revenue. The typical consumer views these taxes as part of product price and reduces purchases. If a tax increase is imposed in order to generate more revenue, sales volume will decline somewhat, reducing the base on which the tax is levied. If the tax base shrinks, tax revenue increases only slightly or may actually decline. Government policy-makers must factor in responsiveness to tax changes – and it is the price elasticity that provides this important information.

Scandinavian countries traditionally impose high taxes on hard liquor, but the effect has generally been ineffective as a revenue raiser considering the costs associated with collecting the tax. Swedes avoid the national liquor store monopoly and buy in Denmark; the Danes purchase liquor in Germany. In October 2003, Denmark slashed its excise tax on Scotch whisky by 45 percent, reducing the price per bottle by more than $5. Finland is considering a reduction, and Norway has cut excise taxes on liquor in recent years. Reducing excise taxes could actually raise revenue as individuals purchase more hard spirits domestically at lower prices.

4.11   USING ELASTICITIES TO ANALYZE TAX BURDENS

Some members of the general public and many students are convinced either that sellers can pass on the full amount of excise and sales taxes to consumers of, for example, gasoline. We now consider on a deeper level what actually occurs in competitive markets when government imposes sales or excise taxes. Who really pays the tax? Is it the buyers of any item paying the original price plus an amount equal to the per-unit tax at checkout? Or, do sellers absorb the per-unit tax and keep the price down for consumers? The correct answer is somewhere in between. Consumer and producer surplus is a powerful analytical device that cuts to the core of these questions.

Consider a competitive market represented in Figure 4.6. The equilibrium price and quantity are P_0 and Q_0. Now suppose that the government decides to impose a tax of T dollars per unit on each unit sold.

What is the effect on price and quantity? Obviously, the price buyers pay is no longer the amount received by producers (as it would be in a purely competitive market). Now there is a third party involved – the government. The dollars paid by the buyer are divided between producer and government.

The quantity supplied after tax is determined in the following manner. The demand curve (D) indicates amounts buyers purchase at various prices. Buyers do not care whether their fees go to the producer or government, or are split between the two. Producers' supply depends on price received as displayed on the supply curve (S). Obviously, the number bought equals the number sold. The answer to how many are sold is found by looking for a price P_b paid by buyers and a price P_p paid to producers *such that the difference between the two is equal to T*. This solution occurs at Q_1 in Figure 4.6. At Q_1, the buyers pay a price equal to P_b, the producers receive

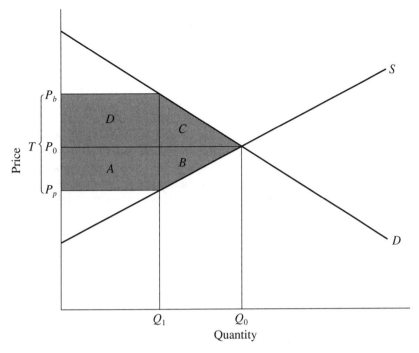

Figure 4.6   A tax analysis with consumer and producer surplus. P_0 and Q_0 represent
the competitive equilibrium before any tax is imposed. After the tax is imposed, P_b
represents the price buyers must pay and P_p represents the proceeds that sellers receive.
The tax per unit is represented by T. In this particular case, the burden of the tax is
borne slightly more heavily by the buyers and less so by the sellers. Producers lose the
value represented by $A + B$ and buyers lose the value represented by $C + D$.
The deadweight loss to society is equal to $B + C$.

a lower price, P_p, and the difference between the two equals T, the tax per unit
paid to government.

We know that the after-tax quantity sold is less than before, and that buyers
pay more and producers receive less per unit. Which group (buyers or producers)
is bearing more of the tax burden? Compared with pre-tax, producers lose a value
equal to the areas of A and B in Figure 4.6. The area B is producer surplus lost
because there are fewer goods sold and A is producer surplus lost due to reduced price.

Buyers are also incurring loss compared to the original pre-tax situation. Buyers
suffer a loss equal to the areas of C and D. The area of C represents consumer
surplus lost by receiving less of the good, and D is consumer surplus lost due to
a higher price. The area of B and C combined is a deadweight loss resulting from
the tax. Note that the areas of A and D are not part of the deadweight loss because
that amount is what the government receives in tax receipts. Therefore, it is not
considered a loss to society.

In Figure 4.6 a larger burden is borne by the buyers because the sum of the
areas of D and C (the loss in consumer surplus) is larger than the sum of the areas
of A and B (the loss in producer surplus). The relative size of the burden changes

depending upon the elasticities of the demand and supply curves. Generally, the burden of the tax will fall mostly on the buyer if $|e_d/e_s|$ is small; the burden will fall mostly on the producer if $|e_d/e_s|$ is large. A particularly useful way of looking at tax burdens in the real world is to calculate a measure called the pass-through rate:

Pass-through rate $= e_s/(e_s - e_d)$

The pass-through rate is simply the fraction of the tax levied that is passed through to the purchaser of the product. For example, assume a product is sold that has a price elasticity of demand of −0.5. This same product has a supply elasticity of +0.3. Demanders are more elastic that suppliers. The government decides to levy a tax of $1.00 per unit on the item. What percentage of that dollar would be translated into a price increase for consumers? We could calculate the answer as follows:

Pass-through rate $= 0.3/[0.3 - (-0.5)] = 0.375$

In other words, the market price of the good would be expected to rise by 0.375 or about $0.38. The buyer pays $0.38 more for the product and the supplier receives $0.62 less.

The burden on any payroll tax, such as Social Security contributions, is divided between employer and employee. Suppose that firms face a $100 a year per employee increase in payroll taxes on either the federal or local level. Recall that in this example employers are the buyers (demanders) and employees are suppliers. Each firm is required to remit $100 per employee to the government. Firms, given a pass-through rate like the one calculated above, would face a wage increase of $38 per employee per year. Firms will pass through a $62 cut in take-home wages to employees. Deadweight loss is the decrease in employment demanded due to higher wages and the withdrawal of employees from the labor force due to reduced compensation.

The above examples of excise taxes, remitted to the government by sellers, and of payroll taxes, remitted by employers, highlight a particularly important point. It is our goal to demonstrate that taxes result in an efficiency loss and that the burden of the tax is shared by both buyers and sellers. This holds regardless of whether suppliers or purchasers are required to remit the tax to government.

In Figure 4.7, the diagram on the left (a) shows the most common case in which suppliers reduce their supply because at every possible price the value of the excise tax is remitted by them directly to the government. The equilibrium price that buyers pay rises to P_b, but the producer earns P_p and remits areas A and D to the government. In the diagram on the right (b) in Figure 4.7, the purchaser is responsible for remitting the tax to government. Knowing that a per unit tax has to be paid, for example, on a new automobile, consumers reduce their demand, causing equilibrium quantity and price to fall. The price that producers receive is P_p and buyers pay P_b and remit areas A and D to the government. In both cases, deadweight loss is equal to B and C, and, in both cases, buyers pay more and sellers receive less per unit.

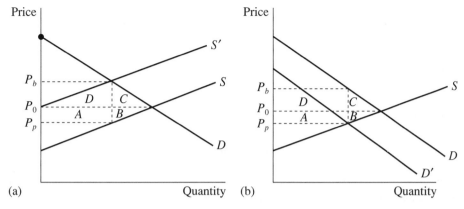

Figure 4.7   Deadweight loss and tax burden with seller (a) or buyer (b) remitting the tax. In (a), the supplier decreases supply because part of the revenue received is remitted to government. In (b) the buyer decreases demand for a particular item because in addition to price paid, a per unit tax must be remitted to government. In both cases, deadweight loss is equal to area C plus B, and the net price received by the seller is less and net price paid by the buyer is more than before the tax is levied.

4.12   FORECASTING CLIENTS AND REVENUE

How do NFP administrators make staffing and other decisions when revenue depends on client choice? Using standard forecasting tools, they estimate the number of clients and per capita revenue from client fees and sponsor subsidies. Forecasting involves making the best possible judgment about the future value of some variable. It is based upon a thoughtful analysis of past, present, and future factors influencing that variable. Forecasting analyses typically include both subjective (judgmental) and objective (quantitative) considerations.

Judgments are made in choosing method(s) and how they are applied, in intepreting the results, and in incorporating the results into managerial decisions. **Quantitative forecasting** uses statistics and mathematical techniques to add precision and accuracy to **qualitative forecasts** which are subjective and judgmental. With computer software, NFP administrators validate their subjective judgment on the future values of important variables such as number of clients, revenues, and costs.

Forecasting is both art and science. Administrators making intuitive forecasts based solely on their "gut feelings" do disservice to their firms. A blending of managerial experience along with sophisticated quantitative models yields the most reliable forecasts.

Our primary focus here is on client numbers and user fee revenue. However, the techniques apply to a wide variety of government and nonprofit activities, such as:

- school enrollment;
- employment;
- population;
- tax revenues;
- entry and exit of NFP firms;

- response to prices of complements and substitutes;
- the unemployment rate;
- automobile registrations;
- law school graduates;
- new housing starts;
- open-heart surgeries;
- national income;
- number of child-abuse cases.

Techniques depend on the series to be forecasted and the environment in which the forecast is prepared. A useful forecast is prepared for those who have confidence that the forecast provides a better estimate of future occurrences than they would have otherwise. Ideally, decision-makers and forecasters work together throughout the process.

Forecasting assists managers in making decisions under conditions of risk or uncertainty. Better forecasting reduces risk. Profit-seeking firms often commit a percentage of their annual expenses to their forecasting effort.

Responsibility centers, preparing budgets within any NFP forecast, consider four areas:

1 *Management.* The NFP director forecasts client numbers to budget staff, programs, and marketing-related functions.
2 *Production.* Forecasts are needed to plan for material needs, equipment needs, staff, and other production activities.
3 *Human resources.* The forecasted level of activity assists human resource managers in planning the hiring, releasing, and placement of personnel.
4 *Finance.* The forecast of clients determines the firm's expected cash flow and the potential need for outside funds. Long-term forecasting is needed for capital budgeting.

Being facetious, we can say for certain that future clients will equal this year's number, plus or minus! Seriously, how does one forecast next year's client revenues? One way is to observe techniques used by practicing administrators.

4.13   TYPES OF FORECASTS

At the highest level of aggregation firms do macroeconomic forecasts. *Macro-economic forecasts* are national or regionally prepared forecasts of aggregate measures such as gross domestic product, the unemployment rate, inflation, interest rates, and other macroeconomic variables. Values for economic variables on a national level assist in preparing lower-level forecasts. A social service administrator aware of how her region traditionally responds to a national recession can factor this information into forecasting client demand.

One level down from national statistics is the *industry*. For example, a public housing administrator may find the expected increase in the availability of rental units throughout the country relevant. If he is fortunate, useful information is available for certain types of housing on a state, county, or city level. Ultimately, however, the administrator has to assess linkages between available macroeconomic

information and his firm. For administrators, *firm level* forecasts are the most important. School districts and hospitals refer to demographic data, but they need,
respectively, a reliable forecast of their own pupils and their own admissions.

Forecasts can be categorized by **time horizon**. Short-term forecasts are generally for less than two years and most often, for one year or less, into the future.
Long-term forecasts extend more than two years out, with five years being a typical outer limit for reliable forecasts. Projections are sometimes made 10 and 20
years ahead, but it is usually recognized that such forecasts are tentative "ballpark
figures" for strategic planning.

A typical NFP firm earns revenue for each client to whom it provides service.
User fees, as defined by office of Management and Budget (OMB), are paid directly
by clients or private insurance. **User charges** is a broader term referring to user
fees plus any per client subsidy paid for by a sponsor or government. There are
qualitative and quantitative approaches to forecasting revenue or clients ranging
from the most naïve to the most sophisticated. We cannot say that any single approach
is the best. It is best to employ at least two different methods and then use managerial judgment to reconcile results.

Let's look briefly at some of the qualitative or subjective methods used.
First, consider what is usually called the *jury of executive opinion*. The subjective
opinions of key administrators may be gathered on an individual basis, discussed,
and collected by the person ultimately responsible. A group estimate, allowing for
interplay of ideas, has the advantage of stimulating deeper insights, but carries a
potential disadvantage. The opinions of dominant individuals could be given dis-
proportionately more importance in the consensus.

To eliminate the undesirable effects of group interactions, a procedure called
the *Delphi method* can be used. The Delphi method can be summarized by the
following steps:

1   Participants are selected (from inside or outside the firm).
2   Questionnaires on the variables in question (such as expected number of
    clients) are distributed to each participant.
3   Results are collected, tabulated, and summarized.
4   Summary results are distributed to participants, who are asked to revise
    their previous responses in light of this new information.
5   Steps 2–4 are repeated until no significant changes result.

The group forecast is not necessarily a consensus but built on the results from
the participants' final round of responses. Written questionnaires make the data
collection, distribution of results, and revised response sequence time-consuming.
However, computer networks make the Delphi method more efficient, especially
when geographically dispersed personnel are involved.

The *composite* method of developing a forecast is another qualitative approach.
Members of each division are asked to estimate the following period's clients for each
program. These estimates are then combined by the manager for a given program
(or geographic area). The person responsible for final forecasts ultimately arrives
at the firm's total. This method has the advantage of incorporating grassroots information. A major disadvantage is that future clients are sometimes overestimated
or underestimated, especially when budget or staffing is done on the basis of forecasts.

Surveys of users' expectations are also helpful in preparing a client forecast. This method works well when users form an easily sampled, well-defined population. For example, a congregation can survey members to identify next year's Sunday school class. Surveys within and outside a NFP firm provide valuable insight into the preparation of qualitative forecasts. However, some forecasts, such as acute care hospital services, are done on a day-by-day basis. In such cases, it may be worthwhile to develop an in-house time tested quantitative model, such as the one presented in Application 4.2 for natural gas.

APPLICATION 4.2
Forecasting Daily Demand for Natural Gas

Vermont Gas Systems, Inc., serves some 26,000 customers who rely on the company for a dependable supply of fuel to heat their homes and businesses. Vermont Gas buys gas from suppliers in western Canada and along the trans-Canada pipeline and must specify the amount of gas they need 24 hours in advance. Having an accurate daily demand forecast is essential.

The company uses a regression model that incorporates weather data (supplied 5 times daily), as well as other independent variables. Weather data include wind speeds, temperature, sunshine, and temperature of the local water supply. Individual models are developed for 24 large-use customers, such as schools, factories, and hospitals.

Source: Mike Flock, "Forecasting Winter Daily Natural Gas Demand at Vermont Gas Systems," *Journal of Business Forecasting*, spring, 1994, 23.

4.14   USING DATA TO ESTIMATE CLIENT DEMAND
AND REVENUE

Quantitative data are classified as time series data or as cross-sectional data. *Time series data* are numerical values and pertain to a given population observed at different evenly distributed points in time. For example, a time series could consist of the total number of students enrolled each year over several years or, in the case of secondary school drop-outs, the number of initially enrolled students continuing over several years. Time series data may be quarterly, monthly, weekly, daily, hourly, etc. *Cross-sectional data* pertain to units of different populations observed at the same point in time. Cross-sectional data could consist of the number of employees at different social service agencies on a particular date or within a certain time period. Most survey data are cross-sectional. Application 4.3 is an example of cross-sectional data used to assess factors explaining attendance at zoos and aquariums. Application 4.4 is a model using multiple regression to forecast the demand for nurses (the dependent variable y) in New Jersey.

In this section, we will use simple regression to present a time series forecast using 11 years of enrollment data for a hypothetical inner-city school district. In addition, we will discuss forecasting meals served in nonresidential care centers using multiple regression, a statistical tool reviewed in the appendix to Chapter 1.

APPLICATION 4.3
Using Quantitative Analysis to Estimate Elasticity and Forecast Demand: A Study of Zoo and Aquarium Attendance

Two economists set out to determine what factors tend to increase or decrease attendance at zoos and aquariums. In particular, they were concerned with how these institutions could remain accessible to low-income citizens given increased costs for transforming traditional zoos into ones with the secondary mission of species preservation.

To evaluate admission fees as a potential revenue source, they collected data in 1994 from 111 nonprofit accredited institutions. Eight of these were exclusively aquariums. Their model hypothesized that museum attendance is related to admission fees, to population in the institution's metro area, to median income of families, and age. Additional factors are the number of exhibits, stand-alone aquariums, and competitors in the area.

The researchers use multiple regression to test their hypothesis. Some of the variables, such as attendance, price, and income, are in logarithmic form. They use logs because of mathematical properties that permit regression coefficients to be interpreted as elasticities. Their results are shown in the table.

Explaining the logarithm of annual attendance for zoos and aquariums

Dependent variable		Dependent variable	
ln price	−0.0838	ln no. of specimens	0.5138[a]
	(0.7672)		(9.0958)
ln population	0.2916[a]	Aquarium	−0.3598[b]
	(3.7945)		(−1.4636)
ln income	0.2010	No. of competitors	−0.1528[b]
	(0.3578)		(−2.2641)
% under 18	0.0044	Constant	3.9288
	(0.1827)		(0.6714)
% over 65	−0.0237		
	(−0.8433)	R^2	0.667
% low income	−0.0050		
	(−0.4063)		

t-values are in parentheses; [a] means that the variable is significant at the 0.01 confidence level; [b] means that the variable is significant at the 0.05 confidence level, two-tail test.

What can we conclude from this work? The authors were able to explain about 67 percent of the difference in attendance at zoos in their sample. The elasticity of attendance with respect to price seems to be negative as expected and inelastic. Zoo attendance is a normal good in that attendance increases with income. The younger the general population, the greater is attendance. Institutions that are larger with more specimens have greater attendance. Institutions that are exclusively aquariums have lower attendance. Zoo attendance declines with other sources of entertainment such as museums, parks, and malls. Given natural log coefficients that are statistically significant, these numbers can be used to forecast attendance. For example, if there is a 10 percent increase in the number of specimens offered, there will tend to be a 5 percent increase in attendance, all other things being equal.

Source: Louis Cain and Dennis Meritt, Jr. "Zoos and Aquariums," *To Profit or Not to Profit*, 217–32, ed. Burton A. Weisbrod, Cambridge, UK: Cambridge University Press, 1998.

APPLICATION 4.4
The Demand for Nurses

In 2002, New Jersey hospitals experienced difficulty in budgeting Registered Nurses (RNs) due to uncertainty about future needs. Geri Dickson, RN, used multiple regression to research demand for nurses in New Jersey.

The New Jersey Model forecasts demand for RNs at the state and county level; demand is used in the study to mean the number of nurses that employers would hire given their availability. It was based upon a longitudinal (sometimes called panel) set of data that held constant many economic variables thought to change over the time period.

Prior to generating the final RN forecast, some independent variables had to be forecasted. For instance, the growth rate in HIV/AIDs was predicted to be 7 percent over the forecast horizon using time-series forecasting methods applied to past data. HIV/AIDs patients were found to be a significant predictor of nursing demand. Health maintenance organizations (HMO) penetration into healthcare supply is also relevant. Once again, time series methods are used first to forecast HMO penetration, an independent variable. Because HMO penetration was growing at a nonlinear rate, a nonlinear regression was used.

Some variables turned out to be insignificant. For example, mortality rate and per capita income in New Jersey seem to have little effect on nursing demand. The model estimated for predicting hospital employment of Registered Nurses (in full-time equivalents: FTEs) is shown in the table.

Dependent variable: hospital employment of registered nurses (FTEs)

Variable	Coefficient	Std. dev.	T-statistic	P-value
Constant[a]	−0.947	0.415	−2.278	0.023
HIV/AIDS rate[a]	0.001	0.000	4.180	0.000
Employment/ population ratio	−0.543	0.732	−0.742	0.458
HMO penetration rate[a]	0.024	0.006	4.304	0.000
Population over 65 rate[a]	0.064	0.017	3.743	0.000
Birth rate[a]	0.093	0.018	5.103	0.000
Surgery rate[a]	0.010	0.003	5.103	0.000
Inpatient days rate[a]	0.853	0.162	5.278	0.000

R square 0.861; adjusted R square 0.848; [a] significant at the 95 percent confidence level.

The significance and sign of some variables is obvious, like that of the "population over age 65" increase relative to the general population. This group often requires extensive hospital stays, and therefore we expect a positive sign. Likewise, if the "birth rate" increases we expect the demand for RNs' services to increase positively. In the equation above both these variables have the expected sign and both variables are significant at the 99 percent confidence level (as shown by the P-value).

The most useful characteristic of using multiple regression in forecasting is the ability to conduct "what if" exercises. For instance, in this forecast, New Jersey's employment to population ratio is expected to increase. But what if this proves unfounded and the ratio falls by 1 percent? Multiple regression models allow the researcher to use the coefficient on this ratio (here it is 0.543 in the forecasting model) to predict that as the ratio falls there will be increased demand for Registered Nurses; the researcher is even able to place a magnitude on the increased demand if the change in the ratio is known.

Source: Geri Dickson, Ph.D., RN, Executive Director of the New Jersey Center for Collaborative Nursing, Forecasting the Demand for Nurses, March 2002, www.njccn.org; M. Biviano, T. M. Dall, M. S. Fritz, and W. Spencer, What Is Behind HRS's Projected Supply, Demand, and Shortage of Registered Nurses?, Rockville, MD: National Center for Workforce Analysis, Bureau of Health Professions, Health Resources and Services Administration, September 2004.

You will recall that simple linear regression involves two variables x and y in which y is dependent on x:

$$y = f(x)$$

Multiple regression involves two or more dependent variables:

$$y = f(x_1, x_2, \ldots x_n)$$

From the simplest relationships to the most complex, regression analysis is useful in determining the way in which one variable is affected by one or more other variables.

It is the responsibility of the analyst to select variables for the model and to select an appropriate measurement for each variable. At times, a dummy variable is used to account for some qualitative event or a seasonal pattern in the independent variable. For example, gender can be represented by a dummy variable with "1" representing females and "0" for males, or vice versa. The dependent dummy variable in Application 4.3 represents different types of facilities; zoos with aquariums are "1" and those without aquariums as "0."

Figure 4.8 and Table 4.2 represent 11 years of enrollment data for a hypothetical school district. Can quantitative forecasting assist in planning for a certain number of students?

In this example, simple linear regression is used to model a relationship between pupils enrolled as a function of time:

$$\text{Pupils} = a + b \ (\text{time})$$

Excel and other software computer programs calculate the regression relationship to be:

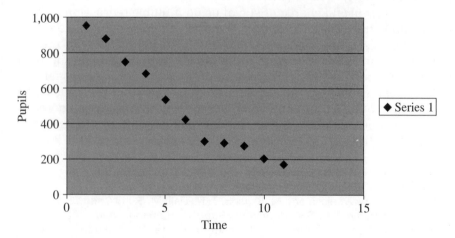

Figure 4.8   Plotting enrollment over time. The negative and almost linear slope of data, based on Table 4.2, indicates that simple regression could be used to forecast declining enrollment.

Table 4.2   A hypothetical inner-city school district with declining enrollment

Year	Pupils
1	950
2	880
3	750
4	680
5	540
6	420
7	300
8	290
9	280
10	200
11	170

Pupils = 990 − 82.27 (time)

(2.7272)

Any software program, such as Excel, can be used to calculate the coefficient of determination (R^2). In this example, the coefficient of determination is 0.95, indicating that 95 percent of the variation in student enrollment can be explained by time. The value of the slope (b) of the equation is negative (−82.27) confirming that the trend is definitely downward.

This type of model is often extended with some reservation to project into the future. A simple forecast for year 12 would be:

Pupils = 990 − 82.27 (12)

= 2.73

How disconcerting! Is a forecast of 3 pupils in the district for year 12 realistic? Probably, it is not. What then is wrong with this forecast? It is time to reevaluate if regression is useful in this instance.

The following three-step process is a guide for evaluating regression:

1   Does the model make sense? (That is, is the model consistent with a logical view of the situation being investigated?) In this case, it is reasonable to assume that enrollment is declining.
2   Is there a statistically significant relationship between the dependent and independent variables? It is possible that student enrollment could drop by 82 students any given year but unlikely that it would drop by this amount consecutively. The standard error of the estimate for this regression would be so large that the confidence interval around any point estimate is too large for planning purposes. A projection indicating 3 students plus or minus 130 is not helpful! See Chapter 1, Appendix section A1.4, for point and interval estimates.

3   What percentage of the variation in the dependent variable does the regression model explain? Using the coefficient of determination (0.95) indicates that time explains a large percentage of the variation in enrollment.

Our model supports the conclusion of declining enrollments over time but more work is needed if we wish to use regression to forecast enrollment. If we had data for the past 30 years we might observe enrollment cycles or a more gradual long-term decline. Research on the community's demographics may indicate that houses, presently occupied by the elderly, are in the process of being sold to younger families. This hypothetical example clearly shows that simple regression analysis using 11 years of data is not a substitute for judgment, other forecasting methods, or more sophisticated quantitative analysis. If, in the above example, enrollment in some years increased and in others declined, regression might indicate the overall trend. However, without more information and data, the point estimates presented in this example using simple linear regression are inadequate in forecasting future enrollment.

Sometimes, after plotting data, we observe that forecasting requires a statistical technique incorporating both trend and periodic cycles. To show this, we use actual data from the United States Department of Agriculture's Child & Adult Care Food Program (CACFP). Each day, 2.9 million children receive meals and snacks through CACFP. It also provides food to 86,000 adults in nonresidential adult centers and to youths participating in eligible after-school programs. The School Lunch Program is also part of CACFP.

Our specific example uses data from the childcare center program of CACFP. Public and private nonprofit childcare centers, Head Start programs, and other approved institutions are included. Profit-seeking firms may participate as well in the childcare center program based on the percentage of clients eligible for free and reduced price meals.

Four years of data, available from the United States Department of Agriculture website (http://www.fns.usda.gov/cnd/Care/CACFP/aboutcacfp.htm), provide adequate history for forecasting month-by-month future meals served. First, we plot a graph to identify visually any pronounced pattern in the data.

The time series in Figure 4.9 shows little trend but suggests a pattern of seasonal behavior. Seasonal behavior is a consistent pattern that occurs in many time series within a year; that is, it is a pattern that occurs every year in a data series.

Although Figure 4.9 does not show a very accurate forecast model, we can still estimate a trend or regression with meals forecasted as the dependent variable (i.e., the "Y" variable) and an index of time as the independent variable (i.e., the "X" variable). The estimated equation for the childcare center data is:

$$Y = 90,637,924 + 130,405 \text{ (time index)}$$

The number of meals served is growing over time as indicated by the positive sign of the X variable. However, we know from Figure 4.9 that there is a great deal of variation from this trend. The low coefficient of determination (often called "R-squared") reflects the percentage of the variation (i.e., up and down movement) in meals served explained by the model. The coefficient of determination for this

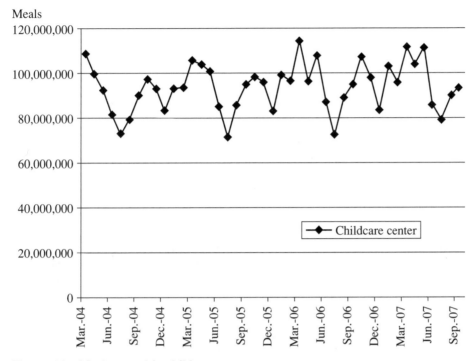

Figure 4.9   Meals served in childcare centers
Source: USDA: http://www.fns.usda.gov/cnd/Care/CACFP/aboutcacfp.htm.

model is 2.3, accounting for merely 2.3 percent of the variation observed in meals served.

We need a forecasting technique that fits the seasonal pattern exhibited by the data. Fortunately, many good statistical models are able to do this; the one most commonly used is called Winters exponential smoothing. Applying a Winters model to the meals served data gives the results provided in Figure 4.10.

In the historical period (the data between March of 2004 and September of 2007) the actual and fitted values are quite close; it is difficult to see both lines because they often overlap. After September of 2007 the model is used to predict meals served for the next 12 months. Note that the patterns of seasonality and trend are both replicated into the future period. The lines drawn above and below the forecasted meals served are the 95 percent confidence intervals for the forecast; the fact that they are very close to the forecast is one way of seeing the accuracy of this particular model. The coefficient of determination using seasonal variation and trend is 0.92, indicating that the model now explains 92 percent of the variation in meals served. A manager would be much better off using this model than a simple trend model in order to forecast meals served in childcare centers.

In conclusion, forecasts are made using qualitative methods, such as a jury of executive opinion, the Delphi method, and the sales force composite method. Prior to relying on quantitative models, such as simple or multiple regression forecasts,

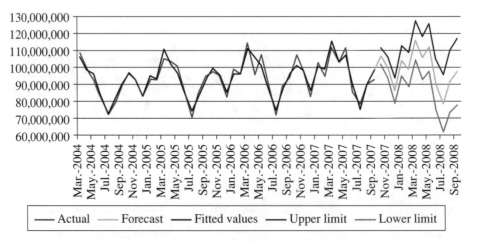

Figure 4.10   Forecasted meals served in childcare centers with seasonal variation.
Winters exponential smoothing is used to fit actual data for seasonal variation and trend.
The upper and lower limits of the forecasted meals represents a 95 percent confidence
interval.

the NFP firm should plot a graph to inspect data for obvious patterns. It is strongly
suggested that firms use a combination of qualitative and quantitative forecasting
techniques. More than one method reduces error in the final forecast.

CONCLUDING NOTES

- Consumers control neither the prices paid for various commodities nor in
  the short run their earned income. Consumers allocate income to maximize
  satisfaction.

- Subsidies reduce user fees for education, health, and social services. Clients
  substitute subsidized services for those paid out-of-pocket. Unless satiated, clients
  increase consumption of fully subsidized services.

- It is possible to estimate client response to user fees. Whenever response to a
  price change (up or down) is high, the demand is price elastic. Whenever response
  to a price change (up or down) is low, demand is price inelastic.

- When demand is price elastic lowering (raising) price increases (decreases) total
  revenue and when demand is inelastic lowering (raising) price decreases
  (increases) total revenue. Sales taxes increased (decreased) with the intention
  of raising tax revenue could potentially result in actually lowering (increasing)
  tax revenue.

- Income elasticity of demand measures percentage increases or decreases in
  quantity purchased to changes in income.

- Elasticities of supply and demand determine whether buyers or sellers bear the
  greatest burden of a new sales tax. Even when government tax revenue

increases, reduced output and consumption imposes a deadweight loss on society.

- Quantitative models may improve forecasting accuracy over purely subjective or judgmental forecasts.

- Industry and firm level forecasts are the most common type prepared in or for a given firm.

- Historical, judgmental, and client surveys are used to estimate demand. Estimates of client demand may be biased if budgets are allocated on the basis of these forecasts.

- Regression analysis, reviewed in Appendix A1, is one type of quantitative forecasting tool.

- A forecaster is responsible for ensuring that regression assumptions are met, that the variables included in the model are appropriate, and that the results are statistically significant.

KEY TERMS

Model

Utility

Law of diminishing marginal utility

Budget constraint

Indifference curve

Maximum utility

Elasticity

Price elasticity of demand

Marginal revenue

Price elasticity of supply

Income elasticity of demand

Quantitative forecasting

Qualitative forecasts

Macroeconomic forecasts

Time horizon

User charges

Client fee

Time series data

Cross-sectional data

SUGGESTED READINGS

Armstrong, J. Scott 1985: *Long-range Forecasting: From Crystal Ball to Computer*, 2nd edn., New York: John Wiley & Sons.

Braley, George A. and Nelson, P. E. Jr. 1973: "Effect of a Controlled Price Increase on School Lunch Participation: Pittsburgh, 1973," *American Journal of Agricultural Economics*, February, 90–6.

Gwartney, James D., Stroup, Richard L., Sobel, Russell, and Macpherson, David 2002: *Economics: Private and Public Choice*, 10th edn., Cincinnati, OH: South Western.

Kennedy, Peter 1992: *A Guide to Econometrics*, 3rd edn., Cambridge, MA: MIT Press.

Pindyck, Robert S. and Rubinfeld, Daniel L. 1991: *Econometric Models and Economic Forecasts*, 3rd edn., New York: McGraw-Hill.

Wilson, J. Holton, and Keating, Barry 2007: *Business Forecasting*, 5th edn., Homewood, IL: McGraw-Hill.

Working, E. I. 1927: "What Do Statistical Demand Curves Show?" *Quarterly Journal of Economics*, February, 212–35.

END OF CHAPTER EXERCISES

Exercise 4.1

Calculate all of the meaningful arc elasticities (mid-point formula) of demand (price and income) based on the following observations.

Observation	Quantity	Price	Income	Elasticity coefficient
A	10	100	3,000	
B	20	90	3,000	
C	30	80	4,000	
D	40	80	5,000	
E	50	70	6,000	
F	60	70	6,000	
G	70	60	7,000	
H	80	50	7,000	

For each of the elasticities you calculate, explain in one or two sentences what your result means.

Exercise 4.2

$$P = 400 - 5Q_D$$

a. Complete the table:

P	Q	Total revenue	Marginal revenue
180			
160			
140			
120			
100			
80			
60			
40			
20			

b. What is the arc price elasticity between the prices of 180 and 160 (mid-point formula) and what happens to total revenue if price decreases?

$E_p =$ _____

What is the arc price elasticity between the prices of 120 and 100 and what happens to total revenue if price decreases?

$E_p =$ _____

What is the arc price elasticity between the price 60 and 40 and what happens to total revenue if price decreases?

$E_p =$ _____

Explain the relationship between elasticity coefficients and total revenue when price increases or decreases.

Exercise 4.3
Use the following data (see table) and a standard spreadsheet package, such as Excel, or a statistical program to estimate a simple linear regression function of users as a function of income:

Observation	Users	Income ($)	Observation	Users	Income ($)
1	1,000	4,000	6	800	2,900
2	800	3,000	7	1,000	4,600
3	900	3,700	8	700	2,700
4	1,100	4,400	9	1,200	5,000
5	1,500	5,900	10	600	2,400

a. Write the regression equation using U to represent users and Inc to represent income:

Users $= f$ (income) $=$ _____

b. Interpret the value of the constant (or intercept) term and of the slope term in the equation.
c. Is the coefficient for the income variable significantly different from zero at a 95 percent confidence level?
d. What level of users would you predict if income were $4,200? What if income were $6,800? Are there any problems with making the latter estimate?
e. What 95 percent confidence interval would you estimate for users at an income level of $4,200?

Exercise 4.4
(Advanced analysis required.) Janis Brown is the new director of parks for the state. She has been concerned about the amount of money being budgeted for promoting usage of the park system. Her total budget has been cut, and she wants to revise the promotional budget downward but is fearful that usage may drop so much that the park system will no longer be fulfilling the governor's objective of having at least 18 million people per year use the state's parks. Before her arrival as director of parks, the department had developed the following linear relationship showing how use (U) was related to promotional expenditures.

This function was estimated based on the following set of 14 observations, where usage (U) is in millions of park visitors and promotional expenditures (PE) are in thousands of dollars (see table):

Year	Usage	Promotional expenditures	Year	Usage	Promotional expenditures
1981	6	320	1988	16	1,320
1982	14	400	1989	17	1,410
1983	12	500	1990	17	1,700
1984	10	590	1991	19	2,010
1985	14	700	1992	17	2,190
1986	14	900	1993	18	2,400
1987	17	1,100	1994	19	2,720

a.   Using linear regression, estimate the number of park visitors Janis could expect if she cut the budget to $1,500.00

   Number of visitors = usage = _____

Will this satisfy the governor's objective?

b.   Plot the usage and promotional expenditures data on the following grid:

Usage

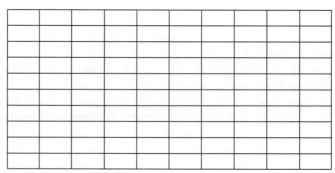

Promotional expenditures

After plotting, you will note that a nonlinear function may fit the data better than a linear function.

Exercise 4.5

Suppose that the elasticity coefficient for the quantity of Y with respect to the price of X is negative. What does this indicate about the relationship between products X and Y?

Exercise 4.6
Suppose that the elasticity coefficient for the quantity of Y with respect to the price of X is positive. What does this indicate about the relationship between products X and Y?

Exercise 4.7
Healthcare spending is nondiscretionary. The theory of diminishing marginal returns, therefore, offers little insight into household healthcare expenditures. True or false? Explain.

Exercise 4.8
An increase in the price of tuition at state schools, tolls on public highways, and entrance fees at public parks reduces the real income of households. Explain using a budget constraint diagram.

Exercise 4.9
A household cannot increase its income in the short run and has no control over the prices of individual goods and services. Therefore, if fees increase on a particular service, the household has no choice other than paying the increased price. True or false? Explain in terms of an indifference curve diagram.

Exercise 4.10
Suppose that the elasticity coefficient for the quantity of Y with respect to the price of X is negative. What does this indicate about the relationship between products X and Y?

Exercise 4.11
Suppose that the elasticity coefficient for the quantity of Y with respect to the price of X is positive. What does this indicate about the relationship between products X and Y?

Exercise 4.12
Explain how it is possible for a NFP firm to increase its user charges and simultaneously lower client fees.

Exercise 4.13
Explain if the statistics listed below represent time-series or cross-sectional data.

    a.   Recent changes in enrollment.
    b.   Enrollment in different academic majors.
    c.   Spending on durable goods, nondurable goods, and services.
    d.   Classification of students with respect to age, gender, and ethnic group.
    e.   Survey results of clients who are very, somewhat, not, and definitely not satisfied with service provided.
    f.   Causes of death in a hospital in a given year.
    g.   The percentage of deaths primarily due to cancer and complications from cancer over a 10-year period.

Exercise 4.14
Explain if the following forecasts for the number of clients next year are quantitative or qualitative.

    a.   Clients will increase because good sources indicate that competing providers are increasing their fees.

    b.   Our clients have increased every year for the past 10 years.

    c.   Ten institutions providing similar services are closing.

    d.   Clients will decrease because three of our best councilors are retiring.

    e.   Our client caseload increases by 10 percent for every 1 percent increase in the unemployment rate and GDP is expected to decline next year.

    f.   A survey of our caseworkers indicates that they expect caseloads to increase in the next two quarters of the present year.

5
Market Failure and Public Choice

5.1   INTRODUCTION

Microeconomists deal with markets and efficiency. They insist that resources be put to the best use, that neither too much nor too little of a particular product be provided, and that all this be done at least cost. Markets tend to approach productive and allocative efficiency through what Adam Smith, author of *The Wealth of Nations* (1776), calls the *"invisible hand."* The invisible hand suggests that markets shift resources toward producing goods and services that individuals demand and away from things they no longer want. Increasing or decreasing prices determines profits, firm entry into and exit out of a given industry, and total output. Clearly defined ownership, profits, and competition point profit-seeking firms toward efficiency. Private markets adapt providing nutritious food, fashionable clothing, and much of whatever people need or desire. But, at times, markets fail.

We have seen that markets fail to produce public goods, due to the nature of the demand for them because of their unique characteristics. In this chapter, we continue the discussion of market failure due to information asymmetry and externalities. A more extended discussion of how market failure affects the cost structure of a firm is postponed to a later chapter. Some economists reduce public administration as a necessary correction for market failure. Most economists, even those favoring a limited role for government, accept that whenever markets do not provide what clients need or desire, private or state sponsored NFPs should.

Market failure is a term that specifically refers to cases where an economy's resources are incorrectly allocated because prices do not reflect true costs and benefits. The market operating freely does not produce, for example, the optimal amount of healthcare and education. The uniqueness of the demand for public goods, discussed in Chapter 2, is part of market failure, but the term also includes situations where the market, due to technological factors, lack of competition, as well as inadequate demand, does not optimally provide certain goods and services. There might, for example, be over-production and hence deflated prices for goods that create pollution, such as gasoline-guzzling automobiles. Or, on the other hand, there may be underproduction and/or overpriced production for goods and services that create social benefits, such as inoculations for contagious diseases. In this textbook, we focus on quasi-public goods produced in nonprofit and government organizations in which users do not pay full cost and government units, sponsors, and private donors subsidize provision. In this chapter you will see that NFP organizations specialize in producing services that markets fail to produce.

The concept of market failure assists in defining the role of each sector in the economy, but to begin we need a framework for analyzing firms in general. In this chapter, we speculate on why firms are needed in any sector. A *firm*, public or private, is an invisible and intangible artificial being, created by law, and possessing the properties of immortality and individuality. In economic terms, every firm is a going concern with a purpose, governed by common rules of its own making or professional norms. It may be viewed as a nexus of contracts between suppliers, producers, clients, and sponsors. In practice, however, organizations are managed by persons, referred to as agents, acting on behalf of sponsors, referred to as principals. Admittedly, administrators operate at times in the interest of their own personal goals as well as those of the organization, and these goals often conflict and are mutually exclusive. After describing the function of NFP firms in addressing market failure, we address the motivation of individuals administering these organizations.

Owners and sponsors need some way of monitoring the behavior of decision-makers within firms. In the profit-seeking sector, competition, with regulation, provides the monitoring role, however imperfectly. In the not-for-profit sectors, it is often assumed that intelligent, well-trained leaders with strong moral character know what is right for the firm and consistently act on this knowledge. Right? Fortunately, NFPs, like all firms, are able to rely on law, customs, practices, habits, precedents, and, whenever possible, competition to act as a check on individual behavior.

Therefore, we begin to examine the role of unique NFP firms in their quest to address market failure in the context of the general theory of a firm.

5.2   CHARACTERISTICS OF MARKET FAILURE

Some industries, such as education, healthcare, and social services are populated by large percentages of government and nonprofit firms. This is so because in these areas individual contracting is impossible, costly, or inefficient due to *market failure*. The failure flows from four sources:

1   The good in question is a public good characterized by non-rivalry or non-exclusionarity.
2   The market lacks a large degree of competition.
3   Contracting for the product involves asymmetric information.
4   Production or consumption of the product involves externalities affecting third parties.

In Chapter 2 we identified the nature of public goods and in Chapter 3 discussed the unique nature of collective demand. Costs are outlined in Chapter 6, and a detailed discussion of imperfect competition is postponed until Chapter 7. Here, we focus on the two remaining characteristics of market failure, namely informational asymmetry and consumption externalities. We start in Application 5.1 in which an overview of market failure is used to justify government's support and operation of a vast network of national parks in the United States.

APPLICATION 5.1
Making the Case for National Parks in Terms of Market Failure

Who doesn't love national parks with their beautiful vistas, soaring mountains, shimmering lakes, and historical treasures? Market failure can be used to justify ownership of the parks by the National Park Service, a government agency. U.S. voters have collectively revealed their intention through a process of public choice to provide an appropriate amount of these services, believed to be unobtainable in private markets even with government subsidies.

Consider whether or not national parks are *pure public goods*. National parks meet the *nonrivalry* characteristic of a public good in that the same good can be consumed by more than one person without diminishing the enjoyment of others. This is true up to the point of congestion. However, unlike pure public goods, national parks can easily exclude visitors with entrance fees. Thus national parks to some degree are public goods, but could also be considered *club goods* which are provided privately and are free to exclude The Nature

Conservancy, which purchases land and protects it from development, is a private organization providing services similar to national parks. If private efforts are deemed to be insufficient, the public could simply subsidize nonprofit provision without directly owning and operating national parks.

Is there some technological aspect of national parks requiring a monopoly government provider? Does the efficient scale needed for provision require a single supplier? Parks provide two main services, preservation and recreation. As we shall see in Chapter 6, cost functions are difficult to calculate and especially so in the case of firms engaged in simultaneously producing multiple goods with multiple benefits.

Do visitor entrance fees sufficiently reflect benefits to taxpayers and future generations? Would private markets take into consideration the value of conserving natural and historic resources? National parks have *non-use values* in that one might get satisfaction from knowing that parks exist even if he or she never intends to visit. This places national parks in the category of a *pure public good*. It does not determine, however, if each park provides benefits over and above maintenance costs. Cost–benefit attempts to estimate preferences for national parks are inconclusive.

Do positive and negative externalities justify public provision of national parks? Park advocates argue that, in addition to being a public good, national parks provide positive spillover benefits, or externalities in the form of education and scientific research. Private parks are less inclined to engage in these activities unless they provide a private return to ownership.

Private parks survive only if the stream of income for park use exceeds the benefit from selling the property. Mining, logging, drilling, and electrical generation often encroach on park land creating negative externalities affecting private park owners and their clients. According to the Coase Theorem, a complete assignment of property rights and transaction costs along with private negotiations should be able to handle negative spillovers without government intervention or ownership. If this is true, government could encourage park owners and encroaching firms to negotiate privately. The Coase solution works when the number of firms affected is small, bargaining costs are negligible, and ownership of the environment is clearly established.

Even when theoretical arguments justify public versus private ownership of national parks, the scale and scope of their services require case-by-case considerations. Theoretical arguments clarify, but do not ultimately determine, if national parks should be privately owned with or without taxpayer subsidies or be publicly owned and operated. One solution is government ownership of large national parks with year-to-year operations contracted out to profit-seeking firms.

Source: Robert W. Turner, "Market Failures and the Rationale for National Parks," *Journal of Economic Education*, fall, 2002, 347–56.

5.3   INFORMATION ASYMMETRY

Asymmetric information is a situation in which one party to a market transaction has much more information about a product or service than the other party. A patient does not know if a heart stent will significantly improve his quality of life; a student does not know if learning calculus will increase her lifetime earnings. Both clients are in a position of having to accept information provided by professionals who personally benefit from the client agreeing to these procedures. Lack of full knowledge leads to contract failure in that clients are unable to make appropriate choices that maximize their wellbeing. In some situations, it is providers who lack complete information. Taxpayers and donors cannot be certain that students will put in the necessary effort to benefit from subsidized tuition, and disability insurers cannot be certain that claimants are incapable of work. In all of these situations, at least one of the parties, provider or client, enters into a transaction with an uncertain outcome. Patients, in general, have neither sufficient information to evaluate services nor to determine what procedures are necessary. Likewise, other parties, such as sponsors of the clinic or insurance companies, are hindered in assessing the quality of the service rendered. When asymmetric information leads to contract failure, sponsors as well as clients trust public administrators of government and nonprofits to provide the service more effectively. If the non-distributional constraint holds, public administrators have less incentive to lower quality in order to enrich themselves.

How can information asymmetry be circumvented in the case of for-profit health facilities? Conceivably a client could hire a knowledgeable professional, such as a private family practice physician, to accompany him or her to the clinic and monitor service. Or, an insurance company could own and operate its own clinics. Both options increase the cost of contracting. In such situations, Henry Hansmann (1987) argues that nonprofit firms have evolved to meet the need for trust by clients with insufficient information. This assumes that the non-distributional constraint eliminates the potential for personal enrichment due to asymmetric information. In other words, a NFP organization is not telling clients to purchase the service in order to make administrators rich.

Trust on behalf of donors, sponsors, and clients

Let us examine the Hansmann hypothesis. Do NFP firms exist because the non-distributional constraint protects donors, sponsors, and clients in certain industries? In certain situations, clients are incapable of accurately evaluating the product or of enforcing a contract. The charter of a NFP is designed to protect the patron (user) from those who control (administrators) in the same way that corporate law protects shareholder interests in the profit sector from those who control (agents). Certainly, an unconscious person entering a hospital emergency room or trauma center cannot choose, evaluate, or insist that best practices be followed in his or her treatment.

Given contract failure due to informational asymmetry, nonprofit or government provision may be necessary to prevent administrators from engaging in excessive cost-cutting and low-quality services. NFP provision may not be absolutely necessary but merely preferred for non-standardized services not easily evaluated by the user.

5.4   MARKET EXTERNALITIES

Externalities are positive or negative effects accruing to individuals who did not choose to participate in the exchange; they are third-party effects. A negative externality is a *social cost*. Automobile pollution is a negative externality imposing a cost on individuals who may not even choose to use a vehicle. A positive externality is a *social benefit*. Inoculating yourself or your children against disease creates a positive externality. Those inoculated provide a social benefit to anyone susceptible to the disease, even if he did not bear the costs of being inoculated. Transactions between buyers and sellers of polluting products fail to account for negative effects on third parties. Conversely, those benefiting from others' inoculations do not pay for this positive third-party effect. Straightforward supply and demand analysis can be used to demonstrate the harm/benefits of externalities and their effect restractively on resource allocation.

Negative externalities and supply and demand

In Figure 5.1, market supply (S_0) and demand (D_0) intersect at point *A* with a price equal to $1 and a quantity of 100. In the absence of externalities and assuming perfect competition, this outcome represents productive and allocative efficiency. Suppose, however, that considerable social costs, such as pollution, are created in the production process, such as causing pollution in the atmosphere. The low market price, which does not reflect full social cost, encourages consumption and expanded output. Resources are overly allocated to this particular good. If, by law, producing firms are expected to pay for damages to the environment, then production costs are increased and the industry supply curve shifts from S_0 to S_1. The new intersection of S_1 with D_0 at point *B* increases price to $1.20 and reduces output to 80 units; this outcome is preferable because it restricts resources from being over allocated to something harming individuals who were not part of the pollution-creating transaction.

Now, let's consider negative externalities from the demand side. Suppose that the consumers, represented in Figure 5.1, do not take into consideration full social costs created by consuming this product, such as medical expenses due to their decision to use tobacco. Therefore, market supply (S_0) and demand (D_0) intersect at point A with an equilibrium price of $1 and an equilibrium quantity of 100. Then, suppose that each consumer were required to have a license or pay a tax upon purchasing the product. Overall demand for the product would decrease. The demand curve shifts from D_0 to D_1 in Figure 5.1, reducing output to the new equilibrium intersection of S_0 and D_1 at point *C*.

In the absence of negative externality correction, the amount of resources allocated and output purchased is excessive and inefficient. A better allocation is achieved by either reducing the amount supplied and/or reducing the amount demanded. Price increases if suppliers are forced to internalize both private and social costs and

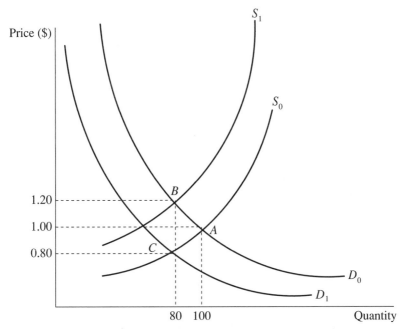

Figure 5.1   Correction for a negative externality. A regulation forcing suppliers
to internalize pollution costs decreases supply. A tax on consumption decreases demand.
Either measure reduces the equilibrium quantity of the good associated with a negative
externality.

decreases if the consumers are required to pay for them. In both cases, the equilibrium quantity decreases reducing the production and use of a good with a
negative externality.

Positive externalities and supply and demand

In Figure 5.2, market supply (S_0) and demand (D_0) intersect at point A with an
equilibrium price of $1 and an equilibrium quantity of 100. In the absence of extern-
alities and assuming perfect competition, this outcome represents productive and
allocative efficiency. Suppose, however, that the product in question creates social
benefits on being purchased and consumed, such as education or inoculations.
Economists sometimes use the term ***merit goods*** for items insufficiently produced
if left to private markets. Health, education, and housing up to a certain level may
be considered merit goods. Expanded output and consumption is desired and can
be achieved by either increasing demand or supply. In one case, suppose consumers
are provided with a voucher or tax credit. In Figure 5.2, this would shift D_0 to D_1,
and the new equilibrium with S_0 (point B) is at a price of $1.20 and a quantity of
120. In another case, suppose suppliers are subsidized to provide the product. If
supply is increased from S_0 to S_1, then the new equilibrium intersection with D_0
(point C), decreases price and increases purchases. With uncorrected positive externalities, the amount of resources allocated and output purchased is insufficient and

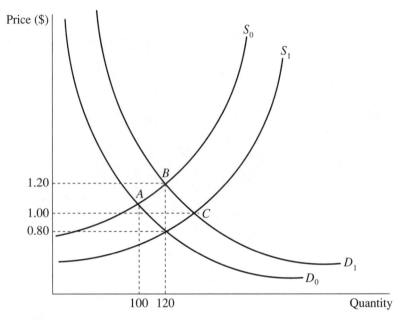

Figure 5.2   Correction for a positive externality. A voucher or consumer tax credit increases the demand for a good. A producer subsidy increases the supply. Either measure increases the equilibrium quantity of the good associated with a positive externality.

inefficient. A better allocation is achieved by either increasing the amount supplied and/or increasing the amount demanded. Increasing supply directly reduces price and increasing demand increases equilibrium price, but in both cases the equilibrium quantity rises, increasing benefits derived from the positive externality.

Property rights and regulations

By what authority should any person or organization direct a market to produce more or less of a given product? Later in this chapter, we discuss collective decision-making, but now we propose the assignment of property rights as one solution in deciding if external inefficiencies exist and how they can be corrected. *Property rights* are the legal protection given to the acquisition, holding, and transfer of ownership. When property rights are unassigned or held communally, anyone can freely use the property if no one else is already using it. Who decides how much industrial and agricultural emission, sewage, and fishing a specific river can absorb without harm? Given clearly established property rights, the prices firms are willing to pay in order to pollute and the pollution that communities are willing to accept determine emission levels. Clear ownership internalizes the costs and benefits associated with the production of the final product. According to the Coase Theorem, mentioned in Application 5.1 with respect to commercial encroachment on park land, a complete assignment of property rights and transaction costs should be able to deal with negative spillovers without government intervention.

Consider, for example, residents that have clearly established property rights to the quality of air or water in their community. A firm attempting to emit pollutants into the air or water is barred from doing so or needs to compensate residents per unit for each emission. The town could sell and thus create a market for "pollution" rights. The immediate effect of this, aside from the revenue earned by the town, is that the amount of pollution remains at or below the level acceptable to the community.

This theoretical argument for controlling pollution is not merely an academic proposal; power plants in the United States trade and pay for such rights. Certainly, this increases the cost of doing business and these costs are passed through to customers in the form of higher prices. Consumers, facing higher prices for goods and services that create negative externalities, have an incentive to conserve usage. Clearly defined property rights protect the environment, conserve resources, and limit consumption. The market and property rights approach is at times preferable to imposing general bans and restrictions.

5.5   CORRECTING MARKET FAILURE WITH TAXES AND SUBSIDIES

Remember, any taxed activity declines and any subsidized activity expands. Economists tell the story, which may or may not be true, of a town that began to charge double the fee to license dogs compared to cats. The dog population declined dramatically and the cat population increased. However, there were reports of registered cats barking! Nonetheless, taxes and subsidies can change behavior in ways desired and intended by policy-makers. Given market failure, taxes can be used as an instrument to reduce social costs and subsidies used to increase social benefits. If this is executed correctly, people's wellbeing increases.

Public finance is that branch of economics dealing with government taxation and spending, including specific taxation on cigarettes, gambling, gasoline consumption, etc., supposedly designed to reduce these activities. These are sometimes called "sin taxes." Your understanding of elasticity and tax revenue maximization may cause you to legitimately question the intention of the policy-maker. Do we really tax addictive activities to change behavior and lessen the consumption of these activities? Or, do we tax these particular activities because addiction limits response and thus increases tax revenue? You recall that inelastic demand allows more of the tax burden to fall on consumers. Suppliers, facing inelastic demand, are able to shift most of the burden of the tax in the form of higher prices, incorporating the tax.

Public finance, in addition to developing tax policy, also studies subsidies, tax deductions, and credits designed to increase health, education, and savings. Consider some indirect subsidies offered to private nonprofit firms. Lower postal rates reduce the price of mass mailings for nonprofits. In addition, they may be exempted from local property taxes. Thus, the value of social benefits created by nonprofits should at a minimum equal the cost of legislating and administering subsidies and the value of tax revenue foregone.

A *tax deduction* lowers the cost of giving to charity. Nonprofit firms benefit from the personal income tax deductibility of charitable donations to 501(c) 3 organizations. The economic justification for allowing tax deductible contributions hinges on the assumption that nonprofits create social benefits.

The extent to which nonprofit deductions treat all taxpayers fairly is of special concern to public administrators. Consider the United States' progressive income tax in which higher-income earners pay more taxes at a higher rate. This means the out-of-pocket expense for each dollar given to charity is less for affluent taxpayers. For example, a person earning a million dollars yearly may pay 45 percent of the last dollar earned in taxes; one earning $50,000 yearly might pay 25 percent. Suppose each person contributes a dollar to a nonprofit firm. The affluent individual is forfeiting 55 cents that he or she could have spent on personal consumption; the less affluent is forfeiting 75 cents. This distortion is not merely academic. Consider a congregation sponsoring a pre-school in which members' children are given priority. For tax advantages, high-income earners prefer low tuition with the congregation providing a large subsidy per child. Affluent families therefore pay fewer taxes on their donations but not for tuition. Consequently, social pressure may be exerted on the less affluent to donate time in the form of coaching, baking, painting, etc. because they are unable to make large donations. Admittedly, lower tuition makes the school more accessible to all. In any case, volunteering is not treated as favorably as donations in the present U.S. tax code. Some public finance economists suggest that a *tax credit* based on some percentage of the value of all donations of time and money would be neutral and allow for better decision-making. A tax credit is an amount subtracted from taxes owed; a *tax deduction* generally reduces taxable income.

Taxes and subsidies can affect behavior in unintended ways. For example, the California Department of Motor Vehicles tried to stimulate demand for hybrid automobiles in order to reduce emission of pollutants from gasoline powered vehicles. They did this by issuing a limited number of stickers to allow drivers of hybrid vehicles to use lanes restricted to cars with two or more passengers. To save on commute time, those with longer commutes were willing to pay premium prices for hybrid vehicles, creating congestion in the restricted lanes. Because the stickers remained with the car, the second-hand value of these cars initially increased. However, with lane crowding and counterfeit stickers, the price of hybrids fell. The net impact on automobile pollution is difficult to assess (McKenzie, 2007). Nevertheless, straight-forward supply-and-demand analysis demonstrates that society's scarce resources can be redirected through appropriate taxation and subsidies.

5.6   CORRECTING MARKET FAILURE WITH NOT-FOR-PROFIT FIRMS

When free markets fail to achieve optimal provision, other institutions arise to bridge the gap. This often takes the form of government and private nonprofit firms. Some argue against viewing NFP firms in this limited role. Are NFPs nothing more than a corrective for market failure? Rather, is the existence of NFPs due to elaborate non-economic social mechanisms, which economists often fail to appreciate?

Peter J. Hammer of the University of Michigan Law School (2001) criticizes Kenneth Arrow and others for using economic theory as the benchmark for analyzing healthcare institutions and professional services. For example, eco-nomists accept government licensing for healthcare professionals merely due to asymmetric information where trust is needed. Otherwise, licensing is perceived as merely raising cost and creating product uniformity rather than excellence. A strictly market approach, according to Hammer, has negative consequences because it fails to accept human beings' altruistic motivation. Blood donations and professional norms for determining trustworthiness are dismissed by concentrat-ing on the market approach.

Not all economists reduce NFPs to the reductionist role of correcting for mar-ket failure. Social economists position all nonprofits and profit-seeking firms as essential intermediate organizations between family and state in a free society. Whether you view the NFP role as essential or merely residual, economics is helpful in assessing effective provision of certain goods and services in whatever type of insti-tutions is preferred by clients.

Regardless of how we justify the existence of NFP firms, history, social norms, and government policy affect their financing and internal decision-making. Who really is in charge of the local community hospital? How do we measure the effectiveness of local schools? To address these questions, we turn to the microeconomic theory of the firm to determine if NFP firms behave in ways that profit-seeking firms could not and do not. And, do they minimize cost?

Theories of the firm in general and NFP firms in particular

Let us begin with the supply side of the market. All firms engage in the produc-tion of a good or a service. What exactly is a firm and why do we believe the firm plays such an important role in the economy?

A firm is any group of individuals who form together and act as a unit to pro-duce a good or a service. Most firms are organized as corporations; some attempt to make a profit (like Ford and General Electric) while others are not-for-profit organizations (like the Red Cross or the University of Texas). Some firms are large, employing thousands of people, while other firms are owned and run by only a few people. While it is clear that the primary organizational unit for producing goods and services is the firm, it is less clear why this is so.

Managed coordination is one reason why firms exist at all, and the firm is also a mechanism for redistributing risk. Although risk may be less a factor in NFP firms than for profit-seeking firms, market production of any kind is risky. A sup-plier may renege on a deal to deliver inputs. A purchaser may renege on orders placed. An employer may renege on employee benefits. Consider if, after a week of hard work, workers' salaries are reduced or suspended because clients have failed to pay fees. A firm assists its owners in absorbing market fluctuations while honor-ing contracts to pay relatively stable wages. Staff is then partially insulated from economic fluctuations. This is a reallocation of risk; owners accept more risk and employees accept less. Without the mechanism of a firm to reallocate risk, both parties are worse off. In a nutshell, this is the first reason why firms exist: they redistribute risk efficiently.

In return for the offer of stable wages, owners expect employees to permit them to supervise and guide their work. Employee supervision is in part the desire to manage risk efficiently and arrange for orderly supply. A hospital can offer service around the clock every day of the week; an individual nurse or physician cannot. This is sometimes called the "productivity explanation" for the existence of the firm.

There is another reason why firms exist. Firms exist because buying from others, as compared to self-sufficiency, is efficient. This benefit results from economies of scale, specialization, and lower transaction costs. Two people (or a much larger group) coordinate production better than if they acted independently. Coordination that takes place within the firm is much closer than the cooperation observed between buyers and sellers. A family could certainly contract separately with math, language, music tutors, etc. for their children. However, a better-quality education at less expense may be found in a school that coordinates an age-appropriate comprehensive curriculum.

Individuals in a firm work together more productively than if they operated independently. The division of labor (each individual specializing in a particular procedure or part) eliminates the need for each individual to perform every task in turn. Can you imagine a single individual, no matter how skilled or well-equipped, doing heart surgery without a team? Exceptional individuals at times do this, but consider the time and cost of contracting separately for nursing services and facilities.

In a hospital, division of labor occurs within the firm as different units accept responsibility for testing, cleaning, and meal preparation, as well as pre- and post-operation care. However, some of this division of labor may take place between firms as independent firms contract to provide specialized services such as laundry or anesthesiology. A firm, then, is a coordinating unit deciding how best to convert inputs (raw materials, labor, machinery, etc.) into output (the final product or service). Obviously, firms differ depending on the sector of the economy in which they operate, but each firm operates as a coordinating unit.

Profit-seeking firms have three features that make them easier to model than nonprofit firms (Speckbacher, 2003):

1   They have clearly defined owners guiding business decisions.
2   These owners share the common goal of maximizing profits.
3   Profits are relatively easy to measure.

Government and nonprofit firms, on the other hand, focus on their specific missions, they serve potentially conflicting constituencies, and their output is not easily measured. All producers, however, share some similar internal characteristics highlighted by the following three distinct models of economic behavior.

Traditional optimizing theory

Consider the following two statements that apply to all firms. First, scarce inputs are used to produce goods and services. Second, optimization implies minimizing costs for a given level of output, or maximizing output for any given level of inputs. In the profit-seeking sector, profit maximization in the absence of market failure leads to optimization. Costs are minimized and output maximized through the invisible hand of market competition. Of course, we are speaking ideally. Not all profit-seeking firms function efficiently or are well managed.

A profit-seeking firm can translate the goal of profit maximization into subgoals, delegate responsibilities, and decentralize decision-making. On the other hand, profit-seeking goals in the NFP sectors are neither relevant nor appropriate, even though from time to time some projects generate cash surpluses. Hence, profit-seeking accounting methods do not translate well into the nonprofit or government sectors.

An even more important issue concerns which NFP group (donors, the board, administrators, clients, etc.) decides on what it is that the firm wishes to maximize. Given these considerations, we nevertheless maintain that traditional optimizing theory (minimizing costs for any given level of output or producing the greatest output with fixed resources) is a valuable benchmark objective for any NFP firm.

An approach based on *optimizing theory* applies cost minimization and output maximizing techniques to the nonprofit firm. This is justifiable when costs can be approximated by direct observation or by comparing like outputs in various sectors of the economy. For example, the cost of producing a hamburger, fries, and soft-drink meal in a school cafeteria should approximate the cost of a similar meal in a local restaurant. Similarly, the cost of producing modest housing in the profit-seeking sector should act as a benchmark for public housing. Allowances, of course, need to be made for different specifications.

Regardless of sector, it is always appropriate and often possible to identify opportunity costs. Nonprofit accounting may not be able to place a precise rental value on space in a single purposed building such as a church or a school, but one can approximate by considering the potential gains if the same space were used for some other activity. The space used for a hospital's gift shop, for example, has value in terms of other uses for the same space. On the revenue side of the balance sheet, especially when users are paying close to full cost and have alternatives, it is easier to measure value created. In many situations, traditional cost minimization and output optimization can be approximated and applied in NFP managerial decision-making.

Complete contracts approach

A firm can also be viewed as a nexus of interrelated contracts among and between input suppliers and purchasers of outputs. With the *complete contracts approach*, these contracts are fully specified; they protect as well as limit a firm's suppliers and purchasers. For example, an employee knows precisely what salary and benefits will be provided in return for a given amount and quality of work. Suppliers of inputs to the firm know when and how much they will be paid for services and goods rendered to the firm. Clients have full information both of what they will receive and of what they will be charged. On the other hand, firm owners are not guaranteed fixed returns. In return for assuming this risk owners have the right to control the firm and to appropriate any residual between costs and revenue. Profit-seeking owners of a tutoring center, for example, contract with teachers, financiers, property owners, and clients with the expectation of earning profit. To avoid losses, owners of the center have a strong incentive to write complete, well specified contracts ensuring, for example, that tutors and students do not enter into subcontracts at reduced prices.

Consider the case of the pure Knightian entrepreneur, named for Frank Knight, a University of Chicago professor who modeled it. Such a firm's capital needs (for machinery, plant, tools, and equipment) are met entirely by borrowing rather than by issuing stock. All factors of production needed are purchased in the market rather than being hired internally. Its output is sold in the marketplace. The Knightian entrepreneur acts as prime mover and owner who controls the firm and receives all its residual earnings. In such a firm, costs reduce to expenses and contracts with a range of suppliers; the entrepreneur assumes all risk.

Consider how NFPs differ from the pure Knightian entrepreneur. NFP firms often lack clear ownership rights and fully specified contracts. Although the NFP sponsor, public or private, owns the facility, subsidizes the mission, and acts as overseer, control is not as absolute as it is in the case of the Knightian entrepreneur.

In nonprofit firms, such as private colleges, trustees select top administrators and make major policy decisions. In public organizations, such as the U.S. Department of Commerce, the President as Chief Executive appoints top-level administrators. This assumes that the priorities of the organization reflect the platform of the political party voted into office. However, in setting NFP priorities internally, it is often not clear which group has the residual right or expertise to interpret the mission, to specify objectives, and to monitor performance, unlike a firm headed with a Knightian entrepreneur.

The nebulousness of NFP contracting does not necessarily attract either more or less committed employees than profit-seeking firms. The rewards, however, tend to be different. NFP firms, obviously, use more non-financial performance criteria and rewards than profit-seeking firms. The CEO of a profit-seeking home health-care agency with higher than average profits generally receives higher compensation relative to industry peers. On the other hand, in NFP firms, salary differentials do not correspond directly to financial performance. In the government sector, civil servant pay scales are based largely on credentials and experience, not performance. To motivate managers and employees, NFP firms often substitute *soft incentives*, like job security and unstructured job descriptions, rather than higher salaries. Application 5.2 compares the incentive structure of top administrators at nonprofit versus profit-seeking hospitals.

Viewing a firm as a nexus of specific contracts between the owner/sponsor and other suppliers clarifies the structure of hard and soft incentives used to channel efforts toward mission. This model adapted to the NFP sectors would assign priority in interpreting the mission of a firm to its board or sponsoring organization.

APPLICATION 5.2
A Case Study Based on Nonprofit and For-Profit Hospital Treatment of Altruistic Administrators

Researchers find consistent evidence that both nonprofit hospital administrators as well as for-profit ones face financial performance incentives. Actually, management turnover due to poor financial performance is stronger in nonprofit hospitals than in for-profits. These conclusions are based on a study of 2,134 nonprofit and for-profit hospitals over the fiscal years 1991 to 1995. University affiliated medical school hospitals were excluded.

Nonprofit boards are precluded from writing meaningful incentive contracts due to the nondistributional constraint. Therefore, when returns on assets decline, nonprofit hospitals simply replace their chief operating officers. For-profits, on the other hand, cut bonuses in bad times rather than turnover management.

In addition, the study found little evidence that the CEOs of nonprofit hospitals confront explicit altruistic incentives. Boards pursuing altruistic goals should reward lower prices, higher output, and higher quality of care. We would expect nonprofit hospitals to distribute "profits" altruistically whenever they have some degree of market power and less competition. Nurses per patient, revenue per patient day, and service expenditures represent altruistic variables. Using regression analysis, the researchers conclude that altruistic managers experiencing less market competition were no more likely to be rewarded than managers in highly competitive markets.

Why do clients prefer nonprofit hospitals with boards that fail to reward altruistic managers? How would you design a study to demonstrate differences between nonprofit and for-profit hospitals?

Source: James A. Brickley and R. Lawrence Van Horn, "Managerial Incentives in Nonprofit Organizations: Evidence from Hospitals," *Journal of Law and Economics*, 45 (1), 2002, 227–49.

The stakeholder view

In stark contrast to the firm as a nexus of complete contracts, the *stakeholder view* holds that any firm, profit-seeking or NFP, is characterized by incomplete, or unspecified, contracts. The firm, as a combination of specialized assets and people, mutually benefits owners, employees, and clients, all of whom have implicit, or unspecified, claims on the firm. The stakeholder view of the firm differs from the optimization and contract models in that no one group in the firm has an exclusive right to control.

In light of the stakeholder view, a conventional profit-seeking firm would be nothing more than a special type of producer cooperative – a lenders' or capital cooperative. In practice, ownership in the conventional profit-seeking firms is commonly assigned to stockholders who supply the firm with capital, assume risk, and exercise control. The homogeneity of interest of this group, i.e. profit and wealth maximization, is the significant factor in the success of modern investor-owned business corporations. In contrast, a NFP stakeholder approach suggests that homogeneity of interest is achieved by a joint decision-making process including administrators, employees, consumers, and the general public.

The stakeholder view of the firm in many ways fits the NFP firm. NFP firms do not have clearcut owners exercising complete control over the firm. Stakeholders, such as suppliers, donors, volunteers, employees, clients, and even ex-clients, theoretically share NFP decision-making in proportion to their specific investments not protected or specified by contract. For example, ex-clients such as alumni have a continuing role in a university, because they have a stake in the reputation and value of diplomas issued.

Each of us has his or her personal opinion on stakeholder control. Do you believe that key stakeholders have the right to interpret mission in a controversial situation? Or, do you believe that board interpretation of mission and public good creation should dominate the agendas of various stakeholders? Unfortunately, NFPs face indivisible and conflicting claims, and the interests of stakeholders are not homogeneous. If you agree that nonprofit administrators must strategically balance the interests of donors, employees, clients, and the public at large with a firm's primary goals, you subscribe to a stakeholder view of the firm. If so, you must develop some way of integrating stakeholder claims, extending beyond legal and contractual responsibilities, with the intended mission of the firm.

Thus far, we have outlined three approaches to the firm: optimization, complete contract, and stakeholder theory. Regardless of whichever model approximates your preferred view of the modern NFP firm, two conditions must hold; otherwise, the nonprofit firm will exist only by virtue of the subsidy it receives from its sponsor/taxpayer or by virtue of its tax-exempt status. First, because efficiency and effectiveness are seldom achieved by cooperation among individuals (Buchanan, 1965), some external group needs to set objectives and monitor a firm's activity. Second, effectiveness and efficiency are served whenever those in the organization agree to cooperate (Croteau, 1963). These two conditions do not necessarily conflict. Stakeholder cooperation facilitates internal management and provides benefits but is not a substitute for external direction and evaluation.

Theories of the firm provide a framework for analyzing NFP firms, highlighting the differences between them and profit-seeking institutions. NFP firms do not and should not involve profit maximization, and, unlike profit-seeking firms, they do not have clearly defined owners. Furthermore, NFP firms, operating in highly specialized industries, are unique and cannot be reduced to a single abstract model. Yet, each firm, public or private, has a mission. Economic principles, derived from the theory of the firm, assist NFP organizations as they rationally strive toward specific, mutually compatible, and consistent goals.

Nonprofit by default or historical precedent

It is also the case that firms in certain industries are *nonprofit by default or historical precedent*. The mix of nonprofit, government, and profit-seeking firms varies within and between industries from country to country. For secondary education in the United States, public provision dominates, but healthcare is mainly provided in the private sector. It is almost the reverse in the United Kingdom, where the private sector traditionally dominates in providing elite secondary education but healthcare is nationalized into the government sector.

Often, firms from all three sectors, government, nonprofit, and profit-seeking, coexist in the same industry. There are no compelling economic reasons why some firms are organized as profit-seeking, government, or nonprofit firms, although the last two types dominate in providing public goods and in cases of market failure. Government and nonprofits often initiate services not provided in the market. Not only do NFP firms initially enter markets and create profit opportunities, they sometimes continue in these markets to counter monopolistic profit-seeking practices.

NFP firms also continue to be found in markets where substantial market failure does not exist. In other words, NFP firms produce even in situations where exclusion is possible and consumption is rival, unlike public goods. In many industries, such as postal services, surgical centers, primary education, and collective bargaining, we observe government, nonprofit, and for-profit firms operating successfully. If institutional and historical factors permit, variety and quality are increased when all three sectors compete in a given industry.

Why do some countries have large private nonprofit sectors and others do not? Why doesn't government exclusively produce what the profit-seeking market does not? What added benefit does a private nonprofit sector provide? The uniqueness of nonprofit firms lies in the subsidized production of differentiated goods containing social components. Private nonprofits, by harnessing the energies and creative juices of mission inspired individuals, accomplish what government cannot. We expect private nonprofits to be more flexible than government and on the cutting edge in providing quasi-public goods. The green revolution in agriculture, support for public radio and television, early childhood services, hospice care for the terminally ill, and low-income housing are just a few of the contributions initiated by private philanthropic organizations. Admittedly, like firms in any sector, private nonprofits can metastasize into disorder, randomness, and chaos. The Achilles' heel of private nonprofits is that permanently endowed and largely tax-exempt foundations and firms can lose their focus dissipating wealth in endless studies, conferences, reports, and stakeholder salaries.

Cooperatives

A cooperative, usually nonprofit, is an association of economic units, firms, individuals, or households. *Cooperatives* are self-governing voluntary organizations, and unless a significant portion of revenue comes from government or a sponsor, they should not strictly be classified as NFP firms. As previously indicated, private profit-seeking corporations, such as Coca Cola and General Electric, are in one sense collectives owned by investors who seek a return on their capital in return for risk and uncertainty. However, some group, other than stockholders, sponsors nonprofit cooperatives. A cooperative association itself is not an instrument designed to increase owner wealth, but rather to provide specific services to its members. A farmer's cooperative is designed, for example, to coordinate the sale of a particular agricultural product. This is different from focusing on optimizing individual owners' total wealth. Cooperatives own and operate utility, insurance, agricultural, and condominium associations. Other cooperatives are worker-owned and include professional services such as law, accounting, and marketing. These associations may be classified into two types: producer cooperatives, designed to efficiently market members' output, or consumer cooperatives designed to counter monopoly suppliers. A cooperative generally has no mission beyond that of its owners and, hence, distributes any surplus in proportion to a member's shares.

There are, however, some cooperatives that do have a mission beyond that of its members. They are sponsored by nonprofit or government agencies, and receive part of their funding from donated funds or services. A credit union, for example, may be organized to provide credit and financial services to households ignored by or charged high rates for borrowing from commercial banks. Credit unions, like nonprofits, are subsidized indirectly by taxes and directly by their sponsors.

Nonprofit tax status is given to a cooperative, such as a credit union, based on the assumption that members are provided with insurance, financial counseling, education, or other social services. Legally, tax-exempt cooperatives consist of members having a "common bond." In the United States, the prevalent common bond is that of employment, but it may be neighborhood, church, or industry based. The *common bond*, an association among members required for nonprofit status, is designed to provide an incentive for volunteers to manage the cooperative, with the assumption that one member's interests are closely identified with the interest of all.

Clubs

Clubs consist of people *voluntarily* cooperating for mutual rather than personal or public advantage. In the United States, clubs formed in order to provide private benefits to members pay taxes once their yearly revenue hits a certain amount. Golf courses, swim clubs, and fraternal organizations are taxed nonprofit firms. Individuals form clubs for three reasons. First, clubs share production costs that take advantage of large-scale economies. You may join a swim club and pay dues rather than build a pool in your back yard. Second, people sharing a common interest form clubs. Radio amateurs create clubs to provide members with antennas, repeaters, and fellowship. Finally, clubs form to exclude others from their benefits. A club may own and maintain, for example, a nature reserve where archery, fishing, and picnicking are available to members only.

Economists are interested in decision-making within cooperatives and clubs because as a group they decide on trade-offs between common goods even though the goods and services are internal to the group. Clubs and cooperatives are self-financed and do not receive revenue from an outside sponsor. They differ in one important respect from nonprofit and government firms. Club boards and managers do not have the same type of fiduciary responsibility expected of those organizations providing external public and quasi-public services.

5.7   POTENTIAL FOR GOVERNMENT AND NONPROFIT FAILURE

NFP firms are created to address "market failure." But, is there such a thing as "NFP failure"? Certainly. NFP firms are not exempted from human frailty, and their solutions to market failure are often less than successful. For example, whenever government and nonprofit firms are given exclusive monopoly rights or subsidies, there is a potential for NFP failure. Failure in the NFP sectors generally stems from an almost complete absence of any mechanism for reconciling internal firm policy with successful public good provision.

Having administrators who are honest, well educated, and in pursuit of the public interest is a primary condition for, but no guarantee of effectiveness. The public is legitimately concerned with performance. Performance measurement in the NFP sectors is not very different from similar services in the for-profit sector such as airline safety. However, dissatisfied customers in the for-profit sector generally can and do take their business elsewhere. This option may not exist in the NFP sectors where the risk of error is too great or other options do not exist.

Clients in the NFP sectors have limited choice, and often, in the case of government-provided services, no effective choice. Taxes are coercive and someone who does not like the services provided cannot opt out. In countries with multiple jurisdictions, citizens vote with their feet by moving to communities providing a more suitable package of services and taxation level (Tiebout, 1956). However, this imposes moving costs on individuals and in extreme cases weakens the fabric of communities.

Similarly in the nonprofit sector, one endures poor service whenever provision is bundled with membership. Pre-paid dues at a country club limit client response to poor service. Periodic review takes place in nonprofits but correction comes slowly. Ceasing to exist due to poor performance occurs in the nonprofit sector but less frequently than bankruptcy in the profit-seeking sector. It is sometimes the case, however, that nonprofit sponsors abandon projects that they cannot or no longer wish to subsidize. This generally occurs, even when institutions are well managed and socially productive, whenever client fees together with donations and subsidies fail to cover cost.

NFP accountability and competition, outlined in Chapter 8, are partial solutions to the shortcomings of NFP firms, often characterized by sluggish response and the absence of least cost incentives.

Mechanism design theory

The gap in knowledge between buyers and sellers and the costs and consequences of asymmetric information are at the heart of *mechanism design theory* developed by Hurwicz, Masken, and Myerson, who were awarded the 2007 Nobel Prize in Economics. Mechanism theory suggests that NFP firms may be the optimal mechanism for provision when a non-distributional constraint is needed for client protection. Whenever client protection is needed, the cost of monitoring quality is high, and for-profit managers have an incentive to reduce quality in order to increase profits. Group homes for orphans provide an example. Children (the clients) are incapable of evaluating service and have no one acting as their advocate, even if the government were to sufficiently fund for-profit firms/individuals to provide residential care. Whenever monitoring costs are not exorbitant, such as in processing utility bills or tax payments, profit-seeking firms for government services may actually be preferred. This is not the case with caring for a very young child or invalids. Here, the best mechanism for delivering the service may be in institutions with administrators operating under a non-distributional constraint. NFP status does not guarantee better care, but creates less incentive to skimp on providing service.

The principal–agent problem

Real-world firms in whatever sector are made up of individuals with personal goals. The *principal–agent problem* legitimizes discussion of deviations from profit maximization in profit-seeking firms as well as deviations from mission in NFP firms. The principal–agent problem occurs when one person (the agent) acts on behalf of another individual (the principal).

Consider the owners of profit-seeking firms (stockholders); generally they have little detailed knowledge of the firms they own. Their ownership may be quite divorced from the everyday operations of the firm. Few of General Electric's stockholders, for instance, either work for the company or attend annual stockholders' meetings. It is unclear then why GE managers would constantly work to secure the interests of such a seemingly disinterested group of stockholders. With respect to employee benefits, for example, the interests of managers and workers at GE are in direct conflict with the desire of stockholders to maximize profits. Stockholders, however, expect employees and managers to direct their efforts toward efficient production and to be honest in serving the corporation's interests.

If the contributions of each employee were easily identifiable, the principal–agent problem would not exist. All managers would then have an incentive to continue maximizing profits. Unfortunately, stockholders' (the principals') objectives cannot be assessed in the short run and it is not simple to know when or how to reward or punish each manager (agents). Ideally, however, the interests of stockholders and the desires of the agents work in the same direction. This homogeneity of interest results in firms that are well managed. The principal–agent problem is indeed a problem in practice because the fortunate state of affairs (i.e., a coincidence of desires on the part of the owners, managers, and employees) does not always exist.

Managers and employees often pursue their own goals, even at the expense of a firm's profits. Economists call this *subgoal pursuit*. Obviously, personal goals should be subordinated to the main goal of a firm. It is virtually impossible to eliminate all subgoal pursuit. Few employees work to capacity 100 percent of the time, and they may modify tasks in ways that do not exactly match what is expected.

NFP firms are not exempted from the principal–agent problem, even when they have clearly defined missions that are consistently pursued. Every multi-person firm introduces a host of opportunities for subgoal pursuit and principal–agent problems. In fact, due to fuzzy ownership rights and a variety of stakeholder interests, NFPs may be more susceptible to these problems. Every firm needs to tailor contractual arrangements to address problems created by conflicts of interest. The source of these conflicts may be between employees and owners/sponsors of a firm, between a firm and its suppliers, or between user clients and donors. Even if everyone associated with a NFP firm is well intentioned, we cannot neglect the discussion of principal–agent problems brought about by the difficulties of diffuse ownership plus the multiple and sometimes conflicting goals of NFP stakeholders.

Addressing principal–agent problems

The best solution to any principal–agent situation is for the principal to find an agent with matching goals or create ways to unify goals. In Application 5.3, China created new forms of ownership to solve this problem.

APPLICATION 5.3
Defining Property Rights to Limit Externalities in Chinese State Owned Enterprises (SOEs)

State owned enterprises (SOEs) are "owned by all the people." Therefore, Gary Jefferson of Brandeis University sees SOEs as a common good with inefficiencies resulting from an unclear assignment of property rights. State owned enterprises are over-consumed by some stakeholders creating negative externalities affecting all members of society. The opportunistic behavior of stakeholders extracts value from the firm in excess of their specific contributions. If public revenue is used to cover losses accrued by state owned enterprises, these stakeholders gain indefinitely.

To improve economic efficiency of SOEs, the Chinese government initiated a series of gradual reforms in 1979. It began by permitting SOEs to retain 12 percent of increased profits or reduced losses. Then, managerial autonomy was gradually deepened under a contract-responsibility system in which the SOEs agreed to deliver predetermined amounts of revenue to the state. Formerly, all losses were covered by the state. A modern corporate system evolved by which the state became entitled to dividends on its shares.

An unexpected effect of reform was an emerging Chinese property-rights market. Township and village enterprises (TVEs), foreign and domestic joint ventures, shareholding, cooperative, and privately owned enterprises all entered the market. Allocative and productive efficiency increased because these reforms incorporated the Coasian (Coase, 1960) prescription. Well-specified property rights reduce transaction costs as well as inefficient resource allocation.

Jefferson argues that privatization, merely selling a state's industrial assets, creates fewer benefits. Privatization in Russia resulted in insiders stripping assets, because minority shareholders could not enforce their rights. In China, the emergence of regional non-state firms without access to state funds creates a hard budget constraint. Forcing firms to cover costs clarifies property rights and reduces transaction costs.

Source: Gary H. Jefferson, "China's State Enterprises: Public Goods, Externalities, and Coase," *American Economic Review Papers and Proceedings*, May 1998, 428–32.

Firms cannot easily identify people with like-minded goals. Motivation sessions, provided by an employer, are generally an attempt at changing people's goals. Much of the "team building" and "pride building" modern corporations seem to relish, are seen by economists as goal modification in order to solve principal–agent problems.

To get anyone to do something when they have a better alternative (i.e., meeting their own personal goals), you must offer a reward. Two hundred years before Adam Smith wrote *The Wealth of Nations*, Jean de la Bruyere wrote "the shortest and best way to make your fortune is to let people see clearly that it is in their interests to promote yours."

Economic incentives used to modify an agent's behavior are quite common. The simplest example involves production workers being paid for each piece of finished work. Piece rate contracts are simple attempts to match employees' interests with those of owners. Any differential payment scheme, such as piece rates, commissions, bonuses, or royalties, raises the cost to an employee of subgoal pursuit. Perhaps the most effective incentive would be one that gives managers a financial stake in the success of the firm. However, this is not an option for NFP administrators; the non-distributional constraint precludes most financial incentives other than salary and promotion. However, the NFP sector needs to address principal–agent problems by properly arranging incentives for administrators and employees in terms of mission.

A critique of the principal–agent contract in the government sector

Francis Fukuyama argues that principal–agent theory, emphasizing personal incentives, limits government's ability to devise optimal arrangements for public administrators (2004). He argues that clearcut best practices may not exist in the public sector and that each institution needs to be evaluated in context. This suggests that goals in the public sector are not delegated from the top but evolve through complicated interactions between stakeholders. For example, groups of administrators and public school teachers act as agents for groups of taxpayers, parents, and children. Which group has the ultimate authority? Do these groups agree on learning goals? Can outcomes be precisely specified and measured?

There are literally thousands of classrooms charged with unspecified goals depending on the surrounding culture. Delegation of rules and procedures from top down implies excessive monitoring costs. Fukuyama hypothesizes that, because the most problematic areas of public administration are those characterized with low specificity and high transaction volume, principal–agent analysis yields little insight. Several industries in the government sector are graphed in Figure 5.3 in terms of specificity and number of transactions.

In Figure 5.3, government sector industries most difficult to administrate, such as education and healthcare, have low-specificity and high-transaction volume. In these areas, Fukuyama argues, public administration must rely on a mixture of formal mechanisms of accountability and informal norms that promote cooperative behavior. The diagram is helpful in explaining why many developing countries can have highly competent central bankers, operate national oil companies and airlines, yet fail in providing primary education or rural healthcare. A central banker makes a few clearly specified and easily monitored decisions such as controlling the money stock from month to month. A secondary school guidance counselor, on the other hand, sees many students each with different treatment goals that cannot be easily monitored.

Certainly, some government firms benefit more from a microeconomic or technical approach than others. Yet, even government industries characterized as being

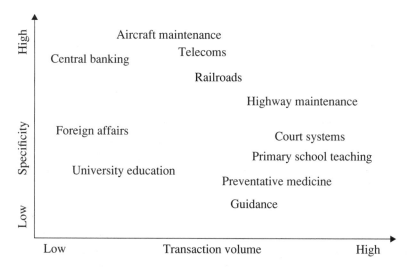

Figure 5.3   Government sector industries characterized by goal specificity and number of transactions. A central banker makes relatively few but highly specified decisions such as controlling money stock from month to month. A guidance counselor sees many clients each with different treatment goals.
Source: Francis Fukuyama, "Why There Is No Science of Public Administration," *Journal of International Affairs*, 48 (1), 2004, 195.

resistant to universal norms and having high monitoring costs require periodic assessment. Comparative research in public administration reveals how various methods improve outcomes.

Government corruption

Whenever market failure is addressed by taxing some activities while subsidizing others, opportunities for official corruption abound. Corruption increases the size of government, the rents of public employees, and the misallocation of resources. This is not to say that government corruption exceeds that found in the profit-seeking or nonprofit sectors. But official corruption is especially serious because government has the power to coerce and because we depend on government to police and discipline private correction. Government agents, motivated by self-interest and pursuing subgoals, are in a position to use this advantage. Therefore, an even larger bureaucracy is needed to monitor official agents. This is not an argument for eliminating government's attempt to correct for market failure. What it does imply is that there may be some optimal amount of government correction. The benefits of government correction should exceed its costs.

5.8   COLLECTIVE DECISION-MAKING AND PUBLIC CHOICE

Group action is one solution to market failure. In *collective decision-making*, a group of individuals agree, through some voting process, to collect funds sufficient to buy or produce public goods. ***Public choice***, a branch of economics, studies how collective decisions are made and then tries to create a formal institutional system that aligns administrators' (the agents) interests with those sponsoring the firm (the principals).

A group can provide anything that is legal by self-producing or contracting for it. In collective provision, however, unless there is total unanimity, the group is transferring resources among members. If your sorority decides to subsidize parties and you need to use that time for study, your dues are transferred to those who like to party. When majority rule is used to make group decisions, percentages of up to 49 percent of voters are overruled in each decision. This explains why individual market choice is preferred whenever possible to collective decision-making.

Voting rules

Whenever the total benefits of providing public goods through voluntary collective action exceed total costs, society's wellbeing is increased. The word voluntary is important because the loss to someone coerced to transfer resources to others cannot be measured. However, even when one making a collective decision has nothing to lose personally, theoretical problems remain in maximizing benefits. Because majority voting does not incorporate the strength of individual preferences, highly beneficial projects may be defeated and ones with fewer benefits approved. For example, if out of three people two benefit on net from a collective decision, the measure may be passed even though the total gain does not exceed costs assessed on each person.

Majority voting can lead to inconsistent outcomes known as the ***voting paradox***. Suppose, for example, that the board of a local family medical clinic consisting of members Anderson, Jones, and Smith are in the process of hiring certain specialists to attend one morning per week. Consider the following preferences:

- Anderson prefers a gynecologist to a dermatologist and prefers a dermatologist to an orthopedist.
- Jones prefers a dermatologist to an orthopedist and prefers an orthopedist to a gynecologist.
- Smith prefers an orthopedist to a gynecologist and prefers a gynecologist to a dermatologist.

At one quarterly board meeting, the three board members are asked to vote between hiring a gynecologist or a dermatologist. The gynecologist is selected by majority vote and employed. At the next quarterly meeting, a vote is taken between a dermatologist and an orthopedist, and a dermatologist is added to the staff. Note that if at the first meeting the board had been asked to decide between a gynecologist and an orthopedist, the orthopedist would have been hired first. Meanwhile, the clinic continues without the services of an orthopedist. The voting paradox demonstrates that getting an issue on or off an agenda (or its position on the agenda) affects outcome more than the intrinsic worthiness of the project. It also demonstrates that voters cannot reflect the intensity of their preferences. Alternatives to a majority voting rule are designed to correct the voting paradox.

These include unanimity, weighted or ranked votes, and more than 50 percent approval to pass on important decisions.

Collective decision-making, in the absence of a rule setting limits, explains the expansion of government goods. Consider a group of individuals periodically meeting at a restaurant. Some prefer expensive wines and high priced items such as lobster and indulge their preferences knowing that the check will be evenly divided. After several such events, nondrinkers who generally choose mid-priced items unaccustomedly order dessert. Costs escalate. This is similar to congressional *log-rolling* in which one elected representative votes for approval of a project against his or her own preferences in the expectation that the favor will be returned.

Even in the private nonprofit sector where legal coercion cannot be used to get funding the *free-rider problem* distorts decisions. Each member of a church, synagogue, or mosque benefits from a beautiful worship space, classes, and other programs. However, many join an organization expecting donors other than themselves to carry the burden. If these individuals donate the bare minimum and still are considered members, the under-funded nonprofit ultimately produces less than the optimal amount of social goods.

Vernon Smith (2002 Nobel Prize Winner in Economics) and other economists use simulations to study individual response to appeals for donations. In one simulation, four members of a group are given $10 and told that they can either keep the money or invest any part of it in a group fund. Everyone who contributes a minimum amount shares equally in the benefits. The simulation is repeated several times to enable individuals to assess probabilities of gain and adapt their behaviors. If the fund grows by $2 in a given round and all contribute, each member receives $0.50. How inclined would you be to donate $1 to the fund in further rounds? An investment in this fund is a donation in support of a public good. Each member benefits from the investment but the individual investor loses some personal assets. The economists conducting these simulations find that those who at first may have been willing to donate a dollar or more will over time reduce their donations and most will never contribute more than the minimum required to share in the benefits.

Interest groups

Special interest groups sometimes referred to as public interest or pressure groups influence the NFP sectors. Special interest groups explain why one local government generously supports education and another emergency medical care. When rational self-motivated individuals realize that they have interests in common they band together to determine the direction of NFP firms. Pressure groups play a positive and useful role in highlighting preferences and grievances and counterbalance one another. At worst, they get others to provide goods from which they personally benefit.

Do pressure groups form whenever and wherever needs and/or benefits are the greatest? Unfortunately, no. It is counter-intuitive but true that pressure group formation does not depend on the size of anticipated benefits. Rather, it depends on the patterns of distributed benefits and assigned costs. Consider student government allocations from required activity fees. An interest group lobbying for subsidized ski trips is more likely to form than one providing some small benefit for the total student body, such as wireless internet connection.

Pressure groups have problems with *free riders* refusing to join in the effort but nevertheless expecting to receive benefits without contributing time and donations. To eliminate free riders, some groups develop a legal mechanism to requiring membership. Labor unions try to ensure that all do not receive the collective bargaining benefits provided by dues-paying members. Offering some divisible individual good in addition to the collective good is an attempt to circumvent free-rider problems. The American Automobile Association, for example, lobbies for better highways but also provides individual members with emergency road and routing services. However, interest groups providing these benefits experience fierce competition from other profit-seeking firms willing to provide similar benefits at lower cost.

Rent-seeking

Rent-seeking behavior is any activity whereby an individual or a group of individuals transfer income or wealth to themselves at someone else's expense. Large guaranteed returns/profit are considered rent and firms and individuals spend valuable resources to place themselves in position to gain or maintain these returns. The following example is one form of rent-seeking, a concept created by Anne Kruger in analyzing trade, corruption, and slow economic growth. Gordon Tullock later extended the concept to public choice.

Suppose you were producing a product that no one else in the country is willing or able to produce. However, the product could be imported from abroad. If you convince the government to place tariffs, quotas, bans, or other entry barriers on the product, you are able to sell at a higher price. The difference in price you receive with and without the restrictions is rent. However, you will probably need to incur some costs in maintaining your entry barrier privilege. Rent-seeking expenditures increase costs of the provider but do not increase or improve output; rather, the cost and effort of maintaining rents could be better used in improving the product. Earnings derived from rent-seeking are economically inefficient.

Governments create rent-seeking opportunities directly or indirectly by laws and rules, in hiring practices, and in purchasing procedures. Wherever liquor and taxicab licenses are set to a certain number, licensees earn higher incomes than they would in an open market with free entry. And clients pay higher prices. Elected officials respond to interest groups that lobby to maintain rent-creating advantages. Rent-seeking occurs when farmers, manufacturers, and other professional groups benefit financially from unnecessary subsidies, trade restrictions, tax abatements, and government licenses. Figure 5.4 shows how taxicab licenses transfer surpluses to producers from consumers.

In Figure 5.4, prior to licensing, consumer surplus is *EAC* and producer surplus, *EAS*. With licensing, taxicab services are reduced and price rises. Consumer surplus falls to *HDC* and producer surplus increases to *SFDH*, although some of the increased producer surplus must be spent in securing a license. A deadweight loss of *FAD* remains. If the intention of introducing licensing was to correct a negative externality, then the deadweight loss may be compensated by social benefits. However, even when the benefits of reduced congestion, for example, exceed deadweight

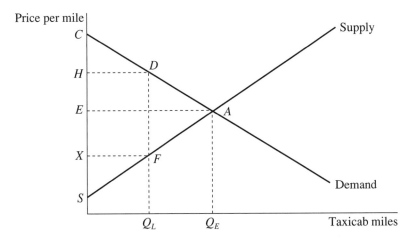

Figure 5.4   Licensing produces deadweight loss and surplus transfers. In the absence of taxicab licensing, price per mile is E and the quantity provided is Q_E. Consumer surplus is EAC and producer surplus is EAS. If taxi services are limited by licensing to Q_L, consumer surplus falls to HDC and producer surplus could rise to $SFDH$. If licensing fees per mile rise to FD, government or holders of existing licenses capture $XFDH$ of the surplus. The deadweight loss of licensing is FAD because the total of producer and consumer surplus is less than it was before licensing.

loss, those potential taxicab operators without licenses and all taxicab users experience a loss.

Well financed political action committees (PAC) often promote government programs that transfer income to certain groups. When PAC behavior transfers large sums of money to small interest groups, the relative cost imposed on each individual taxpayer is small. Because the cost to each individual taxpayer is small, there is little incentive to keep informed or organize groups to counter specific types of rent-seeking.

Rent-seeking is essentially a stratagem for transferring resources from one group to another. Those seeking rents are willing to pay dues to achieve their goals. What they hope to receive, however, is something vastly greater in size or value to rent-seeking costs. A question, never definitely answered, is whether total expenditures by rent-seekers exceed the value of desired rents (Lockard and Tullock, 2001). Given opportunities to earn rents, many seek but not all will succeed.

Rent-seeking represents a net cost or deadweight loss to society limiting output and quality, while needlessly transferring wealth from some to others. Reducing rent-seeking opportunities is generally in the public interest.

A final word must be said about democracy and how it corrects for market failure. This chapter describes how interest groups, log-rolling, rent-seeking, and majority voting distort resource allocation. However, as Amartya Sen has shown, widespread distress from famines does not exist in democratic societies with voting rights for all. Markets may not be able to deal with natural catastrophes, such as droughts and crop failure, but voters can force those in power to respond. Public administrators are on the front line of providing feasible solutions creatively, at least cost, and effectively.

CONCLUDING NOTES

- Given market failure resource allocation is inefficient and prices fail to reflect true costs and benefits. Market failure exists: when public goods are not provided; when competition is lacking; when parties to a contract do not have access to the same information (asymmetric information); and when positive and negative externalities are present.

- Government and nonprofit firms are predominately found in industries characterized by market failure.

- Not-for-profit provision is often preferred as a solution to asymmetric information. NFP administrators due to the nondistributional constraint cannot reduce quality for personal gain.

- Negative externalities are social costs and positive externalities are social benefits. In both cases, third parties are affected by buyer and seller contracting. Markets over-allocate resources to goods characterized by negative externalities. Markets under-allocate resources to goods characterized by positive externalities.

- Clearly defining property rights, taxation, and subsidies corrects market failure due to externalities. Indirect and direct subsidies to NFP firms are designed to increase social benefits; specific taxes are designed to decrease negative externalities.

- NFP firms, like all firms, use scarce resources to produce goods and services. NFP firms do not attempt to maximize the difference between revenue and costs. However, they engage in optimizing behavior when they produce a given amount of output at least cost or produce the maximum amount of output with a given amount of resources.

- All organizations are subject to human failure. Because NFP firms do not have clearly defined owners and serve potentially conflicting constituencies, alternate theories of the firm, such as the stakeholder view, may be more descriptive of their behavior than optimization techniques.

- Economic reasoning alone cannot explain the coexistence of profit-seeking, government, and private nonprofits in certain industries. Various nonprofit institutions such as cooperatives and clubs evolve to meet specific needs, incompletely addressed by families, government, or markets.

- Principal–agent problems present a particular hazard to NFP firms. NFPs lack financial incentives designed to coordinate the interests of owners/sponsors with those of administrators.

- In collective decisions, individuals agree, generally through some voting process, to provide public goods. Majority voting does not incorporate the intensity of individual preferences, and thus is subject to the "voting paradox." Voter outcomes depend on how proposals are presented and may be inconsistent.

- Social benefits provided in the private nonprofit sector cannot coerce free riders. If free riding becomes excessive, donations fall, and few contribute more than minimum dues.

- Public interest groups provide a role in formulating preferences and the means to direct the allocation of resources. Pressure group formation does not depend on the size of potential benefits but rather on the pattern of distributed benefits and assigned costs.

- Individuals engage in rent-seeking behavior rather than in producing value when the expected benefits of rents exceed costs. Rents transfer income or wealth to some at others' expense. Governments create rents directly or indirectly by laws and procedures that limit free entry into a market.

KEY TERMS

Invisible hand
Market failure
Firm
Asymmetric information
Externalities
Social cost
Social benefit
Merit goods
Property rights
Tax credit
Tax deduction
Optimizing theory
Complete contracts approach
Soft incentives
Stakeholder view

Nonprofit by default
  or historical precedent
Cooperatives
Common bond
Clubs
Mechanism theory
Principal–agent problem
Subgoal pursuit
Collective decision-making
Public choice
Voting paradox
Log-rolling
Free riders
Rent-seeking

SUGGESTED READINGS

Acemoglu, Daron and Verdier, Thierry 2000: "The Choice between Market Failures and Corruption," *American Economic Review*, 90 (1), 194–211.

Buchanan, J. M. 1965: "An Economic Theory of Clubs," *Economica*, 32 (February), 1–14.

Croteau, John T. 1963: *The Economics of the Credit Union*, Detroit, MI: Wayne State University Press.

Fukuyama, Francis 2004: "Why There Is No Science of Public Administration," *Journal of International Affairs*, 48 (1), 189–201.

Hammer, Peter J. 2001: "Arrow's Analysis of Social Institutions: Entering the Marketplace with Giving Hands?" *Journal of Health Politics, Policy and Law*, 26 (5), 1081–97.

Hansmann, Henry B. 1987: "The Effect of Tax Exemption and Other Factors on the Market Share of Nonprofit versus For-profit Firms," *National Tax Journal*, 40 (March), 71–82.

Lockard, Alan and Tullock, Gordon (eds.) 2001: *Efficient Rent Seeking: Chronicle of an Intellectual Quagmire*, Boston, Dordrecht, and London: Kluwer Academic.

McKenzie, Richard 2007: "Sticker Shock," *Wall Street Journal*, Saturday/Sunday, February 17–18, A8.

Pincus, Jonathan J. 1977: *Pressure Group and Politics in Antebellum Tariffs*, New York: Columbia University Press.

Sandler, Todd and Tschirhart, John T. 1980: "The Economic Theory of Clubs: An Evaluative Survey," *Journal of Economic Literature*, 18 (December), 1481–1521.

Sen, Amartya 1999: *Development as Freedom*, Oxford: Oxford University Press.

Smith, Adam 1976: *An Inquiry into the Nature and Causes of the Wealth of Nations*, Chicago, IL: University of Chicago Press.

Speckbacher, Gerhard 2003: "The Economics of Performance Management in Nonprofit Organizations," *Nonprofit Management and Leadership*, 13 (3), 267–81.

Tiebout, Charles M. 1956: "A Pure Theory of Local Expenditures," *Journal of Political Economy*, 64 (October), 416–24.

END OF CHAPTER EXERCISES

Exercise 5.1
Use the concept of asymmetric information and the nondistributional constraint to explain why clients may prefer NFP provision in the following situations:

    a.   Childcare nurseries.
    b.   Convalescent and nursing homes.

Exercise 5.2
Individuals in a particular city are willing to tolerate a certain amount of odor emanating from local ethanol plants. However, they wish to be compensated for the distress and use this revenue to subsidize parks.

    a.   Draw and label a supply curve for the right to emit such odors for each 8-hour period (21 periods each week).
    b.   Draw a demand curve on the same diagram and explain why it is negatively sloping.
    c.   Explain the effect of an increase in the price firms receive for ethanol on the demand for emission rights. How could the community respond?
    d.   Do property rights in this situation reduce the negative externality due to market failure? Explain. Discuss the effect of clearly established property rights on the allocation of resources and price of ethanol.

Exercise 5.3
Concrete sidewalks in River Bend, a moderately sized city in the mid-western United States, are crumbling due to age, weather, use, and erupting tree roots.

a. Draw a supply and demand diagram showing an equilibrium price of $100 for each square section of repair. Then, describe the effects on price and quantity of the town council's decision to compensate homeowners for 50 percent of the cost of repaving sidewalks completed by city or private contractors.
b. Use another supply and demand diagram to show the effect of compensating contractors directly if they can demonstrate that they repaired homeowners' sidewalks.
c. In what sense do homeowners' sidewalks provide social benefits justifying a subsidy? Do you think that either of the above proposals is fair to all of River Bend's taxpayers? Explain.

Exercise 5.4
Consider two middle schools (grades 6–8) in your community; one is public and the other a private nonprofit.

a. In what sense are these schools optimizing institutions? How would this compare with a profit-seeking middle school?
b. Do employees, clients, and textbooks suppliers have complete contracts in their association with the two schools? How do these contracts compare?
c. Describe the differences in decision-making in these schools using a stake-holder model.

Exercise 5.5
Economists justify special tax treatment of NFP firms based on theories of public goods and market failure. Because these firms are directly or indirectly subsidized, they are cushioned from market discipline. Discuss cost-effective ways of monitoring their performance.

Exercise 5.6
Interview someone with a checking/draft account at a credit union.

a. On what basis is he or she permitted to be a member of that particular credit union? Who sponsors the organization? Does the sponsor subsidize the credit union in any way?
b. To whom are any residuals between the credit union's costs and revenue distributed.
c. Does the person have a loan from the credit union? Why did he or she borrow from the credit union rather than another financial institution?
d. Does the credit union provide services not available at other financial institutions?

Exercise 5.7
Consider ways that the following firms attempt to align the interests of principal and agent:

    a.   A software start-up company?
    b.   A large Fortune 500 corporation?
    c.   A small congregational church?
    d.   A large religious denomination?

Exercise 5.8

School board member A prefers football to basketball and basketball to synchronized swimming. Member B prefers basketball to synchronized swimming and synchronized swimming to football. Member C prefers synchronized swimming to football and prefers football to basketball.

    a.   The nonvoting chairperson indicates that the district can afford to hire one coach only and proposes a vote determining whether to hire a basketball or football coach. Which will be hired?
    b.   If later, as funds become more available, the chair proposes a vote between hiring a synchronized swimming coach or a basketball coach, which coach does the district hire?
    c.   If the chair had initially in the first vote proposed a vote between football and synchronized swimming, which coach would the district have hired?
    d.   Could you devise a better voting rule in making collective decisions?

Exercise 5.9

Use Public Choice interest group coalition theory to explain if and why the following issues will likely be addressed:

    a.   Residents' desire for public tennis courts.
    b.   Convenient drop off places for hazardous chemicals such as left-over paint.

Exercise 5.10

Consider the case in which locally registered taxi companies have the exclusive right to pick up passengers at the airport. These companies charge $2.00 per mile. In other areas around the state the fare is $1.00 per mile. Describe conditions under which the existence of taxi registration is an attempt to raise revenue, reduce congestion, or rent-seeking on the part of taxi companies. Provide an example of rent-seeking in the NFP sectors.

Exercise 5.11

In the absence of profit-and-loss systems in the NFP sectors, what procedures can be substituted to ensure that public administrators undertake activities contributing to mission?

Exercise 5.12

Provide an example of how the government can require profit-seeking firms to internalize spillover or social costs. Draw a supply and demand curve for this industry in market equilibrium. Then show the effect of the correction. How will this change affect allocative efficiency?

Exercise 5.13

Provide an example of how the government can increase the consumption of a product that has external social benefits. Draw a supply and demand curve for this industry in market equilibrium. How will this change affect allocative efficiency?

Exercise 5.14

Suppose that a public administrator functioning as a university dean is required to engage in a 360-degree assessment process to get feedback on her performance. All subordinates are asked to participate in assessing the performance of the dean. What other stakeholders should be included? Should responses from different stakeholders be weighted differently? Explain.

Exercise 5.15

What reduction is more effective in increasing consumption of a good with social benefits: a tax credit or tax deduction? Explain.

Exercise 5.16

Use the theory of the firm to justify school efficiency compared with home schooling.

Exercise 5.17

Individuals in NFP firms, public and private, have no overall common goal to guide decisions and cannot measure output. True or false? Explain.

Exercise 5.18

Contrast hard and "soft incentives." Application 5.3 discusses two distinct responses to NFP failure by China and Russia respectively. In your opinion, are hard incentives (bonuses and net income sharing) as compared with "soft incentives" appropriate in the NFP framework?

Exercise 5.19

Differentiate and provide examples: A public good that is both financed and produced in the public sector and another public good which is government financed but privately provided.

Exercise 5.20

Suppose you were the nonvoting chair of a committee consisting of three additional members (Smith, Jones, and Yang) responsible for allocating $100,000 each to two out of three projects based on majority vote by the committee. You have a strong preference for option C. What options are funded if the committee votes to allocate the first $100,000 to the choice between A and B and the second $100,000 between the remaining two projects? How would you have structured the voting agenda? Explain your reasoning.

Ranking of preferences of voters:	Option A: cost = $100,000	Option B: cost = $100,000	Option C: cost = $100,000
Smith	1	3	2
Jones	3	2	1
Yang	2	1	3

Part III

Production Theory and Public Administration

6
Production and Costs

6.1   INTRODUCTION

Reed Hastings, the founder and CEO of Netflix, pioneered an online system for renting DVDs delivered by mail. This cost saving innovation led to lower prices and increased convenience for consumers demanding this service. His innovation is significant because service industries experience fewer cost saving innovations as compared with manufacturing. However, Hastings says, "We're finding out more and more that competitive forces can provide great improvement in services –

telephones and airlines being obvious examples. Now, those [airlines and telephones] are [in the] for profit sectors, but you can obviously see this in the nonprofit sector as well. There's not one environmental nonprofit. There are dozens, and they all compete for impact and prestige and donor dollars. And they have different approaches to the problems and that's healthy."[1] NFP firms are primarily low-tech service providers, but, nevertheless, they are being forced to consider or lead the way in effective cost saving innovations consistent with mission. The purpose of this chapter is to provide a framework for analyzing these costs.

All firms produce something, either a good or service, as a means to an end. For profit-seeking firms that end, or objective, is best thought of as maximizing profits. For NFP firms, the goal is undoubtedly more complex, although best summarized as purposeful behavior attempting to further mission. However, all firms are alike in that they seek to minimize costs. Thus, this chapter focuses on production costs, on how to minimize costs for a given level of output, and/or on maximizing output for a given level of inputs. To achieve this goal, decision-makers start with a basic understanding of production economics.

A firm incurs costs because it must pay for all inputs used in the production process. This chapter outlines rules for determining the cost-effective amount of a particular input. Then, we develop a basis upon which an understanding of a firm's costs can be constructed. A NFP child daycare provider, for example, must rent or purchase a facility, buy supplies, and hire staff. These inputs are combined in some manner to produce output. Costs vary depending on the size of the facility and the number of clients served. Understanding the mechanism of production sets the foundation for a study of costs. Fundamental cost assumptions presented in this chapter will be combined in Chapters 8 and 9 with revenue to analyze user fees and the optimal level of output. To begin, however, we must differentiate short- and long-run production/cost horizons and examine the difficulties associated with collecting and analyzing cost data.

6.2   MODELING PRODUCTION

Production involves taking various inputs on site and combining them in such a way as to yield the desired finished product. For example, hospital administrators combine beds, buildings, linen, medical/pharmaceutical/food supplies, and human resources as well as capital (diagnostic equipment, operating theaters, etc.) to yield inpatient services. Some inputs, such as the facility and the existing number of beds, are relatively fixed in supply (at least in the short run). Other inputs vary and, as different quantities of each are used, the level of output is expected to vary.

The relationship between the amount of various inputs used in the production process and the level of output is called a ***production function***. Production functions describe efficient levels of output, getting the most from each given level of inputs. Thus, the output associated with each combination of inputs is the maximum output possible with that set of inputs, given existing technology.

---

[1] Jason J. Reilley, "Movie Man," *The Wall Street Journal*, February 9–10, 2008, A9.

For example, if the institution offers standard childbirth services, it requires some combination of facilities, equipment, and the services from a range of medical providers. As the number of births/admissions increases, the amount of inputs needed increases. Production functions can also change as technology changes. Laundry services needed per client, for example, decline with the introduction of disposable products.

In this chapter, we assume that a theoretical NFP firm is engaged in producing a single good or service. This is merely a simplification making the exposition easier to follow.

6.3   A PRODUCTION FUNCTION WITH ONE VARIABLE INPUT

Production functions may be presented in tabular, graphic, or algebraic form and consist of one, two, or more variable inputs. Let's begin with the tabular and graphic forms of a function that could represent the production of vision screening in a state bureau for driver licensing. We represent the output of vision screenings by the letter Q and the number of employees conducting the screenings per eight-hour shift by the letter L. Table 6.1 shows the output that results for different levels of the labor input.

We assume in this example that the variable labor input combines with other inputs, such as machines and testing space, which are fixed in the short run. Technology, or know-how, is also assumed constant. The relationship given in Table 6.1 between the labor input and the quantity of output is shown in graphic form in Figure 6.1. The production function goes through the origin, indicating that without labor, no output is produced.

The same information contained in the production schedule in Table 6.1 and in the graphic production function in Figure 6.1 can be represented by an algebraic function:

$$Q = 7.5L^2 - 0.5L^3$$

In this form, we see most clearly that if the number of laborers is zero, the level of output is also zero. For positive values of labor input, the corresponding level of output can be determined from the production function. For example, if four

Table 6.1   A production function for vision screenings: $Q = f(L)$

Labor (L)	Output (Q)	Labor (L)	Output (Q)
1	7	8	224
2	26	9	243
3	54	10	250
4	88	11	242
5	125	12	216
6	162	13	169
7	196	14	98

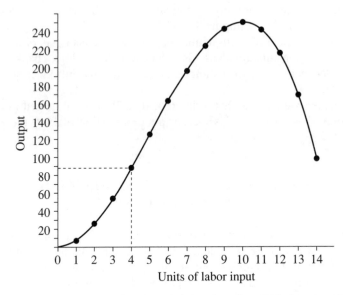

Figure 6.1   Graphic depiction of the production function. This function shows how output, such as the number of vision tests produced, varies as the units of labor employed change.

laborers are hired for a given eight-hour shift, Table 6.1 indicates that 88 vision tests can be processed. Similarly, from Figure 6.1 we see that if four units of labor are hired, the graphic production function is 88 units above (in the vertical direction) the horizontal (labor) axis. Algebraically, we can also see that 88 units of production result from four labor inputs used:

$$Q = 7.5(4)^2 - 0.5(4)^3 = 88$$

What if we wanted to know how many vision tests could be produced if four workers were hired for the full 8-hour shift but one worker was hired for a 4-hour half shift? That is, what output level should be expected from $L = 4.5$? The tabular form of the production function is not helpful in this case, because $L = 4.5$ is not specified. We could estimate the level of output as the midpoint between $L = 4$ and $L = 5$ ($Q = 106.5$), but this assumes that the production function is linear between 4 and 5 units of labor, when in fact it is not. As it turns out, in this case, the production function is very nearly linear in this range, and the estimate of 106.5 units of output for 4.5 units of labor input is not too far off. Using the graph in Figure 6.1 to estimate the rate of output for 4.5 units of labor involves considerable individual judgment. One person might make an estimate of 107 units, while others might select different values.

The most accurate method of determining the output of 4.5 units of labor is to use the algebraic form of the production function:

$$Q = 7.5(4.5)^2 - 0.5(4.5)^3 = 106.3$$

Everyone gets exactly the same result from this calculation.

Three important measures of production

In the above production functions, the measure of output represented by Q has been the total product that results from each level use of labor (L). For example, we see from Table 6.1 that a total of 88 vision tests are produced if we employed four units of the labor input. You will often see total product represented by TP as well as by Q.

A *fixed input* is any input whose quantity cannot be changed by the firm in the short run. A *variable input* is one that can be added to the process to increase output. In the case of the division of motor vehicles responsible for vision tests, the facility itself is a fixed input in the short run. The number of machines and/or personnel may be variable inputs. **Total product** refers to the total output of a particular good or service produced by a firm.

In addition to total output, two other measures of production are important: marginal product and average product. For decision-makers, it is often particularly important to know how production changes as a single variable input is changed or the average output per variable input. For example, we may wish to know if it would be worthwhile to hire an additional unit of labor for some productive activity. Thus, we need to have a measure of the rate of change in total product as the use of any one of the variable inputs is changed. We call this change the marginal product of the variable input. To find the effect that changing one input has on output, it is necessary to hold all other inputs constant while changing only this one. If more than one input is changed at a time, we could not tell how much of the change in output should be attributed to each of the input variables that have been changed.

The **marginal product** (*MP*) of a variable factor of production is the rate of change in total product (*TP* or Q) per unit change in the variable input while holding other factors constant. If the production function is stated solely in terms of a single variable factor of production [for example, $TP = f(L)$], the marginal productivity of labor is equal to the change in total output divided by the change in labor,

$$MP_L = \frac{\Delta TP}{\Delta L}$$

Would you expect output to increase at a constant rate as more of any one input is added to the production process? To help your thinking about this question, assume that you have a small garden plot, say 10 feet by 20 feet. You want to grow beans, tomatoes, zucchini squash, and onions. In preparing the soil for planting, you decide that some fertilizer would improve your yield. So you call a garden supply store for advice about how much to use.

Suppose the gardening expert suggests that, as a rule of thumb, gardeners in your area should apply 1 ounce (by weight) of fertilizer per square foot of garden twice each year. For your 200 square feet of garden, that would amount to 12.5 pounds. You spread that amount over your garden, and then someone suggests that if one application of fertilizer were good, two applications would be better. If two were better, perhaps three or four would be better still. Do you think that each successive application of fertilizer would do as much to increase your yield as the first? Probably not. What would you expect to happen if you bought enough

Table 6.2   Total, average, and marginal product ($TP = 7.5L^2 - 0.5L^3$). Marginal product increases, reaches a maximum, and declines as more labor is added. Total product declines when marginal product becomes negative.

Labor input (L)	Total product (TP)	Average product (AP = TP/L)	Marginal product (MP = ΔTP/ΔL)
0	0	—	—
1	7	7	7
2	26	13	19
3	54	18	28
4	88	22	34
5	125	25	37
6	162	27	37
7	196	28	34
8	224	28	28
9	243	27	19
10	250	25	7
11	242	22	-8
12	216	18	-26
13	169	13	-47
14	98	7	-71

Other inputs and the level of technology are held constant.

fertilizer to spread 6 inches deep over the entire garden? Nothing would grow at all. You could use so much of this variable input that output would be driven down to zero.

It is safe to say that most production functions react in the same general way as more of a variable input is added to other fixed factors (such as the fixed land area in the garden plot example). *Output does not increase at a constant rate.*

Note that the production function graphed in Figure 6.1 at first increases at an increasing rate (for L less than 5), then increases at a decreasing rate (for L between 5 and 10), and finally begins to decline (for L greater than 10). Look also at Table 6.2 to see what happens to the rate of increase in output as more labor is used and the amount of capital is held fixed (that is, reading across any row of the table). You see that as more labor is used, the rate at which output increases becomes smaller.

Many mistakes in economic reasoning result from the failure to recognize that all production processes are subject to **diminishing marginal productivity**; that is, most production processes are not simply linear. The *law of diminishing marginal productivity* states that as additional units of a variable input are added to other inputs that are fixed in supply, the increments to output eventually decline (unless the technology of the production function changes). This principle of diminishing marginal productivity is observed in all production environments including the NFP sectors and has been well documented by empirical research. NFP managers can safely assume that it will operate in all situations if the use of a variable input is continually increased while other inputs are kept constant. As we shall see shortly, the marginal productivity of inputs plays an important part in determining how much will be employed in obtaining an optimal outcome. Diminished marginal productivity is due to increasing labor, for example, when all other factors are held constant. It is not due to employing labor of a lesser quality. Labor inputs in production functions are assumed to be homogeneous or identical. However, Application 6.1 warns that in practice not all labor inputs are equally capable.

APPLICATION 6.1
Substituting Capital for Labor at the Post Office

The processing of over a half a billion pieces of mail daily takes a lot of labor hours. Historically as much as 80 percent of the United States Postal Service's (USPS) budget was for labor costs. However, in recent years the labor intensity of providing mail service has been reduced as automated mail-processing equipment has been utilized. Incorporating more capital intensive means of "production" has been largely related to controlling costs.

A study by the Postal Rate Commission found that over 28 percent of the USPS's mail-processing labor costs were accounted for by "nonproductive time." While management disputes this claim, such a high percentage suggests a labor-productivity problem. Automation has reduced labor costs by incorporating wider use of machines sorting mail into the order needed on a carrier's route.

USPS management also initiated an early retirement program as a way to reduce costs. Their intent was to reduce mainly supervisory personnel who did not directly handle the mail. However, over half of those who took advantage of the early retirement program were letter carriers and clerks, many of whom had to be replaced to maintain customer service. The less experienced replacement workers were less productive and contributed to a further increase in work hours and a decrease in productivity with a corresponding increase in labor costs. This illustrates the need for a careful and thorough economic analysis of likely outcomes before potential labor saving programs are put in place.

As you read the rest of this chapter keep the USPS in mind and think about how the concepts presented in the chapter can be related to the public and nonprofit sectors.

Source: Mark Lewyn, "The Check's Still Not in the Mail," *Business Week*, March 18, 1994, 38.

At times, we want to know the productivity per worker, or per pound of fertilizer, or per machine, and so on. This calls for the use of another measure of productivity: average product. The **average product** (*AP*) of a variable factor of production is defined as total output divided by the number of units of the variable factor used in producing that output:

$AP = TP/L$

This represents the mean (average) output per unit of labor.

The concept of average product is widely used. When people make comparisons of labor productivity between industries or between countries, they are almost always referring to the average product of labor (that is, the average amount of output produced per labor hour). Various political, social, and economic issues, such as inflation and balance of payments problems, have focused considerable attention on the average productivity of workers in the United States. It is often argued that employee wage increases should be tied to increases in productivity (meaning *average* productivity) and that one reason for diminished competitiveness in world markets is that domestic labor has not increased in productivity as fast as has labor in some other countries. The advent of the use of quality circles and other forms of employee participation in management are, in part, attempts to increase the average productivity of the workforce.

Marginal, average, and total product compared

The production function presented in Table 6.1 is reproduced in Table 6.2 along with average and marginal products of the variable factor labor. Remember that the amount of other inputs and the state of technology are assumed fixed. The values for marginal product are between each increment of labor input because those values represent the marginal productivity over the respective intervals. In the table, marginal product has been calculated as $MP = \Delta TP/\Delta L$. The data in Table 6.2 are graphed in Figure 6.2.

In both the table and the graphic representation, we see that both average and marginal productivity at first increase, eventually reach a maximum, and then decline. Note that $AP = MP$ when the average product function is at its maximum. This is necessarily the case. If $MP > AP$, the average will be pulled up by the incremental unit, and if $MP < AP$, the average will be pulled down. It follows that the average product function will always reach its peak where $MP = AP$. We know that average product equals total product divided by the number of units of the relevant factor of production. The average product function reaches its peak at $L = 7.5$. Thus, beyond 7.5 units of labor, both marginal and average products are declining.

Maximum production (total product) is achieved when declining marginal product crosses the labor axis (Figure 6.2); marginal production is 0 at this point. We see from the upper portion of the graph in Figure 6.2 that total product is maximized when 10 units of labor are used. In the example of a licensing bureau conducting vision screenings, maximum output is achieved when the last worker fails to add to the number of screenings completed in a given shift.

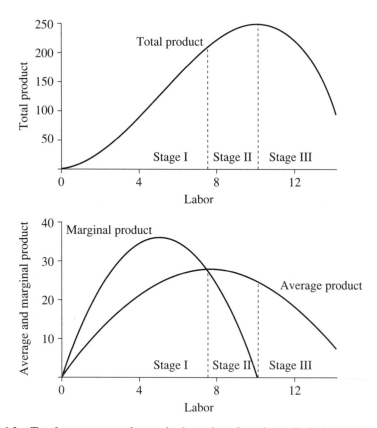

Figure 6.2   Total, average, and marginal product functions. Early in stage I, where marginal product is increasing, total product increases at an increasing rate. When marginal product starts to decline, total product begins to increase at a decreasing rate. Once marginal product becomes negative, total product starts to decline. As long as marginal product is above average product, the latter rises; but when marginal product is less than average product, it pulls average product down. Thus, $MP = AP$ at the peak of AP.

6.4   THREE STAGES OF PRODUCTION

Our examination of the production function in the previous section allows us to divide the production function into "stages." These are the economists' shorthand way of referring to the areas of the production function that a firm should consider for production and other areas which a firm should not consider reasonable for production.

In Figure 6.2, we have divided the graph into three parts; labeled stage I, stage II, and stage III. The first stage includes the region from the origin to the level of labor input at which the average product of labor reaches its maximum. We have shown that this is at $L = 7.5$. So throughout stage I, average product is rising, even though marginal product has begun to fall as we near the end of stage I. In our driver certification example, the average number of vision screenings increases as we add employees in stage I.

Stage II includes the region between the maximum point on the average product function and the point at which marginal product falls to zero. In the example in Figure 6.2, this is the region between $L = 7.5$ and $L = 10$. During stage II, both marginal and average products are falling, but both are still positive. At the end of stage II, the number of vision screening conducted due to adding one more unit of labor input is zero.

Stage III is the entire region for which the marginal product of labor is negative (to the right of $L = 10$). In this stage, the amount of the fixed resource available *per unit of labor* has become too small for efficient production to take place. While we will not prove this here, the same type of problem occurs in stage I. In stage I, the amount of labor is too small for the existing amount of the fixed resource, which results in a negative marginal product for that resource.

This means that of the three stages of production, only stage II has a positive marginal product for all inputs (we will demonstrate this point more thoroughly later in the chapter). The decision-making importance of this relationship is that the *relevant range of production is restricted to stage II*. No administrator would knowingly employ a resource for which the marginal product is negative.

6.5   VALUE TO THE FIRM OF INCREASED INPUTS

Using production tools, we can answer some realistic questions arising in any firm, profit-seeking or NFP. Suppose you were the manager of the state-licensing agency doing vision screening. How much labor would you hire? Answering the question in this naïve situation helps in understanding how production functions work. We already know that the only range of production you should consider is stage II (which occurs between $L = 7.5$ and $L = 10$ in Figure 7.5). We address this problem by first asking ourselves: Under what conditions would we hire additional workers?

Would you hire a worker if the cost of doing so, including wages and all benefits, was more than the revenue you get in fees and state subsidy from the added output attributable to that worker? Probably not. But would you hire another unit of labor if you could receive revenue from the added output for more than the added cost of employing that unit of labor? This type of questioning is the basis upon which a local administrator decides to increase any factor of production or for state planners to determine the optimal number of licensing bureaus. Before formalizing this criterion, let's define two terms that will help us discuss the situation.

From the perspective of a NFP administrator trying to balance his or her budget. *Marginal revenue product* (*MRP*) is the additional revenue the firm receives when the output from one additional worker is provided. It is, then, a dollar measure of the additional output attributable to the efforts of an added worker. It is calculated as

$$MRP = (MR)(MP)$$

where *MR* is marginal revenue and *MP* is the marginal product of labor. *MRP* is a negatively sloped function because *MP* diminishes, and *MR* is either constant or diminishing depending on whether fees and other per unit revenue stay the same or decline as output increases.

Marginal resource cost (*MRC*) is the extra cost to the firm of employing one more unit of labor. *MRC* is made up of the wage rate plus other costs to the firm of employing that additional worker (for example, insurance, social security, and retirement). We assume that the number of workers hired by this firm is small relative to the entire labor market, and so the *MRC* is independent of the number of workers hired. That is, we will consider *MRC* to be equal to some constant dollar amount per additional worker employed.

Now suppose that you receive $4 in total for each vision screening from fees and state subsidy and that the *MRC* for the labor you hire is $6.75 per hour ($5.25 as the wage rate per hour plus $1.50 per hour in benefits). The *MRC* for hiring one more worker is $54 a shift. Further, assume that you can hire workers for less than a full day but that you have an agreement to employ people only in 2-hour blocks of time. For example, 7.75 labor units would be 7 people working an 8-hour shift plus one person working six hours. Based on this information, Table 6.3 can be completed.

As long as *MRP* > *MRC* it pays to continue employing more labor. This is true for up to 9.00 units of labor, as we can see in Table 6.3 and in Figure 6.3. This result can be generalized as shown in the box.

The optimum number of units in any variable resource to employ is determined by the condition that

$$MRP = MRC$$

The optimum number of units of a variable resource employed is of particular significance to a profit-seeking firm. The revenue generated by the last nurse employed

Table 6.3   Marginal revenue product and marginal resource cost for stage II of production

L	MP	MR ($)	MRP ($)	MRC ($)
7.5	28.125	4	112.50	54
7.75	26.156	4	104.62	54
8	24	4	96	54
8.25	21.656	4	86.62	54
8.5	19.125	4	76.5	54
8.75	16.406	4	65.62	54
9	13.5	4	54	54
9.25	10.406	4	41.62	54
9.5	7.125	4	28.5	54
9.75	3.656	4	14.62	54
10	0	4	0	54

MRP = (*MP*)(*MR*); *MRC* = $6.75 per hour, or $54.00 per labor unit (8-hour day).

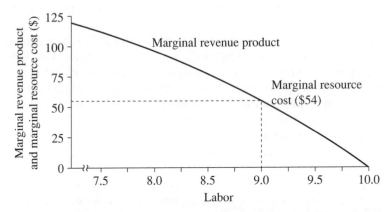

Figure 6.3   Determination of the amount of labor to employ. As long as *MRP* > *MRC* the firm benefits by hiring additional labor and increasing production. If at the current level of production *MRP* < *MRC*, production should be cut back and fewer units of labor employed. In this example, the optimum level of employment is at 9.0 units of labor.

in a profit-seeking institution equals the nurse's salary. Note that each nurse up to the last one employed generates revenue exceeding compensation. Remember, each nurse employed contributes to total profit. A nonprofit hospital, depending on how it defines its mission, may choose to hire more or fewer nurses, because a NFP firm with multiple programs may choose to use one activity to subsidize another. It logically follows, however, that for any activity expected to yield revenue greater than cost, the *MRP* of the last variable input employed must at least equal *MRC*.

6.6   COST THEORY

Some of a firm's costs are obvious. Paychecks are prepared and distributed to employees. Utility bills are received, processed, and paid. Invoices from suppliers of component parts are treated similarly. These are examples of explicit costs. But, not all costs are so obvious. One of the skills of a good administrator is the ability to uncover less obvious and often hidden costs and to assign costs carefully. Application 6.2 provides an example of estimating overhead costs in a university print shop.

APPLICATION 6.2
Quantitative Analysis Helps Allocate Overhead per Job

Consider a private nonprofit or state university print shop that occasionally contracts to do work for outside firms. It is fairly easy to calculate labor and paper costs for each job, but more difficult to estimate overhead costs in deciding how to price the work. In the past it has been common to allocate such costs based only on the amount of direct labor involved. However, with today's more highly automated systems it makes sense to look beyond just direct labor and to consider such factors as the hours of machine use and number of different machine setups in applying overhead costs. Adel Novin has shown how regression analysis can help do just that and in the process facilitates the development of multiple overhead rates per job.

Novin estimates overhead costs, relying on machine hours used and number of setups. First, she determines in single regressions that both machine hours (MH) and the number of setups (NS) are statistically significant in determining overhead costs (OC):

$OC = 72,793.81 + 74.72\ MH$

R-squared $= 0.77$; t-ratio for $MH = 5.79$; $df = 10$

$OC = 74,033.14 + 465.00\ NS$

R-squared $= 0.39$; t-ratio for $NS = 2.55$; $df = 10$.

Then Novin combines machine hours (MH) and number of setups (NS) in a multiple regression model. Her particular study indicates that:

$OC = 19,796.43 + 65.44\ MH + 322.21\ NS$

$$(9.71)\ (5.49)\ (t\text{-ratios})$$

R-squared $= 0.95$ (adjusted R-squared was not reported); $df = 9$

This model, given appropriate historical data, provides a tool with which overheads can be charged per job and product in a manner reflecting actual costs.

Source: Adel M. Novin, "Applying Overhead: How to Find the Right Bases and Rates," *Management Accounting*, March 1992, 40–3.

The manner in which costs are classified or defined is largely dependent on the purpose for which the cost data are being used. Historically there has been disagreement between accountants and economists on how costs should be treated. To a considerable degree, the reason for the difference of opinion was that the two groups wanted to use the cost data for dissimilar purposes.

Traditionally, accountants are concerned with the collection of historical cost data for use in reporting a firm's financial behavior and position, and in calculating the firm's tax liability. Economists and some accountants, on the other hand, are primarily concerned with using cost data as a foundation for managerial decision-making. These purposes called for different types of cost data and classifications. A better understanding of the alternative uses of the data, along with a closer working relationship between cost accountants and managerial economists has reduced the intensity of the disagreement over cost classifications. Accountants, however, still correctly rely primarily on historical cost records in determining the profit or loss of a firm during some past period of time, in establishing the tax liability of the firm, or in assuring that resources are used to fund a particular activity.

Economists use historic cost data but rely as well on opportunity costs in evaluating economic decisions. In this chapter, costs include what economists call normal profit. Normal profit or a *normal return* refers to the opportunity cost to the sponsor/entrepreneur of using the firm's resources in a particular activity. Opportunity cost, you will recall, is the value of the resource in its next best use, that is, if it were not being used for the present purpose. Economic profit/net income is revenue minus costs that include a normal return.

As a specific example, consider the costs to you of taking a course in public and nonprofit economics. The out-of-pocket costs (explicit costs) include the average tuition cost of this course (say, $450) and the cost of books and other supplies (perhaps another $100). One might view this $550 as the cost of the course. However, we should include the opportunity cost concept and consider what you could have been doing instead of taking the course. To attend the course might involve about 45 class meetings per semester, each about 60 minutes in length. In addition, time must be spent getting to and from class, doing homework assignments, test preparation, and so on. The actual total number of hours spent on this economics class may be closer to 135 hours per semester (3 times the 45 60-minute class meetings). Now, what could you have done in lieu of taking this course? One alternative could be to work at, say, $6 per hour. Your time cost in money terms is then $810 ($6 per hour times 135 hours). The total cost of taking the course is then:

Tuition and supplies (explicit):	$550
Time cost (implicit):	$810
Total cost of course:	$1,360

The major portion of the total cost of the course turns out to be the implicit time cost. The implicit cost could have been zero if you had no opportunity to work, or it could have been much higher than $810 if your skills were highly valued in the market.

Accountants typically use only those costs that are recorded in various accounts as representing an actual transfer of money. They do, of course, account for depreciation but most costs are explicit, or nominal, costs and often do not represent the full economic costs relevant to a given decision. In addition to explicit costs, the economist incorporates implicit, or imputed, costs.

Relevant costs for making decisions

To further illustrate the consequences of using opportunity cost, consider the following decision situation. Suppose that Mr. Devitt, owner of Devitt Heating and Air Conditioning Company has contracted with the Darlington City Council to replace an obsolete climate control system in City Hall. The City Council gives Devitt first chance at the job because his company is the only local one with the necessary size and expertise to handle the contract. The climate-control system must be completely installed during 21 workdays in June. Mr. Devitt has been offered $69,000 to do the job.

After careful analysis of the type of system requested by the City Council, Mr. Devitt establishes reasonably accurate estimates of the time and resource requirements to complete the task in the given time period. The best estimate of the labor requirements indicates that 84 labor-days are needed. Since June is one of the busiest months for Devitt, only three employees, trained and experienced in this type of work, are allocated to the job. Thus, from his present workforce, only 63 labor-days can be used for this job (21 days times 3 laborers). Fortunately, Mr. Devitt's brother, Mike, will be home from college at the end of May and can perform much of the unskilled work. Mr. Devitt figures that, for his regular employees, each labor-day costs the company $170 (including wages, hospitalization insurance, social security payments, and other miscellaneous expenses). Thus, the labor cost for his three employees for 21 days will be $10,710 (3 times 21 times $170). Mike expects to be employed at his usual summer job for $50 per day but would be willing to work for his brother if asked.

The Devitt Company has all the necessary equipment for the job and holds most of the materials available in inventory, except one major component. The materials in inventory cost $47,500, and other components can be specially ordered in time at a cost of $8,500. Table 6.4 summarizes Mr. Devitt's first estimate of the cost of the project based on explicit and historical cost concepts. The decision seems obvious: since costs are $2,290 less than the revenue from the project, Mr. Devitt should accept the contract.

Upon seeing these estimates, Mike suggests to his brother that this is not a true depiction of the relevant costs involved. First, Mike notes that his labor time has a net opportunity cost of $50 per day waiting tables at a restaurant down the shore; thus, if he works 21 days on this project, his labor should be included at $1,050 ($50 times 21). Furthermore, the replacement costs of the materials to be used from Devitt's inventory have increased an average of 6 percent. Their replacement cost is $50,350 ($47,500 times 1.06). The increase in value provides a better estimate of the full cost to the Devitt Company of using those materials to install the new climate control system in the Darlington City Hall. Mr. Devitt agrees and reevaluates the situation as shown in Table 6.5. Using the opportunity cost concept (including the imputed cost of Mike's labor), we see that if this project is undertaken, the company would incur a loss of $1,610, rather than Mr. Devitt's initial estimate of $2,290 in profit.

Table 6.4   Explicit costs and revenues of the City Hall project

Revenue	$69,000
Costs	
Labor	$10,710
Materials (inventory cost)	47,500
Special component	8,500
Total costs	66,710
Profit	$ 2,290

Table 6.5   Explicit and implicit costs of the City Hall project

Revenue	$69,000
Costs	
Labor (explicit)	$10,710
Labor (implicit)	1,050
Materials (replacement costs)	50,350
Special component	8,500
Total costs	70,610
Profit (loss)	($ 1,610)

This hypothetical example is fairly simple. It assumes that Mr. Devitt can lay off employees at no cost to the firm when there is no work. The example also ignores whether Mr. Devitt may have been able to use these workers and resources in some alternative way that would have produced more profit than the Darlington project. Or, perhaps, Mr. Devitt should consider that the company might actually gain long-term promotional benefits by incurring a loss on this important project.

We should emphasize two important points. First, there is not always a right and a wrong way to look at cost. The interpretation and determination of costs must be consistent with the use for which the information is generated. For example, the relevant cost data for determining a company's tax liability may be quite different from the relevant data for decision-making. Second, the determination of costs is not always a purely objective matter; considerable judgment must be used, and there is often disagreement among analysts on the appropriate costs in a given situation. This is particularly true when the imputed/indirect opportunity cost concept is involved. Most analysts agree, however, that the full cost of a NFP hospital gift shop, for example, should consider the opportunity costs of the allocated space and some estimation of value of volunteer services. Application 6.3 describes how the Office of Management and Budget deviates from explicit minimum cost estimates in competitive bidding for government contracts.

APPLICATION 6.3
Government Competitive Sourcing: Minimum Costs versus Best Values

The Office of Management and Budget's circular, numbered A-76, governs the process of competitive sourcing in an attempt to improve the performance of the federal government. Periodically, an agency announces full public–private competition, and requires that in-house bids as well as outside firms meet deadlines.

Competitive sourcing is a term that refers to a government agency studying the efficiency and nature of an activity in order to make the best decision about how to provide the agency with a specific good or service. Once it has been determined that an activity is required, agencies must classify each activity as "inherently governmental" or "commercial." Fifteen percent of "commercial" activities were to be opened to competition between government, nonprofit, and private sector vendors by the end of 2003.

"Best value" recognizes that the lowest price bid is not always the best. Performance and quality both constitute the evaluation criteria. Bidders are encouraged to include performance standards in their proposals. This may depart from formal specifications but provides information and incentives to innovate.

Source: Carl De Maio and Vincent Badolato, "Competitive Sourcing: The Wait is Over, the Time is Now," *The Insider*, Heritage Foundation, no. 308, July, 2003, 5–6.

Private costs versus social costs

A further distinction, confounding discussions of costs in public administration, is between private and social costs, which we previously introduced in Chapter 5 as negative externalities due to spillover effects. Private costs are those that accrue directly to the individuals engaged in the relevant activity. Examples include the billed cost of electricity used, the cost of hiring labor, and interest charges on borrowed funds. Social costs, on the other hand, include all costs related to the productive activity regardless of who bears the burden of those costs. Social costs should not be confused with government or subsidized costs. They include negative externalities. *Social costs* are private costs plus implicit costs passed on to third parties not involved in the activity in any direct way; they are not "socialized" costs picked up by government.

Consider the classic case of a manufacturer located on the edge of a lake or river that dumps waste into the water rather than disposing of it in some other manner. The private cost to the firm of dumping the waste is zero. If the waste is hauled away to a landfill or otherwise treated, some explicit private cost would be involved. Third parties located down-current are adversely affected by the waste and incur higher costs in terms of treating the water for their use, having to travel to alternative recreation facilities, and so on. If these external costs were included in the production costs by law, a truer picture of the real or social costs of the output would be obtained. Production costs, in the absence of regulations concerning negative externalities, appear lower than they really are. This results in increased supply and thus an overallocation of scarce resources to expanding the output of goods that generate social costs. Ignoring the full social costs leads to an inefficient and undesirable allocation of resources.

Deriving costs from the production function

You recall that the production function specifies the technological maximum quantity of output that can be produced from various combinations of inputs. The cost function combines this production information with information about input prices to yield the cost of producing various levels of output. The cost function (any cost function) can thus be thought of as being determined by the production function and the prices of the various inputs, as shown in the box.

The
production function
combined with
input prices
yields the
firm's cost function

Consider the following situation. Firm A has a production function with constant returns to the variable inputs (its production function is a straight line). The firm purchases inputs at constant input prices (no matter what quantity of inputs is purchased, the per unit price of the inputs remains the same to the firm); there are no quantity discounts and this particular firm does not affect prices in the input markets. Given all of the above assumptions, firm A's resulting variable cost function would be drawn as pictured in the upper part of Figure 6.4. The production function ($Q = 10L$) is shown in the lower part of the graph. Only one variable input is used just to simplify the analysis. The results hold for two or more variable inputs as long as the production function is linear in all inputs. Firm A's variable cost function is linear because as inputs are increased (say, doubled), output increases proportionately (doubles), and with constant input prices, variable cost increases along the straight line exhibited in Figure 6.4 ($VC = 1.5Q$).

To be sure that the relationship between the production function and the variable cost function is clear, let's look at it carefully:

Production function: $Q = 10L$

Assumed price per unit of labor: $P_L = \$15$

The *variable cost* is equal to the price per unit of the variable input times the number of units of the input employed. For example, as the number of vision screenings increases, the variable cost of labor inputs increases. Thus,

Variable cost: $VC = \$15L$

This variable cost function is the one graphed in the upper part of Figure 6.4.

If the assumption of either a linear production function or of a constant input price is changed, the shape of the resulting variable cost curve will also change.

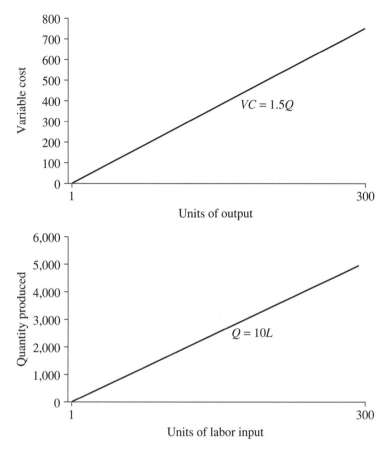

Figure 6.4   Production and cost functions: firm A. This firm has constant returns to the variable input (labor), which results in a linear variable cost function.

The important point to keep in mind is that the shape of the variable cost curve (all the cost curves, in fact) depends on these two pieces of information.

Now consider firm B. It is also faced with a constant input price (we shall assume only one variable input, labor, again with a price of $15 per labor unit), but B's production function exhibits decreasing returns to the variable input. With decreasing returns, each successive unit of production costs (in input terms) a little more than the preceding unit. Thus, Figure 6.5, which depicts firm B's variable cost function, shows that variable cost increases at an increasing rate as the quantity produced increases.

The change in the shape of the variable cost function of firm A to that of firm B is solely the result of a change in the nature of the production function. When there were constant returns to the variable input(s) – case A – the variable cost function was linear, that is, variable costs increased at a constant rate as output increased. When there were decreasing returns to the variable input(s) – case B – the variable cost function increased at an increasing rate as production increased.

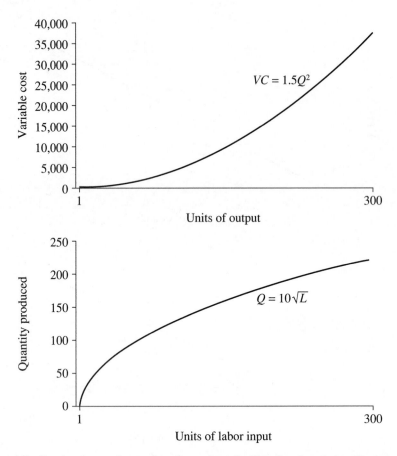

Figure 6.5   Production and cost functions: firm B. This firm has decreasing returns to the variable input (labor), which results in a variable cost function that increases at an increasing rate.

Next consider firm C, with a constant input price (again, $15 per labor unit) but with a production function that has increasing returns to the variable input. Again, the shape of the variable cost curve is determined by the characteristics of the production function ($Q = 10L^2$ in this case) and by the price of labor (which is constant at $15 per labor unit). Firm C's variable cost function is pictured in Figure 6.6; the cost curve increases at a decreasing rate throughout its entire range. In case C there is increasing returns to the variable input(s) and the variable cost function increased at a decreasing rate as production increased. Once again the change in the cost function was determined by a change in the production function.

The cost curves could also change shape in response to a changed assumption about input prices. Firms can often take advantage of quantity discounts when purchasing a resource. If we assume a production function with constant returns to the variable inputs and decreasing input prices (quantity discounts), we would again have a variable cost curve like firm C's in Figure 6.6.

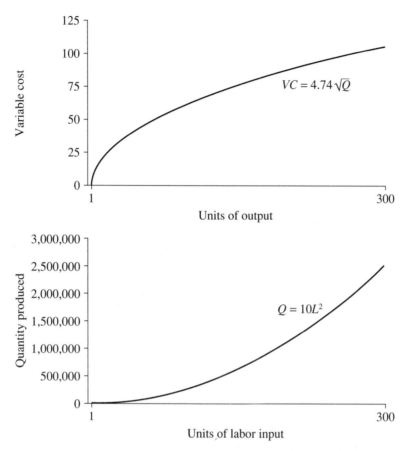

Figure 6.6   Production and cost functions: firm C. This firm has increasing returns to the variable input (labor), which results in a variable cost function that increases at a decreasing rate.

It is also possible for a production function to have different returns to variable inputs over different ranges. The firm represented in Figure 6.7, firm D, first has increasing returns and then has decreasing returns to the variable input along with constant input prices. This combination of assumptions yields the variable cost function in Figure 6.7, which has a shape that is characteristic of many actual variable cost functions: increasing at a decreasing rate and then increasing at an increasing rate. Given that most production functions look like the one in Figure 6.7, most variable cost functions will look like the one depicted in Figure 6.7.

6.7   COSTS IN THE SHORT RUN

The **short run** is defined as a time period during which some factors of production are fixed and others are variable. In the **long run**, all factors of production

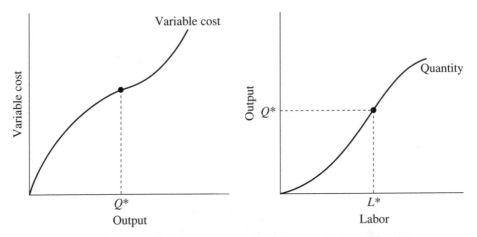

Figure 6.7　Production and cost functions: firm D. This firm has a production function that exhibits increasing returns to the variable factor input (labor) up to $L*$ and decreasing returns after $L*$. The input level $L*$ corresponds to the output level $Q*$. The variable cost function increases at a decreasing rate up to $Q*$ and at an increasing rate beyond $Q*$.

are variable. It is important to note that these periods are not defined by any specified length of time but, rather, are determined by the variability of factors of production. Thus, the time period that one firm may consider the long run may correspond to the short run for another firm. Government and private nonprofit firms generally have time horizons dependent on their budgetary cycles.

Consider South Side High, a small local school, and Electro Power, an electric power generating and distribution company. If the sponsors of South Side should decide to expand their operations, they could hire more teachers and staff and/or add to their capital equipment (with more computers, perhaps) in a matter of a day, a week, or a month. These would be short-run changes because their building (another factor of production) remains fixed in size. However, given six or eight months, they could expand their present facility or move to a new, larger school. This would then represent the long run, because *all* productive factors could be varied.

For Electro Power, the short run extends over a very long timespan. This is because expanding all the factors involved in generating and distributing electric power takes considerable time. Generating funds for expansion and construction, site selection, and environmental impact studies are not done in an instant. A large company such as Electro Power may find it impossible to change all factors of production in less than five years, or even longer. Thus, the short run for such a firm will be far longer, in terms of calendar time, than for firms in some other types of productive activities. We should expect the time span covered by the concepts of long run and short run to vary among industries and, to a lesser extent, among firms within a single industry.

In the short run a firm incurs some costs that are associated with variable factors and others that result from fixed factors. The former costs are referred to as variable costs, and the latter represent fixed costs. *Variable costs (VC)* change as the amount of output changes and can therefore be expressed as a function of output (Q); that is, $VC = f(Q)$. Variable costs typically include such things as raw materials, labor, and utilities. *Fixed costs*, on the other hand, are not a function of the level of output and are constant in the short run; that is, $FC = K$, where K is some constant. Fixed costs may include such things as property taxes, the cost of leases on land, buildings, and some types of equipment, interest on bonds sold to purchase capital equipment, and some kinds of insurance.

We have seen that, when a variable factor of production is added to some fixed factor or factors, the variable factor eventually becomes subject to diminishing marginal returns. That is, as more of the variable factor is employed, output eventually increases at a decreasing rate. With constant input prices, it follows that eventually variable costs increase at an increasing rate, since output is increasing at a decreasing rate (see Figure 6.7).

Consider a typical short-run production function with labor as the variable factor that combines with some fixed factors of production. For such a production function, output will first increase at an increasing rate and then at a decreasing rate when expressed as a function of the variable factor. As a general rule, we should then expect variable costs to increase first at a decreasing rate and subsequently at an increasing rate. To see this explicitly, let's consider a numerical example.

The data in Table 6.6 will help to translate information about production into the corresponding short-run cost functions. The first two columns of this table represent a production function in which daily output at first increases at an increasing rate and then at a decreasing rate as the amount of a variable input, labor, is increased from 0 to 10 units. Some amount of fixed factors with a daily cost allocation of $400 is also used. The per unit cost of labor is assumed to be $160.

The production schedule from Table 6.6 is plotted on the right-hand side of the graph in Figure 6.8. It is drawn as a solid line only up to 10 units of the labor input; since beyond that point total product diminishes (marginal product is

Table 6.6   Determination of variable and total cost from a production schedule

Units of labor (L)	Quantity of output (Q)	Price per unit of labor (P_L)	Variable cost of production $(VC)^a$ ($)	Fixed cost $(FC)^b$ ($)	Total cost $(TC)^c$ ($)
0	0	160	0	400	400
1	8.4	160	160	400	560
2	31.2	160	320	400	720
3	64.8	160	480	400	880
4	105.6	160	640	400	1,040
5	150.0	160	800	400	1,200
6	194.4	160	960	400	1,360
7	235.2	160	1,120	400	1,520
8	268.8	160	1,280	400	1,680
9	291.6	160	1,440	400	1,840
10	300.0	160	1,600	400	2,000

[a] $VC = P_L L = 160L$; [b] FC is given as 400; [c] $TC = FC + VC$.

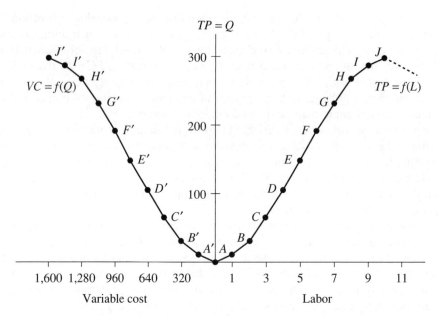

Figure 6.8   Derivation of a variable cost curve. This graph depicts the derivation of the variable cost curve from the production function given in Table 6.6, with a labor cost of $160 per unit.

negative). Each of the 10 points used to plot the production function is labeled with a letter (*A* through *J*).

Assume that each unit of labor costs $160 (that is, a unit equals one 8-hour day at $20 per hour, including fringe benefits, social security, etc.). Then one labor unit, or 8.4 units of output (point *A*), would represent a variable cost of $160. Two labor units, or 31.2 units of output (point *B*), would have a variable cost of $320. Production of 150 units of output (point *E*) would involve five units of labor, or $800 of variable cost. Thus, each point on the production function has a corresponding variable cost. These points are graphed in the left-hand part of Figure 6.8 as points *A′* through *J′*.

We normally think of variable cost as a function of the level of output. Therefore, to see the general shape of a variable cost curve in the manner in which it is most commonly displayed, the diagram should be turned clockwise 90 degrees so that the quantity (*TP* = *Q*) axis becomes the horizontal axis and the variable cost axis the vertical. Doing this, we see that *VC* intersects at the origin because zero output results when no labor is used, and if no labor is used, there is no labor cost (here labor is the only variable factor). We also see that variable cost first increases at a decreasing rate (the slope becomes less steep) and then increases at an increasing rate (the slope becomes steeper). Remember that we are considering the quantity axis as the horizontal, so the slope is measured as the change in variable cost per unit change in the rate of output (or, d*VC*/d*Q*).

Another variable cost function is shown in Table 6.7 and Figure 6.9. We see that variable cost increases at a decreasing rate up to *Q* = 6, and beyond that point, variable cost increases at an increasing rate. This variable cost function is represented by the equation

Table 6.7   Variable cost (*VC*) as a function of output (*Q*):
$VC = 18Q - 2.7Q^2 + 0.15Q^3$

VC	Q
0.0	0
15.45	1
26.40	2
33.75	3
38.40	4
41.25	5
43.20	6
45.15	7
48.00	8
52.65	9
60.00	10
70.95	11
86.40	12
107.25	13
134.40	14
168.75	15

$$VC = 18Q - 2.7Q^2 + 0.15Q^3$$

We have seen that in the short run the **total cost** (*TC*) of production is composed of variable costs and fixed costs (*FC*). That is:

$$TC = FC + VC$$

If fixed costs in this case are equal to 30, we can express total cost as follows:

$$TC = 30 + 18Q - 2.7Q^2 + 0.15Q^3$$

These total and fixed costs are illustrated in Figure 6.9 along with the corresponding variable cost function.

The total cost function has a positive intercept because the firm incurs certain fixed costs (30) in the short run even if output is zero. At nonzero levels of output, the total cost function increases at a decreasing rate up to some point ($Q = 6$) and beyond that increases at an increasing rate. The total cost function always lies above the variable cost function by the amount of fixed cost (30). That is, the vertical distance between the total and variable cost functions is constant throughout and exactly equals fixed costs.

Note that total cost (*TC*) and variable cost (*VC*) at first increase at a decreasing rate and then at an increasing rate. The total cost and variable cost curve may appear to get closer together in this graph as output increases but in fact the *vertical distance* between the total and variable cost functions is constant throughout and exactly equals fixed costs.

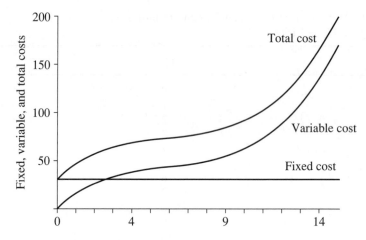

Figure 6.9   Graph of the typical cost functions:

$FC = 30$

$VC = 18Q - 2.7Q^2 + 0.15Q^3$

$TC = 30 + 18Q - 2.7Q^2 + 0.15Q^3$

Costs per unit of output in the short run

Having developed an understanding of fixed, variable, and total cost, we can now evaluate per unit, or average, costs. Dividing fixed cost, variable cost, and total cost by the quantity of output yields average fixed cost, average variable cost, and average total cost, respectively. The term average cost is often used instead of average total cost. We follow the common convention of using the term average cost (*AC*) throughout the remainder of the text. Thus, when referring to the **average cost** of producing some product we mean the total cost divided by the number of units of output. These per-unit cost functions may be written as follows:

$AFC = FC/Q$

$AVC = VC/Q$

$AC = TC/Q = (FC + VC)/Q = AFC + AVC$

There is one additional, and very important, unit cost concept in economic analysis: marginal cost (*MC*). **Marginal cost** represents the rate of change in total cost (or variable cost) as output changes. It is the cost of producing one more unit of output. Thus, marginal cost can be represented as the slope of the total cost (or the first derivative of *TC* with respect to quantity). That is, $MC = \Delta TC/\Delta Q$. Because the only way total cost can change is for variable costs to change, marginal cost can also be considered as the slope of variable cost (or the first derivative of *VC* with respect to quantity). That is, $MC = \Delta VC/\Delta Q$.

If the cost data are given in tabular form, marginal cost is approximated as the change in total cost divided by the change in quantity over each interval ($MC = \Delta TC/\Delta Q$). This is frequently referred to as incremental cost, since it represents the change in cost over an interval rather than at a particular point, as is the case with marginal cost. Since marginal analysis lies at the core of the economic decision process, the concept of marginal cost will be very important in our subsequent analysis throughout this text.

Now let's look into the general nature of each per-unit cost function. The average fixed cost, average variable cost, average cost, and marginal cost functions that correspond to the cost functions graphed in Figure 6.9 are shown in Figure 6.10 and are also given numerically in Table 6.8.

As you see in Figure 6.10 the marginal cost (MC), average variable cost (AVC), and average (AC) cost functions all decrease over some range of output, reach a minimum, and subsequently increase as the level of output expands. For this reason, these functions are referred to as "U-shaped" cost functions. Given the total cost function, we can determine the equations for MC, AVC, and AC and also determine the range of output over which each decreases or increases.

Table 6.8   Unit costs as a function of output. Marginal cost shown in this table refers to an intra-unit marginal cost and not the value calculated from the MC equation at each individual value of Q. That is, the MC values are based on $MC = \Delta TC/\Delta Q$, not on $MC = 18 - 5.4Q + 0.45Q^2$. The values are placed on the quantity (Q) line at the end of each interval.

Q	Fixed cost (FC)	Total variable cost (VC)	Total cost (TC)	Marginal costs (MC)	Average fixed cost (AFC)	Average variable cost (AVC)	Average total cost (AC)
0	30	0.0	30.00	—	—	—	—
1	30	15.45	45.45	15.45	30.00	15.45	45.45
2	30	26.40	56.40	10.95	15.00	13.20	28.20
3	30	33.75	63.75	7.35	10.00	11.25	21.25
4	30	38.40	68.40	4.65	7.50	9.60	17.10
5	30	41.25	71.25	2.85	6.00	8.25	14.25
6	30	43.20	73.20	1.95	5.00	7.20	12.20
7	30	45.15	75.15	1.95	4.29	6.45	10.74
8	30	48.00	78.00	2.85	3.75	6.00	9.75
9	30	52.65	82.65	4.65	3.33	5.85	9.18
10	30	60.00	90.00	7.35	3.00	6.00	9.00
11	30	70.95	100.95	10.95	2.73	6.45	9.18
12	30	86.40	116.40	15.45	2.50	7.20	9.70
13	30	107.25	137.25	20.85	2.31	8.25	10.56
14	30	134.40	164.40	27.15	2.14	9.60	11.75
15	30	168.75	198.75	34.35	2.00	11.25	13.25

$FC = \$30$

$VC = 18Q - 2.7Q^2 + 0.15Q^3$

$TC = FC + VC = 30 + 18Q - 2.7Q^2 + 0.15Q^3$

$AFC = FC/Q$

$AVC = VC/Q$

$AC = TC/O$

$MC = \Delta TC/\Delta Q.$

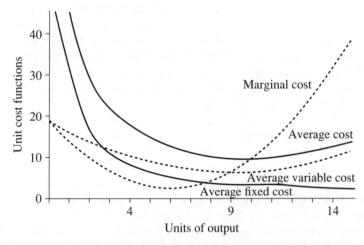

Figure 6.10   Unit cost curves for total cost: $TC = 30 + 18Q - 2.7Q^2 + 0.15Q^3$. This figure illustrates the unit cost functions corresponding to the total, variable, and fixed cost curves shown in Figure 6.9. The data related to these unit cost curves are given in Table 6.8. These functions can also be represented by the following equations:

$$AFC = 30/Q \qquad\qquad MC = 18 - 5.4Q + 0.45Q^2$$

$$AVC = 18 - 2.7Q + 15Q^2 \qquad AC = (30/Q) + 18 - 2.7Q + 0.15Q^2$$

Let us first focus on the marginal cost function. We begin with the total cost function:

$$TC = 30 + 18Q - 2.7Q^2 + 0.15Q^3$$

From this function, we can solve for marginal cost, the change in cost as quantity increases. Given the equation for marginal cost, we can use calculus to determine the output at which marginal cost is at a minimum. This marginal cost has the U-shape shown in Figure 6.10. The minimum point of the marginal cost can be shown to be at a quantity of $Q = 6$.[2] At this quantity $MC = 1.80$. Marginal cost is a decreasing function up to $Q = 6$ and an increasing function beyond that level of output. You should compare this result with the MC data given in Table 6.8 and the MC curve illustrated in Figure 6.10.

---

[2] To find the quantity at which marginal cost is at its minimum we find the first derivative of marginal cost, set it equal to zero, and solve for Q as follows:

$$MC = dTC/dQ = 18 - 5.4Q + 4.5Q^2$$

$$dMC/dQ = -5.4 + 0.9Q = 0$$

$$0.9Q = 5.4$$

$$Q = 6$$

6.8   COSTS IN THE LONG RUN

Many decisions involve short-run cost concepts because they are made in a context in which some fixed input exists. However, long-range plans and decisions are made based on the ability to change the level of use of all inputs. Our earlier example concerned vision screenings in a state licensing bureau. In the short run, the size of the facility was fixed and the tenth worker did not add to total production. In the long run, a larger facility could be built and 10, 11, or more workers employed productively. Thus, all short-run decisions are made within the framework of having certain fixed factors, the level of which was determined by an earlier long-run plan or decision. For this reason, long-run cost curves are often used to depict a firm's planning horizon.

The *long-run average cost curve* (*LRAC*) is sometimes shown as the envelope curve of a series of all the possible short-run average cost curves, as shown in Figure 6.11. Five short-run average cost curves, each representing a different-sized plant (or set of fixed factors) are illustrated, although many more may exist. For any given rate of output, one plant size will accommodate that level of production at the lowest possible unit cost.

Consider, for example, the production of Q^* units in Figure 6.11. That level of output could be produced with the plant size represented by $SRAC_1$, $SRAC_2$, or $SRAC_3$. It represents the optimum rate of output for the size plant represented by *SRAC* (that is, it is at the minimum point of $SRAC_1$). However, if the firm expects to produce at that rate, the best size of plant is the one related to $SRAC_2$. Q^* units could be produced at a cost savings of *FB* per unit over *SRAC*. However, if the firm expanded too much, say, to the plant with $SRAC_3$, the unit cost would be even

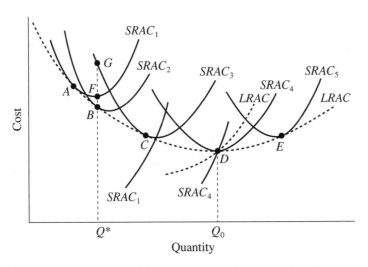

Figure 6.11   Long-run average cost as an envelope curve. The *LRAC* curve is the envelope curve of a series of short-run average cost (*SRAC*) curves, each representing a different size of plant. Economies of scale exist up to Q_0 and diseconomies of scale are evident beyond that level.

higher (at point G) than with $SRAC_1$. The series of points such as A, B, C, D, and E are used to trace out a *LRAC* curve. Each represents a tangency of a *SRAC* with the *LRAC* envelope curve.

The plant size associated with $SRAC_4$ is the optimum size of plant because its minimum point is the lowest of all possible unit costs. In practice, there may be several-sized plants capable of producing at least costs, but the shape of the *LRAC* curve drawn here suggests one level of output associated with minimum per unit costs. Given the *LRAC* in Figure 6.11, we can say that there are increasing returns to scale (or economies of scale) up to Q_0 and decreasing returns to scale (or diseconomies of scale) beyond Q_0.

When all inputs can be varied simultaneously, production may be characterized by increasing, constant, or decreasing returns to scale, summarized as follows:

1   *Increasing returns to scale.* Increasing all inputs by some proportion increases output by greater proportion. Per unit costs decrease.
2   *Constant returns to scale.* Increasing all inputs by some proportion increases output by the same proportion. Per unit costs remain constant.
3   *Decreasing returns to scale.* Increasing all inputs by some proportion increases output by a lesser proportion. Per unit costs increase.

We use the terms **returns to scale** and **economies of scale** interchangeably to explain the shape of the *LRAC* curve. Strictly speaking, this is incorrect. Production and technological factors determine returns to scale. Economies (and diseconomies) of scale may be due to production technology or result from monetary effects alone, as when a larger firm is able to purchase large lots of inputs at reduced cost. For example, a child daycare center sponsored and located on a university campus could gain internal scale economies and lower its per unit costs by increasing the size of its facility. It may also experience external economies in purchasing catering services for a larger number of children. However, in relationship to *LRAC*, it does little harm to think of these lowered costs as representing increasing returns to scale.

Some Reasons for the Shape of the *LRAC*

LRAC typically declines over some range of output for a number of reasons. The most important is that, as the scale of output is expanded, there is greater potential for specialization of productive factors. This is most notable with regard to labor but may apply to nonlabor factors as well. Specialization and the corresponding division of labor contribute to reduced unit costs in several ways. First, labor becomes more adept at the particular task, performs the function with greater skill and consistency and, as a result, produces more output per unit of labor cost. There is also time saved when each worker does not have to move from one job to another at various stations throughout the production facility. Furthermore, specialized workers are more likely to see ways in which their functions can be performed more efficiently.

Other factors contributing to declining *LRAC* include ability to use more advanced technologies such as sophisticated telecommunications equipment and lower costs for some inputs by purchasing large quantities. Furthermore, purely geometric factors, such as the fact that doubling the number of bricks used to build a daycare center, can more than double capacity. Certain administrative costs may not need to be increased over some range of output; for example, one purchasing agent could handle several scattered daycare sites. Technological advances in the technology, including the use of computers, allow management to sort and organize vast quantities of data.

Not all economists agree that the *LRAC* will be U-shaped, implying diseconomies as well as economies of scale. This is in part because the evidence in support of the existence of diseconomies of scale is much less compelling than the evidence for economies of scale. As you will see, many long-run average curves may be L-shaped. Such a shape results from a region of increasing returns to scale that is followed by an extended region of constant returns to scale. Long-run average costs vary depending on the industry in which a firm is engaged. In the public sector, the processing of tax forms and automobile licensing lend themselves to large-scale production. On the other hand, there may be diseconomies (higher costs) associated with larger foster care homes or elementary schools. One should not assume that with expansion per unit costs stay the same. Economies of scale lower and diseconomies increase per unit costs.

6.9   USING QUANTITATIVE ANALYSIS TO ESTIMATE COST FUNCTIONS

Throughout this chapter we have assumed that the quality of output remains constant as output expands. This is not to say that improved quality considerations are not important. However, our emphasis has been on the costs involved in increasing output of a certain fixed quality. Remember, the goal is not to minimize costs. Shutting down is the best way to minimize costs! If the goal is to produce the most output for a given level of expenditure, realize that the level of production affects per unit costs.

The most widely adopted method of determining real-world cost functions is the "statistical" estimation of the relationship between cost and output. The basic technique is that of regression analysis (see the Appendix to Chapter 1). At first glance, the application of regression techniques to the estimation of various cost functions seems deceptively simple: just regress cost on output. However, the job is fraught with difficulties.

Noted econometricians, especially J. Johnston and A. A. Walters, have identified some particularly important and often vexing problems in statistical cost analysis. First, in collecting the cost and output data, we must be certain that they are properly paired; one must be sure that the cost data are, in fact, applicable to the corresponding data on output. For example, if wages paid in a given week are based on the number of hours worked for a previous week, the pairing of accounting data for wages with output for a particular week, say, the nth week, would lead to an incorrect assignment of labor cost to output. A related problem may arise, particularly for short-run cost functions, when the period for which accounting data are available may differ from what might be the most meaningful economic period.

Furthermore, data on costs and output should be obtained during a time period when the output has been produced at a relatively even rate. If, for example, a month is chosen as the relevant time period over which the variables are measured, it would not be desirable to have wide weekly fluctuations in the rate of output. The monthly data would in such a case represent an average output rate that could disguise the true cost–output relationship. Not only should the rate of output be uniform, but it also should be a rate to which the firm has fully adjusted. Furthermore, it should not be contaminated by such external factors as power failures, delays in receiving necessary supplies, and variations in the prices paid for raw materials, labor, and other inputs. These difficulties are exacerbated by the fact that, to generate the data necessary for a meaningful statistical analysis, the observations must include a wide range of rates of output. To observe 24 months of cost–output data when the rate of output was the same each month would provide little information concerning the appropriate cost function.

Still other problems are created by the fact that cost data are normally collected and recorded primarily for accounting purposes and in a manner that makes the information less than perfect from the perspective of economic analysis. Three problems of this nature are particularly widespread. First and most obvious, perhaps, is the use of historic cost for valuation of both assets and inventories.

The second difficulty in this respect is related to depreciation. The distribution of depreciation in profit-seeking firms over the life of an asset is determined, not by what might be reasonable according to economic function, but, rather, by various tax laws. In NFP firms the use of straight-line depreciation, for example, introduces a linearity bias into the estimated cost function. The value of computer equipment, for example, does not decline by the same amount each year. Other depreciation methods create a related bias, since they do not necessarily reflect a true relationship between the asset's productivity and the cost assigned.

Finally, for situations in which more than one product is being produced with given productive factors, it may not be possible to separate costs according to output in a meaningful way. We learn in cost accounting courses that the various ways of allocating costs among products is usually based on the relative proportion each product represents of the total output. These methods are helpful, but in some cases costs may interact such that the methods may not accurately reflect the cost appropriate to each product. In spite of all these difficulties, effective administrators of NFP firms need reasonably accurate knowledge of production factors and estimations of per unit costs.

6.10   THE COST DISEASE

Costs in NFP firms increase rather than decrease due to technological breakthroughs. Baumol and Bowen illustrate the "cost disease" by dividing the economy into two sectors. In one sector, including manufacturing, improved methods increase productivity on average by 4 percent a year. In the other sector, including industries like the performing arts, productivity is relatively constant. All industries compete in the resource market for labor inputs. Rising productivity/output in the one sector affects all industries in two ways: (1) demand for services increases, and (2) firms face higher wages for artists and service professionals. Because productivity remains fairly constant in arts, education, and medicine, these industries experience increased per unit costs as compared to technology-intensive industries.

The *cost disease* refers to the lack of productivity gains in some industries that leads to ever-rising costs. Differentials in productivity gains affect profit-seeking firms, but NFPs are particularly resistant to productivity gains and hence highly susceptible to the cost disease.

Profit-seeking institutions, on the other hand, are not immune to the cost disease experienced in the healthcare industry. One set of researchers (Woolhandler and Himmelstein, 1997) found that hospital ownership (NFP or profit-seeking) is a significant factor in explaining the cost difference between hospitals in the United States. They indicate that administrative costs as a percentage of total hospital costs in the United States between 1990 and 1994 increased in general but were particularly high at for-profit hospitals. They suggest that profit-seeking behavior could result, not merely in higher administrative costs, but in lower hospital stays, reduced clinical staff, and poorer health outcomes. Institutions that economize on high-cost inputs can maintain a higher quality of output.

Does low productivity and high costs make a case for public financing or even public provision? If the service in question is considered a public good, then public financing is certainly justified, but the type of institution in which the service is delivered depends on a careful consideration of outcomes. With for-profit, private nonprofit, and government institutions operating in a given industry, we can at least observe differentials in cost efficiency, outcomes, and production technology. Competition will foster speedier implementation of cost-saving technology and better practices in those industries particularly resistant to productivity gains. Meanwhile, increased living standards along with a willingness to pay higher prices for leisure activities, education, and healthcare permit NFPs to pay the salaries needed to retain service professionals in industries with slow growth rates in productivity.

CONCLUDING NOTES

- Production is the process of providing goods or services that have value to those who use them.

- Production functions describe maximum levels of output associated with different quantities of inputs given existing technology.

- All firms attempt to combine various inputs in such a way so as to improve quality or reduce cost by using the minimum quantity of resources.

- Tables, graphs, and mathematical equations may be used to demonstrate the relationship between output and one factor of production, assuming all other factors of production hold constant.

- Total production depends on the quantity of fixed and variable inputs.

- Most production processes are not simply linear but are subject to diminishing marginal productivity of the variable input(s).

- The relevant range of production is restricted to stage II in which all inputs have a positive but declining marginal product.

- Opportunity cost, in addition to explicit costs, should be included in estimating the full cost of any project.

- Production costs that do not account for negative externalities (social costs) appear to be lower than they actually are.

- Cost functions combine production information with input prices to determine the cost of producing various levels of output.

- Whenever there are decreasing returns to a variable input, average variable cost increases as more units of output are produced.

- In the short run, a firm incurs costs associated with variable and fixed inputs. Marginal cost, average variable cost, and average total cost all decrease over some range of output, reach a minimum, and subsequently increase as the level of output expands.

- In the long run, all factors of production (inputs) are variable and average cost typically declines due to scale over some range of output depending on production technology and input costs.

- Data on costs and output are difficult to synchronize. Historical costs for the valuation of assets and inventories may be inaccurate. Depreciation methods may create bias in cost estimation. In multi-product firms it may be difficult to assign costs to separate activities.

- Productivity increases at different rates. Some industries, particularly in the service sector, experience slow increases in productivity. Higher standards of living, however, increase the demand for these services, which in turn increases costs relative to other industries.

KEY TERMS

Production function
Fixed input
Variable input
Total product
Marginal product
Diminishing marginal productivity
Average product
Marginal revenue product
Marginal resource cost
Normal return
Social costs

Variable costs
Short run
Long run
Fixed costs
Total cost
Average cost
Marginal cost
Long-run average cost curve
Returns to scale
Economies of scale
Cost disease

SUGGESTED READINGS

Baumol, William J. 1977: *Economic Theory and Operation Analysis*, 4th edn., ch. 11, Englewood Cliffs, NJ: Prentice-Hall.

Besharov, Gregory 2005: "The Outbreak of the Cost Disease: Baumol and Bowen's Founding of Cultural Economics," *History of Political Economy*, 37 (3), 412–30.

Dean, Joel 1937: "Statistical Cost Curves," *Journal of American Statistical Association*, March, 83–9.

Johannes, James M., Koch, Paul D., and Rasche, Robert H. 1985: "Estimating Regional Construction Cost Differences," *Managerial and Decision Economics*, June, 70–89.

Johnston, J. 1960: *Statistical Cost Analysis*, New York: McGraw-Hill.

Keating, Barry P. 1984: "Cost Shifting: An Empirical Examination of Hospital Bureaucracy," *Applied Economics*, April, 279–89.

Mansfield, Edwin 1968: *The Economics of Technical Change*, New York: Norton.

McConnell, Campbell R. and Brue, Stanley L. 2002: *Microeconomics: Principles, Problems, and Policies*, 15th edn., New York: McGraw-Hill.

Revier, Charles F. 1987: "The Elasticity of Scale, the Shape of Average Costs, and the Envelope Theorem," *American Economic Review*, June, 486–8.

Walters, A. A. 1963: "Production and Cost Functions: An Econometric Survey," *Econometrica*, January–April, 1–66.

Woolhandler, Steffie and Himmelstein, David U. 1997: "Costs of Care and Administration at For-profit and Other Hospitals in the United States," *New England Journal of Medicine*, 336 (11), March 13, 769–74.

END OF CHAPTER EXERCISES

Exercise 6.1

The manager of a tax return state agency wishes to estimate the functional relationship between the amounts of labor input and forms processed. For a given size of the bureau (and fixed amounts of other factors of production), the following data were obtained:

Output (Q)	15	13	10	10	12	15	11	14	16	9
Labor (L)	10	6	2	1	4	8	2	6	10	1

Output is in thousands of units and labor is in hundreds of labor hours.

  a. Draw a graph representing the production function. You are asked to estimate a production function of the form $Q = a + bL$. Using regression analysis, derive estimates for a and b. Do these estimates have the expected signs? Is b significant at the 95 percent confidence level? What is the coefficient of determination (R^2)?

  b. Write a brief explanation of your production function and related statistics for the production manager, assuming that the manager knows little or nothing about the technique you used.

  c. If 15 labor hours were used, what amount of output would you expect? Could you use the function you estimated to predict the level of output that would be obtained using 160 labor hours? Why or why not?

Exercise 6.2

Med Labs are providers of throat culture diagnoses for several mid-western hospitals. Data for one month have been gathered on the number of labor hours employed (L) and the number of cultures processed (P) for 14 Med Labs. These data are given in the table.

Lab	Cultures processed (P)	Labor hours employed (L)
1	11,000	800
2	13,000	1,600
3	5,000	300
4	8,000	800
5	4,000	100
6	11,000	2,000
7	7,000	600
8	8,000	2,200
9	4,000	300
10	14,000	1,300
11	15,000	1,600
12	4,000	600
13	12,000	1,000
14	14,000	2,000

a.   Plot paired observations on the graph provided.

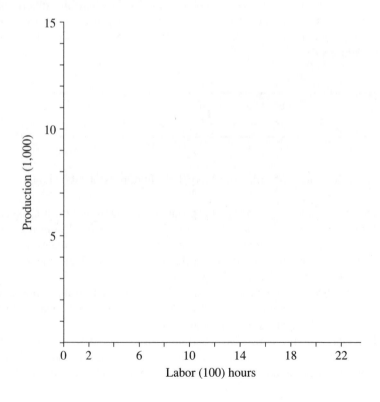

b. From the graph, does there appear to be diminishing marginal pro-
    ductivity for the labor input? Explain.
c. (Advanced analysis.) Use a regression program to estimate the pro-
    duction function in a linear form:

$$P = \underline{\hspace{2cm}} + \underline{\hspace{2cm}} L$$
$$ (\ ) \text{ } t\text{-ratio}$$

$$R^2 = \underline{\hspace{3cm}}$$

Exercise 6.3

Fill in the table using your knowledge of the relationships among the cost functions.

Q	FC	VC	TC	MC	AFC	AVC	AC
1			428.5	—	—	—	
2	340			67.5			248
3						68.5	
4		240					
5				22.5			
6			616			46	
7			623.5			40.5	
8							78.5
9		292.5					70.28
10		300	640			30	

Exercise 6.4

Moreau Shelter Industries employs mentally and physically challenged adults.
   Its administration is trying to classify the following costs as either fixed or variable. To which category would you assign each cost?

a. Office supplies.
b. Electrical bills.
c. Transportation costs for delivery of raw material.
d. Raw material cost.
e. Insurance on the plant and equipment.
f. Insurance on production employees.
g. Costs associated with the customer-billing department.
h. Plant heating and cooling costs.
i. Management office building heating and cooling costs.
j. Management salaries.
k. Maintenance personnel wages.

Exercise 6.5

State University runs flights for varsity athletic teams. This week, its leased
Boeing 737 aircraft sits idle. Are any costs incurred in this decision? If an alumni
group requested the use of the plane for a fee and the university had no other requests
for the craft, what costs are relevant in deciding whether to accept the fee offered

by the alumni? State University pays a licensing fee of $75,000 per year on the 737. Should this fee be taken into account in considering the alumni request?

Exercise 6.6

Cafeteria operating expenses in a private nonprofit or public agency are presently equal to revenue generated from food sales. Should the opportunity cost of its occupied space consisting of the kitchen, serving area, and dining room be considered a cost? How would you go about determining the market value of this space? Under what circumstances should administration contract with a profit-seeking corporation to provide food services?

Exercise 6.7

Use the concept of "cost disease" to explain why medical and educational personnel costs have increased even though it is difficult to justify increases on the basis of productivity.

Exercise 6.8

Draw the long-run average cost curve (LRAC) and explain the shape for the following industries using the concepts of economies and diseconomies of scale:

    a.   Public enterprises supplying water to local residents.
    b.   Maternity wards in community hospitals.
    c.   Community mental health agencies.
    d.   Mechanical vocational training on the secondary level.

Exercise 6.9

Kids' Klubs is an after-school program providing activities for boys and girls. It is one of several programs sponsored by a private nonprofit organization. Kids' Klubs has one administrator earning $18,000, another staff member paid $12,000 a year, and supply expenses of $20,000. The facility, owned by the sponsoring organization and used by Kids' Klubs, could generate $5,000 in rent if leased to a profit-seeking firm. Annual revenue generated by Kids' Klubs in the form of government grants, donations, and user fees is $54,000. Calculate the total explicit plus implicit cost of the program. Is the organization realizing net income from this program? What other costs to the organization, not given here, would you consider in making a decision to continue or expand the program?

Exercise 6.10

Do government and private nonprofits create negative externalities in the form of social costs in the process of providing services? It is generally recognized that uncensored profit-seeking firms in the process of producing steel, for example, pollute the environment. In doing this, they transfer costs to society that do not show up as explicit costs to the firms. Discuss whether NFP firms, such as those treating emergencies, pedophilia, or drug addiction, transfer social costs to communities in which they operate. Should regulations be proposed to minimize NFP social costs?

Exercise 6.11

NFPs rely on fund accounting procedures to assure contributors that funds received are used as intended. Discuss problems associated with assigning overhead expenses to specific programs.

7
Market Structure in Government and Nonprofit Industries

7.1   INTRODUCTION

Firms operate in industries offering a particular service. A particular hospital works in the healthcare industry; a particular university operates in higher education. Clients relative to the number of firms within an industry determine the degree of competition. Although each NFP has a unique mission, most operate within a certain industry. Thus, clients have substitute providers. In this chapter, we address administrators' response to industry competition.

In discussing intra-industry competition, we shift our emphasis from individual client and firm behavior – the emphasis up to this point in the text – to markets as a whole. Likewise, we move from an emphasis on *optimization* to a *description of equilibrium* for a particular industry. We will, however, return to individual firm behavior, decision-making, and optimization within the context of the degree of market competition within which a firm operates.

When economists talk about markets, they are not necessarily referring to grocery stores, farmers' open-air markets, or stock markets. Indeed, the term **market** does not even refer to a place; it refers, rather, to a process. The market is a *process* where the terms of trade – price, quantity, quality, and so on, are agreed upon by the participants.

We can array industries according to the degree of control an individual firm has over its own price/fees, assuming no government interference, as shown in the box.

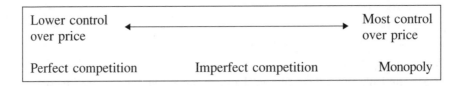

Lower control over price		Most control over price
Perfect competition	Imperfect competition	Monopoly

Although most firms operate in industries characterized by imperfect competition, this chapter focuses on the two extreme cases: perfect competition and monopoly. This is done for two reasons: first, economic theory is complete and more predictive in the two models on the extremes of the competitive range; second, administrators operating in imperfectly competitive markets learn much from the light shed by these two models. Admittedly, the latter reason recalls the joke about economists who look under a streetlight for a coin that was actually dropped down the street in the dark.

Throughout this chapter dealing with pricing and output decisions, you will see the importance of using marginal analysis. In Chapter 9, we will deal with situations in which a public administrator wishes to break even rather than maximize net income. In this chapter we focus on the net income maximizing rule (marginal revenue equals marginal cost) with average-cost graphs that include marginal cost and marginal revenue. Average total cost (per unit) along with marginal analysis is needed to make administrative decisions compatible with strategic goals. A school superintendent approximates the per unit cost of educating various numbers of students each year (average total cost) as well as the extra cost of adding an additional student (marginal cost). Similarly, the hospital administrator needs to estimate the average cost per patient and the marginal cost of additional patients.

The "marginal revenue equals marginal cost" rule is so widely applied in economics that it may be useful to quickly review how this rule is derived. We define net income/profit (π) as the difference between total revenue (TR) and total cost (TC). Recall that the nondistributional constraint does not permit any group of stakeholders in a NFP to claim net income/profit for themselves, but that does not necessarily imply that total revenue is always precisely equal to total costs:

$$\pi = TR - TC$$

Both total revenue and total cost are functions of the quantity (Q) produced and sold; thus, net income/profit is also a function of quantity. Further, any function can be evaluated for a possible maximum by finding where its slope is equal to zero (i.e., in calculus by finding its first derivative and setting that equal to zero). For profit, we have

$$\pi = TR - TC$$
$$\Delta\pi/\Delta Q = \Delta TR/\Delta Q - \Delta TC/\Delta Q = 0$$

Thus,

$$\Delta TR/\Delta Q = \Delta TC/\Delta Q$$

The left-hand term in this equality is the change in total revenue as quantity changes, or *marginal revenue*. The right-hand term is the change in total cost as quantity changes, or *marginal cost*. Thus, if net income/profit increases as output increases and then declines, net income/profit is at a maximum when:

$$MR = MC$$

Note that there is nothing in this rule, or in its development, that is directly related to the form of market structure within which the firm operates. The **profit-maximizing rule** is independent of market structure. You will see the $MR = MC$ principle for decision-making in NFP firms in both perfectly competitive and monopolistic industries.

7.2   THE ROLE OF COMPETITION IN THE GOVERNMENT AND NONPROFIT SECTORS

Some students of public administration resist thinking of NFP firms as competing institutions. This sensitivity is understandable and most of us persist in the belief that core mission, client trust, and the commons must be protected from commercialization. In practice, however, NFPs compete with each other for revenue, board members, grants, employees, donations/volunteers, prestige, political power, and political influence. They compete as well for clients and market share. Private nonprofits compete with government agencies and both compete for alliances with for-profit and other government entities. Some industries such as primary education are almost exclusively NFP. Others, such as campgrounds, are mixed-mode consisting of government, nonprofit, and profit-seeking firms and combinations, called quangos. Application 7.1 discusses the increase in competition caused by the entry of profit-seeking firms into higher education.

APPLICATION 7.1
Profit-seeking Competition in Higher Education

The market for profit-seeking higher education is growing. Profit-seeking educational firms, called proprietary schools, increased their enrollment in the United States by nearly 48 percent between 1996 and 2000. Public and private NFPs experienced less than 6 percent growth during the same time period.

The U.S. Department of Education does not consider these colleges a greater risk for loan defaults than other schools although in the early 1990s a scandal erupted when some proprietary schools failed to deliver the intended job training. Low-income students accumulated debt on which they defaulted. Presently, government money in the form of student loans, research funds, etc. may not exceed 90 percent of a school's revenue. All schools with default rates of 25 percent or more for three consecutive years can lose eligibility for federal financial aid. The overall national default rate is 5.4 percent, with the rate for profit-seeking institutions higher at 9 percent.

Nearly three-fourths of Americans, older than 25, do not have bachelor's degrees, and some type of third-level education, beyond secondary school, is required for many well-paying jobs. For-profits, which cannot offer tax deductions to donors and lack endowments, tailor their courses, schedules, and marketing to these individuals. These schools rely on tuition, often paid by federal financial aid or private employers. Profit-seeking schools tend to spend relatively more on recruitment, accept a higher percentage of applicants, and have higher dropout rates.

Trade schools play an important economic role in providing workers with new skills that assist in acquiring jobs or transferring to better paying ones. Presently, at least one profit-seeking college is lobbying for a repeal of the federal law, aimed at fraudulent correspondence schools. The law prohibits colleges receiving federal financial aid from offering more than half their courses via distance learning.

Do you think that profit-seeking institutions offer a valid alternative to NFP colleges for some students?

Source: "Kaplan Transforms into Big Operator of Trade Schools," *Wall Street Journal*, November 7, 2003, A1.

Industries dominated by NFP firms

Government and nonprofit firms dominate industries characterized by market failure. These industries tend to have three characteristics:

1   The product produced meets the nonrival or the non-excludability criterion for a public good.

2   User fees do not cover all costs and donor and/or tax revenue make up the difference. Trust issues are important in these industries to ensure that funds are not diverted from intended use and that clients are well served.

3   NFP firms enjoy a competitive advantage provided by being part of the public sector or, in the case of private nonprofits, by their favorable tax treatment.

The chosen **basis for competition** refers to the way competitors choose to compete in meeting their client/constituent needs. They may compete on the basis of user fee/price or a range of quality standards. Does a hospital offer a normal childbirth delivery at a lower price than its rivals or does it offer more attractive labor/delivery rooms, massages, sibling visitations, gourmet meals, home visits, etc. Preferences of sponsors, individual donors, taxpayers, and professional mores affect the basis of competition in the government and nonprofit sectors. Profit-seeking firms appropriately concentrate on consumer demand and on increasing the wealth of owners/stockholders; NFP firms concentrate on mission. How and which services are delivered, who provides them, and for what periods of time are determined largely not by the standard of their contribution to net income/profit in NFP firms, but by how the professionals and volunteers interpret the mission of the organization (Tuckman, 1998).

The behavior of any organization operating in an industry dominated by government agencies and nonprofit firms is analyzed in terms of the following five characteristics:

1   *Ease of entry.* The number of firms in a predominately NFP industry and thus the level of competition are affected by start-up capital, certification, and accreditation requirements, as well as the existence of firms with established reputations and large donor bases. These entry barriers explain why one or two hospitals dominate healthcare in small or medium-sized towns.

2   *Bargaining power of buyers.* Markets with one or a few relatively large buyers are called **monopsonies**. This word is not misspelled; it refers to the concentrated market power of buyers, and is discussed at length in Chapter 10 dealing with the demand side of the factor (input) market.

3   *Availability of substitute products or services.* Substitutes influence the prices that firms charge clients and how they appeal to donors. At times, public policy can encourage the development of substitute services, heightening the degree of competition. School vouchers and home-health services, fostered by public policy, encourage the entry of competitors into these respective markets.

4   *Rivalry among competitors.* Competition intensifies in the presence of rivals. There is additional enthusiasm when local high schools play football, as compared to when one of the teams is from out of town. Whenever outputs are hard to measure, a number of equal-sized firms, determined to display their products' uniqueness, compete for clients and donors symbolically through rivalry and in different delivery methods. A university's yearly donations are affected by how they fare with traditional

athletic rivals. NFPs with high fixed costs and excess capacity become intense competitors. At times, a nonprofit firm experiencing losses in a particular program continues to underwrite a less favored activity incapable of meeting its competitors' challenge.

5   *Bargaining power of suppliers of inputs.* NFP firms compete with all firms for supplies with which they produce services. They hire employees who are free to work elsewhere. They borrow funds that are fungible between sectors. Universities offering classes in public service administration compete for students and influence. In Chapter 10, we will discuss the unique resource markets for labor and funds in which NGOs, quasi-public, and public agencies operate.

Industries with inter-sectoral competition

Historically, NFP firms collaborate and compete with profit-seeking firms. Why do some NFPs choose to enter industries dominated by profit-seeking firms? At times, government firms experience a decline in state appropriations and seek other sources of revenue in the for-profit sector. Private nonprofits, faced with increased demand, declining donations, and the power to tax, are pressured to sponsor unrelated business activities. Legal structures, such as holding companies and joint ventures, allow for non-profit, government, and for-profit collaboration. The decision to commercialize some activities with the explicit intent of earning net income/profit leads NFPs at times into direct competition with profit-seeking firms.

Profit-seeking firms, on the other hand, are very much aware that they are often in direct competition with NFPs. Consider restaurants and landlords in a university town. Any move on the part of the university to provide apartments or dining facilities on campus affects the private returns on local investment. Subsidies, such as those received by 501(c) (3) organizations, offer a cushion against competition and tilt the playing field in favor of NFPs. Because a NFP firm receives revenue from sources beyond user fees, it is imperative that NFP firms engaged in commerce do not subsidize profit-seeking activity.

A single overwhelming characteristic of mixed-sector industries is the widespread adoption of profit-seeking business techniques. In healthcare, hospitals have been forced by competition toward a system that has become increasingly oriented toward microeconomic rationality, productivity, and cost containment. This does not necessarily mean that there are not real differences in behavior between profit-seeking and NFP firms in practice, or that the unique role of the nonprofit or government sectors is diminished by the adoption of business techniques (Tuckman, 1998).

7.3   PERFECT COMPETITION IN NOT-FOR-PROFIT INDUSTRIES

Since the time of Adam Smith in the eighteenth century, the perfectly competitive market has been the ideal type of market for economists. In a perfectly competitive market, buyers try to outdo other buyers by offering sellers the most attractive terms, and sellers try to outdo other sellers by offering lower prices. A **perfectly competitive market** exists when the following criteria are met:

1   *There are many buyers and sellers in the market.* The market has so many buyers and sellers that no one participant affects price, and the participants act independently of one another. Actually, there are many cases in which a large number of buyers and sellers are not necessary for perfect competition. It is necessary, however, that the market participants have no control over price. A few NFP industries approach this ideal. In child daycare, for example, a large number of profit-seeking, nonprofit, and government facilities may exist on the supply side of the market, and these providers face a large number of families, on the demand side, seeking service.

2   *All participants have free entry and exit.* Any firm that believes it can earn higher net income/profits by moving from one industry to another has **free entry and exit**. That is, there is complete mobility of productive resources. Congregations, for example, sponsoring daycare facilities can open, close, or contract service and redirect their resources.

3   *A homogeneous or standardized product exists.* A **standardized product** means that one firm's product is neither superior nor inferior to the products made by other firms. There is something about the nature of most but not all NFP industries that resists standardization. It is difficult to reach consensus on best practices and often nonprofits exist precisely to provide differentiated services. Therefore, this condition is seldom met in the NFP sectors.

4   *All participants have perfect knowledge.* All firms have access to the same types of technology, and prospective buyers are familiar with prevailing fees/prices.

Even in the profit-seeking world, examples of perfectly competitive markets are difficult to come by; in fact, there may be few situations that *exactly* match the four conditions outlined. Markets for some agricultural products, bushels of corn or wheat for instance, come very close to perfect competition.

However, the characteristics of perfect competition are equally important in the NFP world as in the profit-seeking sector. Whenever there are many providers in a competitive market, clients easily switch purchases from one provider to another. This ease of transfer encourages providers to compete with one another by attempting to change the terms of trade – to offer lower fees/prices, offer better service, give better quality, and the like. If any one firm refuses to compete with other providers, clients transfer to a competitor. If each provider's products are a perfect substitute for those of every other seller, a single firm offers to sell its entire production at the market price. Thus, in a competitive market an individual firm is said to be a **price taker** and cannot refuse to compete with others offering lower fees: the consequence of doing so would be to lose all one's clients to other providers. NFP nursing homes are often in competition with for-profit providers. Often, nursing home charges per day are determined by Medicare and an institution setting a higher fee could end up with no clients. A public school offering driving instruction

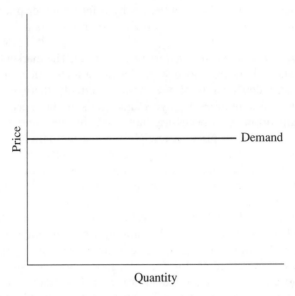

Figure 7.1   The perfectly competitive firm's demand curve. The demand curve facing a perfectly competitive firm is a horizontal line at the current fee/price; thus, it is perfectly elastic. If the firm tries to sell at a higher fee, clients drop to zero as they switch to other providers. Firms have no incentive to provide the service at a lower fee, because they have a full capacity number of clients.

during the summer faces competition with private firms offering a similar product. A daycare center, in an industry approximating perfect competition, cannot charge more than competitors without the risk of losing its clients. Neither does it make sense to charge a lower fee because the firm can fill to capacity at the existing fee. In these competitive situations, an individual firm will perceive its demand curve to be perfectly elastic (horizontal) at the market price, as shown in Figure 7.1. Each client knows he or she is paying neither more nor less than others.

One further attractive characteristic of perfect competition is that the total quantity of goods provided is indirectly decided by clients. Firms have no incentive to cut back in order to raise fees/price. Each has the incentive to produce more units as long as the extra revenue (marginal revenue) received is larger than the cost of the additional units provided (marginal cost). If one provider fails to produce an extra unit yielding net income/profit, another provider will seize the opportunity. Thus, the client has available as many units as can feasibly be produced at this time for a fee equal to cost. Cost, you will recall, includes normal return equal to the sponsor/entrepreneur's opportunity cost.

Supply, demand, and equilibrium in a perfectly competitive market

Perfectly competitive markets are composed of many buyers and sellers; actual competitors and *potential* competitors (those who are ready to enter the market given a particular condition) are both part of real-world markets. Let's assume for

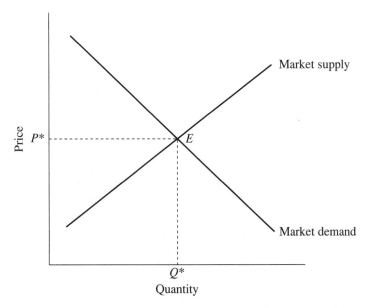

Figure 7.2   Market demand and market supply in a perfectly competitive market.
The balance of supply and demand determines the equilibrium fee/price at point E. This
price is shown as P^*. At P^*, the providers (in total) supply exactly Q^* units of product,
and clients (in total) purchase exactly Q^* units. Thus, the quantity supplied equals the
quantity demanded at the price P^*. The market is in equilibrium.

a moment a perfectly competitive market – one that is unlikely to exist in the
real world. By doing so, we can describe an equilibrium point toward which a
real-world competitive market tends.

In a perfectly competitive market, there is complete freedom of entry and exit:
anyone can enter, produce, and sell a duplicate of what is already being sold. Each
competitor produces but a small share of the industry's total output. The market
supply and demand curves appear like those in Figure 7.2.

The demand for any good, daycare, for example, is downward sloping to the
right and thus follows the law of demand outlined in Chapter 3. This market demand
curve represents the maximum quantities of daycare that would be purchased at
various prices. In a perfectly competitive market, this curve is known with certainty by all. The demand curve in Figure 7.2 is a market or total demand curve
because all clients are represented by the curve. The curve indicates what clients
will do when all providers change their fees/prices.

The market supply curve represents planned production by all actual or potential providers, and its shape depends on how much each provider is willing to offer
on the market at each fee/price. This market supply curve, of course, is dependent
on the cost functions of the individual firms in the industry. For reasons we will
discuss later, the short-run supply curve for any individual perfectly competitive
firm is that portion of the marginal cost curve lying above the average variable
cost curve. If the price given to the individual firm falls below average variable
cost, the firm is better off not producing at all, unless it wishes to subsidize that

activity. Thus, if client fees and a NFP's per unit subsidy fall below average variable cost, shutdown is a reasonable alternative. Even when all fixed costs are paid by the sponsor/government, if client fees are below average variable cost, the NFP firm will be forced to exit the market. For these reasons, the section of the marginal cost curve below the average variable cost curve is not part of an individual firm's supply curve.

The market supply curve is the horizontal summation of all the individual firms' supply curves, which are the marginal cost curves above average variable cost. Since the marginal cost curves are positively sloped in the relevant region, the market supply curve is also positively sloped, as shown in Figure 7.2.

Market price in the perfectly competitive market tends toward an equilibrium where price is P^* and quantity supplied is Q^*. This is shown at point E in Figure 7.2, where supply and demand cross, or are equal. If child daycare is a competitive market, then fees charged in the market tend toward an equilibrium price, such as $120 a week per child. Why does the market tend toward this point? To answer this question, let's see what happens if the price is not at the equilibrium price.

If the fee/price charged is above the equilibrium price, say, at price P_1 in Figure 7.3, the amount of goods suppliers are willing to sell exceeds the amount clients are willing to buy. We could then say that there is excess supply equal to the distance between points A and B in Figure 7.3. There is now a downward pressure on prices and daycare providers will reduce the number of slots available. Several suppliers independently reducing their prices cause market price to fall. As the market price falls, clients increase the quantity they demand, and providers lower the amount they wish to produce. Fees/prices continue to fall until supply equals demand at the equilibrium price P^* in Figure 7.3.

But what happens if at some point the fee/price is below the equilibrium price, say, at P_2 in Figure 7.3? There will be excess demand equal to the distance between points C and D. Upward pressure on price results because some clients are willing to spend more than the current fee rather than forego usage. Suppliers find that they can raise price without losing all their clients. As price increases, the quantities suppliers are willing to offer increase, while the quantity demanded by purchasers falls. This continues until supply equals demand at the equilibrium price P^* in Figure 7.3.

Figure 7.4 represents cost and revenue functions for a representative firm in a perfectly competitive market. Given that there are a large number of such firms all producing the standardized product, it follows that each of these firms will provide their output at the market equilibrium price, P^*. Consider what would happen if this individual firm decided not to sell at the market equilibrium fee/price.

If the firm sells at a lower price than P^*, any net income/profit it currently enjoys would decrease (or their loss would increase). In Figure 7.4, the firm provides Q^* (we shall see why this particular quantity in a moment) at fee/price P^* and earns net income/profit equal to the shaded area, which is $AR - ATC$ times the number sold. If the firm lowers price, the shaded area is reduced in size and the firm loses net income. If, in the daycare example, one center charged a higher fee than P^*, in theory their clients would drop to zero as parents switch children to other centers.

Again, we observe the firm selling at the market equilibrium price and the perceived demand curve is represented as a horizontal line, such as the one labeled D

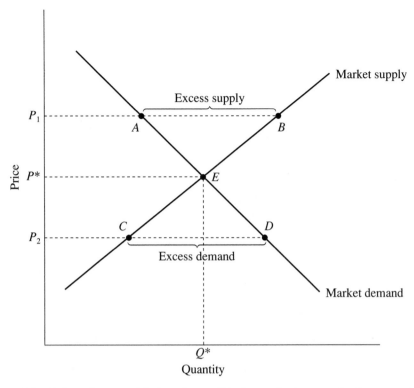

Figure 7.3   Prices above and below the equilibrium price in a perfectly competitive market. High or low fees/prices lead to the reestablishment of the equilibrium price P^*. At the high price, P_1, the excess supply causes providers to lower price, while at the low price, P_2, excess demand causes fees to be pushed higher. Once the price is at P^*, if supply and demand remain stable, price will not change.

in Figure 7.4. Once, for example, daycare fees reach equilibrium at $120 a week, each competitive provider sees his or her demand curve as $120 per child. This same line also represents the marginal revenue (MR) to the firm, since the sale of each additional unit causes total revenue to increase by the price of the product (which is the same, P^*, at every level of output.) This same curve is also the average revenue (AR) curve for the firm, since average revenue equals marginal revenue when the latter is a constant. These relationships can be shown most clearly as follows:

$TR = (P^*)(Q)$

$MR = \Delta TR / \Delta Q$

$MR = P$

$AR = TR / Q$

$AR = [\,(P^*)(Q)\,] / Q$

$AR = P^*$

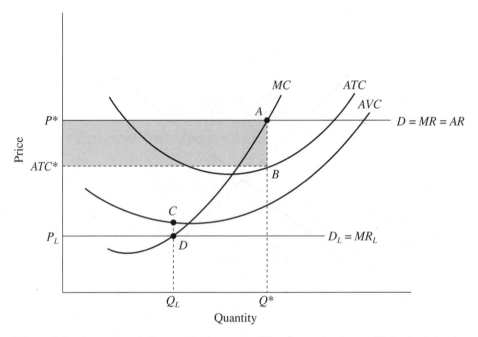

Figure 7.4   A representative perfectly competitive firm: short run. If the fee/price is
P^*, the optimum level of production is Q^*, at which $MR = MC$. The net income/profit
per unit of production is A minus B (or P^* minus ATC^*). Total net income/profit is the
amount per unit times the number of units (Q^*). This is shown by the shaded area. If the
market price falls below minimum of average variable cost (AVC), such as P_L, the firm
minimizes its loss by shutting down. Per unit loss of C to D is avoided, and the total
loss is limited to fixed costs.

Net income/profit maximizing competitive firms operate where marginal revenue
equals marginal cost (point A in Figure 7.4). If a firm operates beyond this point
and provides a quantity in excess of Q^*, the additional units of product add more
to total cost than to total revenue. Note that to the right of Q^*, $MC > MR$. If a firm
moves below (to the left of) point A and provides less than Q^*, the production of
less units decreases total revenue more than the decrease in total costs because to
the left of point A, $MC < MR$.

Before looking at a specific example, let's investigate why a firm shuts down
rather than produces if per unit revenue falls below average variable cost at whatever level of output the firm provides. This is true as well for NFP firms having
all their fixed costs underwritten by sponsors/donors. It is also true for NFP firms
that receive per unit revenue in the form of user charges plus a per client subsidy,
which added together do not cover variable costs. Such a low price is shown as
P_L in Figure 7.4. At P_L marginal revenue (MR_L) equals marginal cost at point D.
The optimization rule that $MR = MC$ seems to call for an output of Q_L units, given
the price P_L. But at Q_L units, the average *variable* cost is greater than the price,
P_L. Thus, the firm does not earn enough revenue to cover even the variable cost
of production. At this fee, the firm is well advised to shut down and not produce.
The fixed cost must still be paid in the short run and represents a loss to the firm,

because total revenues would be zero. But this loss is smaller than the loss of operating, given the P_L price. At that price an additional loss of C to D dollars per unit of production (Q_L) is in addition to all fixed costs. Can you imagine a daycare center surviving when tuition plus any subsidy received did not cover the variable costs of lunches, snacks, and art supplies? Probably not. However, in the NFP sectors, per unit client revenue generally is generally less than full cost including variable supplies, staff salaries, insurance, and rent. Because user fees do not cover full costs in the NFP sectors, most clients in preferred activities benefit from a subsidy.

At prices above the minimum average variable cost, a firm maximizes net income (minimizes losses) by producing the level of output at which $MR = MC$. And because $P = MR$ when the demand curve is horizontal, this means that $P = MC$ is the equivalent criterion for net income/profit maximization (loss minimization). Be aware that even when user fees exceed variable costs, full cost may not be recovered. User fees have to equal total average cost to avoid loss. The collection of points at which $P = MC$ thus shows the quantities that a perfectly competitive firm provides at each price. This is called the firm's supply function, and thus the marginal cost and supply curves are identical for a perfectly competitive firm (but only above the minimum of the average variable cost curve).

The long-run adjustment in perfect competition

In the long run, new providers soon become aware of potential net income/profit to be earned in a particular market. Recall that "perfect knowledge" is one of the characteristics of perfect competition. More firms enter the industry, causing an increase in supply, which drives the fee/price down. This process continues until all net income/profit has been stripped from the market. If, for example, there are profits to be earned in providing daycare services, then new providers enter the market. This drives down daycare fees and eliminates net income/profits.

The market entry process and its effect on a representative firm are shown in Figure 7.5. When price is equal to P_1, the representative firm produces at Q_1 and earns positive net income/profit. Additional firms enter, and the market supply curve shifts to the right, and the representative firm's net income/profit is eliminated. We can see that the long-run equilibrium for the firm is where $MR_2 = MC = P_2 = AC$. Since price equals average cost after this long-run adjustment, the positive net income/profit has disappeared.

If originally $P = MR = MC$ and price was less than AC each firm would have made a negative net income/loss. In such a situation, some firms leave the industry, and the market supply function shifts left. Such a shift would be accompanied by an increase in the equilibrium price, and the amount of negative profit would be less for each firm.

Ultimately, in a perfectly competitive market, the flow of firms entering and leaving an industry establishes an equilibrium fee at which each firm earns only a normal return (that is, no net income or excess profit). In the profit-seeking sector, when net income is zero, the firm is earning no economic profit but is still covering all costs including a **normal return**. A normal return is what a firm would earn if they used their assets to generate income in some other activity. Recall that the full costs for a NFP firm include what they could have received for the use of their property in some other activity. Students in business classes are often surprised

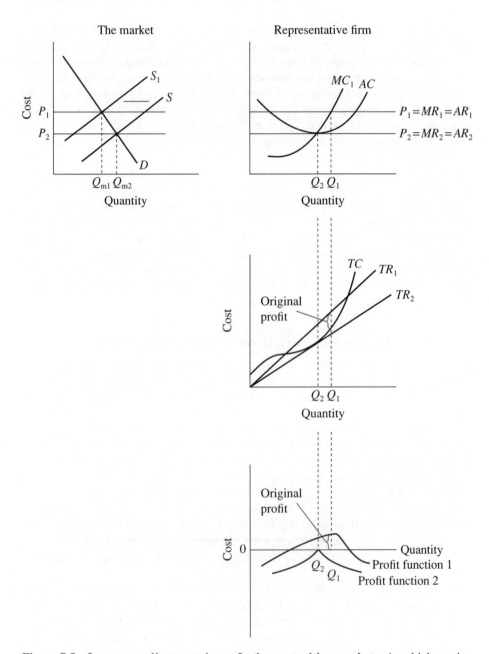

Figure 7.5 Long-run adjustment in perfectly competitive markets. At a higher price of P_1, the individual firm, represented in each of the three diagrams on the right, earns positive net income/profit. The market supply curve in the left diagram increases, reducing price to P_2. The lower price reduces net income/profit to zero.

that the ultimate outcome in the ideal perfectly competitive market is to eliminate all economic profits. NFP administrators are sometimes taken aback when they hope to use net income/profit in some activity in order to cross-subsidize favored activities. The desire for positive net income/profit is not father to the deed; competition reduces fees to cost. Most firms merely cover costs and earn a normal profit. In 2000, pre-tax corporate profits in the United States were less than 11 percent of gross domestic product.

The fee/price in a competitive market in the short run results in economic profit, economic loss, or simply normal profit. However, in competitive industries the market price will settle at a long-run equilibrium in which only a normal return is earned. The long-run adjustment of firms entering and leaving a market places pressure on the market price to move toward our predicted equilibrium.

Perhaps NFP firms are in a position to operate at a loss for a longer period than profit-seeking firms. A chronic loss for a NFP firm indicates that the firm is incapable of covering all variable costs with user fees plus an acceptable per unit subsidy. Inevitably, assets of the firm decline and at some point sponsors cease funding failing activities. Beloved hospitals, schools, and churches close if they continue to generate less revenue than costs. In some instances, as in the case of two environmental organizations described in Application 7.2, a failing institution will merge with an organization having a similar mission.

APPLICATION 7.2
Not All Nonprofits Survive: Some Merge

A nonprofit firm sometimes merges with other firms to increase capacity, to advance mission, and to survive when economic factors fail to support its mission. By merging, a nonprofit firm can potentially increase the size of its donor list, share resources, use space more effectively, relieve debt, and lower costs related to scale. Singer/songwriter John Denver's Windstar Foundation, dedicated to responsible environmental action, merged with the National Wildlife Federation. Windstar's annual financial shortfall threatened dissolution. Similarly, the American Cancer Society merged 57 separate corporate entities into 17 regional organizations. It became obvious that, in spite of good financial health and solid volunteerism, the society would not meet its goal of reducing cancer deaths by 50 percent and cancer incidence by 25 percent.

In nonprofit mergers, one or more firms accept a name change and pledge all their assets to the other corporation. In merging, it is not necessarily the case that one organization is dissolving and the other surviving. However, in dissolution, depending on its charter, a nonprofit's assets are generally turned over to some other tax-exempt entity.

Source: Dan H. McCormick, *Nonprofit Mergers*, Gaithersburg, MD: Aspen Publications, 2001.

Do markets reach long-run equilibrium and remain there? Probably not. The concept of long-run equilibrium is a theoretical construct to assist us in understanding how markets operate. Demand and supply do not remain constant over long periods of time in the real world. Their underlying determinants (such as preferences in demand and technology in supply) are constantly changing. As they change, long-run equilibrium changes. The relevance of long-run equilibrium theory is that it points toward where a market is heading at any point in time; the competitive market is a process of constant adjustment toward equilibrium.

There are some simple rules to be learned from competitive markets. First, a firm entering a competitive market *may* earn positive net income or economic profits for a short time but, if the market is truly competitive, those economic profits dissipate. An early entrant to a new competitive market has some advantages. Second, operating at least cost is an important characteristic of successful competitive firms. If a firm is not a least-cost provider, it cannot survive in that activity. Finally, an effective method of competing is to use a dimension other than price. In competitive markets we assume that all products are alike. One daycare center is as good as another. In the real world, particularly in the private nonprofit sector, a firm differentiating its product survives, and succeeds. Competition takes place in many dimensions. If parents really believe that a particular daycare center is adequate in all dimensions and superior in some, they will be willing to pay higher fees.

7.4   MONOPOLY IN NOT-FOR-PROFIT INDUSTRIES

Markets are a process in which rivals, in pursuit of their own interests, attempt to outdo one another in order to earn net income/profit. However, perfectly competitive markets have the attractive feature that, in long-run equilibrium, each firm earns just enough to cover all costs and sells its product at the market-determined price. This represents allocative and productive economic efficiency. In perfect competition, no one firm can *significantly* influence the outcome of the market process and no one firm earns economic profit in the long run.

Monopoly is the opposite of perfect competition. In a monopoly, there is just one seller and no need to out-perform other firms. As a result, there is an absence of the perfectly competitive outcome. A monopolist does not compete because there are no rivals sharing the market. The real and perceived inefficiency associated with NFP firms is often due to monopolistic power rather than the nature of being NFP. By concentrating on the extreme inefficiency of a single provider, students should learn to recognize waste resulting from less than perfect competition.

Barriers to entry help maintain monopoly power

In order to explain how it is possible for a monopoly to exist, it is necessary to focus on what makes a market competitive. *The necessary condition for a competitive market is freedom of entry.* Since monopoly is the opposite of competition, the *necessary condition for a monopoly (or monopoly power) is a barrier to firms wishing to compete in the market.* A monopolist has what is called *monopoly power.* It can restrict output and manipulate price because it is protected from potential competitors, who find it difficult or impossible to enter the market. Barriers to entry stem from several sources:

1   The firm may have *sole ownership* of a strategic resource (a government may own *all* forest and park land and thus bar others from entry into the market).
2   The firm may have a *patent* or *copyright* on the product produced.
3   Large-scale production may be required to enter the market, precluding potential entrants from starting production (hospitals require immense initial investment). A **natural monopoly** is a special case in which the lowest-cost provider in an industry is a single firm.
4   A well-known name and reputation makes it difficult for new firms to obtain clients.
5   Subsidies in the form of donations and tax revenue are needed to provide services with public-good characteristics.
6   The *government may grant an exclusive franchise* to a provider, precluding competition. Government can designate one utility company or offer landing privileges to one airline. A state university may be the only institution legally permitted to offer accredited programs for teachers or physicians.

By far the most important entry barrier in all sectors of the economy is the last: a government franchise. The reason for this is that all monopoly power derived from entry barriers is subject to decay in the long run – all except an exclusive government franchise. Note how entry barriers have withered away over time:

1   During World War II, the United States lost its supply of quinine because of the occupation by enemy troops in quinine-producing areas. In a short time, a substitute for quinine was found. This synthetic quinine continued to compete with natural quinine even after the war, but the entry barrier due to sole ownership of a strategic resource was broken down.
2   Large-scale production *appears* to preclude entry, but some firms overcome this barrier. Ave Maria University in Michigan did not exist in the 1990s, and now it is opening a second campus in Florida. This requires an immense initial investment. A large donor, Mike Monahan of Domino's Pizza, assisted Ave Maria in jumping over the entry hurdle.
3   Brand names are not effective barriers over the long run. For example, applicants to many universities may submit *either* SAT scores from the College Board *or* ACT (a college entrance exam) scores.
4   Technological change causes some entry barriers to wither away over time. The internet is reducing the Post Office monopoly.

The one entry barrier that does not tend to erode over time is a government franchise. However, it is true that government may revoke an exclusive franchise at any time. It did so recently by permitting charter schools; previously competition for per child state tuition funding did not exist. But government may choose to continue such a franchise indefinitely. Application 7.3 shows how monopolies can operate at a loss with state subsidies. Some government franchises award a monopolist complete monopoly power (such as electric utility companies in most towns), but in other instances the monopoly power granted is incomplete (subsidized state airlines compete with private providers).

APPLICATION 7.3
Balancing Revenue and Costs in Chinese State Owned Enterprises (SOEs)

In Soviet-type economies and in the Chinese economy before 1978, the state provided all inputs to state owned enterprises (SOEs) and covered all costs. The state set wage rates for managers and workers and all activities required state approval. This arrangement was useful in guaranteeing that scarce resources were allocated toward an overall plan with priorities for each project.

To prevent any economic surplus/net income from being arbitrarily distributed, the Chinese introduced reforms to deprive managers of autonomy and to introduce competition. Eighteen years after China initiated reforms, the SOE share in total industrial output declined from 77.6 percent to 28.8 percent. However, SOEs still employ over 50 percent of urban workers and maintain over 50 percent of total investment in industrial fixed assets.

The rise of competing township and village enterprises (TVEs) was expected to eliminate SOEs' waste, looting, and other wrongdoings. It should also have provided overseers with information on competitive costs and expected returns. Still, over 40 percent of SOEs lose money. Some economists argue that the root of the SOE problem is "soft budget constraints" rather than hard market constraints.

Why do so many SOEs lose money. First, SOEs employ large quantities of facilities, tools, and equipment because with priority status they have access to interest free loans. Second, SOEs bear higher burdens for larger numbers of retired and redundant workers. Finally, SOEs, concentrated in energy, raw materials, and other priority goods and services, are not free to adjust price to cover cost. Managers of course ascribe all their losses to policy burdens.

Given policy burdens, the state is expected to cover SOE losses from general tax revenue. State compensation for losses permits SOEs to operate under a "soft budget constraint," such that they do not have to earn revenue equal to costs. For reform to be effective, SOEs must be released from their policy burdens. This would create a level playing field in which poor management becomes transparent.

Source: Justin Yifu Lin, Fang Cai, and Zhou Li, "Competition, Policy Burdens, and State-owned Enterprise Reform," *American Economic Review Papers and Proceedings*, May, 1998, 422–7.

Innovative products are often introduced by entrepreneurs hoping to earn a fortune, but, as time passes, their monopoly power erodes and economic profits are competed away. NFP firms follow a different pattern. NFP firms knowingly enter markets in which there is little prospect of net income/profit. A few NFPs, especially those with government franchises in any sector, have been able to protect their market position over long periods. Some industries, both NFP and profit-seeking, have been effective in enlisting government aid: railroads, electric utilities, the medical profession (through licensing), and the broadcast industry. While almost all real-world markets lie somewhere between the polar cases of perfect competition and pure monopoly, government franchised industries both public and private lie far closer to the monopoly end of the continuum.

The monopolistic firm: a general example

A pure monopolist is pictured in Figure 7.6. The key theoretical difference between a monopolist and a perfectly competitive firm is that the monopolist's demand curve is not horizontal. It slopes downward to the right because it coincides with and is identical to the industry demand curve (if there is only one firm, its demand curve is the industry demand curve).

The monopolist is not a fee/price taker but, rather, a fee/price maker (or price setter). Although the monopolist is still subject to the law of demand (more units may only be sold at lower prices), the monopolist chooses the point on the demand curve at which to operate and thus can set fees/price. A public administrator may be in a position to lower fees to attract more clients, and we have seen that depending on elasticity of demand these lower fees may actually increase total revenue. Note carefully, however, that the decline in fees will reduce the extra revenue PER UNIT below the fee charged. Figure 7.6 graphically explains why this is so.

The upper frame in Figure 7.6 assumes a normal set of unit cost curves for this pure monopolist, and the corresponding total cost curve is shown in the middle frame. The monopolist's demand and average revenue curve coincide, but the marginal revenue curve is now a separate curve. The marginal revenue curve is now downward sloping because more units can only be sold by lowering prices and this always decreases marginal revenue below price. Suppose that there is only one swim club in a small town with 100 season passes selling for $200. Then the only way to induce 20 more families to sign up is to lower price to $180. Since the monopolist must decrease price to increase sales, the additional revenue (marginal revenue) from each successive unit of sales is less than the price at which the unit is sold.

If the swim club lowers price to get new members it must offer the new lower price to returning members. All the previous members that formerly paid $200 will pay the new lower price of $180. The change from the old price to the new one reduces marginal revenue (revenue per unit) below price.

$$TR = PQ$$
$$TR_1 = \$200 * 100$$
$$= \$20,000$$

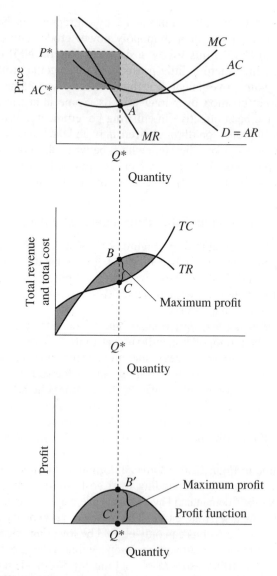

Figure 7.6 Equilibrium for a monopolist. A monopolist maximizes net income/profit by producing the rate of output for which $MR = MC$ (see point A). Since this quantity is Q^*, at which $P^* > AC^*$, a positive economic (or excess) profit results (see shaded rectangle). This net income/profit is also shown in the middle graph by the distance between points B and C. Similarly, the maximum profit is illustrated by the distance between B' and C' in the lower graph.

$$TR_2 = \$180 * 150$$
$$= \$27,000$$

$$MR = \Delta TR / \Delta Q$$
$$= \$7,000/50$$
$$= \$140$$

In Figure 7.6, a profit-maximizing monopolist will choose to operate where $MR = MC$. Its reason is precisely the same as that for the competitive firm. As long as an additional unit of output adds more to the firm's revenue than it does to the firm's cost, profit on that unit will be positive and total net income/profits will be increased (or losses decreased) by producing and selling the unit. This process of producing and selling extra units continues until MR equals MC. There is no incentive to move beyond that point (into the region where $MC > MR$) because producing and selling extra units then reduces profit (or increases losses). Thus, the monopoly firm in Figure 7.6 operates where $MR = MC$, produces the quantity of Q^*, but sets its fee at P^* (found directly above Q^* on the demand curve). Recall that this is very different from a perfectly competitive firm which is a fee-taker and cannot set fee/price.

At price P^*, the monopolist is earning net income/profits equal to the size of the shaded rectangle. In the middle frame, this equilibrium is at the quantity at which the vertical distance by which TR is above TC is greatest. This is also the point where TR and TC have identical slopes. Since the slope of the total cost curve equals MC and the slope of the total revenue curve equals MR, MR must equal MC at exactly the output where TR exceeds TC by the greatest amount, at quantity Q^*.

The monopolist in the long run

In the long run, a firm operating without subsidies can continue only as long as its fee/price exceeds or equals its long-run average cost. For the monopolist pictured in Figure 7.7, the firm's short-run equilibrium is also its long-run equilibrium. The firm in Figure 7.7 is earning economic profit in each short-run period, but since no competitors are able to enter the market, the monopolist continues to produce 8.10 units per period. If a firm is a *natural monopoly,* its profit-maximizing output occurs at a production level at which long-run average costs (not shown) are declining as it increases its scale. This amounts to saying that a single firm can produce the entire supply of the product more cheaply than can two or more smaller firms. Natural monopolies have economies of scale that are large relative to the size of the market. In a small town, the birthing unit in one hospital is considered a natural monopoly, if two smaller-scaled units increase per unit costs.

Government often grants an exclusive franchise to firms thought to be natural monopolies and then regulates fees in order to pass cost savings (from large-scale production) on to clients. Most utilities (electric, water, natural gas, etc.) fall into this category. Many economists are skeptical as to whether natural monopoly characteristics exist over a long period of time. We should question, "Do these industries really need exclusive franchises and regulated fees?"

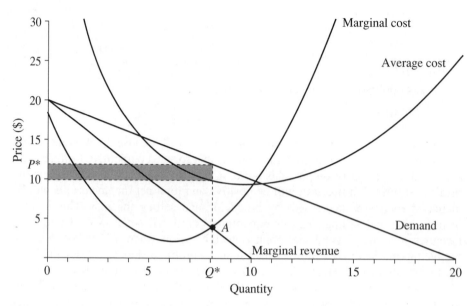

Figure 7.7   A profit-maximizing monopolist. Like all firms, the monopolist maximizes net income/profit by producing the level of output ($Q*$) at which $MR = MC$ (see point A). The profit-maximizing price is then found from the demand curve as $P*$.

Much conventional wisdom about monopolies is not true. Figure 7.7 demonstrates this. Note the point at which a monopolist maximizes profit; this point always falls in the elastic range of the demand curve. Straight-line demand curves are elastic in the upper left-hand half and inelastic in the lower right-hand half. The monopolist always operates in the elastic range because the firm will maximize profit where $MR = MC$, and MC is always positive. Further, when marginal revenue is positive, the price elasticity of demand is elastic. So it would be incorrect to say, as many do, that a monopolist's demand curve is inelastic – that the monopolist can raise price and retain most clients. In fact, a monopolist allowed to operate freely will limit production to the elastic range of its demand curve.

It is also clear from Figure 7.7 that a monopolist does not always charge the highest price the firm can command (that such firms do charge the highest price is perhaps the most common criticism of monopoly). Clearly, in Figure 7.7 there are many prices above $P*$ that the monopolist could choose to charge, say, $16. But the monopolist will *not* choose to charge that price because the firm's profit would be less at that price.

We can also see from Figure 7.7 that monopolists do not *always* make a profit. Suppose the AC curve were $5 higher at each level of output. Then, the monopoly would suffer a loss. The classical cellist in a small town may be a monopolist but cannot cover costs at any performance level, and must pursue opportunities elsewhere. If a short-run loss continues, monopoly firms exit the market. The monopoly firm pictured in Figure 7.7 is, however, earning economic profit, and is expected to remain in the market indefinitely.

7.5   FEE/PRICE REGULATION

What is the solution to monopoly provision in the NFP sectors? Should a monopoly private nonprofit clinic or utility in a small isolated town be shut down? Obviously, no. Would costs per client increase if the clinic were required to spin off into two clinics? Perhaps, depending on the shape of the long-run average cost curve and the number of potential clients. Does it make economic sense to nationalize the clinic and make it part of a state system? Not necessarily. Should the clinic just be left alone and permitted to operate as a monopoly? Over time, monopolies earning profit experience increased competition. Meanwhile, should it be publicly regulated?

Whenever monopolies are regulated, the task is performed by one or more government agencies "in the public interest." Although it is not our purpose in this chapter to provide an exhaustive discussion of regulation, we will look at how a regulatory agency might determine monopoly fees. The objective of a regulator is to make the industry operate in such a manner that the fees and output are closer to those that would evolve if the industry were competitive. Generally, this means reducing monopoly profits and/or improving the allocation of resources.

To illustrate the concepts involved, let's use the diagram shown in Figure 7.8. The diagram represents, for example, the cost curves of an electric power monopoly. Without regulation, the firm makes the profit-maximizing decision to price at P_1 and sell Q_1 units (the price and quantity for which $MR = MC$).

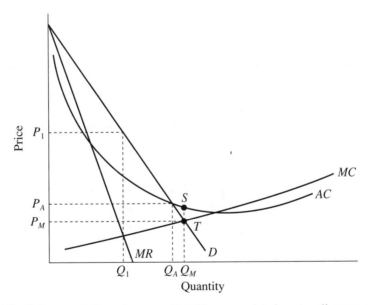

Figure 7.8   Price regulation of monopolist. The unregulated monopolist sets price at P_1 to maximize profits and sells Q_1 units. A regulatory agency that follows the "fair rate of return" criterion sets price at P_A, consumers purchase Q_A units, and the firm obtains zero economic profit, since price equals average cost. For an optimal allocation of resources, it could be argued that the regulatory price should be P_M.

What would regulators see as the "right" quantity of output and price? The most common approach to regulatory pricing is to establish a price that would allow the regulated firm a "fair rate of return" on a risk-adjusted basis. This *fair rate of return* is an opportunity cost concept and ensures that the firm covers all cost, including a normal rate of return. The fair rate of return price is, then, the price that equals average cost. Recall that average total cost includes all expenses plus the opportunity cost of using a firm's resources in this activity. The fair rate of return price is shown as P_A in Figure 7.8. At the price P_A, clients purchase Q_A units, and the average cost of providing that many units is $AC_A = P_A$. Since average cost is equal to price, net income is zero and there are no profits or losses. If economic profit is zero, a fair rate of return is achieved. The regulated firm obtains just a "fair rate of return" equal to total costs. Comparing this result with the unregulated profit-maximizing monopolist, we observe the following:

The regulated fee/price is lower: $P_A < P_1$

The regulated quantity is greater: $Q_A > Q_1$

Guaranteeing a "fair return" results in low client prices and large output, but it presents a serious problem. It provides little incentive for a firm to cut costs and regulators do not have access to information from rival firms on feasible costs. Application 7.4 proposes a solution.

APPLICATION 7.4
AT&T and the FCC: A New Approach to Regulation

Economic logic does not always reign triumphant in public policy choices – but it does sometimes.

Economists scored a victory when the Federal Communications Commission (FCC) moved to a new approach in regulating rates charged by AT&T.

Recall that monopoly firms charge high prices, produce too little output, and earn above-normal profits in the long run. Therefore, regulatory agencies typically focus on a fair rate of return to the firm's assets. If a firm can demonstrate that its rate of return is "too low," it can qualify for a rate increase.

There are problems with this approach. First, it focuses on average, not marginal, costs and thus makes no effort to achieve the efficient solution. Second, it requires that an agency be able to determine what a "fair" rate of return might be. Third, it's impossible to compute with any precision what a firm's assets are worth. Even internal data provide an arbitrary estimate; by inflating asset value, a regulated firm can ensure higher profits.

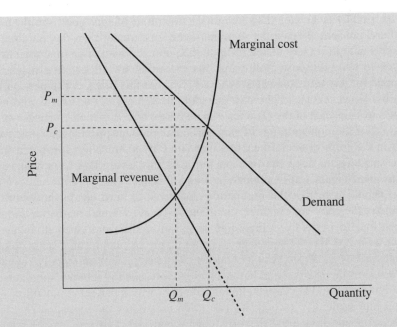

Regulation and the monopolist

A profit-maximizing monopolist charges price P_m and produces Q_m. If a regulatory agency imposes a maximum price of P_c the marginal revenue curve becomes the heavily shaded horizontal line. Output rises to Q_c.

A regulated firm, guaranteed a normal return, has little incentive to reduce costs. A firm that succeeds in lowering its costs has higher profits – and will be ordered to slash prices enough to get profits back where they were. In 1988, however, the FCC adopted an approach to its regulation of AT&T; it was proposed by William Baumol of New York and Princeton Universities and by Robert Willig of Princeton. It sets a relatively simple price cap for the company, such as P_c in the figure. Under the new system, if a firm can cut its costs below the price cap, it gets to keep the profits.

Source: *The Margin*, November/December, 1989, 14.

It is sometimes suggested that society would be best served if the regulatory decision-makers set price equal to marginal cost. The point where $P = MC$, you may recall, represents allocative efficiency. This type of regulation (i.e., price equals marginal cost) mimics pricing in a competitive market. Very briefly, the argument is that price js a measure of the marginal benefit people get from consuming a product. Thus, it follows that as long as price (or fee plus per unit subsidy in the

case of a NFP) is greater than marginal cost, more of that good should be produced and consumed since the marginal benefit is greater than the marginal cost.
The net benefit to society increases up to the point at which price (marginal benefit)
is equal to marginal cost. Following this reasoning for allocative efficiency, the
best price for the regulatory agency to set is P_M. At this price, consumers purchase
Q_m units. However, given the cost schedule in Table 7.8, the firm would have a
loss of S to T on each of the Q_m units, since average cost is that much greater than the
price, P_M. If the consumption of this particular product provides positive externalities in the form of social benefits, there may be justification for increasing the
public subsidies to keep the firm operating at this level. This argument is often
used to justify mass transit regulation with subsidies.

You should note that the regulatory objectives of zero net income/profit plus
allocative efficiency are obtained simultaneously and without regulation in perfect
competition. In perfectly competitive long-run equilibrium, seen in Figure 7.5,
$P_2 = AC$ and $P_2 = MC$. There are zero economic profits, and resources are optimally
allocated. Thus there are serious concerns associated with monopoly regulation.
First, even in theory, the regulation of monopoly cannot achieve simultaneously
both a fair return and allocative efficiency both of which perfect competition approximates automatically. Second, we ask, "Who regulates the regulators?"

Whenever possible, why not offer clients choice? This can be done through
fostering competition and/or providing subsidies or vouchers for use at a variety
of firms, public or private. The lingering concern is that market competition may
be too slow a mechanism in punishing inefficient or dangerous NFP firms. Will
vouchers and subsidies, received by NFPs, be used to further agendas not acceptable to society as a whole? Will firms delivering inadequate service be driven out?
Unfortunately, loosely monitored inefficient NFPs tend not to exit the market as
quickly as profit-seeking firms. Competition alone remains a powerful but imperfect monitoring mechanism in the NFP sectors.

Rent-seeking

While monopolies set higher prices and restrict output compared with competitive
markets, these may not be the greatest social cost of monopoly power. Recall that
monopolies come about and remain active for long periods because of effective
entry barriers. Effective entry barriers are almost exclusively the result of government
action. Beneficiaries of entry barriers have a powerful incentive to lobby government to grant and maintain them. On the other hand, the general public has little
incentive to exert themselves against a specific barrier. Even when the total harm
caused by the barrier is great, each individual is not affected enough to take on
the cost and bother of working for their removal.

The beneficiaries, i.e., firms that gain monopoly power, extract *economic rents*
as a result of entry barriers. Economic rent accrues to the owner of a resource whenever its return exceeds its opportunity costs. In one sense, it is a payment to a resource
owner that is not necessary to keep that resource in its particular employment.
Economic rent is not bad if it triggers a response in the market, encouraging new
firms to enter the market. Such economic rent will ultimately increase output, lower
price, and be self-eliminating. The term ***rent-seeking,*** on the other hand, is used

to describe behavior in a setting where individual efforts to maximize economic return lead to social waste rather than social surplus. Suppose a monopoly hospital spends resources in trying to get the city council to block the entry of a competing hospital. This rent-seeking behavior leads to social waste. An organization with much to gain will lobby to maintain its benefits. The general public has weak incentive to oppose. It is this pursuit by individual firms to the gains of monopoly power through law and government that we call rent-seeking.

Consider the situation in which the government for whatever reason grants monopoly power. Perhaps, exclusive cable television rights are awarded to a particular company. Perhaps, the federal government allocates television broadcast franchises for a particular market area. Or, a state university earns the exclusive right to certify students in a certain profession. The exact situation is unimportant. The recipient of this exclusive (or near exclusive) franchise can expect to earn monopoly returns. Presumably, if a particular firm spends more money, time, and effort lobbying for the exclusive franchise, it has a better chance of being the chosen company. Because monopoly returns can be quite substantial, a lobbying war results.

Only a single firm will actually receive the monopoly franchise. Yet, a large number of firms enter the lobbying war in the hope of being the chosen company. All the time, money, and effort expended by these companies will be wasted except for a single winning firm. Each firm is acting rationally, seeking to maximize its own return, but the total expenditures of the lobbying war will be wasted in the sense that consumers will be no better off with a particular monopoly firm than with any other monopoly firm. Any monopoly firm is in a position to extract the maximum from clients. Thus, lobbying by prospective monopolists is a deadweight loss to society.

There has been some discussion in economics about the size of this deadweight loss to society. Is the deadweight loss larger or smaller than the loss to consumers resulting from the higher prices and restricted quantities of the monopolist? This is an interesting question and current opinion has the costs of rent-seeking being considerably larger than what is commonly thought to be the standard costs of monopoly power (that is, higher prices and restricted quantities).

7.6   FEE/PRICE DISCRIMINATION

In economic jargon, *price discrimination* is usually termed *monopoly price discrimination*. That label is appropriate because price discrimination cannot occur in perfectly competitive equilibrium. *Monopoly power must be present in a market for price discrimination to exist.* This seems a trivial point when you understand the definition of **price discrimination**: the practice of charging different prices to various consumers for a given product. Universities price discriminate when they charge different rates of tuition. Grants, which effectively reduce the price for some students, differentiate between students on the basis of merit or family incomes. In a competitive market, consumers would simply buy from the cheapest seller, and producers would sell to the highest bidders, and that would be that. In our competitive daycare example, a provider is unable to charge higher-income parents more than others because of the easy option of transferring the child to another daycare provider. In less competitive industries, such as hospitals, NFP administrators negotiate with third party payers such as insurance companies or Medicare to charge less. In these instances, they engage in price discrimination to increase net income and thus shift costs to other clients.

With monopoly power, a firm offers different terms (of which price is only one component) to different purchasers, thus dividing the market, a practice known as market segmentation. Or it may be possible for the firm to charge many prices to a single purchaser by creating a price schedule such that the consumer pays a different price for each block of purchases, a practice called *multipart pricing*. The ultimate in the ability to engage in price discrimination is termed ***first-degree (or "perfect") price discrimination***, in which a different price is charged for each unit sold to each customer. This form of pricing charges the client the maximum amount he or she is willing to pay for each unit; the supplier captures all consumer surplus. What is the maximum you would pay for a soft drink right now? How much for an appendectomy if you had acute appendicitis? While first-degree, or perfect, price discrimination is not common, milder forms of price discrimination abound.

For one example, consider utilities, which in most areas of the United States charge a different kilowatt-hour price for different customers: households, farms, businesses, and so on. Consider a theater charging different prices for matinees and evening performances. A number of opportunities for potential price discrimination are presented in Table 7.1.

True price discrimination exists whenever the price differences do not reflect cost differences. For instance, an insurance company may require a medical examination of its prospective customers and, based on that examination, charge people in poorer health higher rates than people in good health. Clearly, the insurance company is charging different prices, but the firm's future costs in serving the policy will be different. We must be certain in identifying price discrimination that the goods sold at different prices are truly identical. In order to do so, we must reference the marginal cost: if the marginal costs of providing insurance to the two customers differ, then the goods are not the same, and the situation is perhaps not a true case of price discrimination. However, if the difference in the marginal costs of provision is not proportional to the difference in prices charged (such as premiums), then it is a case of price discrimination. Note that charging different prices for two seemingly identical products may not be price discrimination. Therefore, some of the examples listed in Table 7.1 may not represent true price discrimination. The test then is whether the differences in the marginal costs of provision are in proportion to the differences in prices charged. For example, if a full-time undergraduate is charged $20,000 per semester and part-time students are charged $10,000 for an equivalent number of credit hours, then the cost of university provided services to full-time students should be double those provided to part-timers. Otherwise, full-time students could rightly claim price discrimination.

We should also be careful to note that not all price discrimination is necessarily undesirable. Price discrimination may perform a desirable service by allocating a scarce resource over some base, such as time or geographic location. A university is better able to utilize its facilities by discounting tuition for evening classes in

Table 7.1   Representative situations conducive to price discrimination

Type	Basis for discrimination	Examples of goods and services in which suppliers charge different prices/fees
Individual or personal	Ability to pay in terms of income, wealth, or amount of insurance	Natural gas, electric, and telephone prices for residential versus corporate customers; senior citizen discounts at theaters, supermarkets, etc.; physicians' low fees for needy patients
	Relatives and friends of wealth and fame, trade classification	Jobber and wholesale discounts; club purchasing; lower credit and interest rates for friends
	Personal appearance, habits, mannerisms, health, size, weight, skill level	Conditions of purchase requiring a tie, shoes, cleanliness, no swimming or sports attire; different insurance premiums based on health
Group membership	Age, sex, race, religion, marital status, military status, employer, club	Group life insurance; special prices on student football and basketball tickets; "corporate days" at amusement parks; charter bus and airline trips; free senior citizen public transportation in off-peak hours; low video rental rates for members; Medicare client
	Geographic location	Higher prices for purchasers living outside the country, state, city limits, or zone; base-point pricing; out-of-state/in-state student tuition differences
	Use of product	Transportation rates based on size, weight, and value of goods shipped; use of milk for drinking, making ice cream, and processing cheese
Product classification	Qualities of product	Relatively higher prices for gourmet foods and drinks, stylish clothes, fine furniture, deluxe models and accessories, and full- versus part-time tuition
	Labels and trademarks	Low prices on generic products
	Quantities of product	"Buy-two-get-one-free"-type offers; quantity discounts
Time sequencing	Time of day	Lower electric rates during midnight to early morning hours; golf course greens fees
	Season of year	Low motel rates during the off-season; high costume rentals near Halloween

which traditional students would not enroll. The term price discrimination, then, has a neutral connotation when used in this context.

We will discuss the three forms of price discrimination in turn: (1) market segmentation, or third-degree price discrimination; (2) multipart pricing, or second-degree price discrimination; and (3) perfect, or first-degree price discrimination.

Third-degree price discrimination

Third-degree price discrimination, or market segmentation, requires that the seller be able to (1) segment, or separate, the market such that goods sold in one market cannot be resold by the buyers in another; and (2) identify distinct demand curves with different price elasticities for each market segment.

An example of such a market could be a campus bookstore. These stores may sell items to students at one price and the identical items to faculty at different (lower) prices. The individuals in each market segment are easily identified by an ID card, and their price elasticities are usually quite different (higher price elasticities for faculty). The price differential must not be enough to make it worthwhile for faculty to buy at their lower price and then resell to students at a higher price! Providers of medical services (doctors, dentists, hospitals, etc.) commonly charge different prices to different customers, who would clearly find it difficult to resell the product (consider, for example, trying to resell a dental fluoride treatment). Theaters sell tickets to children at lower prices than they do to adults (and few adults can enter on a child's ticket).

The question confronting the seller when market segmentation is possible is how best to take advantage of the separate markets. The seller may wish to maximize profits, but what price should be charged in each market in order to accomplish this?

If a seller has a certain quantity of output to sell and wishes to allocate it between two separate market segments, what information is relevant? First, realize that this is a revenue maximization problem; maximizing revenue in this case is the equivalent of profit maximizing because the costs remain the same regardless of which market segment gets more product. Revenue can be maximized by dividing the output between the two markets in such a way that marginal revenue is the same in both markets. Let's look at a very simple example that involves just two markets, both being served by a single plant.

In Figure 7.9, the separate demand curves for each market segment are labeled D_A for market segment A and D_B for market segment B. The marginal revenue functions, of course, are MR_A and MR_B. Since the two demand curves have different slopes, at each price, the elasticities differ in the two market segments.

The marginal revenue curve for the total market (MR_T) is shown in the right-hand frame of Figure 7.9 as the horizontal summation of the two market segment marginal revenue curves ($MR_A + MR_B$). Total output (Q^*) is set where this marginal revenue (MR_T) equals marginal cost at point T. The marginal cost curve is simply the marginal cost curve for the entire firm regardless of where its output is sold.

The firm thus decides to produce and sell Q^*. Now, it must decide how to allocate Q^* between market segment A and market segment B. At any level of Q, the

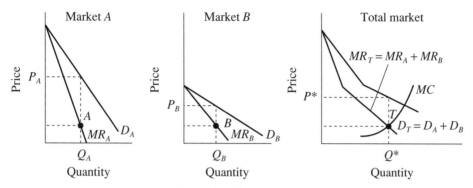

Figure 7.9   Third-degree price discrimination: market segmentation. In this model, the demand and marginal revenue functions for submarkets A and B are added horizontally to get the total market demand (D_T) and marginal revenue (MR_T). The optimum rate of output (Q^*) is found where $MC = MR_t$. Those Q^* units are allocated to the submarkets such that $MC = MR_T = MR_A = MR_B$, and the products are priced from the market segment demand curves $(D_A$ and $D_B)$. Thus, we find for markets A and B the price-quantity combinations P_A, Q_A and P_B, Q_B, respectively. If the firm simply aggregates the market instead of segmenting the market, the price P^* is charged for all Q^* units. Consumers in market A then buy more, consumers in market B buy less, and net income/profit is lower. (Demonstrate this for yourself by drawing a horizontal line from P^* through each market segment and noting where that price line crosses each demand curve.)

seller wants to allocate output in such a way that the marginal revenue is the same in both market segments $(MR_A = MR_B)$. If this was not true, the seller could increase revenue by reallocating more units to the market segment with the higher marginal revenue and fewer units to the market segment with the lower marginal revenue. Thus, the optimality condition is

$$MR_A = MR_B$$

The firm pictured in Figure 7.9 would then produce Q^* units in total and sell Q_A in market segment A and Q_B in market segment B. The prices in each market segment would be set with reference to the demand curve in that segment. Thus, price P_A would be charged in market segment A and price P_B in market segment B.

The key to Figure 7.9 is the curve labeled MR_T (the horizontal summation of the separate marginal revenue curves, $MR_A + MR_B$). It is the intersection of this curve with the marginal cost curve that determines the optimal output $(MR_T = MC)$. The segmenting of the optimal output is then determined from the market segment marginal revenue curves $(MR_A$ and $MR_B)$ such that MR_A and MR_B both equal MC at the same level as $MR_T = MC$. This is found by drawing a horizontal line from the point T across to each submarket. Where this line intersects the MR_A and MR_B curves (points A and B, respectively) determines the appropriate allocation to each submarket $(Q_A$ and Q_B, respectively).

Finally, fees/prices are determined by reading up from the quantities Q_A and Q_B to their respective demand curves (D_A and D_B) and then over to the vertical axes where we find the prices P_A and P_B. In this example, market segment B has the greater price elasticity and so receives the lower price, P_B. The market segment with the more elastic demand always receives the lower price. In other words, clients with the higher elasticity are charged lower user fees even though the cost of producing the services is the same for the other group of clients.

Market segmentation explains the phenomenon of different prices for residential students and faculty in college bookstores. The bookstore has considerable monopoly power with students on campus but much less power with faculty, who may do more shopping off campus. With many stores competing for faculty members' purchases, their demand tends to be much more elastic. If the bookstore is able to separate the students from the faculty, it is generally more profitable to charge a lower price to faculty than to students. It may not be fair but it is the logical outcome of any firm wishing to maximize its profits and able to successfully discriminate between two sets of clients.

Second-degree price discrimination

Second-degree price discrimination is also referred to as multipart pricing. It is a block, or step, type of pricing in which the first set of units is sold at one price, a second set at a lower price, a third set at a still lower price, and so on. Note that this is different from a quantity discount in which the lower (discounted) price applies to all units purchased. In second-degree price discrimination, the lower price applies only to units purchased in that block. The buyer must have already paid the higher price for the earlier units. Some familiar examples should make this clear:

Electricity

In many parts of the country, residential electricity users are billed at different rates for different blocks of consumption. For example, the first 100 kilowatt-hours may be priced at $0.062 per kilowatt-hour, the next 100 kilowatt-hours may be priced at $0.059 per kilowatt-hour, and everything over 200 kilowatt-hours may be priced at $0.057 per kilowatt-hour. This is an example of three-block second-degree price discrimination. You cannot buy the second 100 kilowatt-hours at the lower price until you have already purchased the first 100 at the higher price.

Long-distance phone calls

When you make a long-distance phone call, you are sometimes charged a higher rate for the first three minutes than for subsequent time. It is impossible to buy just the second three minutes of a phone call. You must first have used the initial three minutes. This is second-degree price discrimination.

First-degree price discrimination

Economic theory tells us that if demand curves are negatively sloped and if price is a reasonable measure of a consumer's marginal benefit from purchasing a good, there will be a consumer's surplus when all units of the product are priced the same. That is, we often get more than we pay for in terms of satisfaction. This means, in turn, that we may have been willing to pay more than we are actually charged.

Suppose, for example, that it is a hot summer day and you have just finished your daily three-mile run. You come upon a lemonade stand where you can buy a glass of cold lemonade for $0.25. You drink one, then another, then a third. And you have spent $0.75. But you very well might have been willing to pay $0.50 or $0.60 for just one glass of that cold refreshment. If the seller knew something about your demand, he or she could have sold you the three glasses of lemonade at perhaps $0.60, $0.40, and $0.25, respectively. After all, we do know that a third glass was worth at least $0.25 to you. The seller would then have captured some of your consumer surplus and received $1.25, rather than $0.75.

Perfect, or first-degree, price discrimination occurs when a firm knows the maximum price that each individual is willing to pay for each successive unit. Each appendectomy client, for example, is charged the maximum that he or she would be willing to pay for the service . . . or face the grim alternative. Board members and the financial officer of a private high school could practice first-degree price discrimination by meeting privately with each parent to negotiate tuition in terms of what the family could afford. The firm is then charging the highest price for each successive unit and capturing the entire consumer surplus. Recall that all forms of price discrimination involve some monopoly power, but perfect price discrimination involves a degree of monopoly power rarely found in the real world. The degree of monopoly power determines the length of time such a situation could exist.

Peak-load pricing

Peak-load pricing is a type of third-degree price discrimination in which the discrimination base is related to the time when the service is provided (temporal). We single out this particular form of price discrimination in part because of its widespread use. But remember that all forms of third-degree price discrimination, including peak load pricing, involve a seller attempting to capitalize on the fact that buyers' demand elasticities vary. In the case of peak-load pricing, customer demand elasticities vary with time.

Most utilities experience regular fluctuations in demand creating peak load problems. Natural gas utilities are expected to have sufficient capacity to meet demand during cold winter months but need only a fraction of that capacity during the warmer summer months. City water departments are frequently pressed to capacity during warm and dry periods. The telephone communications industry also has a regular pattern of peak and low demand. During business hours, cell towers are very busy compared to the load during the rest of the day. Similarly, universities experience lower demand during the summer.

Peak-load pricing can be economically efficient, if it directs limited capacity in favor of those who are willing to pay more and rewards those making an effort to use the service at off times.

CONCLUDING NOTES

- Firms may be categorized into industries providing a particular service. An industry's market is any place or means by which the process of exchange occurs.

- NFP firms face competition affecting preferred as well as less favored activities. They compete on the basis of quality, price, and reputation with each other and for alliances with profit-seeking entities. In certain industries, profit-seeking firms are at a disadvantage compared to firms in the NFP sectors operating with tax preferences and donor/taxpayer subsidies.

- Generally, the fee/price charged as well as the output provided by a NFP firm is affected by industry competition. Ease of entry, the bargaining power of buyers, the availability of substitutes, rivalry, and suppliers of inputs determine the degree of competition in a given industry.

- The firm's profit maximizing rule (producing at that output where marginal revenue is equal to marginal cost) is independent of the competitive structure of an industry.

- Perfectly competitive and monopolistic industries are theoretical models. Most industries are characterized by imperfect competition, combining aspects of competition and monopoly. Competition is a dynamic process with client tastes and supplier constraints constantly changing.

- Only in perfectly competitive markets can we expect natural economic forces to lead to productive and allocative efficiency. If a NFP firm operates in a perfectly competitive market, its fee tends toward an equilibrium fee established in that industry. Because each provider's products are perfect substitutes, a single firm offers its entire output at market price. The process of firms entering and leaving the industry reduces each firm's earnings to a normal return; net income/profit is zero.

- Allocative efficiency is achieved in perfect competition because the fee charged plus per unit subsidy, representing the value of the service to the client/donor, equals marginal cost, representing society's cost in providing the product.

- In monopoly, there is a single seller. The firm's demand curve is identical to the market demand curve and as such has a negative slope. Thus, the administrator of any monopoly has significant control over price and the quantity sold. An unregulated monopolist can have positive net income/profit in the long run, as long as there exists a significant entry barrier.

- Much inefficiency associated with NFP firms is due to their monopolistic power rather than their NFP status. A government franchise to any type of firm, profit-seeking or NFP, is the most enduring entry barrier.

- A natural monopolist exists wherever per unit costs are lowest when one firm produces total industry output. Government often grants an exclusive franchise to firms thought to be natural monopolies and then regulates their fees.

- The regulatory objective is to make the industry's price and output similar to that which would prevail if the market were competitive. It is unlikely in theory or practice that regulation can achieve both a fair return and allocative efficiency simultaneously. Monopolies are regulated "in the public interest," usually with the intent of limiting profit. A common regulatory criterion is the fair rate of return doctrine, indicating that price should be set equal to average cost.

- Price discrimination between clients is not effective if a firm's cost of segmenting clients is high or if clients have other choices.

- Peak load pricing is a type of third-degree price discrimination, and in cases in which there is no marginal cost difference between peak and off-peak use, peak load pricing is an exact application of third-degree price discrimination.

KEY TERMS

Market	Monopoly
Profit-maximizing rule	Natural monopoly
Basis for competition	Fair rate of return
Monopsonies	Rent-seeking
Perfectly competitive market	Price discrimination
Free entry and exit	First-degree price discrimination
Standardized product	Third-degree price discrimination
Price taker	Second-degree price discrimination
Normal return	Peak-load pricing

SUGGESTED READINGS

Baumol, W. J. 1977: *Economic Theory and Operation Analysis*, 4th edn., Englewood Cliffs, NJ: Prentice-Hall.
Bork, R. H. 1978: *The Antitrust Paradox: A Policy at War with Itself*, New York: Basic Books.
Clark, J. M. 1961: *Competition as a Dynamic Process*, Washington, DC: Brookings Institution.
Cohen, K. and Cyert, R. 1975: *Theory of the Firm*, 2nd edn., Englewood Cliffs, NJ: Prentice-Hall.
Demsetz, Harold 1982: "Barriers to Entry," *American Economic Review*, March, 47–57.
Henderson, J. M. and Quandt, R. E. 1980: *Microeconomic Theory: A Mathematical Approach*, 3rd edn., New York: McGraw-Hill.

Stigler, G. J. 1957: "Perfect Competition, Historically Contemplated," *Journal of Political Economy*, February, 1–17.

Tuckman, Howard P. 1998: "Competition, Commercialization, and the Evolution of Nonprofit Organizational Structures," *To Profit or Not to Profit: The Commercial Transformation of the Nonprofit Sector*, 25–46, ed. Burton A. Weisbrod, Cambridge, UK: Cambridge University Press.

END OF CHAPTER EXERCISES

Exercise 7.1

Explain why price (*P*), marginal revenue (*MR*), marginal cost (*MC*), and average cost (*AC*) are equal for a perfectly competitive firm in long-run equilibrium. Why do we say that the perfectly competitive firm is a "price taker"? Draw one graph showing *P*, *MR*, *MC*, and *AC* for a perfectly competitive firm that makes a positive net income/profit, and draw another graph with these curves showing a negative net income/profit. In each case, explain the adjustment process leading to zero net income equilibrium. Draw the same four curves in a third graph so as to illustrate equilibrium.

Exercise 7.2

Draw average revenue (demand), marginal revenue, average cost, and marginal cost curves for each of the following situations:

    a.   Perfect competitor with a positive net income/profit.
    b.   Perfect competitor with a negative net income/ profit.
    c.   Monopolist with a positive net income/profit.
    d.   Monopolist with a negative net income/ profit.

Write a brief paragraph explaining each of the four graphs. Also explain what, if anything, might be expected to happen in each case changing the situation you have depicted (for example, the existence of positive net income/profit).

Exercise 7.3

Which of the following firms or professions is likely to be able to price discriminate? Explain why you answer as you do and indicate the basis for price discrimination in each case. Which groups of clients do you think would be charged the higher price in each situation? Why?

    a.   University.
    b.   Physician.
    c.   Soft-drink producer.
    d.   A college-sponsored daycare center.
    e.   Concert promoter.
    f.   University bookstore.

Exercise 7.4

How is first-degree price discrimination similar to second-degree price discrimination, or multipart pricing? Physicians often charge older and younger patients smaller fees than other patients. Do you suspect this is because physicians wish to help those groups? What kind of price discrimination are physicians engaging in?

Exercise 7.5

The allocation of duplication services in one university is accomplished by allocating users a certain amount of "play money" each month. Users pay for jobs on the systems according to a schedule of prices:

Overnight processing: 2 times the base rate.
"When computer idle" processing: 3 times the base rate.
"End of cue" processing: 1 times the base rate.
"Priority" processing: 2 times the base rate.
"Immediate" processing: 5 times the base rate.

a. Could this type of peak load pricing be an efficient way to distribute mainframe resources even though no real money is used? Would the demand curve for duplicating services be negatively sloping?

b. What type of price discrimination would you call this? What problems would be encountered in administering this system? What other resources could be allocated in a similar manner?

Exercise 7.6

Electric utility rates are usually set by a utility after approval by some government body; requests for price increases and/or changes are often the subject of heated debate. The rate schedule given here is typical in many respects of utility rate schedules for residential users:

	Winter rate	Summer rate
Fixed charge	$1.50	$1.50
First 100 kilowatt-hours	0.030	0.030
101–500 kilowatt-hours	0.025	0.025
501–1,000 kilowatt-hours	0.022	0.023
1,001 + kilowatt-hours	0.015	0.020

The difference between the winter and summer rates is a form of peak load pricing designed to discourage extensive use of electric air conditioning.

a. What is the average price for a household that uses 1,200 kilowatt-hours in the winter? In the summer?

b. If a household in winter purchases 1,500 kilowatt-hours, how much would it pay in total? How much would the same household pay if all kilowatt-hours are charged at the $0.015 rate? Is price discrimination evident here?

Exercise 7.7

Explain how the concept of price elasticity is related to peak load pricing. What are some examples of goods or services that you believe represent examples of this type of pricing policy?

Exercise 7.8

Q	MC	ATC	TC	AVC
2	4.88	6.44	12.88	4.94
4	4.78	5.64	22.55	4.89
6	4.69	5.34	32.03	4.84
8	4.62	5.17	41.34	4.79
10	4.55	5.05	50.50	4.75
12	4.50	4.96	59.54	4.71
14	4.45	4.89	68.49	4.68
16	4.42	4.84	77.37	4.65
18	4.41	4.79	86.20	4.62
20	4.40	4.75	95.00	4.60
22	4.41	4.72	103.80	4.58
24	4.42	4.69	112.63	4.57
26	4.45	4.67	121.51	4.56
28	4.50	4.66	130.46	4.55
30	4.55	4.65	139.50	4.55
32	4.62	4.65	148.66	4.55
34	4.69	4.65	157.97	4.56
36	4.78	4.65	167.45	4.57
38	4.89	4.66	177.12	4.58
40	5.00	4.68	187.00	4.60
42	5.13	4.69	197.12	4.62
44	5.26	4.72	207.51	4.65
46	5.41	4.74	218.19	4.68
48	5.58	4.77	229.18	4.71
50	5.75	4.81	240.51	4.75

Q = Quantity; MC = Marginal cost; ATC = Average total cost; TC = Total cost; AVC = Average variable cost.

a. If this is a single firm in a competitive industry, what price must prevail for the industry to be in long-run equilibrium?
b. Suppose that there are 100 firms identical to the one depicted in the table. Plot the supply curve for the entire industry for a range of prices.

Exercise 7.9

You are employed by a hospital that has succeeded through some innovative contracts in dividing its market into three distinct segments; each segment is completely sealed off from the other. The demand curves for the hospital's output are

Customer group 1: $P_1 = 63 - 4Q_1$ $MR_1 = 63 - 8Q_1$,

Customer group 2: $P_2 = 105 - 5Q_2$ $MR_2 = 105 - 10Q_2$

Customer group 3: $P_3 = 75 - 6Q_3$ $MR_3 = 75 - 12Q_3$

where P_1, P_2, and P_3 are the prices charged in each market, Q_1, Q_2, and Q_3 are the amounts sold in each market. The hospital's total cost function is

$$TC = 21 + 16Q \qquad MC = 16$$

where

$$Q = Q_1 + Q_2 + Q_3$$

a. Suggest what the hospital's pricing policy should be, assuming the hospital is a profit maximizer.
b. How many units of output should be allocated to each market? What prices should be charged?

Exercise 7.10
Assume the hospital in Exercise 7.9 has a changed cost function:

$$TC = 21 + 16Q + Q^2 \qquad MC = 16 + 2Q$$

What quantities of product are now allocated to the three groups of customers?

Exercise 7.11
Compare the long-run equilibrium of competitive and monopoly firms. What are the differences in their long-run equilibrium positions? Explain in terms of productive and allocative efficiency.

Exercise 7.12
A "natural monopoly" usually exists only for some finite period of time; natural monopolies do not exist forever. Are there some real-world examples of this phenomenon? Does government stifle the decay of a natural monopoly by granting a franchise to a particular group?

Exercise 7.13
A monopolist has no supply curve. The supply curve for a perfectly competitive firm shows the relationship between the price the firm receives for its output and the quantity of that output it is willing to supply; but no such curve can be drawn for a monopolist. How can this be explained?

Exercise 7.14
A monopoly firm has the following total cost and demand functions:

Total cost: $TC = 100 + Q^2$ $\qquad MC = 2Q$

Demand: $Q = (600 - P)/4$ $\qquad MR = -8Q + 600$

What quantity of output will the firm produce? What price will it charge for the output? What profits will it earn? If the government limited this monopolist by imposing a $200 price ceiling on the product, how would the firm react? What would be its new price, output, and profit?

Exercise 7.15
Price discrimination in the sale of services (college credit, haircuts, airline fares, physicians' fees, etc.) is far more common than price discrimination in the sale of goods. Explain why.

Exercise 7.16
If larger firms produce goods and services at lower average costs, why do economists argue that monopolies are inefficient? Discuss the potential trade-off between increasing client choice with more providers and higher per unit costs.

Exercise 7.17
Is a comprehensive secondary school offering a full range of athletic, music, vocational, academic, and counseling services a natural monopoly? Explain.

Exercise 7.18
In what sense are elementary education and childbirth delivery standardized services? Does differentiating services necessarily increase per unit costs? Third-party payers, such as government or insurance companies, paying a set amount for a given service increase standardization. Discuss and give an example of how NFPs providing differentiated services can compensate for set payments?

Exercise 7.19
Advertising increases costs and indirectly fees paid by sponsors, clients, or taxpayers. If one institution advertises, its competitor may have to advertise as well in order to survive. Should tax-sponsored or subsidized firms be permitted to advertise in order to increase clients? Does advertising artificially increase the demand for subsidized services? Discuss.

Exercise 7.20
What premium above competitive price are clients willing to pay for a differentiated service? Provide an example. In this case, to what extent are potential clients willing to trade off quality in purchasing a differentiated or geographically convenient service?

Exercise 7.21
Oligopolies are characterized by sticky prices. Discuss whether price rigidity in the NFP sectors is due to imperfect competition? Discuss the extent to which NFP firms can pass increasing costs onto client fees? Are user fees set in terms of what the market will bear? Do administered prices requiring legislature or board approval follow or anticipate inflation?

Exercise 7.22
Does competition play a role in providing discipline to firms operating in the NFP sectors? Describe how this works in the delivery of a particular service.

Exercise 7.23
Discuss and provide an example of the potential trade-off between higher per unit costs and more competition in a particular NFP industry.

Exercise 7.24
Provide an example of a discriminating NFP monopolist charging two different user fees to different groups of clients. What circumstances enable the firm to do this? Does this increase the total amount of the service provided as compared to charging the same fee to all clients?

8
Selecting the Right Niche and Setting Client Fees

8.1 INTRODUCTION

Profit-seeking firms strive to be efficient not because they have an intrinsic desire to do so, but because competitors take advantage of them if they are not. There is always another firm waiting in the wings to do a better job. Even in markets with few firms there is the threat of new entrants. Potential competition exists as well in nonprofit and government industries but cannot be counted on to move these sectors toward efficiency or even effectiveness. NFP firms often work in markets without competition and are subsidized.

Theoretically, mission driven NFP administrators should be pleased if other firms enter into their respective industries and should even be willing to collaborate with them. After all, with the entry of new firms output expands and the social mission is furthered. More output, on the other hand, increases supply and equilibrium client fees decline, making if difficult for a particular NFP firm to pay expenses. But not-for-profit managers, again theoretically, do not set fees to generate maximum revenue but, rather, to support expenses. Ignorance concerning the competitive environment may work out well for a few government agencies and perhaps highly endowed nonprofits. In practice, however, NFP administrators are called on to make daily decisions about output and user charges/fees. Recall that user fees represent what the client pays out-of-pocket or through private third parties and total charges include these fees plus the amount billed per unit to sponsors. This chapter continues exploring the competitive environment in which NFPs operate with respect to pricing (fee setting).

Much revenue earned by NFP firms comes in the form of user fees, and its lenders and employees expect to be paid. In this chapter, we first consider the decision to enter into a particular market and then the setting of realistic user fees, the "price" of output produced in government and nonprofit firms.

8.2   PRODUCT DIFFERENTIATION

Most industries fall in the broad middle ground between perfect competition and monopoly. Within this range economists define two market structures known as *monopolistic competition* and *oligopoly*. Monopolistic competition is closer to the perfectly competitive end of the spectrum of market structures, while oligopoly is toward the monopoly end. The degree of competition in the NFP industry determines the control a firm has over fees charged.

In monopolistic competition, there are many sellers. Monopolistically competitive firms compete in industries that sell products that are similar, yet differentiated, and entry into the industry is relatively easy. The firm has some control over price due to product differentiation, which may be actual or simply perceived. For example, some might be willing to pay more for essentially the same service in a religiously affiliated elder care facility compared to a for-profit facility. The success of a wide variety of nonprofit colleges and universities illustrates the range of client preferences. These consumer preferences present the firm with a negatively sloped demand curve for differentiated services. Thus, if the firm raises fees, some clients remain; this would not be the case for a perfectly competitive firm. A particular university can get away with charging more in tuition than others as long as some clients prefer the slightly different product it offers. Given the large number of close substitutes, however, monopolistically competitive demand curves tend to be relatively elastic over a considerable range. In other words, some clients substitute the services of one NFP firm for another as fees increase. Within limits, then, a firm can set a fee and retain clients. Because of product differentiation, university tuition varies between institutions for similar degrees. If fees become excessive, clients abandon their loyalties to certain NFP providers and markets create substitutes. Administrators of NFPs ignore at risk the potential competition of profit-seeking and other institutions providing similar services for lower fees.

Monopolistically competitive profit-seeking industries tend toward long-run equilibrium in which zero net income/profit is the rule. Whenever there is the opportunity to earn net income (economic profit), new firms enter the industry. This reduces or eliminates economic profit. The opposite dynamic results when there are negative economic profits (losses). Higher education in the United States approaches the conditions of a monopolistically competitive market with many firms, free entry, and a differentiated product. It is likely, therefore, that institutions remaining in the market merely cover their expenses, neither earning net income nor a normal return on assets. NFP mission driven institutions do not have to earn the normal return on assets required by profit-seeking firms.

An *oligopoly,* representing another imperfectly competitive model, has few firms relative to total market demand. In the NFP sectors, two hospitals providing service to a whole community are considered oligopolies. Oligopolistic institutions recognize their mutual interdependence. Game theory analyzes this interdependence. Equilibrium prices in competitive industries are constantly changing; this is not so in oligopolies. The "stickiness" of price observed in oligopolistic industries may be due to mutual interdependence. In industries where firms have some control over price, prices change slowly, because competitors meet most declines in price and ignore raises. Application 8.1 discusses various hypotheses on how firms set fees/price.

APPLICATION 8.1
Sticky Prices

Blinder used a novel method to deduce how profit-seeking firms set prices – he asked them! Economists usually watch what people actually do, rather than what they say they do, in order to understand their behavior. However, Blinder translated a number of pricing theories into plain English and then asked managers whether their pricing policies corresponded to these descriptions. Blinder's purpose in this research was to explain a question that has troubled the economics profession for some time: Why are businesses so slow to change their prices when economic conditions change? Stable day-to-day prices are more understandable in the NFP sectors. Government agencies like the U.S. Postal Service need prior approval for rate increases, and private nonprofits are reluctant to pass on increased costs to needy clients. However, we observe that firms in all sectors maintain "sticky prices," even when costs and inflation in general are increasing.

Blinder finds that many firms change prices only once a year, or not at all. Three-quarters of the companies surveyed change their prices two times a year or less. Even when expenses and client demand change appreciably, businesses often wait three or four months before changing prices. It would seem that a profit-maximizing firm could clearly benefit from rapid adjustments to market conditions.

Blinder divides the responses of his surveyed firms into three categories: those explanations that are given most often as the actual reasons for sticky prices; those reasons that are sometimes given; and, finally, those reasons that are losers in what economist Robert Gordon of Northwestern called a "beauty contest among theories."

Winning theories

Winning theories were:

1   *Changing terms*. When demand is strong, firms have a tendency to cut back on freebies or delay delivery, rather than raise prices to take advantage of increased demand.
2   *Implicit contracts*. In order to maintain relationships, firms have an "invisible handshake" with customers to keep prices steady, such that, even when demand is increasing, they do not raise prices.
3   *Coordination*. Firms are lax to raise prices due to uncertainty about competitors' reaction.
4   *Costs*. Firms base prices on costs rather than demand and cost increases take time to work their way through the system.

Mediocre theories

Mediocre theories were:

5   *Explicit nominal contracts*. Firms have explicit contracts that preclude price changes in the short run.
6   *Price adjustment costs*. Changing prices involves costs, such as printing new price sheets, advertising the new price structure, etc.
7   *Pricing points*. Clients have assumptions or "pricing points" that firms need to consider in changing price.
8   *Procyclical elasticity*. Businesses are uncertain about long-run elasticities, the lagged response of quantity demanded to price changes.

Losing theories

Losing theories were:

9   *Hierarchies*. According to this theory there are many people in each firm who must sign off on a price change, and this process is a slow one.

Selecting the Right Niche and Setting Client Fees 269

10 *Constant marginal cost.* The perception on the part of firms that they have constant marginal costs prevents them from responding to external stimuli.

11 *Inventories.* Firms monitor inventory changes and then change prices to achieve desired inventory levels.

12 *Quality.* Firms are reluctant to cut prices because clients view price cuts as cutting quality (about one-half of the firms in Blinder's study said prices reflect quality, but only one-quarter agreed that it is an important issue in changing prices).

The issue of sticky prices is relevant to the NFP sectors as well. Private nonprofit contracts, such as those between hospitals and health maintenance organizations, are negotiated infrequently. Higher fees are often assessed on new clients only, such as tuition increases for first-year students.

Source: Alan Blinder, "Why Are Prices Sticky?," *American Economic Review*, 81 (2), 1991, 89.

Cartels evolve in oligopolistic industries and would be much more common if such formal arrangements to set price were not illegal in some countries such as the United States. A *cartel* is a group of firms that collude and thereby function as a monopoly. When cartels are formed (legally or illegally), their objective is to impose monopoly control over the market. If a few firms cooperate completely, they can generate the same profit as a monopolist. If two hospitals in a small town claim they are cooperating to keep cost down, clients beware! Economic theory suggests that they are colluding to impose monopoly control over the market. To judge whether or not the community benefits by an agreement between two local hospitals to divide specialties between themselves, we must answer several questions. Will two hospitals pass on cost savings from reduced expenses for specialized equipment into lower client fees? Will the one hospital, now guaranteed all clients seeking a particular service, continue to invest in that specialty? Do the cost benefits of one hospital not duplicating the services of another out-weigh the benefits of firm rivalry?

At first, cartel arrangements appear desirable to firms, because industry net income/profits are indeed maximized. However, cartels lead to other problems that contribute to their dissolution. Consider a cartel agreeing to a certain amount of output in order to maintain high prices. A state university system may decide to target and limit the number of students pursuing teacher training on all branch campuses; this is like a cartel. NFPs generally justify cartels in terms of maintaining quality. The cartel may allocate only a very small amount of production (or possibly none) to some firms, leaving them with high average costs and low (or possibly negative) net income/profit. These firms then have an incentive to break from the cartel, setting a price slightly below the cartel price to increase their own clients, thereby weakening the cartel. Larger firms in the cartel may attempt to put pressure on the central committee (or governing board of the cartel) for preferential treatment in the allocation process. In addition, there is always incentive for firms to "cheat" on the cartel by offering lower fees, or, in the case of universities, lower entrance requirements, because each firm perceives its demand under these conditions as being very price elastic. Such price cutting reduces the level of overall cartel net income/profit/quality and can be expected to weaken the cartel, perhaps leading to its eventual breakup.

Price leadership

Cartels lead to an equalization of prices within an industry. Even less formal arrangements than a cartel may lead to similar (or identical) prices charged in an oligopolistic setting. One such arrangement is price leadership. In price leadership the leading firm is usually one that has developed successful pricing strategies in the past. Other firms are willing to follow that firm's lead rather than do price analysis themselves saving time and expense. In addition, following the leader reduces friction and uncertainty in the marketplace. The barometric price leader, testing the market climate, is not necessarily the largest firm in the industry. But such a leader must have a proven record of successful operations in order to develop a following of other firms respecting its policies enough to continue to match the price signals it offers.

NFPs can have one large firm dominating an industry. Such a firm often functions as the price leader for the entire industry. This is known as dominant-firm price leadership. Again the price leader sets the industry price and then allows the other (now smaller) firms to sell what they wish at that price. In both types of price leadership the followers behave as though they were perfectly competitive. They become price takers.

Commercial banking provides perhaps the best example of price leadership. Although commercial banking is in the profit-seeking sector, its pricing policies are critical to firms in the NFP sectors borrowing funds. Banks compete with one another in making loans, but most of the competition is nonprice competition, such as advertising and bonuses for opening an account. The prime interest rate (the rate banks charge on loans to large corporate customers) tends to be the same across all of the major banks, as shown in the following example. When one of the major banks lowers its prime rate other banks follow fairly quickly. Consider one period of falling rates and the speedy sequence that occurred (see table).

Date	Bank	Rate change
Mid-December	Manufacturers Hanover	11.25 ⇨ 10.75
One day later	Bankers Trust	11.25 ⇨ 10.75
Two days later	All others	11.25 ⇨ 10.75
Mid-January	Manufacturers Hanover	10.75 ⇨ 10.50
One day later	All others	10.75 ⇨ 10.50
Mid-March	Bankers Trust	10.50 ⇨ 10.00
One day later	Citibank and Chase Manhattan	10.50 ⇨ 10.00
Two days later	All others	10.50 ⇨ 10.00

This example illustrates price leadership in one particular service industry. The next time you hear a news report about a bank lowering its prime interest rate you might want to watch *The Wall Street Journal* over the next several days to see if other banks follow.

Whenever one NFP firm assumes the role of a price leader, such as raising tuition, others follow closely even if the respective administrators did not enter into an explicit agreement to collude. A study of tuition increases at elite universities in the United States follows a similar pattern. Seldom do we observe a major university lowering tuition or increasing it at a higher rate than rivals. This suggests that universities behave somewhat like oligopolies following a price leader.

8.3   GAME THEORY AND NFP STRATEGIC BEHAVIOR

Oligopolies engage in strategic decision-making. Consider a town with two competing universities offering programs in business administration. As an administrator of one of the programs, will you advertise for students? Will your competing university advertise? What will be the effect on your enrollment if they advertise and you do not? To deal with such questions, we turn to a branch of mathematical analysis called game theory which studies decision-making in conflict situations. Such a situation exists when two or more decision-makers (competitors) with different objectives act on the same system or share the same resources. Game theory provides a mathematical process for selecting a best strategy (that is, an optimum decision or an optimum sequence of decisions) in the face of an opponent who has a strategy of his or her own. For example, a community hospital can use game theory to analyze the effects on net income of initiating a new program in alternative oriental medicine when the rival NFP hospital in town either does or does not open up a similar program.

The key link between economics and game theory is rationality. Economics is based on the assumption that human beings operate rationally in their own best interest. Game theory, in addition, assumes that firms can calculate probabilities of their competitors' choices and respond accordingly. Application 8.2 shows how the Federal Communications Commission estimated the demand for radio frequencies to determine their auction strategies.

APPLICATION 8.2
Game Theory Helps Sell the Electromagnetic Spectrum

In late 1994 the Nobel Memorial Prize in Economics was awarded to three pioneers of game theory. The prize, awarded to John Nash of Princeton, John Harsanyi of the University of California at Berkeley, and Reinhard Selten of the University of Bonn, was jointly awarded because each played a role in creating the foundations of game theory. The film *A Beautiful Mind* is based on the life of John Nash.

Economic theory has been dominated by the concept of perfect competition – competition with many participants and no dominant buyers or sellers. This conception of the real world has been useful in predicting the outcomes of market economies and market-like situations. However, game theory has changed economics since the late 1980s by shifting the focus of study from markets with thousands of buyers and sellers to situations in which there are only a few buyers and sellers with a great deal of give and take.

Game theory applications received a test in December of 1994 when the Federal Communications Commission (FCC) auctioned off radio licenses for new wireless communications services. The FCC auctions opened bidding in the first-ever auction of licenses to use the electromagnetic spectrum. Bidding in this auction was for licenses in the narrowband Personal Communications Service (PCS), expected to be used for advanced paging and data transmission services such as two-way pagers and networked palmtop computers.

The FCC wanted to raise as much money as possible with the auction, at least $10 billion, and used game theory to help it achieve its goal. The FCC had to predict how each bidder would respond, lacking full information as to what a particular frequency was worth. The FCC had to consider the possibilities of buyers strongly or weakly demanding space and its own policy of charging relatively high or low prices for use of the same space. Then, the FCC had to calculate revenue raised for each combination of possible outcomes in order to develop its sales strategy.

In economic theory, rational decision-makers have information about costs and can estimate demand. Choices are made and outcomes follow depending on the market in which the firm operates. Interactions with other individuals or firms and their responses to decisions are generally ignored. Firms consider only their own situation and "conditions of the market."

Game theory, on the other hand, is intended to analyze agents interacting directly with one another and affected by one another. It addresses serious interactions using the metaphor of a game. The single important assumption in game theory is that the outcome for a given NFP firm depends not just on what strategy it chooses, but also on what strategies competitors choose (Gardner, 1995).

Game theory, therefore, is complex, because the outcome depends not only on my own strategies but also directly on the strategies chosen by others. However, the problem is still a rational choice problem in figuring out what options individual firms choose when it is possible to estimate the behavior of interacting decision-makers with different possible outcomes.

Most of the early work in game theory concentrated on the simplest of all games, a zero-sum game. A zero-sum game is a situation in which every possible outcome of the game results in a total value of zero when you add the winnings (losses) of the players. Clients or net income gained by one institution are lost to another. Consider the game of football. There are only three possible outcomes to a game:

1   *A* wins (+1 for *A* in the won/lost column) and *B* loses (−1 for *B*).
¹/₂   a draw (each team gets a 0 in the won/lost column).
¹/₄   *B* wins (+1 for *B*) and *A* loses (−1 for *A*).

In every one of the cases the sum of the outcome values is zero. Zero-sum games are just a special case of a wider class of games called constant-sum games. In constant-sum games the outcome values always add up to the same amount.

Consider a game in which there are two players, each selling a similar product; suppose two small town hospitals share the market for childbirth deliveries. Each firm may use one of two advertising mediums, television or magazine advertising. The outcome of importance is market share. Each makes its decision on advertising independently. Firm 1 has an advantage in using television advertising, while firm 2 has an advantage in using magazine advertising. When both firms use television (represented in Figure 8.1 in the upper left-hand corner), firm 1 receives a 55 percent market share and firm 2 a 45 percent share. Likewise, when both firms use magazine advertising (represented in Figure 8.1 in the lower right-hand corner) firm 1 receives a 45 percent share and firm 2 a 55 percent share. If firm 1 uses television while firm 2 uses magazine advertising, the outcome favors firm 1 by 52 percent to 48 percent. If firm 1 chooses magazine advertising while firm 2 uses television, the market is evenly divided.

We can solve this simple constant-sum game by using the convention of attaching arrows to indicate the preferred option of the various choices. For instance,

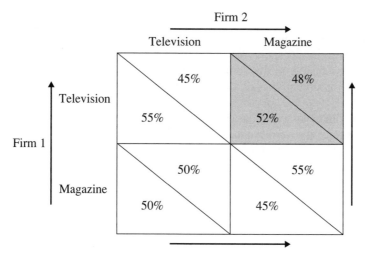

Figure 8.1   Game theory. Firm 1 chooses television advertising and captures 55 percent of market share when its opponent also chooses television. If, however, its opponent chooses magazine advertising, it captures 52 percent. The percentages in the upper triangles of each box represent firm 2's market share. In this example, each firm has a dominant strategy.

the arrow pointing up on the left of the diagram indicates that firm 1 would rather use television and have a 55 percent share or 52 percent share *regardless of what firm 2 does*. This is called a **dominant strategy**, whereby, regardless of the option chosen by a rival, one option is in the firm's best interest. The arrow on the bottom of the diagram pointing toward the right indicates that firm 2 would rather use magazine advertising and receive a 48 percent share rather than 45 percent *when firm 1 has a dominant strategy*.

In this game there is only one situation which both arrows point to and that is in the upper right-hand corner where firm 1 uses television and firm 2 uses magazine advertising. This is the shaded box. This represents equilibrium for this game because neither firm is willing to adopt another strategy from the equilibrium position. The equilibrium is then the pair of strategies which is the solution to the game.

Very few economic situations can be represented by simple one-round constant-sum games, where one or both players have a dominant strategy. The analysis of game theory goes far beyond such simple games and game theory provides a rich understanding of much of economic reality.

8.4   THE PRISONER'S DILEMMA

Consider a NFP application of game theory in the area of criminal justice. This game is called the "prisoner's dilemma." We begin with a short description of the situation. Suppose two suspected criminals, both carrying concealed weapons, are apprehended near the scene of a burglary. The two are placed in separate interrogation rooms and questioned. The interrogator prefers that each simply confess that they are indeed the burglars. The game is modeled in Figure 8.2, using the same conventions we used in Figure 8.1.

If both prisoners confess, each will get a sentence of 10 years in jail; if each clams up and say nothing they can only be given a sentence of one year each for carrying concealed weapons. But one may confess at the same time as the other clams up; this results in the confessed burglar (who has agreed to testify against her partner) receiving no jail time while the soon-to-be convicted burglar gets 20 years!

Using the arrow conventions, it would appear that both burglars would confess; this appears to be the equilibrium. But there appears now to be a discrepancy between the rational choices of each individual taken separately and the rational choice for the two burglars taken together, each considering the response of the other. What appears to be rational for each person (confessing), appears to be irrational when viewed jointly (implicitly colluding by clamming up). This is a remarkable result for game theorists and it has led to some very interesting analyses. Are there any real-world situations which mimic the prisoner's dilemma?

Many coalitions we might expect or even hope for in the real world never actually occur – just as in the prisoner's dilemma. The nuclear arms race with many countries each trying to outdo the other at great expense is such a case. Why don't the "players" collude and choose the rational group choice (i.e., the lower right-hand corner in our diagram)? Asking similar questions in the context of game theory has turned to consideration of what affects the formation and stability of

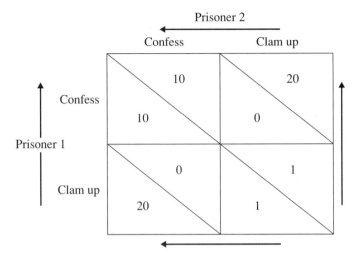

Figure 8.2   Prisoner's dilemma. Collusion with both clamming up reduces the amount of time that each prisoner spends in jail, but each faces 20 years in jail if the other confesses. Do you believe that each prisoner has a dominant strategy to confess?

coalitions. Competing hospitals might enter into an agreement one year to collude on fees charged for a normal delivery (prohibited by U.S. law in the profit-seeking sector). However, collusion can backfire. What happens in the next round of the game, if one or the other hospital reneges on the agreement and charges lower fees?

8.5   A REVENUE MAXIMIZATION MODEL

Maximizing total revenue is not the same as net income (profit) maximization. In fact, net income/profit can decline even as revenue continues to increase. For example, the hotshot new manager of the museum's coffee shop could increase sales with a dynamic and expensive marketing campaign. Total revenue in the coffee shop would increase but not necessarily net income/profit (revenue minus expenses). This is an issue if net income/profit from the coffee shop is expected to cross-subsidize the museum's collection. Per unit costs are not constant and are likely to increase as output increases. NFP firms, unfortunately, are inclined to maximize revenue, unless subject to a minimum net income/profit constraint on unrelated business enterprises. Revenue maximization may be rational if a high sales volume makes it easier for a firm to obtain capital, or if it produces a better image with clients, employees, suppliers, or distributors. Revenue maximization for retaining or expanding staff is not necessarily rational if the expansion results in reducing focus on a firm's mission. NFP firms, more so than profit-seeking firms, are more likely to increase output and maximize revenue, even when this behavior reduces net income generated from a particular activity expected to cross-subsidize preferred mission related projects.

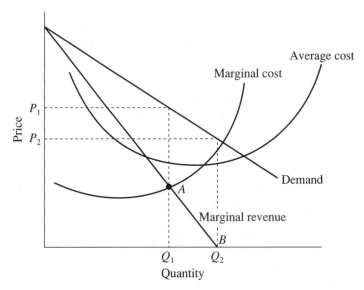

Figure 8.3   Sales revenue versus profit maximization. A net income/profit-maximizing firm produces at Q_1 determined by the equality of marginal revenue and marginal cost (see the point marked A). This rate of output can be sold at price P_1, as determined by the demand curve. A revenue-maximizing firm's management wants to produce and sell additional units as long as marginal revenue is positive. It increases quantity up to Q_2, where marginal revenue is zero, and sells this output at price P_2.

The determination of price and output under the alternative assumptions of net income/profit maximization as compared with revenue maximization is illustrated in Figure 8.3. Note that the negatively sloped demand curve implies that the firm has some control over price and is imperfectly competitive. The price-output combination that maximizes net income/profit is shown as P_1 and Q_1, determined by the intersection of marginal revenue (MR) and marginal cost (MC). However, the price-output combination in **revenue maximization** is achieved when marginal revenue is zero and is represented by P_2 and Q_2 in Figure 8.3.

Note that this revenue-maximization solution is determined by finding where marginal revenue is zero (see point B in Figure 8.3). At this point, the price elasticity of demand is unitary. For a linear demand curve, if demand is elastic, a decrease in price results in an increase in total revenue, and if demand is inelastic, a decrease in price causes a decrease in total revenue. Thus, revenue is maximized by setting price where demand is unit elastic.

8.6   THE MACMILLAN MATRIX

In the profit-seeking sector, firms that cannot make a normal profit in the long run are forced to exit the market. A similar mechanism does not exist in the NFP sectors, when taxpayers/donors subsidize programs indefinitely. However, certain programs are a drain on scarce resources and should be discontinued. What if a

MacMillan Matrix		Program is very attractive to funders and/or community participants		Program is not attractive to funders and/or community participants	
		Several organizations offer similar programs	Few/no organizations offer similar programs	Several organizations offer similar programs	Few/no organizations offer similar programs
G o o d f i t	High organizational capacity and credibility	1 Keep and compete	2 Keep and grow	5 Keep and collaborate	6 Keep and subsidize
	Weak organizational capacity and credibility	3 Give away to other organizations	4 Grow your capacity or give away	7 Give away to other organizations	8 Collaborate or stop

Figure 8.4   MacMillan Matrix: a tool used for classification of programs.
Source: Adapted from: Community Technology Centers' Network, "Tool–MacMillan Matrix," *Ctcnet Guide Access to Action*, www.ctcnet.org, April 4, 2007.

NFP firm offers a program earning less than cost over a long period of time with declining client interest? Or suppose the program barely covers cost plus subsidy? Alternative programs offer more potential. The MacMillan Matrix, developed by Prof. Ian MacMillan of the University of Pennsylvania, is a tool designed to assist strategic NFP decision-making in selecting the correct niche with respect to specific programs. Potential programs are categorized in terms of mission, comparative advantage, and donor/client support. A modified MacMillan Matrix, presented in Figure 8.4, deals indirectly with two of this chapter's topics, namely competition in NFP industries and the amount of revenue needed to cover cost. In the matrix, a program consistent with NFP mission is considered a "good fit." A program compatible with the expertise, experience, and reputation of the organization is thought to be one for which the organization has "high organizational capacity and credibility." Finally, programs are categorized as either "attractive" to donors and clients or "not attractive."

Most NFPs are multi-product firms operating several programs at the same time. Those responsible for strategic thinking are called to periodically review existing and potential programs. Each program can be placed in an appropriate MacMillan cell according to the three criteria as well as the degree of industry competition. Note that a particular program may not be considered attractive in terms of revenue but could represent a preferred mission activity in which the firm has expertise and experience. As such, it would be placed in cells 5 or 6 in Figure 8.4 and a decision must be made to cross-subsidize the activity within the organization (cell 6) or find an existing organization with which to collaborate (cell 5).

The MacMillan Matrix, as it is sometimes presented, assumes that a NFP should avoid duplication of services and exit an industry in which it is not a dominant or least cost provider. Specialization in providing services seems to make sense in that resources are limited and some organizations can provide them better and at lower cost. However, this ignores the fact that competition generally benefits clients. There is a strong case for programs falling into cell 3 in Figure 8.4 to consider leaving the industry. However, consider cell 7 in Figure 8.4. It may be in the best interest of the individual firm to leave the market, but doing so will probably disadvantage some clients, such as those living nearby and benefiting from the subsidy. There is an additional concern associated with collaboration between providers, such as that suggested in cells 5 and 8. U.S. anti-trust law forbids profit-seeking firms from colluding on price, and restrains universities, hoping to prevent a bidding war on scholarships, from sharing information about specific desirable applicants. Is collaboration in the NFP sectors in the interest of clients? Or is it merely a type of price fixing? Competition on price and between firms certainly reduces both the net income/profit and revenue of NFP firms, but it may also reduce fees and increase the number of clients served. In addition, NFP competition provides valuable information on costs needed to produce the service. With multiple providers, administrators are forced to answer the question, "If a competitor can provide the service at that fee, why can't you?" Regulators can only guess at legitimate costs in the case of a monopoly provider.

Overall, the McMillan exercise encourages self-knowledge and honesty in answering questions about mission preferred activities, the capacity of programs to sustain themselves, and the skill of an organization in providing the intended service. A major benefit is that the McMillan Matrix encourages strategic planners to consider exiting from certain donor/taxpayer subsidized markets and reallocate resources to projects yielding higher value.

8.7   COST-PLUS PRICING

In the day-to-day operations of many firms, fee setting does not mirror theoretical pricing practices. This is not to say that the pricing models we have reviewed thus far are not useful. Rather, we recognize simple "rules of thumb" employed in the real world and suggest that some are *similar* to theoretically correct practices. In practice, the cost of becoming "theoretically perfect" may outweigh small enhancements to revenue. One of the most widely used rules of thumb used in pricing is *cost-plus pricing*.

At first glance, this approach seems very simple. With **cost-plus pricing**, the firm needs only to determine the cost of producing a unit of output and then price it at that cost *plus* some markup. The actual process in use, however, is really much more complex. The firm must decide what costs should be included, at what volume of output the costs should be determined, and how large a markup is appropriate. These problems are addressed in this section.

For our discussion of cost-plus pricing, let's consider a nonprofit medical foundation that is planning to market a product, donated whole blood. These blood products could be packaged in a cold pack, which is a double-walled container with

Table 8.1   Preproduction investment costs in providing blood packs

Research and development	$75,000
Plant and equipment	150,000
Preproduction overhead	50,000
Training of blood collection personnel	12,000
Training of distribution personnel	4,000
Certification expenses	9,000

a chemical mixture between the walls that provides an endothermic reaction (a reaction that causes a reduction in temperature) upon opening.

Determining costs

In determining relevant costs in pricing a given-sized blood pack (we shall simplify the problem by assuming that only one size is produced), the cost-plus method takes into account expenditures that go into a product before it is ready for market. Expenditures include the cost of research and development, investment in plant and equipment, special training costs for medical and distribution personnel, promotional activities, and the cost of obtaining certification. These costs are summarized in Table 8.1.

How should the information on costs in Table 8.1 be used to determine the fee per blood pack charged? The question evokes disagreement, particularly between economists and nonprofit accountants. Both agree that the cost of plant and equipment should be depreciated (or replaced as used), but beyond this point, they often do not see eye to eye. Economists view the training of production and sales personnel as an investment in human capital that will also yield a stream of benefits to the firm over some period of years. Research and development expenditures have always been difficult to evaluate and allocate. However, without these expenditures, blood packs would not be available and they thus represent a direct investment in the product. Therefore, all costs in Table 8.1 should be included in the analysis.

Costs discussed thus far are of a fixed nature; that is, the expenses will not vary as the volume of output changes. Other fixed costs typically charged to the production of blood packs include the salaries of medical personnel, such as the manager assigned to the project, and salaries of liaison persons handling this product exclusively. These costs also include insurance on the building, equipment expenditures, and the overhead charge to cover this product's share of firm administrative expenses.

In addition to all of the above fixed costs in producing and marketing blood, the firm also incurs direct variable costs for each blood pack. The most important are direct labor costs, the cost of materials used in collecting blood, the carrying cost for inventory, the charges for general supplies, and utility costs. This group of expenses is directly related to the volume of output and, in this example, we will assume a fairly constant per unit average cost.

Table 8.2   Unit cost of blood packs for three projected levels of sales

	Sales (units)		
Costs	8,000	10,000	12,000
Variable costs			
Labor	$1.50	$1.50	$1.50
Materials	0.30	0.30	0.30
Inventory	0.20	0.20	0.20
Supplies	0.20	0.20	0.20
Utilities	0.10	0.10	0.10
Total variable costs per unit	$5.00	$5.00	$5.00
Fixed costs			
Depreciation	$2.50	$2.00	$0.17
Salaries (collection manager and sales)	3.75	3.00	2.50
Insurance	0.25	0.20	0.17
Taxes	0.10	0.08	0.07
Overhead	3.50	3.50	3.50
Total fixed cost per unit	10.10	8.78	7.91
Average total cost	$15.10	$13.78	$12.91

Table 8.2 summarizes the firm's estimates for all costs (fixed and variable). Each of the columns represents a different projected annual output volume. Note that the average total cost per unit is different for each level of output. This illustrates one of the important difficulties in using costs to establish the product charges: the unit cost changes as the quantity produced varies. The data given here implies decreasing per unit costs as volume increases.

Determining the rate of output

Unit cost of blood packs depends on the scale of production in Table 8.2. What quantity should the firm use in establishing the unit cost? Most firms routinely use a "standard or normal" level of output set at 70 to 80 percent of capacity. In this NFP example, the firm may have no historical data, so per unit cost estimation is based on subjective forecasts of the demand for blood.

The depreciation costs in Table 8.2 are simplified somewhat for illustrative purposes. A straight-line depreciation of all the investments in Table 8.2 over a 15-year period has been applied. Overhead has been figured as 70 percent of unit variable costs. Using this method to determine the charge for general corporate overhead, we see that it could act like a variable cost.

The problem is further complicated because the expected annual sales will be to some extent a function of the fee charged; thus, to determine fee from cost seems to be putting the cart before the horse. Nonetheless, showing general corporate overhead as a type of fixed cost is preferable since it represents a way of allocating fixed corporate costs (such as the administrator's salary) that are not directly chargeable to any product.

Determining the markup

If we assume that the most likely sales volume is 10,000 units per year, we can proceed with a cost-plus determination of the fee. Thus, we approach another critical problem: Plus what? Often the percentage markup is determined by industry tradition. That is, in many cases a standard markup is established outside the firm. If no standard is clearly appropriate for a given product, the firm must ask what return on investment is necessary to attract the funds needed for the project. The manufacturers of blood packs need an initial investment of $300,000 as indicated in Table 8.1.

For our present example, suppose that the standard markup is 12 percent. For a sales level of 10,000 units, the average total cost is $13.78. The firm's fee would then be $13.78 times 1.12 (i.e., 112 percent), or $15.40 per unit. If this firm wished to establish a markup designed to achieve a specific return on investment (that is, a target rate), they would determine the desired rate of return and convert it to a dollar amount. That amount divided by the volume of output is the required dollar markup per unit. Assume, for example, that the firm desires to earn an average rate of return of 20 percent on its investment of $300,000. This implies a target net income/profit rate of $60,000. Note that in this formulation the net income/profit is really just a return on a firm's assets (normal profit) as compared with excess/economic profit. With the expected output rate of 10,000 units, the normal return per unit must be $6.00. Adding this to the average total cost per unit at that level of output, the target rate of return fee is $19.78 (or $19.80) per unit. A target fee/price such as this may be used as a guide and adjusted up or down depending on demand conditions, corporate objectives, extent of competition, and other factors.

Should price ever be below cost?

Note carefully how important the determination of the *relevant costs* is for the pricing decision. To illustrate this importance, assume that blood packs are a success and that the foundation produces approximately 10,000 units per year, as anticipated. In addition, assume that the clinic was built to handle at least 12,000 units and thus there is excess capacity available. Given these conditions, suppose that a new hospital contacts the foundation with an offer to purchase 1,000 *extra* units per year at a fee of $12.50. Should the foundation accept this offer at a fee that we have determined to be less than the cost plus normal return price? In fact, $12.50 is less than average total cost.

The answer is yes *as long as there is no effect on existing or future regular sales.* The *relevant costs* now consist only of the variable production costs. The fixed costs have been fully allocated to the existing level of production and will not change. The desired rate of return on the capital investment is being achieved. Thus, if the added revenue from sales exceeds the additional cost of producing those 1,000 units, the foundation will find the venture profitable. This variant of cost-plus pricing, based only on the additional revenue and costs, is called **incremental analysis** and may be appropriate to any decision of this type.

The incremental cost for the new contract is total variable cost per unit ($5.00) times the number of units (1,000), or $5,000. The incremental revenue is the fee $12.50 multiplied by 1,000 units, or $12,500. The firm, therefore, increases its net income/profit by $7,500, even though the product is sold substantially below the original cost-plus fee and even below average total cost.

Disadvantages of cost-plus pricing

In whatever form it is used, cost-plus pricing has some clear shortcomings. First, the use of historic cost information rather than current cost data may set the price lower than the price necessary to achieve the firm's objective. Furthermore, this method of pricing overstates the ability of most firms to accurately allocate fixed costs among various products. In the blood pack example, this is somewhat less of a problem, since most of the fixed costs are directly attributable only to this product. The somewhat arbitrary allocation of corporate overhead is a manifestation of this problem. Most public administrators are keenly aware of the difficulties associated with assigning overhead costs to particular programs.

In addition, this type of fee-setting strategy is virtually useless if variable costs fluctuate significantly. Table 8.2 assumes that variable costs are constant at $5.00 per blood pack. Unless the producing firm is confident that existing (or forecasted) prices for materials and supplies, as well as labor cost, will remain stable for its planning horizon, the use of cost-plus pricing can be very expensive. Many suppliers of industrial products have built escalators into their pricing structures so that the actual price is the price at the time of delivery rather than at the time of sale.

Finally, cost-plus pricing does not take into account possible changes in demand. Basing price on cost may have little relationship to what consumers are willing and able to pay. This can result in the firm's being unable to sell the "standard or normal" volume at the established price, or the firm may have set the price too low to be able to meet additional demand instantly with new blood donations. Recall that the "standard or normal" volume at the established price is covering all the fixed costs and assumes that variable costs are constant. If the foundation is not able to supply additional units on the spot, ill-will may accumulate, affecting long-run demand.

Advantages of cost-plus pricing

Cost-plus pricing has advantages outweighing its shortcomings as evidenced by industry use of the practice. First, cost-plus pricing leads to relatively stable fees. For industries in which the output is used by others as a material input, price stability may be very important. Blood is an input into hospital services. Textbooks are an input into education. In negotiating contracts, many buyers prefer a stable price, since it reduces the time and expense they must exert in trying to get the best buy. Some managers may prefer a relatively high but stable fee to a somewhat lower but fluctuating price because that stability makes their own planning a little easier.

Cost-plus pricing may also make price increases more acceptable to clients. If the clients can be convinced that an increase in price is simply a reflection of increased costs, they are less likely to develop feelings of ill-will toward the seller. This rationale for fee increases has been used when material and resource costs have pushed up the prices of goods and services in periods of high inflation.

Also, cost-plus pricing is compatible with the objective of many firms to achieve a specified rate of return on investment. Obtaining a target return on investment is the dominant objective of many large firms and used for comparing alternative programs. A target rate of return was incorporated in the determination of a cost-plus price in the previous example for blood packs.

Finally, once the methods to be used in determining the relevant costs and markup are established, this fee-setting strategy becomes fairly simple. This alone may account for the widespread use of cost-plus pricing in many NFP firms.

8.8   ECONOMIES OF SCOPE

Most NFP firms produce more than one good or service. In some cases the products are joint products. One example of joint production in a NFP firm is concerts and lectures scheduled in a university auditorium and financed through student activity fees and general admission tickets. Education (lectures) and recreation (concerts) are jointly produced. Another example is when a national park sets aside acreage for both recreation and forest preservation. In these cases, the NFP is required to make price and quantity decisions about alternate goods. A community college allocates staff and facilities between college transfer and vocational students. The firm probably receives some production or cost advantages from the fact that it is producing two products rather than one. An *economy of scope* can be said to exist when the cost of producing two (or perhaps more) products at the same time is less than the cost of producing each one alone. *Economies of scope* benefits result in cost savings due to spreading overhead costs between products and/or to a reduction in marketing costs per product. Social service agencies generally provide a range of services out of the same facility. Additional advantage may result from joint production facilities or through the sale of a by-product. Economies of scope situations call for special treatment of product pricing.

Consider the actual case of a chancellor of a state university who agreed to increase each student's activity fee by $30 for one year to make up the athletic department's deficit. Several state legislators were concerned that the additional fee would become permanent and suggested instead that basketball tickets be increased by $3 each. The institution provides two different products: education and basketball entertainment. There are cost savings in providing both in the same institution. Should the user fee for each activity reflect relative costs of the two activities? Or, should more costs be shifted to those whose demand is relatively inelastic, i.e., those with less choice? These questions cannot be addressed without reference to the priority that each activity has to firm mission, the responsiveness of each set of clients to fee/price, and the extent to which one activity subsidizes the other.

8.9   PRICING IN THE PUBLIC INTEREST:
HOW PRICING CAN ALLEVIATE CONGESTION

Public agencies engage in setting fees/prices with certain desired outcomes. The goal may not be to maximize net income/profits, usage, or total budget. They may be seeking an objective external to the firm, such as protecting the natural environment.

The Puget Sound Regional Council (PSRC) in the state of Washington deals with transportation policy in the crowded Seattle region. They routinely take an economic modeling approach in order to analyze the effects of various pricing measures on the quality of life in the area. The regional council begins with an examination of the potential impacts of transportation pricing on travel behavior both in the short run and over time. They then review alternative modeling approaches for pricing. Finally, they produce an analysis of outcomes for a set of hypothetical pricing measures identified by the regional council and the study team. They use regression analysis to construct models that mimic the ways families use transportation. The reason for constructing the model is to forecast the effects of various state pricing strategies. Once the model is constructed and "calibrated," fees in the model are varied and results examined. If the model is accurate, these results will be the same as those expected if real-world fees change. The state could potentially adjust fees to reach desired goals. The PSRC model studied four potential *pricing concepts* for the Puget Sound region, including:

- *Congestion fees*. Congestion fees target certain highway spots. *Congestion fees* could vary hour to hour or day to day, or be set at levels in reference to "average" congestion (perhaps with seasonal adjustments).
- *Parking fees*. This fee could be a daily charge on all employees who do not currently pay for parking. Workers who drive alone to work would pay daily parking fees above some threshold level.
- *Fuel fees*. This fee is directed toward reducing fuel consumption and greenhouse gases.
- *Mileage fees*. This fee is aimed at reducing miles of vehicular travel in the region. The easiest way of collecting a mileage fee would be through an annual charge concurrent with vehicle registration, based on odometer readings.

An interesting result of their model is that when congestion decreases due to increased fees, higher-income individuals may actually drive more, purchase more cars, and move further away from work. All of this frustrates the environmental goals. What other results do such models produce? In the 1994 PSRC study, a 40 cent tax per gallon of gasoline was estimated to have the following effects on the target variables:

- Mileage decreased by 1.4 percent.
- Trip frequency decreased by 3.2 percent.
- Time of travel decreased by 3.6 percent.

In contrast, the model predicted far different results if a $2.00 per gallon tax on gasoline were used:

- Mileage decreased by 6.5 percent.
- Trip frequency decreased by 5.8 percent.
- Time of travel decreased by 6.4 percent.

The direction of change in the second set of results from the same model should not surprise anyone familiar with the law of demand, but the PSRC model not only indicates the direction of the changes but also the magnitude of the changes. Estimates of the magnitude of change make such models quite useful. Is such an increase in the gasoline tax (or such goals as a desired decrease in mileage driven) really in the public interest? The economic modeling is straightforward and value free, but the use of the information is not quite so straightforward and not so value free.

CONCLUDING NOTES

- Product differentiation, the hallmark of monopolistically competitive markets, represents NFP firms marketing to a particular niche. In oligopolistic industries, fees/prices are sticky and could follow the behavior of one firm, a price leader.

- Game theory is a mathematical process for selecting a best strategy in the face of an opponent with a strategy of his or her own.

- A bureaucracy, setting fees to maximize revenue, produces where marginal revenue is zero given a linear demand curve.

- A MacMillan Matrix assists multi-product organizations in strategic decision-making involving program choice.

- Cost-plus pricing is a common form of price determination based on the cost side of the ledger, with little attention to the effect of fees/price on demand. All explicit and implicit costs are included. Once the appropriate cost basis is determined, the correct markup is established. An industry norm can be followed, or a markup is set to achieve a specified rate of return.

- An economy of scope can be said to exist when the cost of producing two (or perhaps more) products at the same time is less than the cost of producing each one alone. The advantages that the firm receives from economies of scope are the results of cost savings because of spreading overhead costs over several products. The advantages may also result from a reduction in costs per product due to joint marketing programs.

- The desired outcome of public agencies in setting fees may not be to maximize net income/profits, usage, or total budget but rather an objective external to the firm, such as protecting the natural environment. They can do this by modeling the relationship between various fees and outcomes.

KEY TERMS

Monopolistic competition
Oligopoly
Cartel
Dominant strategy
Revenue maximization

Cost-plus pricing
Incremental analysis
Economies of scope
Pricing concepts
Congestion fees

SUGGESTED READINGS

Alliance for Nonprofit Management 2007: "How Can We Do a Competitive Analysis? Frequently Asked Questions," www.allianceonline.org/FAQ/strategic_planning, accessed April 4, 2007.

Bailey, Elizabeth E. and Friedlander, Ann F. 1982: "Market Structure and Multi-product Industries: A Review Article," *Journal of Economic Literature*, 20 (September), 1024–48.

Burck, Gilbert 1972: "The Myths and Realities of Corporate Pricing," *Fortune*, April, 85.

Clemens, E. 1950–1: "Price Discrimination and the Multiple Product Firm," *Review of Economics and Statistics*, 19.

Gardner, Roy 1995: *Games for Business and Economics*, New York: Wiley.

Griffin, James M. 1977: "The Econometrics of Joint Production: Another Approach," *Review of Economics and Statistics*, 59, 389–97.

Lovel, C. A. K., and Sicklen, R. C. 1983: "Testing Efficiency Hypotheses in Joint Production," *Review of Economics and Statistics*, 65, 51–8.

Panzar, John C. and Willig, Robert D. 1981: "Economies of Scope," *American Economic Review*, 71 (May), 268–72.

Puget Sound Regional Council 1994: *Modeling Congestion Pricing Alternatives for the Puget Sound Regional Council*, Technical Paper MTP-17c, August.

Silberston, Aubrey 1970: "Surveys of Applied Economics: Price Behavior of Firms," *Economic Journal*, September, 511–82.

Weston, J. Fred 1972: "Pricing Behavior of Large Firms," *Western Economic Journal*, March, 1–18.

Wheeley, Otto 1968: "Pricing Policy and Objectives," *Creative Pricing*, 27–38, ed. Elizabeth Marting, New York: American Management Association.

END OF CHAPTER EXERCISES

Exercise 8.1

Butterfly Wings, a nonprofit community theater, produces a performance that currently sells tickets for $16. The performance costs per viewer are:

Materials	$5.10
Direct labor	3.20
Overhead	4.00
Sales expenses	2.10
	$14.40

These unit costs are based on an audience of 100,000 units per year. Butterfly Wings' capacity is generally accepted to be 150,000 tickets per year. An out of town tourist agency has contacted Butterfly Wings with an offer to purchase 60,000 tickets on a short-term basis during the next year at a price of $13.00 each. Sales of these units in the tourist market would not have any effect on Butterfly's local market. Should the offer be accepted? Explain why or why not. Identify any assumptions you make in answering this question.

Exercise 8.2

Brown Laboratory, that processes medical tests, has considerable competition in the marketplace, since there are a number of close substitutes and little substantive product differentiation. Brown has fixed costs of $200,000 and average variable costs of $5. The total potential market is estimated at 1 million units. The lab's administrator would like to maintain a 10 percent share of the market; and the plant has ample capacity.

    a.   What price would enable Brown to break even at a sales volume representing 10 percent of the market (you may want to refer to the discussion of break-even analysis)?

    b.   Suppose that Brown wants to obtain a profit equal to 20 percent of fixed cost. Now what price should be charged?

Exercise 8.3

A laboratory that usually processes its own tests has run short due to a flood that curtailed processing in its labs. Mr. Callup, the purchasing agent for the large lab calls Mr. Lavue, the sales manager for Brown Laboratory (see Exercise 8.2), and offers to contract 2,000 tests at $5.50 per unit. Mr. Lavue tells him that such a deal is out of the question, since their current average cost is $7 per unit. However, since Brown has excess capacity, Lavue makes a counter-offer to process 2,000 tests at $7.35, just 5 percent over cost. Mr. Callup refuses the offer and strikes a deal with another lab. At a weekly staff meeting, Mr. Lavue relates the events to the administrator of Brown and others. If you were Brown, what would you say about Lavue's actions? What would you have done in Mr. Lavue's position? Why?

Exercise 8.4

Test Prep is currently the only producer of an innovative method that can be used to make exceptionally strong pass rates on professional tests, but at roughly the same dollar cost as for the conventional test prep program. From related production experiences, the industry long-run average cost has been estimated and is graphed here as $LRAC$ (see figure). The current short-run marginal and average cost functions for Test Prep are also graphed and are labeled $SRMC_B$ and $SRAC_B$ respectively. A new entrant into this industry could probably not enter at a scale greater than that represented by $SRMC_N$.

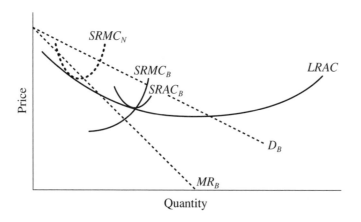

a. Based on these graphs, indicate on the graph the profit-maximizing level of output for Test Prep and the corresponding price.
b. Could a new firm profitably enter the industry at this price? Why or why not?
c. Indicate on the graph a price that would allow Test Prep to make a profit but that would prevent the new entrant from operating at a profit.
d. Suppose someone suggested that Test Prep should operate with the objective of maximizing revenue rather than profit from the sale of this new innovative method. Indicate the corresponding price and level of sales on the graph. What effect would this have on profit?

Exercise 8.5

Two firms in the medical imaging industry must each decide on whether to offer rebates in the coming third quarter of the year. The third quarter is typically a slow quarter for medical imaging and so some added incentives are sometimes offered at this time of year. The following matrix shows the possible outcomes from decisions to either offer a 2.5 percent rebate or not to offer a rebate. You can assume that these are the only available options.

	Firm 2 strategy No rebate	Firm 2 strategy 2.5% rebate
Firm 1 strategy No rebate	A Firm 1 profit = 200 Firm 2 profit = 120	B Firm 1 profit = 140 Firm 2 profit = 160
Firm 1 strategy 2.5% rebate	C Firm 1 profit = 220 Firm 2 profit = 40	D Firm 1 profit = 160 Firm 2 profit = 140

a. What outcome do you expect? Explain why you think that outcome is the likely result.
b. What is firm 1's dominant strategy? Firm 2's?

9
Strategic Goals:
If Not Profit, What?

9.1   INTRODUCTION

Government and nonprofit firms do not maximize profits. Does this mean that they maximize nothing? Certainly not; every organization faces scarcity-requiring trade-offs to achieve the most cost-effective level of output. Cost-minimizing behavior implies minimizing costs for any given level of output and thus is an efficiency principle for any type of firm. Optimal output, on the other hand, requires different rules for determining what level of output should be produced. A public administrator examines, in terms of the firm's mission statement, trade-offs between different outputs, different production functions, and different assessment measures.

Consider a community college offering majors in three divisions: allied health, engineering technology, and business management. Suppose it is "losing" money in one division, meeting most of its costs in another, and earning "profit" (net income) in yet another. Should it discontinue, contract, or expand course offerings in each of these divisions? Another related issue asks, "What are the potential effects on college donations from hosting 'profitable' unrelated activities such as catering events or popular music concerts?"

One researcher studied 386 strategic decisions made from 1879 to 1979 by the private nonprofit Art Institute of Chicago, operating an art museum, library, and school of art. Like most NFPs, strategic decisions were hybrid solutions combining economic, political, institutional, and social strategy. The study found common threads holding the Art Institute together: mission, precedents, strategic issues, administrators' tenure, and reversals/refinements of previous decisions. In this way, the institute was successfully able to customize its activities to sweep in new members, to expand into new programs, and to protect against drains on its income sources (Nathan, 1994).

Government and nonprofit firms, like the Art Institute, are part of the culture and society in which they operate and constantly need to consider and reconsider options, short-term goals and the measures used to evaluate performance change. Overall, however, an organization periodically needs objective evaluation: does it do what it says it does and does it say what it does. Institutional economists factor in a firm's social, legal, and transactional environment but also analyze the incentives facing an administrator with respect to cost, quality, and services provided.

Once strategic decisions are made in terms of what the firm seeks to accomplish, we can combine revenue with cost functions. In this chapter, we compare NFP objectives not in terms of profit but in terms of service provided, introduce break-even analysis, and propose methods of evaluating success.

9.2   THE INSTITUTIONAL APPROACH

Using organizations to achieve certain outcomes is one of humankind's most important accomplishments. *New Institutional Economics* studies how economic institutions, broadly defined, emerge. Stressing transaction costs, this approach attempts to focus micro-analytical reasoning and statistical observation toward understanding how firms operate. As a way of understanding complex organizations, Oliver Williamson differentiates levels of the social environment providing feedback to organizations (Williamson, 2000).

On one level, ***embeddedness*** studies how informal institutions, customs, traditions, norms, and religion are woven into a society. A part of NFP behavior reflects general culture, develops over centuries, and does not lend itself to mathematical calculations. For example, private donations support nonprofit firms in some parts of the world but the practice is not customary in most societies.

Another Williamson level, the ***institutional environment***, deals with formal rules of the game, especially those concerning the political, judicial, and bureaucratic treatment of property. The environment, although it can adapt somewhat over long periods of time or change abruptly, determines the potential for developing efficient and effective institutions. Private nonprofit hospitals and schools may be completely prohibited or suddenly expropriated. In other societies, legal charters for private nonprofit hospitals and schools exist and these organizations are supported with tax advantages and deliberately crafted features, such as the non-distributional constraint. Formal rules, promoting and constraining nonprofit firms and the professions, ultimately determine how social services are provided.

Within an organization, a level of *governance* affects how an institution operates. ***Governance*** is the internal oversight effort to create order, to avoid conflict, and to realize benefits between parties into which it enters agreements. Consider the governance environment of NFP firms in the United States. In September 2004, the chairman and ranking member of the Senate Finance Committee, Charles Grassley (R-IA) and Max Baucus (D-MT), sent a letter encouraging INDEPENDENT SECTOR to assemble a group of leaders to strengthen governance, ethical conduct, and accountability within public charities and private foundations.

The INDEPENDENT SECTOR is a nonprofit, nonpartisan coalition of approximately 500 national public charities, foundations, and corporate philanthropy programs, collectively representing tens of thousands of charitable groups in every state across the nation. The INDEPENDENT SECTOR responded to the senators' letter by creating the *Panel on the Nonprofit Sector*, consisting of members from large and small public charities and private foundations from around the country. The final report issued in June 2005 included more than 120 recommendations to Congress, to the Internal Revenue Service, and to charities themselves (*Panel on the Nonprofit Sector*). Congress and the IRS have an interest in examining abusive practices such as inflated tax deductions for donations, excessive pay for nonprofit officials, and "self-dealing." Self-dealing refers to conflict-of-interest situations. Whenever donors, board members, or related parties receive inappropriate benefits from an organization, the integrity, credibility, and success of the nonprofit sector is undermined. In addition to more government oversight, the *panel* calls for improved internal self-governance.

Understanding Williamson's environmental levels allows us to make comparisons between NFP sectors globally and to contrast performance between NFP firms.

9.3   NOT-FOR-PROFIT CONTRACTS AND GOVERNANCE

Governance describes the way in which a NFP chooses to operate. It aligns contracts and structures step by step at each separate transaction. When governance works effectively, the board merely looks over the shoulders of public administrators who handle day-to-day business decisions. The board in turn provides sponsors and donors with a full accounting of the firm's operations and finances. NFP stakeholder contracts are complex and checks are required to determine if actual practice contradicts intentions. Standard accounting practices, with external auditors, assist in governance, but, as indicated in Application 9.1, small private nonprofits are less likely to have external audits.

APPLICATION 9.1
Internal Control Systems in Nonprofit Firms

Internal controls are designed to safeguard assets, to provide accurate and reliable information, to promote and improve operational efficiency, and to encourage adherence to management policies. Church budgeting practices were the focus of one research study.

Wooten et al. (2003) tested two hypotheses: (1) larger nonprofit congregations differ in their internal control systems compared with smaller ones; (2) congregations audited by an external certified accountant differ from those that do not. They based their work on 548 churches of one denomination responding to a survey of 1,927 churches.

The researchers concluded that churches do an adequate job of providing controls over cash receipts flowing into an organization, probably in order to provide proper tax reporting to individual donors. Controls on disbursements were weaker perhaps due to focusing primarily on mission rather than internal controls.

Larger congregations have stronger internal controls and are more likely to have external audits by a CPA firm (17 percent of the sample). In addition, larger organizations appear to have a greater level of accountability to boards of directors or to society as a whole. For example, having an external CPA audit makes churches more aware of safeguarding their physical assets by such practices as tagging each asset with identification numbers.

Source: Thomas C. Wooten, John W. Coker, and Robert C. Elmore, "Financial Control in Religious Organizations: A Status Report," *Nonprofit Management and Leadership*, 13 (4), 2003, 343.

NFP governance differs from corporate profit-seeking governance in that stakeholder interests are not as sharply defined. Profit-seeking boards are charged with maintaining and increasing owners' wealth. In the NFP sectors, public trust requires that the board be less focused on owners and more on seeing that clients are well served. In the NFP sectors, therefore, governance is really about setting and maintaining high standards for output. Even if larger organizations have more formal controls, as suggested by Application 9.1, smaller ones may be equally effective. Good NFP corporate governance is essential but not sufficient and should not become the enemy of effective performance.

9.4   OPTIMIZATION IN A NFP FIRM

Economic optimality concerns allocating resources, aligning incentives, and responding to prices so as to produce the best feasible output with minimum cost. The process is continuous. Constant adjustments are needed for any firm to approximate the maximization of mission objectives with limited resources.

Production functions and marginal analysis assist in assessing firm output. Technology or "know-how" bridges the relationship between costs and revenue to determine if the firm is viable and will survive. Within the cultural, legal, and governance environment, a NFP firm seeks the greatest quality and quantity of output for a given level of inputs, or so we hope.

9.5   OUTPUTS AND OUTCOMES

Outputs are directly controlled variables and relatively easy to quantify because they depend primarily on inputs. Examples of outputs are hospital stays, prescriptions filled, office hours, caseload assignments, student test results, class size, etc. *Outcomes* by contrast represent the social impact of outputs, are difficult to quantify, and depend not only on the outputs but on other independent variables as well. Examples of outcomes are health, safety, life expectancy, infant mortality, literacy, economic self-sufficiency. It is much easier to measure outputs than outcomes, and NFP managers focus on outputs if that is the basis on which performance is judged. The board, donors, and other interested parties need to set priorities to ensure that a firm's output is positively associated with desired outcomes

Preferred, neutral, and distasteful outputs

An extremely useful technique for understanding a multi-service NFP firm is to classify its activities as favored, neutral, and distasteful outputs (James, 1983). *Favored or preferred outputs* are most closely related to core mission and competency of the firm. Schools teach, hospitals heal, police agencies protect, bureaus record and process, etc. Favored activities are subsidized by donors/taxpayers. *Neutral outputs* are unrelated to core mission but generally complement it. A client/ employee cafeteria and student apartments are neutral activities. The hospital cafeteria or student apartments do not necessarily heal or teach, but complement mission. Revenue generated from neutral activities should at a minimum cover cost or even generate net income. *Disfavored outputs* have the potential for changing the direction of the firm and thereby impede core mission. Disfavored outputs are tolerated because net income generated from them subsidizes preferred outputs. Soft drink machines in the lobby of a NFP, a disfavored activity, should not affect core mission and should generate net income. A congregation engaging in a disfavored activity is described in Application 9.2.

APPLICATION 9.2
Infinity, the Good Life, and Distasteful Activities

The lacy and delicate spire of Grace Church, downtown from the New York City theater district, is visible for miles. Built in 1846, the beautiful neo-gothic Episcopalian church spire had begun to lean about two degrees southwest; the metal anchor holding the cross in place was corroding. Stones had to be replaced.

The congregation raised $500,000 for repairs, with additional funds coming from foundations. The church is "land marked" and thus is not permitted to cut corners on restoration. And so the congregation entered into an unseemly commercial arrangement to fund the $2 million restoration.

Above the portico rises a huge billboard, 140 feet long. A Citibank logo with its "live richly" ad replaces a luxury-car photo of Infiniti G-35 coupes. Billboard revenue so far has provided $200,000 for scaffolding. Reverend Rider says, "We could whine, or we could get creative."

Source: Naomi Schaefer, "Pray and Pay," *The Wall Street Journal*, September 12, 2003, W17.

Profits (net income) from neutral and disfavored outputs should increase output of preferred services. In this way, NFPs internally subsidize their output of preferred activities.

Transferring net income/profit from one output to support another is ***cross-subsidization***, a common practice in NFP firms. Cross-subsidization takes place between clients, between less preferred and preferred activities and also between preferred activities. Profit-seeking firms cross-subsidize to some extent when they divert income from "cash cow" products to developing those with the potential of earning higher returns. However, their motivation is clearly on maximizing long-term profits and long-term wealth of stockholders. Profit-seeking firms are generally neutral with respect to product type; the goal is to direct resources to earn, over time, the greatest amount of profit. Remember that profit-seeking firms attempt to maximize profits but their behavior is ideally constrained by two binding constraints. First, profit-seeking firms are subject to law and, second, domestic and international competition requires that firms produce the best product at least cost. The legal and market constraints facing NFP firms are different; they are mission, not profit, driven; also, the social benefits produced are not wholly financed by users.

APPLICATION 9.3
Retirement Living at Universities

The following ad appeared in *The Wall Street Journal*:

> **We're Reinventing Retirement Living: Oak Hammock at the University of Florida**
>
> Want to check out a Life Fulfilling Community – one based on a 21st century model that focuses on life-long learning, fitness and health . . . all wrapped up in a resort-style environment with intellectual stimulation and interesting neighbors? Then take a look at Oak Hammock. Here, you'll have campus privileges similar to university faculty – with access to sports, performing arts events, library and research facilities, and more. You'll also enjoy a host of world-class amenities, along with the guarantee of unlimited on-site short- or long-term healthcare if needed . . .

Oak Hammock, a nonprofit retirement community located near the University of Florida, has entered into an affiliation with the state-sponsored university.

Are you aware of similar arrangements at other universities? From the point of view of a university, would you consider this to be a preferred, neutral, or distasteful activity? What would a university's motivation be for entering into an agreement with a nonprofit retirement community? What are the benefits and costs to a university of these agreements? Is cross-subsidization taking place?

Source: *The Wall Street Journal*, Monday, August 11, 2003, R6.

The classification of activities as preferred, neutral, and disfavored is particularly helpful when NFP firms partner with profit-seeking or other NFP firms. Application 9.3 describes a partnership between two nonprofits. Costs and benefits of such agreements must be assessed in terms of the objects of each firm.

9.6 OBJECTIVE FUNCTION OF NFP FIRMS

Abstract NFP mission statements hinder but do not obviate an enterprise's clear statement of objectives. The *objective function* establishes in specific goal-related results that which a firm is attempting to provide. For example, is a state mental health agency trying to identify those needing service or is it seeking to provide a certain level of care for X number of clients given the budget allocated? Goals, or objectives, are generally multiple as are strategies to move the organization toward desired results. In all but the simplest NFP firm, objectives are elusive and difficult to translate into goal-related results.

Consider the following economic goals for a NFP manager determined to operate effectively. Minimizing costs sounds great. But as previously noted, the best way to minimize costs is to turn off the lights, close the doors, and have everyone in the firm go home! Is maximizing revenue a proper objective? Probably not. If, for example in the case of a firm soliciting contributions, the cost of raising those funds equals the amount coming into the organization, nothing remains for mission objectives. A fully funded government firm in maximizing revenue is engaged in raising taxes or reallocating funds from other agencies. Finally, maximizing the difference between costs and revenues (profits/net income) is what profit-seeking firms do and is therefore inappropriate for any tax exempt or government firm. Fortunately, the preferred, neutral, and distasteful distinction offers guidance in addressing these issues.

Consider a congregation debating on whether or not they should conduct a vacation scripture school. First, it must consider if the proposal is integral to its mission. Second, it must be determined if the project follows legal and community standards and if the internal skills needed are available. Third, governance for the program within the organization must be established. Any economic decisions must feed back into these prior levels of institutional understanding.

Suppose that data for the vacation school project looked like that presented in Table 9.1. The data raises further issues: Is there a rental market for the congregation's facility that could be used to estimate the opportunity cost of using the premises for a vacation school? Does the facility have value for some other congregational activity? The hypothetical data in Table 9.1A shows fixed costs of $500, representing the opportunity cost of a congregation's facilities.

Table 9.1, part A, indicates that, beyond an enrollment of 40 students, cost per student rises. Therefore, the board must determine if the summer school is a "preferred output." Assume that children of members are the preferred target group. Therefore, the congregation may be willing to subsidize enrollment out of general funds. Suppose, however, that nonmember enrollment is a "neutral" outreach to the community. In this case, user fees for nonmembers should approach full cost per child with no cross-subsidies from the congregation.

Let's suppose that the board decides to subsidize tuition for members' children, and charge nonmembers full cost. This makes the school very attractive to members, but less so to nonmembers. If members are subsidized, enrollment could expand, driving marginal and average costs up beyond the intended subsidy. The congregation in this case could have overallocated funds to this project. The decision may also lead to a nonmember decline depending on their response to paying full cost. In this case, enrollment may be sub-optimal, raising per unit costs. Calculating the net effect is tricky but the direction of the effects cannot be ignored because they affect expected outcomes.

Table 9.1 Vacation scripture school. Part A lists the projected costs for difference levels of enrollment. Part B lists revenue for different levels of enrollment with a competitively determined tuition fee of $220. Part C lists revenue for different levels of enrollment that depend on the tuition fee set by the congregation.

Part A: costs

Enrollment	Fixed cost	Variable cost	Total cost	Average total cost	Marginal cost
0	500	0	500		
20	500	3,700	4,200	210	185
40	500	7,000	7,500	187.5	175
60	500	12,700	13,200	220	285
80	500	18,000	18,500	231.25	265
100	500	25,000	25,500	255	350
120	500	33,000	33,500	279.17	400
140	500	42,000	42,500	303.57	450

Part B: revenue – assuming a competitive market and tuition set to market

Enrollment	Tuition	Total revenue	Marginal revenue	Net income/profit
0	220	0		−500
20	220	4,400	220	200
40	220	8,800	220	1,300
60	220	13,200	220	0
80	220	17,600	220	−900
100	220	22,000	220	−3,500
120	220	26,400	220	−7,100
140	220	30,800	220	−11,700

Part C: revenue – assuming an imperfectly competitive market and firm-set tuition

Enrollment	Tuition	Total revenue	Marginal revenue	Net income/profit
0	300	0		−500
20	280	5,600	280	1,400
40	240	9,600	200	2,100
60	220	13,200	180	0
80	200	16,000	140	−2,500
100	180	18,000	100	−7,600
120	160	19,200	60	−14,300
140	140	19,600	20	−22,900

Table 9.1, part B, provides hypothetical revenue information. Suppose the market for such services is competitive and similar programs in the area charge $220 per child, at which the demand for services exceeds capacity. If the summer school is a "neutral activity" and charges full fee both to members and nonmembers, it enrolls 40 students, and earns net income of $1,300 to cross-subsidize a "preferred activity" of the congregation. This output represents a net income (profit) maximizing objective.

Now assume that the board considers the summer school to be a "preferred activity." In that case, they would increase enrollment to 60 and break even. Or, they could increase enrollment beyond 60, take a loss, and subsidize the activity from other sources of revenue. Economic options in NFPs cannot be addressed without reference to a firm's objective function.

Part C, in contrast to part B in Table 9.1, assumes a negatively sloping demand curve in which enrollment varies with tuition fees. The assumption underlying section C is that the summer school can raise price above the norm for the area and still retain students. In other words, the congregation has market power and functions like an imperfectly competitive firm, and within limits it can set price. Note, that although quantity demanded increases as price declines, the marginal revenue received is lower than price. If the firm lowers tuition in order to gain more students, it generally has to lower tuition for all those clients who would have been willing to pay the higher price. Given the demand and revenue data in part C, the firm maximizes net income (profit) by capping enrollment at 40, setting tuition at 240, and using net income of $2,100 to subsidize preferred activities. Alternately, if the summer program is a preferred activity, it would increase enrollment to 60, lower tuition to 220 and just cover cost.

It is relatively easy to outline options in a simple hypothetical case assuming complete cost and demand information. However, even when complete information is not available, it is possible to do rough calculations taking into account client response and costs relative to scale. In all cases, core mission, not economic considerations, determines the objective function of the NFP firm in terms of preferred, neutral, and disfavored activities. Present IRS nonprofit guidelines indicate that a substantial part of any tax-exempt organization's activities should be directed toward its
primary mission not unrelated businesses.

Strategic maximizing objectives

The strategic objectives of a particular NFP firm or industry are not always apparent. Application 9.4 identifies two subtly different strategies in higher education: maximizing prestige or maximizing reputation. All colleges and universities need revenue to cover expenses but in doing this they select from a variety of maximizing strategies.

APPLICATION 9.4
What Is It That U.S. Institutions of Higher Education Try to Maximize?

Three economists set out on a two-year descriptive study of the post-secondary education industry in the United States. Universities compete in markets for revenue from four sources: student tuition, government funding, public and private research funding, and alumni giving. Universities compete in each of these markets by being better or by differentiating themselves.

The study concluded that a university will either try to maximize "prestige" or "reputation." "Prestige" oriented universities try to maximize revenue from all four sources by focusing on excellent faculty and students, world-class research, and successful sports teams. "Reputation" oriented universities focused on students hoping to acquire market skills. Pedagogical innovation in "reputation" schools was focused on tuition revenue and/or government funding based on enrollment.

What drives the institution to seek prestige? Students at highly endowed/prestigious universities benefit from an improved peer group and possibly increased job opportunity. Faculty at prestigious institutions enjoy a select student body, lower teaching loads, and higher salaries. For-profit universities, at the other extreme, are reputation oriented and faculty tends to have less influence in institutional governance.

The pursuit of prestige is expensive, and if the university is unsuccessful faculty, students, administrators, and taxpayers absorb the costs. What are the benefits? According to one reviewer of this study, the focus on excellence at top universities creates positive externalities for all of society and prestige merely follows good performance.

Source: H. Lorne Carmichael, "Review: *In Pursuit of Prestige: Strategy and Competition in U.S. Higher Education* by Dominic J. Brewer, Susan M. Gates and Charles A. Goldman (New Brunswick, N. J. and London: Transaction, 2002)," *Journal of Economic Literature*, 41 (1), 2003, 233–4.

Let us summarize a few maximizing strategies:

Net income (profit) maximization

The firm will produce that output at which total revenue exceeds total costs by the greatest amount. To do this, output is increased up to the point at which the marginal cost of producing the last unit equals the marginal revenue received. Note, in reference to Table 9.1, that a profit-maximizing firm will not enroll 60 students because, given the existing facility/staff, marginal cost exceeds marginal revenue at this level of output. This is true for each of the revenue schedules (parts B and C), even though the firm with monopoly control over price in part C can set tuition rather than merely respond to the market rate. Whenever marginal cost exceeds marginal revenue, a user is either unwilling or unable to pay the extra cost. If clients insufficiently value the service, it is not worth providing. However, if the client simply cannot afford it, a sponsor may be found to subsidize the amount that the client can pay. In this case, the sponsor values the fact that someone is consuming the product. From the point of view of a NFP firm directly subsidizing or indirectly receiving the subsidy from outside donors, the client user fee *plus the per unit subsidy* must at least equal the marginal (extra) cost of the last unit produced. A state university, for example, is neither able nor should continue to increase credit hours if student fees and the state subsidy per credit hour are less than the extra cost. Allocative efficiency requires that the total value of a good or service to user and sponsor at least equal the cost of producing it.

Output maximization

A firm may decide to expand output up to the point where all costs are covered but zero "profit" (net income) is generated. At this level of output, total revenue equals total costs and net income is zero. In the summer school example, output maximization takes place at 60 rather than 40 students in Table 9.1, parts B and C. We calculate this level by increasing output up to the point where the fee received for each unit of service provided is equal to its average total cost. This strategy suggests that the sponsor of the organization is willing to provide the product to clients as long as all costs are covered by revenue collected from user fees, donations, and budgeted sponsor contributions.

Obviously, there is a tendency for users to over-consume services that are subsidized. If out-of-pocket costs to the client are less than the full cost, why not get in line for more? Suppose the congregation in our example was willing to contribute general church funds to reduce tuition for any student willing to enroll. Output maximization strategies with guaranteed per unit subsidies tend toward over-allocation or waste of society's scarce resources. We sometimes hear people say that there is no such thing as too much of a good thing such as education or preventative healthcare. This may be true but generally an organization has to choose between several good programs. Economists warn that, if the marginal cost of providing a service exceeds value received by donors and fee-paying clients, an organization should evaluate its commitment to the program.

Social benefit maximization

From society's point of view, a NFP balancing revenue and expenses could under-allocate resources to activities with social value. Marginal revenue from user fees incorrectly reflects the full value to society. For example, the price one is willing to pay for inoculations may be less than the potential value of preventing illness in the individual as well as society at large. Whenever a positive externality is associated with consumption, the maximization of net income leads to resource under-allocation for this product. Technically, it is possible to boost a firm's revenue in such a way to include a subsidy reflecting total social and private benefits.

The state could offer to pay a municipal waste water and sewage department a certain amount for each household agreeing to be connected to the system. Increased revenue encourages the firm to expand production to a more socially optimal level. Subsidizing production is theoretically justified in order to reallocate resources to take advantage of social benefits. In Table 9.1, output could be expanded beyond the net income or output maximizing amounts if additional revenue were provided by a source external to both clients and the congregation.

Budget maximizing

In general, administrators, whose compensation depends on the number of employees supervised, have a tendency toward budget maximization. Incentive structures often nudge nonprofit and public administrators to operate as revenue or output maximizers. Sponsors measure output, and could interpret an enrollment of 140 students in Table 9.1 as success, even when they are forced to make up for $11,700 or $22,900 in negative net income. A bureau that performs better than expected in terms of output is often rewarded with even higher budgets. Overlooked is the fact that users and sponsors value additional units less. Budget maximization behavior without checks and controls leads to higher costs and poor client service. This is especially so when the optimal scale of production given existing technology suggests a smaller scale of operation. A seemingly successful program with sufficient revenue equal to cost does not necessarily warrant expansion. All NFP firms are subsidized and choosing where and how to use their facilities and staff should be made in terms of mission, not staff/insider expediency.

Equity accumulation

Income is a flow concept calculated over a period of time; wealth is a stock. Profits (net income) represent a flow each year equal to the difference between cost and revenue. If the assets of a firm accumulate over time, the total value of these assets can be evaluated at any point in time. Assets are a stock concept. Some nonprofits and government firms engage in wealth-maximizing behavior. National Parks purchase large tracts of land. Universities increase their endowments. Equity accumulation goals may or may not be consistent with the mission of the organization or with nonprofit privileges. Additional problems are created when the benefits of an organization's wealth are redirected to activities and individuals unrelated to firm mission. This issue is directly addressed in the tax code that seeks to eliminate pseudo-nonprofits by requiring that a certain percentage of assets be used for program expenses.

Suppose an institution experiences a drain on its net worth. Should mission-directed administrators be penalized monetarily in times of general financial distress? Economists like to observe what individuals and firms do rather than accept what they say they are doing. Application 9.5 tests the degree to which executive compensation in nonprofit hospitals is associated with altruistic goals.

APPLICATION 9.5
Measuring Managerial Performance and Providing Incentives: Do Nonprofit Hospitals Operate Differently than For-profits?

Concentrating on just the hospital component of the nonprofit sector, two researchers found consistent evidence that the managers of for-profit and nonprofit firms face incentives to concentrate on financial performance. But they also found no evidence that nonprofit hospital CEOs have explicit incentives to focus on altruistic activities. In fact, the threat of management turnover due to poor financial performance appears stronger in nonprofit hospitals than in for-profit hospitals. They studied 2,134 nonprofit and for-profit hospitals over the fiscal years 1991–5, excluding all university affiliated medical school hospitals.

Boards of nonprofit hospitals, representing donors and other stakeholders, find it difficult to measure managerial performance and to write meaningful incentive contracts. The authors suggest that this explains why nonprofit hospitals rely more heavily on management turnover when returns on assets decline. For-profit hospitals, not precluded from paying bonuses, can cut bonuses rather than replace management whenever returns on assets decline.

The researchers theorized that boards pursuing altruism would have lower prices, higher output, and higher quality of care. In other words, although nonprofit hospitals target financial returns in competitive markets, they would distribute "profits" altruistically in markets where they have some control. Nurses on duty per person, revenue per patient day, and service expenditures were used as altruistic variables. Using regression analysis, the authors concluded that hospitals with little competition were no more likely to reward altruistic managers than those in highly competitive markets.

Why do you suppose that some individuals prefer nonprofit hospitals if it cannot be demonstrated statistically that nonprofit boards reward managers based on altruistic behavior? How would you design a study to demonstrate the difference between nonprofit and for-profit hospitals?

Source: James A. Brickley and R. Lawrence Van Horn, "Managerial Incentives in Nonprofit Organizations: Evidence from Hospitals," *Journal of Law and Economics*, 45 (1), 2002, 227–49.

9.7   BREAK-EVEN ANALYSIS

One of the simplest, yet most useful, techniques of all economic analyses for public and nonprofit administrators is break-even analysis. A **break-even point** is a level of output consistent with total revenue (*TR*) equal to total cost (*TC*). This section presents the fundamental break-even model with two variations, linear and nonlinear cost and revenue curves. First, linear revenue and cost functions simplify break-even analysis. For many practical applications, this is often satisfactory because these cost and revenue functions are very nearly linear in the relevant range of output. Nonlinear functions should be used whenever the use of linear approximations is accompanied by unacceptable errors. We start with two simple assumptions: (1) total revenue consists of user fees combined with subsidies per unit of output, which is a function of the level of output produced, and (2) costs increase with output. A special case, not discussed below, is when an organization is allocated a fixed budget independent of its level of output.

Linear and nonlinear break-even points

A typical break-even graph is presented in Figure 9.1. Several facts become apparent in viewing Figure 9.1. First, the vertical distance between the total-cost line and the horizontal fixed-cost line represents the variable cost of alternative levels of output. Second, since total revenue (*TR*) is linear, price (*P*) must be constant over the relevant range of output.

Furthermore, average variable costs (*AVC*) must also be constant over this range in order for total cost (*TC*) to be linear. Finally, note that the break-even level of output (*BEQ*) is at the point on the horizontal axis directly below the intersection of *TR* and *TC* (this intersection is the break-even point).

If the only use of break-even analysis were to determine the level of output at which the firm breaks even, given price and costs, the technique would not be so widely adopted. A single break-even graph also shows how much net income/profit (for $Q > BEQ$) or loss (for $Q < BEQ$) the firm will realize at each level of output. Now, suppose that a NFP firm has a target net income of *X* dollars designed to pay interest on bonds, over and above present fixed and variable costs. By adding the targeted net income to fixed costs, we use break-even analysis to determine how great an output volume is necessary to pay interest on bonds.

The formula for break-even analysis is derived in the footnote.[1] We illustrate break-even analyses with numerical examples first for an increase in fixed costs and then for different revenue schedules. First, suppose that a firm presently has

---

[1]   Net income $= TR - TC$

$TR = P * Q$

$TC = FC + VC$

$TC = FC + AVC * Q$

$0 = P * Q - FC - AVC * Q$

$FC = (P - AVC) Q$

$Q = FC/(P - AVC) = BEQ$

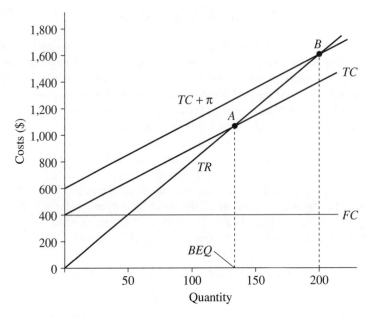

Figure 9.1   Break-even analysis. This is the graphic determination of the break-even level of output (*BEQ*), given fixed costs of $400, an average variable cost of $5 per unit, and a price of $8 per unit. The break-even point is *A*, where *BEQ* = 133. If additional net revenue is needed, the necessary level of output is determined at *B*, or 200 units.

fixed costs of $400, a constant average variable cost of $5, and charges clients $8. The break-even level of client sales is calculated as:

$BEQ = FC/(P - AVC)$

$BEQ = 400/(8 - 5)$

$BEQ = 400/3$

$BEQ = 133$

This result is shown in Figure 9.1 at point *A*, the intersection of total revenue (*TR*) and total cost (*TC*). Now if the firm incurs additional fixed costs of $200, how many units must be provided to achieve that objective? When price (charges for service) and average variable cost are both constant, price minus average variable cost (*P − AVC*) is referred to as the **contribution margin per unit** because that value represents the portion of selling price that contributes to paying the overhead fixed costs (and to profit, if appropriate). If the contribution margin is $3 per unit, then a firm needs to provide 67 more units to cover increased fixed costs of $200. To demonstrate the added output needed to break even, we simply calculate

$BEQ = (FC + \text{additional net income})/(P - AVC)$

$BEQ = (400 + 200)/(8 - 5) = 200$

This result is identified at point *B* in Figure 9.1.

Now extend the problem a little further. Suppose that the firm has a fixed cost of $200 and an average variable cost of $10 per unit but the administration is uncertain about the user fee/price to set for this product. The marketing and economic research personnel have found that the demand for the product is negatively sloped (as would be realistically expected). Collected data indicates expected purchases at three alternative user fees:

User fee	Quantity
$20.00	25
15.00	60
12.50	110

Each user fee/price gives rise to different total revenues, as shown in Figure 9.2 (TR_1 for P (user fee) = 20, TR_2 for P = 15, and TR_3 for P = 12.5).

If net income (profit) maximization is the objective, a fee of $15 is best. However, if the objective is related to mission, then a larger output is preferred and the $12.50 fee is chosen.

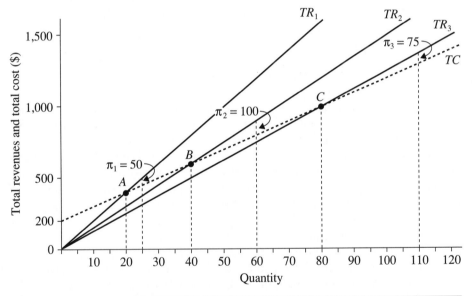

Price ($)	BEQ	Expected sales	Expected profit ($)
20	20	25	50
15	40	60	100
12	80	110	75

Figure 9.2 Break-even levels and potential net income/profit for three total revenue functions. With a fixed cost of $200 and an average variable cost of $10 per unit, we find the above break-even levels for the three possible prices along with the profit based on expected sales at those prices.

Note in this example that as price is reduced, the break-even level for client sales increases from 20 (at A, for $P = 20$) to 40 (at B, for $P = 15$) and finally to 80 (at C, for $P = 12.50$). More important, we see that as price is reduced and purchases increase, net income increases from $\pi_1, = 50$ to $\pi_2 = 100$ and then decreases to $\pi_3 = 75$ for the user fees $20, $15, and $12.50, respectively. Thus, an administrator selects a fee of $15 if the objective is to maximize net income/profit. Other objectives lead to different decisions. For example, if the objective is to further mission and increase availability subject to a minimum $50 net income/profit per time period then a price of $12.50 would be appropriate.

Nonlinear break-even analysis

So far we have assumed that total revenue (TR) and total cost (TC) functions were both linear. In real-world situations this will often be a good approximation because decision-makers operate within relatively small segments of the actual total revenue and total cost functions.

A linear total revenue function assumes that a firm can sell as many units of output as it might like at a constant user fee/price. This ignores client response to price and contradicts the law of demand in which a lower price is needed to increase clients. Likewise, a linear total cost function assumes that production underlying that cost curve exhibits constant returns to variable inputs and thus variable cost remains constant. These assumptions may be misleading.

Consider break-even analysis with nonlinear revenue and cost functions. In Figure 9.3 total revenue is concave downward; in order to sell more units the firm must reduce price. If price is reduced for all (including previous clients willing to pay a higher fee), marginal revenue per unit declines and the TR function increases at a decreasing rate. The total cost function in Figure 9.3 has the traditional double curvature reflecting diminishing rather than constant returns.

With both the TR and TC curves drawn in this more realistic fashion, we can see two break-even points, rather than one. To produce to the left of the lower break-even point at Q_1, the firm incurs a loss. By producing exactly Q_1 units, the firm breaks even. If the firm chooses to produce more than Q_1 units, say Q_2 units, it earns net income/profit. By increasing production, the firm reaches output level Q_3. Here the firm is again just breaking even and any further production forces the firm into loss territory as indicated by the area to the right of Q_3.

Given the information available in Figure 9.3, a firm could choose a particular level of output to maximize profit or, if this were a mission preferred activity, the firm could maximize output subject to breaking even. Any level of output between Q_1 and Q_3 earns net income/profit, but at one point only is net income/profit maximized. If the NFP firm decides to transfer net revenue from a neutral or distasteful activity in order to subsidize preferred activities, it produces at the point where total revenue exceeds total cost function by the greatest amount. This point is shown in Figure 9.3 as Q_2.

How can one determine which output level corresponds to Q_2 in the diagram? The answer is to draw lines that are tangent to both curves and find the point where TR and TC have the same slope. The slope of TR represents marginal revenue and the slope TC represents marginal cost. If the two slopes are equal, then it follows that:

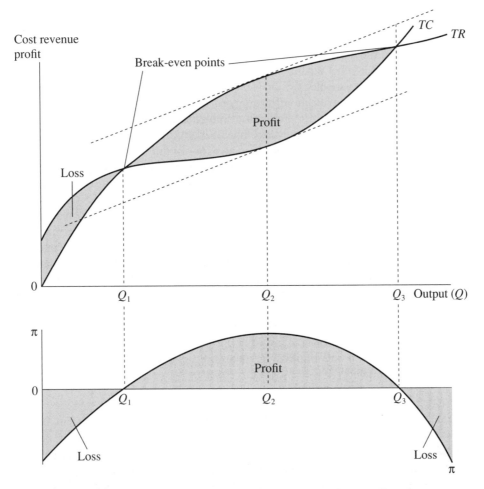

Figure 9.3   Generalized break-even analysis. Nonlinear total cost and total revenue functions are shown in the top panel. The bottom panel depicts the resulting net income/profit function. A profit-maximizing firm chooses to operate where the total revenue function is furthest above the total cost function (at quantity = Q_2). This corresponds with the quantity at which marginal revenue equals marginal cost.

$$MR = MC$$

Given nonlinear total revenue and total cost curves, the bottom panel in Figure 9.3 depicts the net income/profit function. A profit-maximizing firm chooses to operate where the total revenue function is furthest above the total cost function in the top panel. This corresponds with the quantity at which marginal revenue equals marginal cost. A firm seeking to maximize output will produce at the break-even point of Q_3, yielding zero net revenue.

The equalization of marginal revenue and marginal cost condition which maximizes net income underlies the market analysis presented in Chapter 7.

What if breaking even is impossible?

Suppose that total revenue fails to exceed total cost at any level, and that resources, unfortunately, have already been committed to a program in progress. In the short run for most businesses, a firm will continue producing if revenue is sufficient to cover all variable costs and some fraction of fixed costs. The firm absorbs a loss, but would lose even more by immediately shutting down the program. A profit-maximizing firm ceases production immediately if average revenue (equal to price or user fee plus subsidy) is less than average variable costs. No firm, profit-seeking or NFP, can continue to produce at a loss in the long run.

A word of caution is needed for decision-makers in multi-service nonprofit and government firms. Unrelated business or fundraising activities can seem profitable $(TR > TC)$. However, when an activity's average variable revenue (AVR) is less than its average variable cost (AVC), then resources allocated could perhaps create more value in some other activity. For example, in the hypothetical summer scripture school, we did not assume funding from sources other than user fees, to cover all costs, fixed and variable. Suppose donations, endowment income, and volunteer services add revenue or reduce costs to the operation. Or, suppose that advocates for the vacation school fail to include certain implicit costs, such as wear and tear on the facility and the redirection of existing staff's efforts. In these cases, calculated break-even points and "profit" mislead the congregation. Break-even analysis is a powerful tool for decision-making in nonprofit and public firms, but it assumes that all costs, explicit and implicit, be taken into consideration and that revenue be correctly estimated.

9.8   MANAGERIAL DISCRETION

Managerial discretion theory proposes that a manager, consciously or unconsciously, tends to subvert mission by redirecting objectives away from donor/sponsor and client interests and toward his or her own interests. This tendency to subvert is successful if managers are not held accountable either by law, regulation, or competition.

Managerial discretion theory is useful in highlighting differences between NFP and profit-seeking firms, even assuming that all managers act similarly. The lower wages paid to NFP administrators versus those for similarly qualified in profit-seeking firms suggests that the nondistributional constraint prevents net income transfers to insiders. The nondistributional constraint's intention is to screen out employees motivated purely by financial rewards. In practice, managerial emoluments, another name for perks, augment the wages of NFP administrators; thus they may merely appear to be rewarded less than those in the profit-seeking sector. The compensation package in NFP firms may be different but not necessarily lower.

One study found salary differentials between nonprofit and profit-seeking daycare centers not significantly different from zero. In fact, federally financed/regulated daycare salaries in nonprofits are approximately 5 to 10 percent higher than those paid by for-profit centers (Preston, 1988).

Who's in charge of ensuring that government agencies and nonprofits provide quality output and reflect the aspirations of their mission statements? Ideally, upper management mirrors the goals of sponsor and board. However, administrators are human beings with personal goals. The unhindered pursuit of personal goals may be inappropriate, unless they reflect mission.

Recall that the essential characteristic of a NPF organization is the ban on distributing net earnings, if any, to those exercising control, such as members, officers, directors, and trustees. However, the nondistributional constraint is a rather crude client protection device that most states make little or no effort to enforce. NPF managers, like those in the profit-seeking sector, have the potential to enrich themselves with excessive salaries, low-interest loans, personal services and amenities, and generous contracts to businesses in which they have an interest. How can a society protect itself from this type of NFP abuse? Suggestions include entrusting the government with NFP oversight, fostering competition between all three sectors, requiring better internal governance, and monitoring by clients and accrediting organizations.

Those in favor of government oversight argue that clients are not in a position to evaluate quality, and therefore legal sanctions and regulations are required. NFP organizations enter into a trust relationship with clients who avail themselves of critical services. These contracts are incomplete and different from those between customers and profit-seeking firms. The inability to completely specify what clients receive and what firms provide is called *contract failure*.

When contracts are incomplete, there is a need for legal oversight representing the interests of users and donors. NFP regulation corresponds to corporate law designed to protect shareholders (owners) from those who control. Regulations give government the right and duty to eliminate incentives allowing administrators to engage in excessive cost-cutting or quality deterioration in services provided by NFPs.

Financial checks and balances alone are insufficient when contracts are incomplete. Transparent accounting fails to detect mission drift. This is especially so when the problem does not rest with an isolated firm but is widespread and systemic in certain industries. Herding behavior explains how clusters of firms observe and interpret other firms' behavior and follow it. In other words, leading trends may not represent best practices. Firms emulate rather than assess the effectiveness of certain practices.

Suppose, for example, that a few high schools initiate open classrooms (several classes sharing the same space) or block scheduling (students attending core classes twice a week rather than daily). Changes are difficult to execute and schools that do so are perceived to be on the cutting edge. Schools failing to adopt these innovations are perceived by clients to be nonresponsive. There is an incentive to follow trends, without assessing whether a particular innovation is effective or appropriate. Involuntary trial programs involving people are understandably discouraged, and professionals are unwilling to admit doubts. Therefore, untested practices become policy.

Clustering behavior pressures firms unwilling to change. Accrediting associations jump on the bandwagon and penalize institutions reluctant to adopt new practices. Herding also works in the opposite direction, when current practices fail to deliver expected results. Then, institutions shift in tandem and abandon a practice without due consideration. Clustering behavior in the NFP sectors is more serious than marketing fads because NFP clients do not have as many choices as customers in profit-seeking firms.

Whose preferences dominate?

In much of microeconomics, products are assumed to be homogeneous (standardized); in other words, quality does not vary from one product to another. In the NFP sectors, counseling, medical services, and, to some extent, education are best provided as uniquely as possible rather than homogeneously. Who decides how to fit a particular service to a particular client?

Research suggests that administrators dominate decisions on the nature of production, the amount of output provided, and product attributes. NFP managers typically have freedom in defining goals. Consequently, there tends to be more variance in the quality of output over time and across firms competing in these sectors than in the corporate sector. Administrators of universities, hospitals, and art museums are free to choose a certain level of quality and in doing so may be strongly influenced by elite stakeholders. Faculty, for instance, may prefer that resources be allocated to research rather than instruction. Physicians may insist on advanced laboratories in hospitals rather than additional beds. Curators may prefer one expensive work by a famous painter rather than several pieces representing different schools of art. Certain groups within NFP firms, including the head, have opportunities to further personal agendas (Glaeser, 2003).

How does dominance by some stakeholders in NFP firms manifest itself? It could lead to higher salaries and benefits and even widespread looting of the organization's assets. On the other hand, elite workers supporting the mission could internalize the goals of the organization and produce a higher-quality output. Administrators in association with certain workers are left free to interpret firm mission in terms of their own preferences. This tendency is strongest in wealthy endowed institutions. Although this freedom may lead to increased quality in one dimension, the type and quality of output chosen could be at odds with what donors or clients prefer. Managers and top professionals have opportunities to pursue their own interests rather than focusing on donor and client interests. The managerial discretion model suggests that private nonprofits and government agencies have a lifecycle whereby they are originally controlled by boards representing sponsors, donors, and taxpayers. Over time, according to Glaeser, a NFP adapts to the preferences of particular administrators and elite employees.

Negative external shocks, such as a stock market decline affecting endowment income, tax revolts, or technological and demand shifts reduce NFP firms' revenue sources. In these instances, elite worker preferences become less important, and the firm may revert to mission. In other words, competition in the market for clients, donors, and tax dollars can act so as to discipline nonprofit and government firms.

Figure 9.4 contains four categories of NFP firms classified by two criteria (Hansmann, 1980). The first criterion distinguishes firms on sources of revenue. *Donative NFP firms* receive most of their revenue from donors, taxpayers, or sponsors. *Commercial NFP firms* receive the bulk of revenue from the sale of

	Mutual	Entrepreneurial
Donative	Box A: *Non-endowed:* Common Cause National Audubon Society Political parties United Way *Endowed:* American Economics Association	Box B: *Non-endowed:* March of Dimes CARE *Endowed:* Art museums Ford Foundation Roman Catholic Church
Commercial	Box C: American Automobile Association (AAA) TIAA-CREF Pension Plan Country clubs	Box D: National Geographic Society Educational Testing Service Community hospitals Nursing homes Encyclopedia Britannica

Figure 9.4   A two-way classification of NFP firms. In mutual firms, member owners exercise control. In entrepreneurial firms, managers control. In donative firms, donations are the primary revenue source. In commercial firms, client fees dominate as the primary revenue source.

Source: Hansmann, Henry B., "The Role of Nonprofit Enterprise," *Yale Review Journal*, April 1980, 842.

services. A second criterion distinguishes firms on the basis of control. Firms controlled by sponsors and clients are called ***mutual NFP firms***. Those free from the formal control of sponsors and clients are called ***entrepreneurial NFP firms***.

Figure 9.4, box C, identifies cooperatives as mutual/commercial firms. These are atypical NFP firms because they receive virtually all of their revenue from sales. The "donative" versus "commercial" classification is extremely useful but organizations cannot be classified easily into just two categories. Donations as a percentage of revenue are a continuous quantitative variable. Therefore, most NFPs fall in the middle between "donative" and "commercial." A university, for example, may receive approximately 50 percent of its revenue from tuition and 50 percent from endowment income and donations. A classical government or private NFP firm receives a major portion of its revenue other than from the sale of its services. The exercise of formal control by sponsors (mutual) versus managerial discretion (entrepreneurial) also presents categorizing difficulties. Hospitals, for example, are most likely commercial/entrepreneurial institutions (box D); however, in some cases they are closely supervised by local government or founding sponsors.

The single important characteristic of firms in each box of Figure 9.4 is the degree of administrative discretion. However, there is no easy way to measure the degree of control. We are left with the difficulty of separating overlapping groups attempting to influence decisions. For example, you may be simultaneously paying tuition for your children at a school from which you graduated, donating to its annual fund, and subsidizing it with taxes. In addition, you may sit on the board and have relatives employed there!

9.9   COMMERCIAL ACTIVITY

NFP firms depending almost exclusively on user fees behave like commercial entrepreneurial firms, according to the Hansmann classification. After the Tax Reform Act of 1986 eliminated charitable contributions for those taxpayers not itemizing deductions, NFP administrators initiated commercial activities to make up for lost revenue (Schiff and Weisbrod, 1987). With declining revenue sources in the form of donations, tax revenue, and direct subsidies, NFPs are observed turning to commercial activities. This suggests that it is the source of a firm's revenue that, in part, defines its behavior.

Commercial activity links the profit-seeking and NFP sectors, and it becomes more difficult to determine the lines dividing them. Corporate alliances between NFP and profit-seeking firms can entail conditions contrary to primary mission, creating conflicts of interest. Examples include: agreements not to publish research adversely affecting a corporate sponsor, engaging in research and practices contrary to the beliefs of its sponsoring organization, and redirecting facilities and other resources away from preferred activities. Another moral hazard is alliances designed to permit profit-seeking firms to evade taxes.

NFP commercial activity, at times, creates an unfair competitive environment for local businesses. The White House Conference on Small Business and a Subcommittee of the U.S. House of Representatives addressed the issue of "unfair competition" between nonprofit and for-profit competition. Application 9.6 offers examples in which a nonprofit recreation center and a government library compete with local businesses. Is the playing field for each of the three sectors level? This is a legitimate concern.

APPLICATION 9.6
"Unfair Competition" When Nonprofit Firms Become Commercial

The Metro YMCA in downtown Portland, Oregon, offers a fitness club for a substantial initiation fee plus monthly payments. In return, one can use the equipment, track, racquetball, basketball courts, Nautilus, and sauna. Very close to the Metro YMCA is Frank Eisenzimmer's Cascade Athletic Club. It offers roughly the same facilities at a slightly higher price. While there are likely minor differences in equipment, staff competency or cleanliness, the major difference is that the Cascade Athletic Club pays $75,000 per year in property taxes while the Metro YMCA pays nothing. Eisenzimmer is, of course, free to retain the profits for his athletic club but the YMCA must use its quasi-profits by subsidizing other activities. Over the years it appears that the YMCA has received less and less of its income from donations and more income from fees for services.

The YMCA originally was intended to provide facilities for the poor and has been doing so since the late nineteenth century. At present, the YMCA is one of several organizations leading the way nationally on innovative pre- and after-school programs for children of working parents. However, the Nautilus machines in the Metro YMCA are behind locked doors and available only to fee-paying members. The special memberships available at the Metro YMCA are not for the needy. Eisenzimmer, the owner of a competing for-profit facility, says, "The free enterprise system has been around a lot longer than the YMCA. Tax exemption is a gift from the community to an organization that provides charitable good deeds in return. If the organization is straying from its original intent, the community should remove the tax-exempt status. If the YMCA is truly interested in serving the community, why is it against paying a fair share of taxes?" Has the organization become too entrepreneurial? Is it in the administrators' expansionary interest to align themselves with a different, more affluent group of patrons? Or, is it the case that survival and cross-subsidies to preferred programs require income generating activities?

YMCAs receive less than 20 percent of their income from donations and need to respond to clients. On the other hand, consider public libraries, which are almost totally dependent on their government sponsors. Few libraries earn more than a pittance from fees charged for fines, duplicating, or computer usage. The local government sponsor usually reviews performance and budget requests, and then allocates a yearly block grant from which the institution funds their programs.

Even when private video rental is available, public libraries have branched out into lending DVDs and CDs. It cannot be argued that libraries expect to earn income by lending these items, because borrowing fees are minimal. Although librarians might argue that their selection of DVDs has value, a library's objective may have more to do with increased traffic. Increased traffic maps into increased demand for service and funding by its sponsoring agency.

In Dayton, Ohio, for instance, the public library loans videos free of charge. Using standard cost-accounting methods, it was estimated that the cost to the Dayton public library of circulating an average item is $1.73, not including costs of library capital. The average rental price at a profit-seeking store was $2.40.

Clients of the library incur waiting costs. The Dayton public library rarely buys multiple copies, while Video Towne stores of Dayton carry multiple copies of popular videos at its seven locations. U.S. public libraries are open fewer than 40 hours per week on average while the comparable number for a private video store is 74 hours per week.

The motivation of NFP firms to enter into commercial activities varies. The YMCA enters the health club market to seek revenue as donations shrink and the Dayton public library circulates videos to demonstrate to its sponsor increased user demand.

How would you make the case that the YMCA and the Dayton public library continue to provide public goods that entitle them to nonprofit tax advantages? Has managerial discretion allowed the managers of these firms to change the firms' orientation?

Source: Nancy M. Davis, "The Competition Complex," *Association Management*, August, 1986, 25; William B. Irvine, "The Private Video Library: A Bright Beginning, an Uncertain Future," *Heartland Policy Study*, no. 20, March 31, 1988, 3.

9.10   ASSESSING NFP FIRM PERFORMANCE

The bottom line in any nonprofit or government agency is faithfulness to mission, to the intentions of those that support and sponsor it, and to client trust. A necessary but insufficient condition for the stewards and civil servants, staffing these organizations, is to be well intentioned. But good intentions are not enough. Any organization, nonprofit, public, or profit-seeking becomes inward looking without external discipline. Oversight, competition, and the need to respond to clients provide this discipline. Civil servants and nonprofit administrators, however well intentioned, can act in their own self-interest, boost their budgets, protect their power, and resist outside scrutiny. Of course, profit-seeking managers would do the same in the absence of stockholder pressure. When markets work, profit-seeking CEOs earn increased compensation for good and downward adjustments for inadequate performance. NFPs, on the other hand, rely on trust, and therefore the "carrot and stick" approach is seldom used for employers in the NFP sectors. The key for all types of firms is to focus on objectives and for sponsors to recognize the value of external competition and/or effective oversight.

A commercial restaurant provides service, sometimes well and sometimes poorly. It is not essential to define precisely what that service means: nutritious or low priced food, friendly or formal atmosphere, pleasant employees or unobtrusive catering. Profit and loss statements as well as competition with other restaurants discipline a firm and indicate whether the proper trade-offs are being made. Without these controls, profit-seeking corporations would not be any more efficient or effective than NFP firms. It is undeniable that competition and client choice in the NFP sectors also leads to increased effectiveness. In certain situations, admittedly, these conditions are neither feasible nor appropriate.

Given a lack of competition between providers as well as an inability to use financial incentives, nonprofit and government boards must explore unique ways to exercise their obligations. Because they oversee firms financed by funds other than client fees, NFP boards combine two roles: first, they need to make sure that firms remain true to mission, and, second, they have a duty to monitor quality. This latter role is most critical when clients have few options or none at all.

Against what standards should a nonprofit or government firm be evaluated? How does one measure success when there are multiple objectives? Conflicting objectives? Intangible and unquantifiable objectives? Are professionals within the firm in a position to better evaluate programs even though board members have the legal responsibility? Are detailed guidelines necessary for measuring output?

Three essential points must be made about the evaluation process in general:

1   The struggle to agree upon assessment criteria, including some measurement of output, should take place along with the process of specifying objectives.
2   It is essential to distinguish between two types of evaluation: a process-measuring program outputs and showing how they relate to preferred outcomes should be followed by a process measuring how programs reflect the sponsor's moral constraints.
3   Internal evaluations are helpful but seldom accurate. Internal data systems are often biased justification for the firm's survival or expansion. They attempt to show proof of demand. This is misleading given NFP subsidies to clients. Whenever possible an adversarial approach, certification of standards, and an external audit assist the board, sponsor, donors, and clients in assessing performance.

Accountability

Clients and society as a whole benefit from the unique characteristics of the NFP sectors. Firms in these sectors provide services subsidized through donations, tax revenue, and at times committed employees willing to work for less. The subsidies, however, do not guarantee high quality and altruistic performance. Accountability is still needed to maintain the stream of social benefits and to keep these institutions out of the hands of incompetents and charlatans (Rose-Ackerman, 1996).

External watchdogs consist of government, the news media, and sponsoring boards. Federal and state-level agencies have been established to oversee private nonprofits. These bodies essentially enforce laws requiring that funds be used to pursue mission and to prevent insiders from enriching themselves. Internal Revenue Service regulations guide charitable organizations on what constitutes appropriate financial compensation for top employees and assess penalties if they are not followed. *Good Governance Practices for 501(c) (3) Organizations* is a document issued by the IRS in early 2007. These, at present, voluntary recommendations include:

• adopting a mission statement, code of ethics, conflict of interest policy, whistleblower policy, document retention policy, and fundraising procedures;
• ensuring board members, officers, and employees comply with their duties of care and loyalty to the organization and, if compensated, are paid no more than reasonable compensation;
• providing full and accurate information to the public about the nonprofit's activities and finances; and
• when the size of a nonprofit's revenue or assets is substantial, hiring an independent auditor to conduct an annual financial audit.

States hold primary responsibility for overseeing nonprofits but vary greatly in resources allocated to this task. State laws differ in whether they permit state attorney generals or other agencies to enforce oversight, institute suits, require reports, etc. At present, about 40 of the 50 states require charities that solicit funds in that state to be registered within the state. Registrations expire and are further complicated with state and federal requirements that are inconsistent. Although government oversight provides useful information to all stakeholders, compliance costs can be large. Furthermore, although a government bureaucracy can eliminate the worst offenders, it cannot measure the effectiveness of a particular NFP firm.

Journalists and other information sources contribute useful information about NFPs. The Better Business Bureau and GuideStar are just two of many organizations providing online information regarding program spending as a percentage of fundraising, executive compensation, and board structure.

The American Institute of Philanthropy publishes and makes its *Charity Rating Guide* available at a nominal fee for those trying to determine if a particular charity is worthy of their contributions. The *Guide* reports whether or not an organization is eligible to receive tax-deductible contributions, noting those charities which may have incorporated entities subject to a different tax status. Depending on the availability of information, each organization is listed by industry, its financial performance measures, and given an overall grade. Ratios used to calculate the letter grade are: (1) percentage of revenue received that is spent on charitable purposes, and (2) the cost the organization incurs in raising $100 in donations. A grade is reduced if a charity retains available assets exceeding three years or more of current program expenses. Organizations with "years of available assets" exceeding five years are considered least in need of charitable contributions and receive an "F" grade regardless of other measurements.

Universally, private nonprofit activity is generally associated with a free press, because both require similar rights and freedom. Unfortunately, the role of the media in private and public sector oversight comes at a cost. Inaccuracies and false rumors can increase expenses and limit service when NFP firms are put in the position of constantly defending their policies.

What drives foundation expenses compensation?

Boris et al. (2008) summarize the results of a three year study on ways that independent, corporate, and community foundations differ. Smaller foundations generally have few or no paid staff, community foundations employ professional staff more intensively, and corporate foundations may not report staff compensation because it is absorbed by the parent company. These differences can lead to the appearance of over-spending on administrative versus program expenses, because IRS-990 type documents fail to properly inform the public about the full cost and categories of foundation expenses.

Boards of trustees hold the ultimate decision-making rights over the assets of NFP institutions. Donors on the board are expected to monitor on behalf of the overall donor community. Voting rights of sponsors and donors are diluted, however, if board composition includes members with personal agendas but little stake in the organization. Unfortunately, we do not as yet have sufficient information to evaluate how the three watchdogs of government, media, and board interact. Does strong government regulation augment strong media and board oversight or does it substitute and replace it?

Standard-setting organizations

A NFP firm may opt for accreditation by a national or international independent nonprofit agency. It does this to demonstrate that procedures and qualifications of those providing the service meet certain standards. Accreditation does not certify product quality. When a university, for example, meets the standards of the Association to Advance Collegiate Schools of Business (AACSB), curriculum and staffing procedures are scrutinized but the output (graduates) are not tested or certified. The accreditation process involves a review of the organization, including service standards, personnel, financial and risk management, and continuous quality improvement. Numerous specialized accrediting bodies promote best-practice standards. *Best practices* is a term that refers to professional procedures believed to be effective in dealing with certain situations given existing know-how. Conducting a test for streptococcus, for example, is considered a best practice whenever a patient presents with a sore throat. The consistent application of best practices should statistically be directly linked with improved outcomes.

9.11   OPERATIONAL TARGETS AND INDICATORS

Some metrics are needed to determine if output is increasing or decreasing and if a firm is meeting preferred outcomes. It is acknowledged that assessment tools in the hands of incompetent or unethical administrators decrease social welfare but measurement is still needed. Perfect assessment measures do not exist. However, for individuals motivated by mission and willing to face reality, even deficient tools are useful. A NFP firm will never be able to guarantee individual results in return for payment, but it can provide information on the group as a whole. Thus, a private nonprofit school, for example, with a unique creative curriculum, can agree to external standardized testing of its students, provide results, and permit comparison with mainstream approaches. Application 9.7 discusses the controversy of relying on external national student examinations compared with internal assessment tools.

APPLICATION 9.7
External Examinations versus Internal Assessments

Internal conflicts of interest suggest that institutions will often fail even though they are staffed by well-prepared and highly motivated staff with state-of-the-art facilities and best practices.

Superintendents of school districts face powerful incentives to set low standards in order to make them easier to reach, to defer maintenance on facilities, and to raise budgets. They are often paid according to the number of people who report to them, and therefore have a strong temptation to become budget maximizers.

Principals are judged on inconsistent assessment standards. They may be unable to select their staff, and internal pressure prevents them from retaining good teachers by awarding differentiated salaries. In large school districts, students and competent teachers without seniority often are not free to transfer to more effective environments.

Whenever academic standards call for top-down "accountability," some school districts, being evaluated, are permitted to produce their own tests to determine acceptable levels of progress. This is sometimes referred to as "authentic outcomes-based" or internal assessment. On the other hand, external curriculum-based examinations measure what is actually taught in school. These are produced and administered by persons outside, or external to, the school district.

Are there conflicts of interest inherent in having a school district simultaneously set standards, measure performance, and take responsibility for results? Is vocational training geared to the needs of a specific region negatively impacted from one-size-fits-all national exams? Do external curriculum-based exams address these problems?

Source: Joseph L. Bast and Herbert J. Walberg, *Let's Put Parents Back in Charge*, Chicago, IL: Heartland Institute, 2003.

We stress the importance of external indicators in this section knowing that national organizations providing these services are also subject to error and increase costs. Data generated externally about graduates' performance on certifying exams for employment in medicine, education, and civil service is a valuable instrument in assessing a university's performance. They may also be valuable filters protecting health and safety.

The indicator-operational target approach is a pragmatic methodology for improving performance in the nonprofit and government sectors. It originates in the assumption that no one has complete information to determine output as policy filters through an organization. Pharmaceutical companies are aware that they often do not know how a specific drug acts on the body, even when they test and monitor results. Similarly, the "mechanism of action" between policy and results is unknown. The nonprofit or government agency has to set up targets and indicators to test the intensity and direction of effort. We will first discuss indicators measuring outputs and then backtrack to targets, the link between policy and outputs.

An *indicator* is defined as a variable that provides information about the effect of current firm activity on future movements in the ultimate objective. The choice of an indicator involves selecting some variable that consistently provides reliable information about influences of present actions on the status of the ultimate objective. *Indicators* are assessment tools that are easily observable, accurate, and cost-effective. Suppose that a school district's ultimate educational objective is that students have the skills needed for entry-level jobs or higher education. To achieve this, they initiate a new program increasing the time spent on core classes. The percentage of students performing at a certain level on standardized tests used for job placement could be an indicator of school policy. The usefulness of an indicator hinges on whether or not it consistently supplies reliable information.

An *operational target* is a measure observable shortly after a policy change. The target reflects needed policy adjustments, and in the short run dominates changes in indicators. Hours of instruction in math and language could serve as an operational target between curriculum and students' ultimate performance on standardized tests.

Inappropriate indicators provide improper incentives. Some professors argue that student course evaluations are an inappropriate indicator of teaching effectiveness. Although student course evaluations act effectively as a target for measuring client satisfaction, they do not lead to better academic outcomes. Application 9.8 supports this argument. It may be the case, on one level, that student course evaluations help identify faculty whose performance is indeed consistent with a preferred goal of administrators, e.g., student retention.

APPLICATION 9.8
Student/Teacher Course Evaluations: An Indicator of Teaching Effectiveness or Threat to Educational Standards?

Faculty promotion, tenure, and salary in colleges and universities increasingly depend on teaching effectiveness as measured by student course evaluations. Do these evaluations measure the effectiveness of a particular instructor? Do these evaluations relate to the mission of the college or university as a NFP firm? Student course evaluations highlight the general problem that NFP firms have in choosing appropriate indicators.

An educational institution is legitimately concerned with accurately assessing the performance of faculty members as well as increasing the amount of learning taking place. If the amount of learning that takes place is related to grading policies, it is imperative that the instrument used to evaluate its faculty does not provide incentives to manipulate grades and thereby degrade the quality of education.

Thousands of articles on student course evaluations have been written which confirm that higher student grades are associated with higher teacher course evaluations. Are students learning more in these classes? Highly motivated students enrolled in small elective upper-level classes evaluate a given faculty member higher than he or she would receive in large lower-level required classes. It is, of course, possible to compare faculty members' performance in similar situations. However, this still does not necessarily imply that higher evaluations are associated with more learning resulting in higher grades or that higher evaluations result in some way from higher grades and, perhaps, less learning.

In an attempt to separate the effects of grades on student evaluations of teaching from other variables, Valen Johnson compared two sets of Duke University evaluations of first-year students before and after they received their final grades for the semester. These paired evaluations enabled researchers to compare how a given student tends to rate all instructors compared with how they rate those classes in which they received higher or lower than average grades. Both grade expectations and received grades caused a change in the way students perceived their teacher and the quality of instruction. In general, however, higher grades resulted in higher evaluations.

Even if it were possible to evaluate individual faculty members by comparing them with others teaching similar classes and giving similar grades, the unintended effects of higher grades and lower levels of learning are factors that must be taken into consideration or monitored in some other fashion.

Source: Valen E. Johnson, "Teacher Course Evaluations and Student Grades: An Academic Tango," *Chance*, 15 (3), 2002, 9–16.

The implementation of targets and indicators is modeled in Figure 9.5. Transmission of mission within the firm consists of policy instruments, such as procedures and practices, and operational targets. A target might be a specific number of professional staff per client. Indicators, outside the firm's control, connect firm output to ultimate policy objectives, which lie in the "real" world. Third graders' performance on reading in a nationally normed test is an indicator. The real world in our example consists of all those things over which the sponsor does not have control, such as students' ability or patients' general health, motivation, values, and other socio-cultural conditions. Implied in this methodology is the assumption that policy decisions work through the firm to provide results, which to some extent can be controlled and accounted for.

The Naval Supply Center in Newport, Rhode Island, has as its principal mission to receive, store, and issue material for clients, consisting of ships, navy battalions, naval shore facilities, shipyards, and aircraft overhaul facilities. Material supplied includes everything from fuel and electronic repair parts to frozen meats: approximately 50,000 items in inventory. Headquarters of the Navy in Washington, DC, use the percentage of processed requests completed within 7 days as an indicator of the supply station's effectiveness. Processing involves recording requests and storing the goods in a suitable location for delivery. The number of shipments and receipts are reported periodically and used as operating targets. Because the objective of any organization is to provide service at minimum cost,

How to operationalize a mission statement

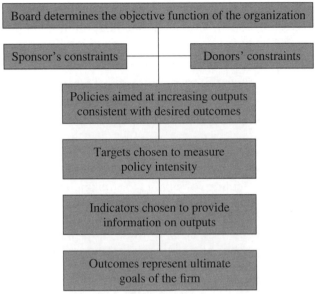

Figure 9.5   The use of targets and indicators. Administrators establish a firm's policy and operational targets as part of the transmission mechanism. Indicators and outcomes take place in the "real world."

operational targets, along with indicators, which are largely output measures, are used in conjunction with cost information to determine operational efficiency.

Targets and indicators are not perfect substitutions for market efficiency and effectiveness, but chosen carefully they provide government and nonprofit agencies with alternatives to the all-inclusive profit measure used by corporations. Application 9.9 deals with organizations using targets and indicators to provide online quality rankings for U.S. hospitals.

APPLICATION 9.9
Keeping the Patient Informed

Any institution, public or private, profit-seeking or nonprofit, will be shunned and/or shut down if clients are harmed and the institution receives negative publicity. This only occurs after terrible things have happened. Is there a way of providing patients with good information about those hospitals adopting standards to prevent poor outcomes and to avoid mistakes such as X-ray mix-ups and medication errors?

A variety of organizations provide free online quality rankings for U.S. hospitals, and the Joint Commission on Accreditation of Healthcare Organizations actually audits hospital-quality data. Due to asymmetric information in choosing hospitals, clients have difficulty evaluating hospital services and limited expertise in interpreting rating systems. One such rating system, The Leap Frog Group, ranks hospitals for both quality and safety. It was created by 150 company employers who purchase billions of dollars of healthcare on behalf of their employees.

Leap Frog's safety rankings are based on a survey of 1,300 hospitals on 30 key practices. The goal is to determine if hospital managers are creating a "culture of safety" for making safety a top hospital priority. Note that this survey does not inspect hospitals. It is based on self-reports. Therefore, some doctors and hospitals have resisted these types of surveys as arbitrary, unfair, and resource consuming. As is the case with other social service providers, it is always easier to measure processes and inputs than effective outcomes. Corporations desiring higher quality and cost-effective healthcare apparently believe that raising consciousness about safety improves safety; otherwise these profit-seeking firms would not pay for Leap Frog information.

Source: Laura Landro, "Report Card to Rank Hospitals on Safety," *Wall Street Journal*, April 22, 2004, D1.

Targets and indicators need to be consistent. If a school district, for example, uses standardized testing as an indicator of student learning and teacher certification as a target, then there should be firm evidence that increasing the target (certified teachers) is directly related to improvements in the indicator (student scores). At times, multiple indicators of quality are required because a single indicator is focused at the lower end of an acceptable range for certain activities. In the case of the Naval Supply Center, different time targets for various types of requests would lower overall average response time.

Suppose a university uses, as one of its indicators of quality, the percentage of new students who excel on entrance examinations. While this indicates something about the admissions office, it does not reveal anything in particular about value added in the form of learning or skills acquired by attending the institution. It could mean that already educated, high-performing test-takers seek to be part of a select student body and hope to benefit from the institution's networking opportunities. Can a school use its athletic program to attract high performers? Is it conceivable that targeting a university's performance in athletics affects the number of applications from top students? Application 9.10 offers some clues to answering these questions.

APPLICATION 9.10
Do University Athletic Programs Significantly Influence Institutional Quality?

Average SAT entrance test scores are perceived as evidence of institutional quality. Some suggest that high-performing athletic programs have a strong influence on enrolling better students. This has led to investigations of factors influencing the enrollment of students with high test scores. It is hypothesized that athletic programs exert a strong influence. Bremmer and Kesselring use multiple regression to evaluate this proposition. Their model is summarized below:

Dependent variable is average freshman SAT score

Variable	Coefficient	t-ratio
Constant	966.734	11.588
Sports (in a major conference or well known = 1)	11.003	0.659
Level of tuition	0.010	2.705*
Volumes in library	−0.001	−0.215
Salary of faculty	0.353	3.096*
Age of the school	−0.007	−0.047
Students/faculty	1.782	1.095
Enrollment	−0.001	−0.275
Endowment/student	5.036	1.862*
Ph.D./student	−0.191	−0.453
Average state SAT	0.016	0.340
Acceptance %	−310.133	−7.530*
Football (number of bowl appearances in prior 10 years)	0.802	0.280
Basketball (number of NCAA tournaments in prior 10 years	0.030	0.013

Adjusted R-squared = 0.817; $n = 119$.

In any regression study, the researcher must decide beforehand on a level of significance. In this study, only variables with t-ratios large enough to be significant at a 95 percent level are considered important. Just four variables for which the t-ratios are marked with a * are significant at a 95 percent confidence level. In this particular study, institutions having higher average SAT scores for students tend to have higher levels of tuition, higher faculty salaries, high endowments, and lower acceptance rates. Using "acceptance rate" to explain SAT scores of those presently enrolled is probably a misspecification which leads us to dismiss its significance. In fact, "acceptance rate" could have been substituted as the dependent variable in place of SAT scores as the measure of student academic quality. This suggests another hypothesis yet to be tested: good athletic programs increase the number of applications. In this study, however, none of the sports related variables have statistical significance and thus these researchers conclude that athletic programs are not an important determinant of the quality of the institution.

Source: Based on Dale S. Bremmer and Randall G. Kesselring, "The Advertising Effect of University Athletic Success: A Reappraisal of the Evidence," *Quarterly Review of Economics and Finance*, winter, 1993, 409–21.

Warning!

At times, private nonprofit firm and government personnel appear to be totally unresponsive to their clients, donors/taxpayers, and communities. Sponsors, administrators, and users seem powerless in moving an organization toward consistent objectives. The proverbial "kicking a dead horse" comes to mind. This inertia could be due to conflicting operational targets within an organization or the absence of effective incentives. In other cases, NFP employees run around like untamed broncos to demonstrate high performance on any indicator they believe is monitored. In both cases, persons within the firm are reacting to incentives. In India, for several years, the operational target of the population control agency was the absolute number of males sterilized. Administrators filled their tallies with old men and young boys. Insufficient incentives and inappropriate indicators contribute little to a sponsor's ultimate objective.

Individuals in NFP enterprises respond to incentives and quickly learn to manipulate targets and indicators used to measure their performance. The *U.S. News and World Report*'s yearly rankings of colleges and universities use the annual percentage of alumni contributing as an indicator of alumni satisfaction. Therefore, some colleges began to count room deposits forfeited by graduating seniors as donations spread out over several years. This practice reduces annual gift size but is an expected response by fundraising staff from pressure to meet annual targets for the percentage of alumni giving (Golden, 2007). Targets and indicators are necessary but cannot replace the endless conversation on achieving excellence and interpreting firm mission.

CONCLUDING NOTES

- NFP firm behavior is embedded in informal institutions, customs, traditions, and societal norms. In addition, a country's formal rules and regulations determine how public goods, including social services, are provided.

- Institutional governance is a process by which the board of a NFP firm provides administrative oversight as well as an accounting of activities and finances to sponsors and donors.

- Given the constraints of culture, law, and mission, an effective NFP firm attempts to provide the greatest quality and quantity of output for a given level of inputs.

- Favored or preferred outputs are closely related to core mission and competency. Neutral outputs complement preferred outputs. Disfavored outputs can either subsidize or hinder mission. NFP firms cross-subsidize between activities.

- Given full cost and revenue data, a firm may choose: to produce a level of output consistent with maximizing net income (profit), to break-even and cover all costs, or to operate at a loss and cross-subsidize with donated funds or less favored activities.

- The net income (profit) maximizing level of output is where total revenue exceeds total cost by the greatest amount. In the production range where marginal costs are increasing, net income is maximized where marginal cost is equal to marginal revenue.

- An output maximizing strategy is achieved at a production level where total revenue equals total cost and net income is zero. At this point, the client fee plus per unit subsidy equals average total cost.

- Allocative efficiency is approximated if the NFP firm produces but does not exceed the point where the marginal cost of the last unit equals the value to the user (the user fee) plus the value to the sponsor (the subsidy).

- The incentive structure facing bureaucrats often leads to budget maximizing behavior, which discounts higher costs and reduces marginal benefits below social marginal cost.

- There are generally two break-even points given total revenue (TR) and nonlinear total costs (TC). Any level of production between these points produces some net income (profit), but maximum net income (profit) is earned at one point. At this point, the slope of total revenue (MR) equals the slope of total costs (MC).

- If revenue earned per unit of output is constant, we can calculate the level of sales necessary for the firm to break even. The level is found by dividing fixed cost by the difference between price and average variable cost (called the contribution margin). This break-even rule can be extended to calculate the production volume necessary to obtain any specified level of net income or to determine which of several price-quantity combinations will yield the maximum net income for a given cost structure.

- At times, total revenue fails to exceed total cost at any level of output. If resources have been committed, it is reasonable to continue the program in the short run as long as revenue from fees and donations is sufficient to cover variable costs and some fraction of fixed (overhead) costs.

- Upper level administrators, at times, use managerial discretion to pursue personal goals contrary to those of the sponsor.

- Quality of output over time and across firms varies more in the NFP sectors than in the profit-seeking sector. The preferences of elite workers in NFP firms tend to dominate more so than those similarly employed in the profit-seeking sector.

- The Hansmann classification divides NFP firms into four categories by two criteria: donative versus commercial and mutual versus entrepreneurial.

- The movement of NFP firms into commercial activities blurs the line between the NFP and profit-seeking sectors. Profit-seeking alliances may conflict with primary mission. Commercial activities offer untaxed NFP firms an advantage over profit-seeking firms.

- Specifying objectives and assessment measures should be determined together as part of the same process. Assessment measures coordinate output to preferred outcomes and sponsor preferences. Accreditation and external audits supplement internal evaluations.

- Federal and state-level agencies exist to ensure that NFP funds are used to pursue mission and to monitor corruption. Media sources such as newspapers, the Better Business Bureau, GuideStar, etc. provide information on program spending. NFP boards hold ultimate decision-making rights and responsibility.

- A NFP firm cannot guarantee individual results in return for a fee. The "mechanism of action" between policy and results is often unknown. However, operational targets test the intensity and direction of a firm's efforts, and indicators measure the extent to which a firm achieves its objectives.

KEY TERMS

Embeddedness
Institutional environment
Governance
Outputs
Outcomes
Favored or preferred outputs
Neutral outputs
Disfavored outputs
Cross-subsidization
Objective function
Break-even point

Contribution margin per unit
Managerial discretion
Contract failure
Donative NFP firms
Commercial NFP firms
Mutual NFP firms
Entrepreneurial NFP firms
Best practices
Indicator
Operational target

SUGGESTED READINGS

Benjamin, Lehn 2006: "Review: *Measuring Performance in Public and Nonprofit Organizations* by Theodore Poister," *Nonprofit and Voluntary Sector Quarterly*, 35 (1), 152–5.

Boris, Elizabeth, Renz, Loren, Hager, Mark A., Elias, Rachel, and Somashekhar, Mahesh 2008: *What Drives Foundation Expenses Compensation?*, Report of the Urban Institute, Foundations Center, and GuideStar.

Glaeser, Edward L. 2003: *The Governance of Not-for-profit Organizations*, Chicago, IL: University of Chicago Press.

Golden, Daniel 2007: "To Boost Donor Number, Colleges Adopt New Tricks," *Wall Street Journal*, Friday, March 2, A1.

Hansmann, Henry 1980: "The Role of Nonprofit Enterprise," *Yale Review Journal*, April, 835–98.

James, Estelle 1983: "How Nonprofits Grow: A Model," *Journal of Policy Analysis and Management*, 2, 350–65.

Nathan, Maria Louise 1994: "One Hundred Years of Strategic Decision-making: Building the Art Institute of Chicago, 1879–1979," *Short Takes on Nonprofit Governance*, ed. M. M. Wood, Indianapolis, IN: Indiana University Center on Philanthropy.

Niskanen, William A. 1971: *Bureaucracy and Representative Government*, Chicago, IL: Aldine Publishing Company.

Panel on the Nonprofit Sector Convened by INDEPENDENT SECTOR 2005: "Strengthening Transparency, Governance, Accountability of Charitable Organizations," a final report to Congress and the nonprofit sector, June, www.nonprofitpanel.org/final, accessed June 23.

Preston, Anne 1988: "The Effects of Property Rights on Labor Costs of Nonprofit Firms: An Application to the Day Care Industry," *Journal of Industrial Economics*, March, 337–50.

Rose-Ackerman, Susan 1996: "Altruism, Nonprofits, and Economic Theory," *Journal of Economic Literature*, 34 (June), 701–28.

Schiff, Jerald and Weisbrod, Burton 1987: "Competition between For-profit and Nonprofit Organizations in Commercial Markets," paper presented at the American Economics Association Meetings, Chicago, IL, December.

Weisbrod, Burton A. (ed.) 1998: *To Profit or Not to Profit*, Cambridge, UK: Cambridge University Press.

Williamson, Oliver E. 2000: "The New Institutional Economics: Taking Stock, Looking Ahead," *Journal of Economic Literature*, 38 (September), 595–613.

END OF CHAPTER EXERCISES

Exercise 9.1

In higher education, many costs and revenues are nearly linear with relation to the level of activity, as measured by enrollment. It has been suggested that break-even analysis may be a useful management tool for the combined analysis of costs and revenue in higher education. Suppose that fixed cost for top-level administrative salaries, maintenance, building and grounds expenses, and so on for the South Central State University (SCSU) totaled $1.2 million per year. Also, assume that revenue per student is composed of a tuition charge of $25 per credit hour for in-state students and $65 per credit hour for out-of-state students, plus a state appropriation of $50 per in-state student credit hour and $10 for each credit hour for out-of-state students. In addition, SCSU has some revenue from sources not related directly to student credit hours, such as federal grants and private research grants, which amounts to about $300,000 per year.

SCSU is divided into two colleges: the College of Arts and Sciences and the College of Agricultural Studies. Each college has four departments. The college and department budgets for variable costs, such as faculty salaries and supplies, are given in the following table, along with the number of credit hours taught by each department:

	Faculty salaries	Other variable costs	Total variable costs	Credit hours taught	Allocation fixed cost
College of Arts and Sciences	$1,900,000	$320,000	$2,220,000	$39,690	
Department 1	600,000	100,000	700,000	14,000	
Department 2	450,000	70,000	520,000	9,450	
Department 3	500,000	90,000	590,000	9,440	
Department 4	350,000	60,000	410,000	6,800	
College of Agricultural Studies	1,800,000	310,000	2,110,000	34,400	
Department 5	400,000	80,000	480,000	8,400	
Department 6	700,000	110,000	810,000	10,200	
Department 7	200,000	50,000	250,000	4,000	
Department 8	500,000	70,000	570,000	11,800	

Assuming that the fixed costs should be allocated on the basis of each unit's share of total credit hours, complete the final column of the table.

a. Determine the break-even level of enrollment for each college and each department (for now, ignore the $300,000 of revenue that is not related directly to enrollment).

b. Rank the departments according to profitability. How many departments operate at a net loss? Does each college "pay its own way"?

c. Suppose that the $300,000 of grant revenue is obtained by departments as follows:

> Department 1, 10 percent.
> Department 2, 12 percent.
> Department 3, 28 percent.
> Department 4, 0 percent.
> Department 5, 10 percent.
> Department 6, 15 percent.
> Department 7, 10 percent.
> Department 8, 15 percent.

Which departments break even?

d. The faculty in department 6 is concerned because the Board of Regents has been under pressure to cut costly programs. The faculty argues that their work and their graduates are vital to the agricultural base of the state's economy and that, because of the positive externalities they create for the rest of the state, their state appropriation per credit hour should be increased by $5. If this was done, would department 6 still have a deficit, would they have a net surplus, or would they break even? If they would not break even, how much revenue per credit hour would be necessary for them to break even with the current enrollment?

e. Is it reasonable to expect each department to "pay its own way"? What about each college? Who should decide this?

Exercise 9.2

University Press is considering publishing one of two manuscripts (A and B), both of which it will sell for $10 per copy. The well-known author of manuscript A insists on a large pre-payment. Manuscript B involves a large number of colored illustrations. University Press will decide shortly on which of the two manuscripts to publish this year. It estimated the following data for publishing each book, and management believes that 150,000 units will be sold of each book:

	Manuscript A ($)	Manuscript B ($)
Sales	1,500,000	1,500,000
Variable costs	800,000	950,000
Fixed costs	400,000	250,000
New income/profit	300,000	300,000

a. Calculate the break-even point for both processes.
b. Which manuscript would be preferred if management felt there was a high probability of exceeding sales of 150,000 units? Why?
c. Which manuscript would be preferred if management felt there was a high probability of selling considerably less than 150,000 units? Why?
d. On what basis to you think University Press should decide between the two manuscripts? Explain.

Exercise 9.3

Moreau Shelter Industries, employing mentally and physically challenged adults, produces a single product, which sells for $25 per unit. Its variable operating costs are $10, and its fixed operating costs are $2 million.

a. Calculate Moreau's profit for 100,000 units and 200,000 units.
b. Calculate the break-even volume.
c. Draw the break-even chart for Moreau Industries.

Exercise 9.4

The administrators at Moreau Shelter are considering changing its operations. Using the information provided in Exercise 9.3, calculate both the profit level and the break-even point under the following conditions:

a.   10 percent increase in selling price.
b.   10 percent increase in selling price coupled with a 10 percent increase in variable costs.
c.   10 percent increase in selling price coupled with a 10 percent increase in fixed costs.
d.   10 percent increase in variable costs coupled with a 10 percent decrease in fixed costs.
e.   10 percent decrease in variable costs coupled with a 10 percent increase in fixed costs.

Exercise 9.5
Does the dominance and survival of the private nonprofit sector in a particular industry depend on embeddedness or Micro-analytic considerations? Provide two examples and explain.

Exercise 9.6
Identify each of the following issues in terms of Oliver Williamson's analysis of the environment (embeddedness, institutional, or governance) in which NFPs operate. Explain why you choose to consider the issue as part of more than one environmental level:

a.   Whether or not the university's board members are given gratis tickets to athletic events.
b.   The extent to which property owned by a private nonprofit is exempt from property taxes.
c.   A fireworks display takes place each year on Independence Day over the town's river.
d.   An established religion receives state subsidies.
e.   Professionals do not release information about clients outside the organization.
f.   In emergencies, police and other government officials occupy the property of private nonprofits.
g.   Organizations may not discriminate between clients on a particular characteristic.
h.   Off-duty police officers are given use of department vehicles.
i.   Hospitals may choose to qualify as nonprofit organizations. Physician practices cannot.
j.   Bonuses are paid to workers in the Admissions Office of a University for the number of applications received.
k.   Pomp and Circumstance is played as gowned graduates enter to receive their diplomas.

Exercise 9.7
Explain why performance on standardized tests and graduation rates are used as operating targets. What indicator(s) would you use to measure school effectiveness?

Exercise 9.8
In evaluating public health, explain, in terms of targets and indicators, measures that could be employed as operational targets and others as indicators.

Exercise 9.9

Why do the authors of this text suggest that some internal assessment instruments, such as student course evaluations, are biased? What about surveys of golf club members or adolescents in foster care? Use the two-way classification of mutual/entrepreneurial firms to discuss this.

Exercise 9.10

Why do university students move off campus when subsidized residential facilities are available? Deal with this as the reverse of examples in the text in which profit-seeking firms operate at a disadvantage with respect to NFP firms? What measures could a budget maximizing administrator take to discourage students from moving off campus? Relate these measures to preferred, neutral, or distasteful activities.

Exercise 9.11

Carefully discuss, in terms of preferred, neutral, or distasteful activities, the pros and cons of a full-service hospital with a pedestrian walkway linked to an adjacent hotel operated, owned, or leased by the hospital.

Part IV

Input Markets and Cost–Benefit Analysis

10
Employing Labor and Capital

10.1   INTRODUCTION

In Part II of this text the market for the services of a NFP was analyzed in terms of clients' responsiveness to price. In this chapter, we turn to a different market but, as usual, supply and demand determine price and quantity of exchange. The market that we now wish to focus on is the one for resources, sometimes called the input or factor market. NFP firms, in the supply and demand framework, are suppliers of services to clients in product markets, but in resource markets they are demanders/employers of people, facilities, and loanable funds.

Of course, there are an almost infinite number of input markets in which firms demand inputs from the household sector supplying them. NFPs enter factor markets as demanders of nurses, teachers, attorneys, plumbers, volunteers, internet technologists, buildings, short-term loans, donations, etc. To organize our analysis, we will first discuss NFP employment of human resources, followed by the demand for funding with which firms purchase capital. Capital, in economics, refers to the actual machinery, plant, tools, and equipment needed to produce goods and services. Corporations account for and replace depreciated assets from funds received from current sales, but expansion is financed through undistributed profits, bank loans, bonds, and the sale of stock. NFP firms cannot issue stock, and they are forced to compete with all firms for funds in the loan market.

10.2   INPUT MARKETS AS DERIVED DEMAND

NFP firms have less control purchasing supplies in the resource market than they have in selling their unique services which are often subsidized. Most inputs are purchased in competitive markets where a firm pays the going rate or does without. In a few cases, NFPs access labor for below-market wages, subsidized by private or government employment programs. Generally, however, NFPs hire competitively in open resource markets.

The resource demand for facilities, equipment, and labor is called a *derived demand*, because it follows client demand for a firm's output. NFP demand for professional employees, school buildings, hospitals, and other facilities mirror the demand for primary goods and services such as education, healthcare, etc. Recall that, high compensation is not based exclusively on years of study in a rigorous field. It also depends on the demand for the services provided. An expert in baroque music will not earn much unless there is a demand for baroque music. Teachers' salaries are derived from the demand for education which in turn depends on demographics. Similarly, the demand for therapists is derived from the demand for therapy.

Economic theory offers some insight into two critical issues confronting NFPs in the resource market. How many inputs at each price level should a firm hire? How should a firm decide between hiring more labor and/or purchasing more equipment?

To begin, we assume that units of capital (equipment and facilities) and labor may to some extent be substituted one for another in the production process. The example works as well for substituting one type of worker with another. The old saw about the many ways to skin a cat suggests that substitutes can be found for many resource inputs.

Optimal combination of inputs

Within any organization, managers employ inputs in certain combinations. Administrators, for example, within some range can substitute licensed practical nurses for registered nurses. To minimize unit costs and maximize output, decisions are made to perhaps hire more workers and purchase less equipment or vice versa. With a fixed budget, an administrator selects inputs at prices (costs) over which he or she has no control. What combination of workers and equipment will achieve the highest possible level of output? The goal is to ensure that the last dollar spent on one input yields no more or less productivity than the last dollar spent on another. Otherwise a reallocation would realize more output for the same expenditure.

Let's consider the allocation between labor and capital equipment. Inputs are allocated efficiently if the ratio of marginal productivity of the last worker (MP_L) hired over the cost of that worker (C_L) is equal to the ratio of the marginal productivity of the last piece of equipment (MP_E) purchased over the cost of equipment (C_E):

$$\frac{MP_L}{C_L} = \frac{MP_E}{C_E}$$

This assumes (quite reasonably) that marginal productivity falls as subsequent units are employed and that the two inputs are independent. This is a reasonable assumption because rational firms operate in stage II of the production function. Economists call this relationship the **equimarginal principle** or the **least-cost criterion**.

Consider a case in which the output per dollar cost for the last unit of labor exceeds that for the last piece of equipment. In this situation, output is not optimally produced. By reallocating expenditures to labor (causing MP_L/C_L to fall) and decreasing equipment expenditures (causing MP_E/C_E to rise), more output is produced at no additional expense. Employing more labor *reduces* the productivity of the last dollar spent on labor. Employing less equipment *increases* the productivity of the last dollar spent on equipment.

Table 10.1 represents a simplified set of options for a hypothetical public radio station soliciting pledges either by mail or telephone. Potential donors are drawn randomly to receive either a phone call or letter soliciting pledges. In Table 10.1, by allocating $100 of expenditures incrementally, an organization seeks to maximize pledges by employing the two methods.

The public radio station attempts to maximize pledges for money spent. If initially a total of $500 were allocated for soliciting, pledges are maximized where:

$$\frac{MP_M}{C_M} = \frac{MP_P}{C_P}$$

$$\frac{10}{\$100} = \frac{10}{\$100}$$

This equilibrium occurs with $400 spent on mailings and $100 on phone solicitations. The total number of pledges (73) is the sum of the marginal productivities $(20 + 18 + 15 + 10 + 10)$.

NFPs should adopt the best means of raising funds, but most donors, rightly so, are concerned with expenditures relative to donations. Suppose the budget in the above example is increased to $1,000. The station could then expand to a different optimal combination. After spending a total of $900 ($400 on mailings and

Table 10.1   Allocating a pledge drive budget between two methods. Each incremental spending of $100 reduces the extra pledges made for both direct mailings and phone calls. The goal, in this example, is to allocate the budget in such a way so as to maximize the number of pledges.

Direct mailings		Phone calls	
Funds allocated ($)	Additional pledge yield (MP_M)	Funds allocated ($)	Additional pledge yield (MP_P)
100	20	100[a]	10
200	18	200	9
300	15	300	8
400[a]	10	400	7
500	5	500	6
600	4	600	5
700	2	700	4
800	2	800	3
900	2	900	2
1,000	1	1,000	1

[a] Note that if $500 were allocated to the pledge drive, then the maximum number of pledges (73) would be gained by allocating $400 to direct mailings and $100 to phone solicitations.

$500 on phone calls) the firm is indifferent between spending the last $100 on either mailings or phone calls and arbitrarily chooses one or the other. This yields a total of 113 pledges. Due diligence requires monitoring solicitation costs relative to funds received. In this case, the 113 pledges need to raise on average an $8.85 contribution ($1,000/113) merely to cover variable fundraising costs. Best NFP practice requires full transparency on reporting expenditures as a percentage of funds raised.

10.3   DEMAND AND SUPPLY OF HUMAN RESOURCES

From an economic point of view, a worker is not paid based on credentials, experience, character, intelligence, or work ethic but on his or her contribution to the firm over a certain period. Employees need to generate value at least equal to their compensation. Underlying this economic concept is the fact that the derived demand for any input is based on the demand for the final good or service produced by the firm. All firms, nonprofit or profit-seeking, exist to create value for clients and/or sponsors and cannot afford to compensate on the basis of perceived intrinsic value.

Therefore, each input neither can claim nor receive more than it creates. This economic proposition is counter-intuitive, because it sometimes appears as if those actually doing the work are on the bottom of the pay scale! This perception arises from the difficulty of quantifying the contributions of administrators in terms of patients seen, students taught, or caseload size. Also, most employees feel that they generate net value over and above compensation received and they are generally correct. However, as output and employment expand, marginal output per employee tends to decrease as does additional revenue brought into the firm per worker. Economists are looking at the value created by the last nurse, the last teacher, or the last social worker hired. The last employee should not be hired unless he or she creates in value what they are paid. Another misleading perception is that some professionals are underpaid. A firm generally will not compensate more than the market requires, and therefore a large supply of professionals in a particular field depresses compensation in that field for all practitioners. However, none of these perceptions negate the fact that the demand for a particular resource reflects value created relative to cost.

Marginal revenue product represents revenue coming into the firm from the sale of output produced by the last resource employed. Marginal revenue product analysis provides insight into many NFP decisions. It determines the average size elementary class, the number of critically ill patients cared for by a single nurse, and the social worker's caseload. In these cases, the value created by a NFP input is represented by the total revenue generated. Recall that, for NFPs, revenue includes client charges, state subsidies, and all fees from third parties per unit of output.

In Table 10.2, a given resource such as labor is added in single increments from zero to seven. Note that total product or output increases but marginal product declines. For simplification, we assume that each unit of output can be sold for $2.00. Beware! A NFP manager, in many markets, cannot sell additional units without reducing price, but the analysis holds for small changes in output. In Table 10.2 we multiply the constant price ($2) by the marginal product to get marginal revenue product which is the value of the extra output generated by the last resource employed. The first unit employed generates $18.20 of revenue and the seventh unit, $2.00.

The graph drawn in Figure 10.1 puts resource price (wage rate) on the vertical axis. At a cost of $14 per worker, one input is demanded because he is responsible for increasing revenue by $14. At a lower cost of $10, 2 additional units are

Table 10.2   Calculating marginal revenue product (MRP). Marginal revenue product is the change in total revenue that results from selling additional output produced by adding one more unit of valuable resource.

Units of labor	Total product	Marginal product (MP)	User fee/charge received per unit ($)	Total revenue ($)	Marginal revenue product (MRP) ($)
0	0	—	2	0	—
1	7	7	2	14	14
2	13	6	2	26	12
3	18	5	2	36	10
4	22	4	2	44	8
5	25	3	2	50	6
6	27	2	2	54	4
7	28	1	2	56	2

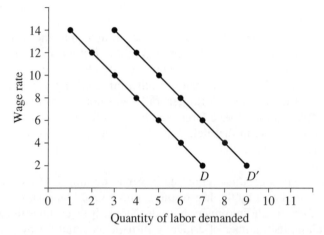

Figure 10.1   A firm's demand for resources. If each additional worker contributes less revenue to diminishing marginal productivity, a firm will not hire more labor unless the wage rate declines. If worker productivity in general increases or the user charges received for the service increase, the demand curve shifts to the right.

hired for a total of 3 workers producing 18 units of output. Note that the firm earns premiums over cost from the first 2 workers hired. The first unit brought $14 into the firm and the second, $12 but cost the firm $10 each.

What factors induce a NFP firm to increase employment of a given resource? Note in Table 10.2 that a lower resource price (wage rate) increases the quantity of resources (workers) demanded, but this price is generally beyond the firm's control. Any increase in marginal revenue product increases demand. Unfortunately, increasing productivity is difficult to achieve in the service sector. Another factor inducing more hiring is an increase in client fees or sponsor subsidies. Increased productivity and/or increased client charges, shift the demand curve to the right in Figure 10.1 to D'.

Professional associations, by restricting entry or negotiating a wage rate above equilibrium, benefit those who hold jobs but exclude others from being employed. If, however, professional associations work to establish best practices, to monitor performance, or to promote the product, then existing wages and employment may be maintained or increased by shifting the demand curve to the right.

Whenever input demand is based on marginal revenue product, each employee generates revenue equal to or more than the amount received in salary. As indicated above, marginal revenue product is difficult to estimate. In the Uuited States, the Taxpayer Bill of Rights charges the Internal Revenue Service with ensuring that charity leaders not receive exorbitant pay and perquisites. In practice, NFP executive compensation is generally justified in terms of comparable salaries at similar organizations, yet Application 10.1 questions the value added by some NFP executive officers. Application 10.2 deals with the difficult problem of assessing individual productivity in teamwork situations.

APPLICATION 10.1
The New York Stock Exchange Is a Nonprofit?

With respect to the compensation of the head of the New York Stock Exchange (NYSE), one reporter writes:

"Critics are shocked! Shocked! Shocked! The head of a not-for-profit, quasi-regulatory concern amassed about $140 million in deferred compensation without putting a penny at risk . . . Not to put too fine a point on it, but this great symbol of American capitalism is not a capitalist institution and its operations, including salaries, are not subject to any usual kinds of market discipline."

Several decades ago, following Securities and Exchange Commission rules, the NYSE was created and became the world's leading stock exchange. It turned into the most liquid market, even when it took longer to complete a trade on the NYSE than elsewhere. No trader wants to be the first to move from the largest market; therefore, the incumbent market had an advantage.

In a corporation where additions or subtractions to shareholder value can be measured. The NYSE, until recently, was a nonprofit firm owned and operated by its members. Thus, its head earned a large salary based on net income earned by an imperfectly competitive company enjoying an unusually dominant position. Resources necessary to perform the NYSE's mission, namely the regulatory function aimed at protecting stock buyers and sellers, may have been reallocated in the form of economic rents to top administrators.

Whoever sits in the executive's chair always looked good, like shooting fish in a barrel. This means the salary awarded the head was economic rent, payment well above the minimum required to make available his or her executive services.

How would you go about measuring the value added by the chief operating officer of a similar NFP firm?

Source: Susan Lee, "The Big Board's Barrel," *The Wall Street Journal*, September 10, 2003, A24.

The Civil Service System

Government bureaucracies are slow in responding to changes in the labor market and changing employee productivity. The Civil Service System in the United States sorts employees into job classifications each containing several different pay levels. The 1949 Classification Act created the General Schedule for setting pay and evaluating federal employees. Annual across-the-board raises are authorized by Congress, and it is generally difficult to fire or suspend employees on the basis of their work performance.

APPLICATION 10.2
Shirking and Team Production

In the world of perfect information, it is easy to know who is actually doing the work. If the actual productivity of each input were known, a firm could determine the factors that are over utilized and those that are underutilized and make the necessary adjustments to maximize output. This is particularly difficult or impossible if workers are formed into teams. Organizations have valid reasons for using teams. An organization has an incentive to use teams, if, for example, 5 people working as a team can produce more than 5 people working individually.

Suppose each worker is compensated based on the average output of the team. If one member of the committee shirks his or her responsibility, the total amount of output declines. The cost of shirking is shared with each team member, and the one reducing his or her work effort receives no less than any other member.

The problem is that every member of a team faces the same incentive to reduce work effort, particularly when they observe other members getting away with it. What can firms do to reduce excessive amounts of shirking? The obvious solution is increased monitoring by managers of each worker. However, the cost of monitoring may be greater than the value of output lost by shirking. In addition, proxies used to measure individual output, such as how many clients seen by a caseworker per day, miss any contribution directed toward increasing group effectiveness. Therefore, shirking is often tolerated.

- Discuss your personal experiences with compensation offered for team projects at home or work.
- Did the team create more value than if the individuals worked independently?
- What techniques could be used to measure individual contributions?
- Should team members assess and report the percentage contribution of their peers?

Source: A. Alchian and H. Demsetz, "Production, Information Costs, and Economic Organization," *American Economic Review*, 62, December, 1972, 777–97.

The Civil Service System, at publication date, is in the process of being modified. House and Senate recently announced an overhaul in the pay and personnel rules for civilian employees of the Department of Defense and the Department of Homeland Security. This means that civil service law will no longer anchor more than half the federal workforce. Some administrators are eager to move government workers into a system that links the timing and amount of pay raises to individual job performance. Will giving managers more discretion over pay increase cronyism and favoritism? Under the new provisions, the disciplinary process is streamlined, and each department sets up an in-house panel to hear appeals. Under the new proposals, employees can continue to take their cases to the Merit Systems Protection Board, an independent agency.

The supply of human resources

Our discussion of marginal revenue product suggests that over the long run a firm cannot pay workers more than the value they create. However, firms in the NFP sectors derive some part of their budgets other than from the direct sale of their services to clients. Consequently, suppliers of human resources to NFP firms have an opportunity to affect payment to themselves through their influence on those funding the budget. The purpose of this section is to discuss collective bargaining and how suppliers of resources use "political" influence to increase their compensation in the NFP sectors.

Public employees are limited in the extent to which they may become personally involved in politics. Federal employees are technically prohibited by the Hatch Act, passed in 1939, from engaging in political campaigns. In 1940, Congress extended this restriction to state and local government employees whose salaries are paid from federal funds. Many states and cities have enacted similar acts intended to avoid this conflict of interest and to protect government employees from being forced to contribute to political campaigns or to work on behalf of politicians. In addition, these acts preclude government employees from running for public office.

Why should we be concerned about the role of public and private nonprofit employees in making policy decisions within a firm about their own compensation? The effectiveness and mission of a NFP firm, whether it is involved in healthcare, education, government, etc., is a separate issue from the financial wellbeing of those who work for the firm. Endowed institutions or those that are in a position to tax the general public or their membership can survive indefinitely as worker-run cooperatives providing clients with poor service.

Since 1965 a rapid and dramatic rise in government workers' unions occurred at the federal, state, and local levels in the United States. Following a decade of intensive organizational activity, the public sector organized a higher proportion of employees into employee associations than private sector unions did in the thirty-five years following the National Labor Relations Act, designed to encourage collective bargaining in the profit-seeking sector. Workers for state, local, and federal government now account for almost half of all union members. Thirty-seven percent of government workers belong to unions, compared to about 10 percent of private-sector workers.

Union contributions to candidates for public office, political parties, and organizations are subject to federal election law. However, in some states, public employee unions, such as the American Federation of State, County and Municipal Employees (AFSCME) and the National Educational Association (NEA) engage in political activities such as as lobbying and testifying before legislative committees.

Employee associations, such as the American Nurses Association and the American Association of University Professors, rarely endorse candidates for elective office, contribute funds to political campaigns, provide manpower to help get out the vote, or mail out campaign literature. However, even when these professional associations use a form of rhetoric that appears to be above political interest, they engage in lobbying, present testimony at legislative hearings, and try to influence votes on specific bills that affect their members financially.

To the extent that professional associations or unions are successful in restricting the entry of workers into the NFP sectors, their members' compensation exceeds market equilibrium. This results in the output of essential goods and services being reduced and costing more than otherwise. NFP employees are often legitimately criticized for lobbying, under the guise of quality and public interest, for increased client fees, taxes, and subsidies to further their own financial interests. However, one must not be too cynical. Employee associations often assist in maintaining quality by setting selection standards and provide value in negotiating appropriate work environments. They support NFP employees in vulnerable negotiating positions, particularly those in the public sector where many workers face a single employer of their services.

The demand for human resource services

In Chapter 7, we defined *monopsony* in the context of firms that dominate a particular industry. Monopsony refers to the market power of *buyers* in determining price and quantity. Dominant firms use monopoly power in *purchasing* inputs as well as in selling outputs. Theoretically, it is possible for a firm that is the sole or one of a few firms employing a particular type of worker, to keep the number hired low and hence pay workers less than the marginal value that they add to revenue. For example, graduates with elementary and secondary school teaching degrees in most towns in the United States face a single school district in the market for their services.

Note that a hospital in a small town may be in a monopsonistic position to hold down the wages of specialized nurses who count on that hospital for a job in their chosen field. However, on the other side of the market, hospitals that supply their services to relatively few third-party payers experience the monopsonistic power of insurance companies and government. Suppliers of monopsonies realize their probability of winning a contract is affected by buyers' price sensitivity. Those offering services to a few purchasers find that they forfeit opportunities if they raise price. The hospital as a supplier of services is forced to accept whatever fee the Medicare and insurance companies permit. A hospital is providing services to a monopsonist whenever a significant percentage of the hospital's clients is enrolled with one or two health insurers. Large service buyers negotiate prices and services for third-party clients from a position of market power. At times, they are large enough to redirect their business to a competing medical facility or even open up and operate one of their own. To prevent this loss, a NFP firm may focus attention less on clients using its services and more on organizations making payments. Forced to cut costs, institutions dealing with monopsonies offer less than equilibrium wages to their employees.

The solution to a monopsonistic purchaser of services is the proliferation of all types of firms both public and private, nonprofit and profit-seeking. This would break up the market power of a large employer. Surprisingly, employees of public institutions often see private institutions as threats rather than potential employment opportunities. This strong opposition to different types of institutions such as charter schools by public employees suggests that the monopsonistic power of government is not being exercised with respect to wages adjusted for the degree of job security.

Administrators err if they overestimate their monopsonistic power and offer wages below equilibrium to certain groups of employees. They incorrectly assume that trained professionals, such as those in mathematics and science, are ready and willing to provide services to NFP firms for fees below those they could earn in the profit-seeking sector. In Cuba, people joke that upward mobility for a medically trained physician is a position as hotel doorman. To model choices that individuals make in supplying labor, economists traditionally discuss the choice as a trade-off between income from work and leisure. NFP employees, in an area with limited job opportunities, are free to opt out of paid work for more leisure. In this context, leisure may involve one adult in a two-earner couple substituting homemaking or childrearing responsibilities for time in paid employment.

A wage rate increase triggers two effects. The opportunity cost of leisure increases because the worker/couple must forfeit more income for each hour of leisure (substitution effect). This effect results in more labor supplied as compensation increases. On the other hand, a worker/couple earning more income from each hour of work can afford to "purchase" additional leisure (income effect). This effect results is less labor supplied as compensation increases. The net income and substitution effect determines the response of free individuals and households to changes in compensation.

Investment in human capital

Human capital is simply the knowledge and skills that make a person productive. The availability of high-tech equipment along with diligent employees is ineffective if employees lack the skills required to use software. Expenditure undertaken with an expectation of improving an individual's education, skills, and, hence, productivity is called investment in human capital. NFP institutions benefit when the labor pool from which they draw includes large numbers of trained individuals. Generally, families or individuals pay tuition or assume loans to acquire human capital. Much human capital is created through formal education subsidized by donors and taxpayers. Firms, as well, find it in their best interest at times to invest in the human capital of their employees.

Firms requiring specific skills not available in the labor pool cannot produce without internal or outsourced training for their employees. It is important to distinguish between firm-specific human capital and human capital that makes the worker more generally employable. For example, a hospital employee paid for attending a workshop on computerized patient charts increases a hospital's efficiency but that employee who now has transferable human capital is more likely to quit for higher compensation elsewhere. Obviously, firms consider the risk of increasing their employee skills but continue to do so either because on net it raises total productivity or skilled employees are unavailable.

Volunteers

Volunteer labor is commonly found in the NFP sectors. Like all employees, volunteers respond to incentives even when motivated altruistically to make a difference in society. Individuals who make charitable contributions are more likely to volunteer their time as well; thus, donor and volunteer motivation is very similar. In fact, those who donate higher percentages of income tend to volunteer more. According to INDEPENDENT SECTOR, an organization that has commissioned surveys on volunteering in the United States, 47.7 percent of Americans volunteered an average of 4.2 hours a week (Brudney, 2001). Not all volunteers are associated with formal organizations but all three sectors (profit-seeking, government, and nonprofit) benefit in some way from those who are willing to work without monetary compensation. Most, but not all, NFP administrators report that volunteers contribute value. About 69 percent of all volunteers are in the nonprofit sector. Another 28 percent volunteer at government agencies in fire and public safety, culture and the arts, health and emergency medicine, food and homelessness, etc.

Volunteer hours in a particular NFP can be summed and divided by total hours in an average workweek to determine the number of *full-time equivalent volunteers*. Multiplying full-time equivalent volunteers by a realistic wage rate approximates the implicit donation of volunteers to the organization. These relatively easily calculated measures are one gage of public support for a particular program.

Volunteer networks assist in identifying potential donors and in staffing special events. Symphony volunteers often donate cash as well as time and even function as clients when they purchase tickets. Volunteers have the potential to create value, but a NFP firm needs to ask if this potential is realized. If volunteers are intended to function merely as a network for donations and clients, full-time equivalent calculations do not represent cost savings in terms of regular full-time staff.

The dollar value of full-time equivalent volunteers may not be an accurate measure of value created by volunteers, although this measure is commonly used. Volunteer selection, training, and placement increase a NFP's costs. Volunteers do not receive a paycheck, but the additional cost of having a volunteer may be thought of as a *shadow wage*. Regular full-time personnel are generally hired competitively from a number of job applicants. In these situations, the hired individual is paid the going market wage for his or her services. Volunteers, on the other hand, usually self-select or may even be court ordered to do community service. Regular workers are required to respond to performance incentives. Volunteers may be less closely supervised and hence have a greater propensity to engage in goals contrary to firm mission. Finally, firms are more fully conscious of employee costs but tend to underestimate the implicit cost of recruiting, training, and supervising volunteers. Volunteers often do not arrive with the same skills as regular employees and have less incentive to acquire them.

Obviously, there are significant rewards, in terms of personal satisfaction, for those volunteering. For some, the experience represents an investment in human capital leading to paid positions. From the point of view of those within organizations, volunteers are generally perceived as contributing net value, as indicated in Application 10.3 outlining the findings of a national study on volunteers.

APPLICATION 10.3
Volunteers Add Value But Are Not Free

The Current Population Survey (CPS) indicates that an estimated 63.8 million Americans (28.8 percent of the population) volunteered in the nonprofit and government sectors in the 12 months preceding September 2003.

Unfortunately, as indicated by a 1998 UPS Foundation study, volunteers do not believe that these experiences use their skills and interests to best advantage. In response, the Corporation for National and Community Service, the UPS Foundation, and the USA Freedom Corps organized the first national study of volunteers. The study was conducted by the Urban Institute in the fall of 2003 based on a sample of 1,753 charities among those filing IRS Form 990 or 990EZ in 2000. This filing is required for those charities with over $25,000 in annual gross revenue. In addition, the study included 541 out of approximately 380,000 congregations of all faiths.

The sample taken from the nonprofit sector concludes:

- Four out of 5 charities use volunteers and 1 out of 3 congregations manage volunteers in social service outreach programs.
- More than 9 out of 10 organizations would like to increase volunteers; the median number of new recruits desired is 20.
- A large majority of charities reported that volunteers are beneficial to the organization and allocating resources to managing volunteers yields benefits.
- The best prepared and most effective volunteer programs are those with paid staff members dedicating a substantial portion of their time to volunteer management.
- Only about one-third of charities reported initiating the "best practice" of formally recognizing the efforts of their volunteers.
- Recruiting volunteers for workday hours is recognized as a problem by 25 percent of the charities and 34 percent of the congregations.
- Some organizations have benefited by using a volunteer full-time coordinator to recruit and manage volunteers. Although full time, some of these coordinators work in return for a living stipend. AmeriCorps members are one example.
- About 40 percent expressed the need for information resources linking volunteers with organizations.

Does your experience as a volunteer or with an organization using volunteers confirm the finding of this study?

Source: Mark A. Hager, "Volunteer Management Capacity in America's Charities and Congregations: A Briefing Report," Washington, DC: Urban Institute, 2004.

Two important points must be acknowledged with respect to volunteers. First, like all inputs, they are subject to diminishing marginal productivity. Second, volunteer labor is not free. In addition to the expenses of training, ID badges, security clearances, coatrooms, lunch vouchers, etc., full-time staff must be reallocated to coordinate volunteers. All costs associated with volunteers need to be compared with value created. A firm is effectively using volunteer labor compared to paid staff when the ratio of the marginal revenue product of the last volunteer (MRP_V) over per unit cost of each volunteer (P_V) equals the ratio for paid employees:

$$MRP_V/P_V = MRP_L/P_L$$

10.4   INTRINSIC MOTIVATION

Economists generally model the relationship between a firm (principal) and employee (agent) as a contract in which a firm offers explicit financial and professional rewards. In return, the employee extends the effort necessary to achieve the firm's objectives. In NFP firms, however, it is likely that individuals care about what they do and derive utility from their work in addition to financial reward. For example, most social workers enjoy seeing children well cared for; most medical professionals delight in seeing patients get well; most professors are excited about sharing their professional insights with students.

The willingness to work for personal satisfaction follows from *intrinsic motivation*. The goal of a NFP is certainly not to extinguish intrinsic motivation but, rather, to design contracts that trigger this willingness and increase an employee's work effort. Kevin Murdock, affiliated with Stanford University and McKinsey & Company, theorizes about optimal incentive contracts fostering intrinsic motivation (2002). In his model, contracts failing to stimulate intrinsic motivation reduce firm output, because optimal contracts incorporating intrinsic motivation provide a potential for increased performance.

Murdock argues for contracts fostering intrinsic motivation even when NFPs' support for the personal goals of professional employees at first absorbs resources. If support for intrinsic motivation causes an agent to work harder, the increased effort will generate positive outcomes for a firm. For example, a secondary school incurs expense in allowing a new teacher to initiate a chess club. If the teacher, who happens to be a chess enthusiast, increases his or her efforts in the classroom, everyone benefits. Effort levels are not observable, but outcomes, such as a functioning chess club and improved student performance, are. Note that the implicit employee contract does not permit an activity incompatible with firm mission, but the activity should be independent of primary mission. For example, if it is absolutely certain that chess clubs improve academic performance, then the school should explicitly contract for a chess club advisor. A firm should be open to subsidizing an employee's intrinsic motivation but not any more than that needed to trigger extra effort plus the uncertain chance that a project turns out to yield secondary benefits. A police officer, permitted to coordinate a neighborhood basketball tournament in the parking lot of the police station, increases cost. If the officer increases his or her effort in law enforcement, then the implicit contract advantages the organization. If neighborhood crime falls due to the tournament, the organization captures the entire bonus. Of course, periodic review is necessary to avoid mission drift, such as turning a police station into a recreation center.

10.5   PERSONNEL ECONOMICS

Economists ask: "How are pay and promotions structured across jobs within a firm to induce optimal effort from employees?" To understand compensation in the NFP sectors, we start, as economists generally do, with several assumptions. First, workers seek to maximize their income and utility and firms seek to maximize output for minimum cost. Second, the NFP firm is employing human resources and offering services in markets that approach equilibrium prices and quantities. Finally, the firm seeks productive efficiency or effectiveness. Obviously, these conditions are never perfectly met because individuals respond to a variety of noneconomic factors, and markets are subject to monopoly power and imperfect information. Nevertheless, the economists' model supported by statistical and experimental studies permit us to understand why firms in general and NFPs in particular adopt different compensation structures.

Lazear and Shaw (2007) note that, compared with the 1980s, compensation for workers now varies more among employees in general. This is due to some extent to pay-for-performance and group-based incentives. These authors define **personnel economics** as a relatively new field of study aimed at modeling firms' use of optimal management practices in employing human resources.

Consider, first, a firm in which high wages are associated with jobs rather than with individuals who hold the job. For example, consider the variation in wages between the superintendent of a school district and a third-grade teacher. Regardless of how effectively or how hard the teacher works, he will not earn wages equal to those of the superintendent. To increase income and/or prestige within the organization, he and others may strive for promotion to superintendent. The larger the compensation spread between teacher and superintendent, the larger the incentive to put forth the effort needed to achieve the position. Only the winner earns the prize. This wage pattern represents the tournament theory of compensation. **Tournament theory** explains large discrete jumps in compensation whereby pay is associated with the position rather than individual performance.

Now consider situations where there is little variation in wages between employees or where wage variations are due to differences in performance. In many if not most NFP organizations we observe compensation compression (little variation in wages plus benefits) among certain types of workers. A straight salary or one consistent with education background is paid because accurate measures of individual output are impossible or too costly to acquire. Pay for output or performance compensation schemes in the profit-seeking sector typically use piecework pay, bonuses, and stock options. Pay for performance requires ease or low costs in measuring output. For example, it is relatively easy to count the amount of revenue a salesperson brings into the firm or the number of credit hours taught by an individual faculty member. What do NFP firms lose when they pay essentially the same salary to individuals with the same credentials? They lose individuals with alternative high-paying and more rewarding jobs. In addition, they are less able to weed out low performers by reduced wages. Finally, wage compression forfeits the possibility of boosting overall effort level with individual incentives. It is not at all clear, however, that pay-for-performance works as effectively in the public and private nonprofit sectors as in the profit-seeking sector. Consider how much effort individuals exert in trying to be perceived by bosses as more productive than their associates! Furthermore, in many if not most NFP situations, pay-for-performance is inconsistent with the nondistributional constraint.

It is essential that appropriate employees be directed into certain positions. Lazear and Shaw propose that small-scale experiments study how to attract suitable employees to increase firm effectiveness. It makes sense that a firm should offer pay packages and benefits attracting the workers it desires. Employees seek flexible hours, comfortable working conditions, enjoyable colleagues, interesting projects, and nurturing bosses in addition to monetary compensation. Benefits raise the firm's total compensation cost; they are not free! However, different benefit packages sort applicants to determine those best suited to mission and those willing to trade off monetary compensation for other benefits. Statistical studies of compensation in the profit-seeking sector, however, do not yet provide clear evidence that employers trade off wages for "positive" job attributes.

From 1987 to 1996, the share of large firms that have more than 20 percent of their workers in problem-solving teams rose from 37 percent to 66 percent (Lazear and Shaw, 2007). Teamwork takes time and certain employees free ride on the work of others. However, teams can be more productive than individuals working alone. Services, provided in the NFP sectors, are particularly adapted to and in some instances require teamwork. Without a doubt, in education, medicine, and social work, etc., a professional's input interacts multiplicatively, such that marginal productivity is enhanced in teams. Should high-performing teams be rewarded with increased compensation in the NFP sectors? The very thought of paying individual civil servants for effort shocks. It is the case, however, that teams of public educators whose students perform well on standardized tests earn performance bonuses in some states.

Optimal production requires choosing appropriate compensation packages from a range of human resource practices. Traditional practice requires close monitoring of employees working alone. Another practice involves innovative pay-for-performance or team performance bonuses. Complementarity of skills, the economic basis for teamwork, is essential for professional groups working together in medical rehabilitation facilities. Typically, teams excel in solving complex problems quickly within a generally designed practice. Team-based decision-making, however, can be costly when a team decision has negative consequences for clients or firm. A team could prematurely agree to change the standard design practice for treating strokes. A highly paid generalist, with overall knowledge, may therefore be required to monitor the design practice of teams consisting of individual experts. Does the increased use of highly specialized experts or the need for a hierarchy of generalists explain the rise since 1987 in wage inequality? Lazear and Shaw suggest that it may be both.

There is substantial evidence in the profit-seeking sector that innovative compensation schemes increase productivity. Will they work as well in the NFP sectors? The transition from one type of compensation to another results in adjustment costs and a short-term fall in output. Ultimately, the choice of compensation packages must be consistent with firm mission based on serious study and experiments.

10.6   DEMAND AND SUPPLY FOR LOANABLE FUNDS

Wouldn't it be lovely if NFP administrators could concentrate exclusively on staffing an organization to deliver high-quality service to clients? Wouldn't it be ideal if taxes, donations, and client fees were sufficient for operating expenses, maintenance of existing facilities, and growth? In practice, the typical NFP administrator needs financial market know-how in order to acquire needed funds offering the lowest possible repayments.

"A bird in the hand is worth two in the bush," goes the old saying. Elevated to the concept of loanable funds, the old saw indicates that money now is worth more than money in the future. This applies both to the risk lenders take in agreeing to future payments as well as the risk borrowers assume in being able to make those payments. NFPs normally enter the loanable funds market as demanders of funds and agreeing to future payments. Program expansion and new facilities generally entail borrowing. In borrowing, the firm commits itself to paying the costs of any new project plus interest. On the supply side of the market, some endowed NFPs lend funds in return for future payments. They are suppliers of funds. Their endowments provide annual revenue to fund certain activities and can balance for a budget deficit. The financial officer of the firm allocates the endowment into financial and real investments yielding the greatest return for the least risk. Application 10.4 discusses institutional endowments used to provide revenue in adverse times when donations decline and demand for service increases.

Administrators make commitments on future payments and agree to endowment earnings based on the time value of money, a financial concept we will attempt to explain in the next section. Realize that a NFP organization seeks the highest possible return on its endowment adjusted for risk and the lowest payout in interest on borrowed funds. Most institutions are *risk adverse* meaning that they are willing to assume risk only for higher returns. A risk-adverse investor will place funds in relatively risk-free accounts and government bonds unless the risk associated with a higher return is acceptable. NFP administrators and boards act in trust for donors and clients, and should be prudent. The funds they borrow and lend are not their own.

APPLICATION 10.4
Do Endowments Permit Not-for-profit Firms to Adjust to Revenue Shocks?

Consider an institution depending on donations to finance essential social services to clients in distress. Whenever client caseloads increase due to economic recessions, donations and tax revenues also fall. But not-for-profit firms by their very nature cannot distribute profits in good years and eliminate them in difficult times. Public and private NFP institutions need some other means of absorbing revenue variability when donations and client fees are uncertain and program expenditures continue or increase. Some institutions hold endowments as a form of savings to protect themselves from these revenue shocks.

Administrators and trustees of large endowments held by non-taxed and donor financed institutions are subject to the moral hazard of excessive accumulation to ensure salaries and the survival of the institution. However, they know that in emergencies the institution is expected to respond quickly without seeking donations and loans. The National Center for Nonprofit Boards suggests that not more than total expenses for two years be held as an endowment. Many organizations exceed this. Fisman and Hubbard studied endowments using a data set, compiled by the National Center for Charitable Statistics, containing all 501(c)(3) organizations with more than $10 million in assets and a random sample of 4,000 smaller organizations. Institutional endowments were calculated from Form 990 that tax-exempt organizations file with the IRS:

Endowment = Total assets – Total liabilities

and

Endowment intensity = Endowment/Total expenses

They found that endowment intensities vary significantly between non-profit industries, with arts and education having on average high endowments and healthcare less. Because NFP industries, relying on donations, cannot easily lay off employees or reduce fixed expenses, those with more volatile revenue streams are most likely to have larger endowments. To test the significant of determinates of 1987 industry median endowment intensity, Fisman and Hubbard used regression:

Endowment intensity = Constant + Volatility + Loan dummy
+ Labor intensity

   1.51   23.41   −0.77   −5.10

(1.99) (7.45) (−1.48) (−2.68)

$R^2 = 0.43$

$N = 23$

Volatility, the standard deviation of revenues, has a positive coefficient (23.41) and with a standard error of 7.45 is significant. Loan dummy refers to whether an organization received a loan during 1987–96; note that the coefficient (−0.77) is negative as expected but with a standard error of (−1.48) it is not highly significant. Labor intensity is the ratio of labor expenses to total expenses and the coefficient (−5.10) is negative as expected and significant.

We can conclude that industries with high variability in revenue and fixed non-labor expenses do indeed depend on endowment income as precautionary savings.

Source: Raymond Fisman and R. Glenn Hubbard, "The Role of Nonprofit Endowments," *The Governance of Not-for-profit Organizations*, 217–33, ed. Edward L. Glaeser, Chicago, IL: University of Chicago Press, 2003.

The present value calculations that follow link a firm's revenue and costs over time. They assist managers in deciding between present costs and future benefits as well as between benefits now for costs in the future. Should an emergency medical and fire department purchase an expensive piece of equipment now that will generate benefits over the next 10 years? Should the university accept a donation now in return for a promise to provide the donor with a yearly lifetime stipend (annuity)?

Discounting and present value

The *present value* of x dollars to be received in n years with the rate of interest equal to r percent is merely the amount that must be invested (or lent) at r percent to receive x dollars in n years. For example, suppose that endowment funds in a bank earn 7 percent and the institution needs to have $2,000 available at the end of two years. How much does it need to have in the account to achieve that goal? In other words, what is the present value of $2,000 to be received two years from today when the current interest rate is 7 percent? If we let PV equal the amount we must deposit, then at the end of one year, the principal and interest due the depositor would be given by $PV(1 + 0.07)$. If this amount is kept on deposit for another year, the principal and interest at the end of the second year, which must equal $2,000, according to our problem, would be expressed as $[PV(1 + 0.07)](1 + 0.07)]$. That is,

$$PV(1+0.07)^2 = \$2,000$$

or

$$PV = \frac{\$2,000}{(1+0.07)^2}$$

$$PV = \frac{\$2,000}{1.1449}$$

$$PV = \$2,000(0.8734)$$

$$PV = \$1,747$$

In other words, if the interest rate is 7 percent compounded yearly, then $1,747 received today is equivalent to $2,000 received two years from today. The procedure for finding the present value of the $2,000 is called discounting, with the rate of discount being 7 percent. Let us look at three other examples to further illustrate this concept.

Example 1

Find the present value of $550 in benefits to be received by the firm three years from now if the interest rate is 8 percent. The present value can be thought of as the amount we must deposit (or lend), now at 8 percent interest, in order to have a total of $550 in principal and interest at the end of three years. If PV represents the amount we deposit, then at the end of one year, the principal and interest at 8 percent would amount to $PV(1+0.08)$. In the same manner, at the end of the second year, the principal and interest would be $[PV(1+0.08)](1+0.08)$, or $PV(1+0.08)^2$, while at the end of the third year, the total amount on deposit would be $[PV(1+0.08)^2](1+0.08) = PV(1+0.08)^3$.

$$PV(1+0.08)^3 = \$550$$

or

$$PV = \frac{\$550}{(1+0.08)^3}$$

$$PV = \frac{\$550}{1.2597}$$

$$PV = \$550(0.7938)$$

$$PV = \$436.61$$

Example 2

The present value of a stream of cash flowing into the firm over a period of years can be found by adding the present values of cash flows for each year. For example, suppose that the problem is to determine the present value of $3,000 to be received two years from now, $4,200 to be received four years from now, and $2,600 to be received five years from now if the interest rate is 7.5 percent. To arrive at the present value for this stream of cash flows, we discount each of the cash flows with a discount rate of 7.5 percent.

$$PV = \frac{\$3,000}{(1+0.075)^2} + \frac{\$4,200}{(1+0.075)^4} + \frac{\$2,600}{(1+0.075)^5}$$

$$PV = \frac{\$3,000}{1.1556} + \frac{\$4,200}{1.3355} + \frac{\$2,600}{1.4356}$$

$$PV = \$2,596 + \$3,145 + \$1,811$$

$$PV = \$7,552$$

These calculations indicate that, if the interest rate is 7.5 percent, $7,525 now is equivalent to $3,000 in two years plus $4,200 in four years plus $2,600 in five years.

Example 3

Suppose that, as winner of a state lottery, you must make a decision concerning whether to receive $10,000 a year for the next 10 years or $70,000 today. Assume that the interest rate is 6 percent and that the cash flows are tax free. You should calculate the present value of the stream of cash flows and compare it with $70,000. Discounting the stream of cash flows is done as

$$PV = \frac{10,000}{(1+0.06)^1} + \frac{10,000}{(1+0.06)^2} + \ldots + \frac{10,000}{(1+0.06)^{10}}$$

These discounting procedures can be accomplished using present value tables for an annuity (Lewellen et al., 2000). An annuity is a series of equal payments made at regular time intervals, for example, yearly. In calculating the present value of an annuity, we are assuming that the interest rate is constant over the 10-year period. Referring to a table that gives the present value of an annuity, we find that the present value of $1 received each year for 10 years is $7.3601 if the interest rate is 6 percent. Therefore, the present value of $10,000 received for 10 years is

$$PV = \$10,000(7.3601) = \$73,601$$

You may also calculate the present value of this stream of cash flows (instead of using a table) by discounting the cash flow in each of the 10 years and summing the discounted values:

$$PV = \$10{,}000(0.9434) + \$10{,}000(0.8900) + \$10{,}000(0.8396)$$
$$+ \ldots + \$10{,}000(0.5584)$$
$$= \$73{,}601$$

The discount factors 0.9434, 0.8900, and 0.8396 . . . 5584 are the present value of $1 received 1, 2, 3 . . . , 10 years from now, respectively, with an interest rate of 6 percent. These discount factors can be extracted from a present-value table and are derived as follows:

$$0.9434 = \frac{1}{(1.06)^1}$$

$$0.8900 = \frac{1}{(1.06)^2}$$

$$0.8396 = \frac{1}{(1.06)^3}$$

$$0.5584 = \frac{1}{(1.06)^{10}}$$

These numbers sum to 73,601, which is the value we found in the present value table; it represents the present value of $10,000 received each year for 10 years when the interest rate is 6 percent.

By multiplying future dollars by these discount factors, we are taking into consideration that a dollar received in the future is less valuable to us than a dollar received today. Therefore, we are putting the cash flows on a comparable basis in order to evaluate the options facing our lottery winner. Obviously, at an interest rate of 6 percent, the better choice is to receive $10,000 each year for the next 10 years, since the present value ($73,601) of these cash flows exceeds the $70,000 you would get if your accepted your prize immediately.

To summarize, the present value of a stream of cash flows $(A_1, A_2 \ldots A_n,$ where A_1 is the dollar amount that will be received at the end of the first period) is calculated by discounting the net payments according to the following procedure:

$$PV = A_0 + A_1/(1 + r)^1 + A_2/(1 + r)^2 + A_3/(1 + r)^3 + \ldots A_n/(1 + r)^n$$

The use of spreadsheets makes such present-value calculations simple. In effect, the information in a present-value table is programmed into the spreadsheet. You should check the results we have shown with your spreadsheet.

Perpetuity formula

There is a shortcut, based on mathematical approximation, in the special case where there is a long stream of identical costs or benefits to a firm. Any project that has the same annual costs or benefits for 20 or more years has a present value close to that given by the **perpetuity formula**:

$PV = {}^{B}/_{r}$ (B is the stream of payments and r, the discount rate)

Example 1

The present value of a cardiac imaging scanner to a hospital providing $4,000 of benefits each year for 20 years discounted at 7.5 percent:

$PV = {}^{B}/_{r}$

   $= \$4,000/0.075$

   $= \$53,333$

Example 2

The present value of an annuity paid by a college to a donor receiving $2,000 a year for approximately 20 years discounted at 6 percent:

$PV = {}^{B}/_{r}$

   $= \$2,000/0.06$

   $= \$33,333$

Whenever a public or private NFP firm uses the present value or perpetuity formula, an interest rate must be chosen for discounting future benefits and costs. Because the interest rate represents the opportunity cost of money, it makes sense to choose and consistently use one of a multiplicity of current market rates. A whole literature exists on choosing an appropriate discount rate. For our purposes here in comparing different projects, consistency in using the same rate is critical. The "best" discount rate is one representing the rate that the firm could receive by selling, for example, a piece of property and placing the funds is a relatively risk free asset. This discussion on choosing a discount rate will be continued in Chapter 11.

Consider just a few NFP implications of an overall hike in interest rates. Many religious organizations, medical institutions, universities, and other nonprofit groups offer retirees a guaranteed stream of lifetime income in return for a large contribution donated in the present. This gift offers the donor an immediate tax deduction and a fixed amount of income every year for the rest of his or her life. A NFP firm typically follows the payout rates set by the American Council on Gift Annuities in Indianapolis, and these payout rates tend to be somewhat lower than those provided by for-profit insurance companies. The NFP firm is able to offer lower returns because, in addition to the immediate charitable tax deduction for the gift, the donor can fund the gift annuity with appreciated property and avoid some capital gains taxes. As with any annuity, the estate loses if the donor dies soon after purchasing an annuity unless the annuity comes with some sort of guarantee. Also, the donor's future income depends on the financial trustworthiness of the NFP, unless the annuity is backed by a reputable insurance company. If interest rates are expected to increase, the discounted value of expected payments declines and NFPs offering annuities will be obliged to offer donors the same payments for smaller initial donations or larger future payments for the same donation.

Whenever high interest rates are chosen to discount future costs and benefits, expansion projects within the NFP firm are affected in several ways. The present value of many projects declines because future benefits are heavily discounted. For example, the projected discounted stream of revenue from a new cardiac scanner yields a lower present value that may be less than the cost of the new machine. In addition, higher interest rates make it more costly for a firm to borrow funds from a lending institution and/or issue new bonds for purchasing facilities and equipment. Furthermore, a higher interest rate forces a firm to forgo higher returns on any cash expended on the project. As previously mentioned, the sensitivity of interest rates used to discount future costs and benefits is discussed further in Chapter 11. We turn now to two ways that NFPs can use options to reduce an organization's risk.

10.7   USING OPTIONS TO REDUCE RISK

Financial economists are fond of pointing out that "options have value." Generally, options refer to a type of financial instrument; in this section we will deal with two kinds referred to as "put options" or "call options." *Options* allow a financial officer to lock in some certainty about the future; it is the ability to trade something at a given price at some future time. Such an opportunity has value. Consider the case of a business manager of any NFP firm, purchasing heating fuel with a price varying from season to season. Suppose the price varies by 50 percent over the course of a year and fuel costs represent 10 percent of a firm's annual budget. Would the manager be willing to purchase a financial instrument guaranteeing the price of fuel when needed? Or suppose an institution seeking funds for a new facility is forced to issue new bonds on which they have to pay a variable interest rate. Could the manager purchase a financial instrument to protect against increases in the interest rate?

Like any item of value, financial options have prices attached to them. How do the business managers in the examples above know how much to pay for a financial instrument guaranteeing a certain fuel price or locking in a constant interest rate? The answer lies in tying the option price to the probable price of the underlying asset at some future date. Nobody knows for certain the value of an asset (like heating fuel) at some time in the future. But there are individuals and companies willing to make a reasoned guess at the future price; it is these individuals and companies who write option contracts which relieve NFPs of some price risk. In Figure 10.2, an option buyer pays a premium to an option writer in return for the right to make a particular choice.

The purchaser of the option pays a cash price for the option but receives risk reduction in return and is better able to budget expenses. Option pricing is a serious business and financial analysts spend a great deal of time and effort in setting the "correct" prices of various options. Options that permit the option buyer to purchase a particular item at a specified price on or before a certain date are called *call options*. Options that allow the buyer to sell a particular item at a specified price on or before a certain date are called *put options*.

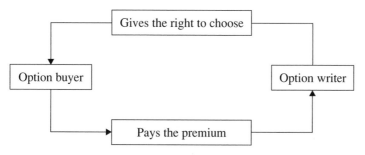

Figure 10.2   Option pricing. The option writer receives a premium for providing a choice to the option buyer. The option buyer receives the choice of exercising or not exercising the choice over a given period of time in return for a payment to the option writer.

Analyzing option prices requires an understanding of why anyone would purchase either a put or a call option. The simple answer, of course, is that you lower risk or save money buying (or selling) options. This is true. You can also lose a great deal of money quickly by not understanding how options are priced. In no way are we suggesting that NFP firms become active traders in options' markets. If, however, the budget of a particular NFP firm suffers due to price fluctuations of a critical product, administrators may wish to reduce risk by purchasing a single option to lock in price.

An option is a contract. It gives the buyer of the option the right to choose during a specified period of time, to buy (or sell) a specified quantity of a specific asset at a given price. The other party to the contract is the writer of the option; that individual has the obligation to fulfill the holder's right to choose.

Options are written with many types of underlying assets. There are options on commodities (corn, wheat, etc.), precious metals (gold, silver, etc.), currency options (pesos, euros, etc.), and stock options (IBM, GM, etc.). The asset on which the option is based is called the underlying asset. Most options in the United States are traded on the Chicago Board Options Exchange (CBOE), which was founded in 1973. The CBOE trades over 700,000 options daily (other exchanges are located in New York, Philadelphia, and California). A full range of underlying assets are represented. The options you see traded on the CBOE are not sold by the companies whose products are being traded but by investors. An investor must be on the opposite side of the contract with a NFP buying or selling at a certain price. Managers of all types commonly use options of one form or another to protect the firm against a variety of risks. An example of how an option works will help explain how it can protect from risk and how it is priced.

Consider the value of a call option for which a business manager in the spring pays $6.50 to purchase a unit of fuel at $90 any time before autumn. Figure 10.3 shows the possible values of this option on the exchange just before it expires at the end of the summer. If the price of fuel at that time is less than the $90 exercise price (also called the striking price), you would not want to exercise the option to buy the fuel for $90. (Why buy the fuel for $90 using the option when you

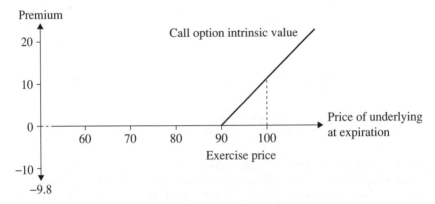

Figure 10.3　The value of a call option. The benefit to a buyer, such as a NFP business manager, of a call option on fuel is shown when the market price of fuel is $100. The exercise price of the option gives the option buyer the opportunity to purchase fuel at $90. The intrinsic value of the option is $10 (also called the payoff to the option buyer); for a call option it is equal to the market value of fuel ($100) minus the striking price of the option ($90). By convention, intrinsic value may not be less than zero and so the value of the option to the left of $90 equals zero.

could purchase it for less on the open market?) In this situation, the value of the option is zero.

If fuel turns out to have a market price greater than $90 at the end of summer, it would be sensible for you to exercise the option to purchase fuel at only $90. The option permits the business manager with funds to cover the difference between the amounts budgeted for fuel and the present higher prices. At expiration, the option is worth the difference between market price of the underlying asset and the exercise price of the option ($90); this is referred to as the intrinsic value of the option. Again examining Figure 10.3, if the market price of fuel (the underlying asset) is $100 just before expiration, then the intrinsic value of the option is $10 (i.e., $100–$90). If fuel is selling for $100, the business manager can obtain fuel out of budget for $90. If the option was purchased at $6.50, the firm benefits. What if fuel prices had decreased? Well, the option will not be exercised and the firm forfeits the cost of the option.

Put options work in a similar manner. Producer cooperatives are a type of NFP firm. Farm producing cooperatives benefit from put options in guaranteeing members a certain price for crops harvested in the future. Our example of a call option allows choice in paying for fuel. A put option, on the other hand, gives a cooperative the right to sell grain at a certain price. Assume that the put option, when seed is dormant in the ground, sells for $2 and grants the coop a selling price of $90. If grain prices are above $90 it would be unwilling to exercise the option. Why sell grain for $90 using the option when it could sell grain for more than $90 on the open market? NFP producing cooperatives benefit from put options in guaranteeing that their products can be sold for a certain price.

However, if grain is selling below $90 just before the option expires, a NFP cooperative would be pleased to exercise the option of selling at $90. Figure 10.4 shows the value of the put option as the price of grain changes.

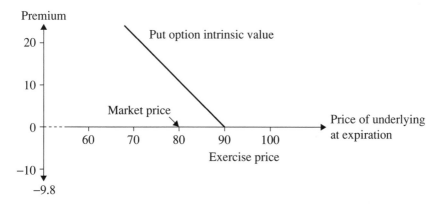

Figure 10.4   The value of a put option. The intrinsic value of a put option to the option buyer, such as a NFP cooperative selling grain, is the striking price ($90) minus the market price of grain ($80). In this case the intrinsic value is $10. The intrinsic value of the option depicted above is zero whenever market grain prices exceed $90.

CONCLUDING NOTES

- The demand for resources and labor in the factor markets is called derived demand because it is based on client demand in the product market. To achieve productive efficiency, economic theory indicates that each factor input should generate revenue equal to or exceeding cost.

- Allocative efficiency requires that the ratio of the marginal productivity of the last worker (MP_L) hired over the cost of that worker (C_L) is equal to the ratio of the marginal productivity of the last piece of equipment (MP_E) purchased over the cost of equipment (C_E).

- NFPs are in a position to induce certain employees to exert more effort when implicit contracts offer support triggering intrinsic motivation. Personnel economics is a sub-discipline to study optimal compensation packages for specific skills and industries.

- Costs and revenue are incurred by a NFP firm over different time periods. This requires discounting of expenditure and revenue flows for decision making. The present value of x dollars to be received in n years with the rate of interest equal to r percent is merely the amount that must be invested (or lent) at r percent to receive x dollars in n years.

- The purchaser of the option pays a cash price for the option but receives a reduction in risk in return and is better able to budget expenses. Options that allow the option buyer to purchase a particular item at a specified price on or before a certain date are called call options. Options that allow the buyer to sell a particular stock at a specified price on or before a certain date are called put options.

KEY TERMS

Derived demand
Equimarginal principle
 (least-cost criterion)
Marginal revenue product
Human capital
Full-time equivalent volunteers
Shadow wage
Intrinsic motivation

Personnel economics
Tournament theory
Risk adverse
Present value
Perpetuity formula
Options
Call options
Put options

SUGGESTED READINGS

Bretz, R. D. Jr., Milkovich, G. T., and Read, W. 1992: "The Current State of Performance Appraisal Research and Practice: Concerns, Directions, and Implications," *Journal of Management*, 18 (2), 321–52.

Brudney, Jeffrey 2001: "Voluntarism," *The Nature of the Nonprofit Sector*, 57–63, ed. J. Steven Ott, Boulder, CO: Westview Press.

Lazear, Edward P. and Shaw, Kathryn L. 2007: "Personnel Economics: The Economist's View of Human Resources," *Journal of Economic Perspectives*, 21 (4), 91–114.

Lewellen, Wilber G., Halloran, John A., and Lanser, Howard 2000: *Financial Management: An Introduction to Principles and Practice*, Cincinnati, OH: South Western College Publishing.

Murdock, Kevin 2002: "Intrinsic Motivation and Optimal Incentive Contracts," *RAND Journal of Economics*, 33 (4), 650–71.

Wolff, N., Weisbrod, B., and Bird, E. 1993: "The Supply of Volunteer Labor: The Case of Hospitals," *Nonprofit Management and Leadership*, 4 (1), 23–45.

END OF CHAPTER EXERCISES

Exercise 10.1

Assume that Corby Hospital Network assigns physical therapists with short-term contracts to three hospitals (A, B, and C) in different locations. The output of physical therapists is subject to diminishing returns as more are assigned to a given hospital. The therapists are paid a fixed monthly salary of $11,500. Based on past data, Corby estimates monthly net income/profit for each hospital, depending on the number of therapists assigned:

Number of therapists	Total net income/profit by hospital ($ thousands)		
	A	B	C
0	0	0	0
1	15	12	14
2	29	23	27
3	42	33	39
4	54	42	50
5	65	50	60
6	75	57	69
7	83	63	77
8	88	65	83

a. What is the total number of therapists Corby will hire? (*Hint*: Calculate MRP for each additional therapist at each hospital.)

b. How will therapists be allocated between the three hospitals? What is the economic basis of these allocations?

c. In a real-world situation, would you expect the assumption used here of diminishing returns to a factor (that is, the therapists) to hold? Explain.

d. What would the corporation do if the market wages of therapists rose to $12,000? How would Corby react if market wages fell to $10,100?

e. Would it make sense for the firm to concentrate on a single market area in order to saturate the area with therapists and capture all therapy revenue from competition in that area? Why might neighborhood hospitals differ with respect to the marginal productivity of therapists of similar ability?

Exercise 10.2

You are a county engineer and want to repair and slurry seal the maximum number of miles of roads between spring and fall of 2008. You allocate $100,000 fund increments between the county's own crew and an outside contractor. Both public and private crew leaders meet privately in one session and alternately trade back and forth blocks of highway miles chosen; each leader selects the easier to repair miles first.

Number of $100,000 increments	County crew miles proposed	Marginal county crew miles per increment	Outside contractor miles proposed	Marginal contractor miles per increment
0	0		0	
1	60		80	
2	80		95	
3	98		109	
4	113		121	
5	123		131	
6	131		140	
7	138		142	
8	143		143	
9	145		144	
10	146		145	

a. Fill in the chart.

b. Presently 3 increments are allocated to the county crew and 3 increments to the outside contractor for a total of $600,000. Is this the optimal combination? If you wished to equalize the "bang per buck," you would reallocate funds from the _____ crew to the _____ crew.

Exercise 10.3

Refer to information in Exercise 10.2.

a. How would you allocate funds between the two crews if your budget permitted $1,000,000 from the county for road repair?

b. How would you allocate funds between the two crews if told to repair 287 miles of roads?

Exercise 10.4

The development officer of the small liberal arts college from which you received your undergraduate degree approached you about contributing $100,000 for their library expansion in return for naming the new wing after you. You are 66 and expect to live until 86, at least. You have considered contributing up to $25,000 to the college but had never considered $100,000. You explain to the officer that your retirement funds are limited and dependent on the 8 percent return you earn on your modest portfolio. At lunch, which the officer expensed to the college, he indicates that the college would be willing to pay you $6,000 a year for life in return for the $100,000. You indicated that you would think about it. Calculate the present value and explain your inclination to accept or reject the offer.

Exercise 10.5

You are on the board of a privately endowed home, Garden View, for physically and mentally challenged adults. All revenue comes either from Garden View's endowment or a flat fee provided by the government for each resident. At the semi-annual board meeting, the financial report is presented indicating that the endowment is fully invested in mid- to long-run government securities earning 8 percent. Two proposals are on the table:

a. Physical Therapy presently uses the pool at Winding Trace across the shared parking lot from Garden View. The annual charge for using the pool is $2,000 yearly plus a small operating fee per client visit. A pool at Garden View could be built for $30,000 and guaranteed to last for 20 years. Calculate the present value of the pool. Assume a zero rate of inflation. (*Show work.*)

b. Will you vote yes or no to approve construction of the pool presented above? Explain.

Exercise 10.6

Garden View, the facility described in Exercise 10.5, is required to hire staff capable of driving residents to medical appointments. However, Garden View has contracted with a local transport service for all client appointments. The transport service charges $40 round trip; total bills submitted to Garden View for this service have averaged $20,000 for the past three years and are expected to remain approximately the same. A seven-year-old fully equipped van with a three-year prepaid lease including insurance (and fuel costs) becomes available at the end of this year from a local auto agency for an initial payment of $60,000.

a. Calculate the present value of the services of the local transport service for next year and the following two years using 8 percent as the discount rate. (*Show work.*)

b. Will you vote yes or no to approve leasing of the available van? Explain.

Exercise 10.7

Why is the demand for nurses, physicians, and teachers referred to as "derived demand"?

Exercise 10.8

Identify and explain "best practice" in terms of compensating employees for expenses incurred in attending a work related conference.

Exercise 10.9

Nearly 30 percent of the American workforce is licensed. Florists, hairdressers, barbers, funeral directors, interior decorators, etc. are licensed in some states. Discuss whether licensing protects public welfare or if licensing is a means of restraining competition and of limiting new entrants. What is the effect on price and the quantity of services provided in an industry with government mandated credentials.

Exercise 10.10

Outline a method for a public administrator to choose between ways of raising $100,000 in donor contributions.

11
Cost–Benefit Analysis

11.1   INTRODUCTION

Most proposals presented to government and nonprofit firms sound good. Who is not in favor of stronger and better bridges, schools, and protective services for children? Who is not in favor of technologically advanced equipment, rehabilitation programs, and medical research? However, resources are limited and thus every society/firm must ask when considering options, "Do benefits exceed costs and what programs yield the greatest benefits?" Ideally, decision-makers should try to assess, given moral and legal constraints, each person's *compensating variation*, the negative or positive monetary value that would make him or her as well off as they would be in the status quo.

Assessing costs and benefits with a consistent methodology is resisted by those who believe that NFP firms can and should spend every dollar allocated to a specific program and seek additional funds. Accountability requires public administrators to question, "What do we get in public benefits as a result of expenditures made?" Breaking even or achieving a modest net income keeps firms operating but NFP survival with subsidies does not measure effectiveness. Profit-seeking firms have traditionally used benefits per dollar to decide between projects. NFP firms, struggling with the question of accountability, can modify benefit analysis for use as an appropriate tool in certain situations. In fact, the Reagan and Clinton administrations required agencies to provide a cost–benefit analysis for all proposals exceeding a certain cost. *Cost–benefit analysis (CBA)* is a tool for attempting to fully account for all costs associated with a new proposal and a detailed calculation of specific private and social benefits. CBA is a method for determining whether or not a proposal should even be considered, and the size of net benefits relative to alternative projects.

Consider the following: In the United States there are 178 separate federal programs designed to help people get back to work. These programs cost $8.4 billion and 2.4 million people actually obtain employment each year as a result of their efforts. But what would happen if we took the most effective programs out of the total 178 and allocated to them the entire budget of $8.4 billion? Maybe, 14 million people would find new employment, a far larger number than the actual 2.4 million. Lack of accountability and tolerance for the status quo are often responsible for poor performance in NFP firms.

Sponsors of NFP firms, lacking clearly defined ownership and simple quantitative measures of outcomes, rely on assessment tools. Return on assets, earnings per share, income after taxes, sales, and stock price, are inappropriate tools to gauge effectiveness in a government or nonprofit firm. On the other hand, some tools used internally in the profit-seeking sector translate well into the NFP sectors. One of these tools is cost–benefit analysis. With transparent accounting and auditing systems, raw data needed for NFP cost–benefit analysis has become increasingly available.

After reviewing net discounted present value in the profit-seeking sector, we extend this tool into cost–benefit analysis for the NFP sectors. The goal is to determine if the benefits of a given project exceed all associated costs. The chapter ends with two applications of cost–benefit analysis.

11.2   NET DISCOUNTED PRESENT VALUE

Net discounted present value (or *NPV*) is a decision-making technique normally used by profit-seeking firms. Public administration students may already be familiar with this technique. Those working for public utilities and hospitals use net discounted present value to decide between different pieces of equipment under consideration. Net discounted present value is so similar to cost–benefit analysis it is sometimes referred to as *private cost–benefit analysis*. The technique depends upon comparing various projects and programs on the basis of how they affect the "bottom line" of net income/profit. Projects and programs that make positive contributions to overall profit are candidates for implementation while those failing to meet the ironclad standard of profit contribution are discarded. It is helpful for students to understand the net present value approach toward profit before proceeding to NFP cost–benefit analysis with social objectives rather than profit maximization.

Net discounted present value

The *NPV* methodology involves a comparison of the value or worth of an investment with its costs. An investment's net present value can be expressed in the form of the following equation:

$$NPV = \sum_{t=1}^{n} \frac{R_t}{(1 + K)^t} - C$$

Where

R_t = the projected after-tax cash flow in time period t,
K = the risk-adjusted discount rate,
C = the dollar amount or cost of the initial investment, and
n = the number of periods for the project or asset.

The first term on the right-hand side of the equation is the mathematical form of the discounting technique used by financial analysts, such as the time value of money presented in Chapter 10. The value of any project can be measured as the present value of its projected revenue flows. The difference between its present value and its cost (measured as "C" above) indicates whether the project is a candidate for implementation. If *NPV* is positive, the project is a candidate; it may not be implemented because other projects are even better candidates, but it is a possibility for implementation. If *NPV* is negative, the project would not contribute to profit and so is not a candidate for implementation. This procedure, as used by profit-seeking firms, is simple and straightforward.

The *NPV* technique assumes that a dollar in hand today is worth more than a dollar in hand tomorrow. At any positive interest rate, a dollar today can be deposited in a bank account and becomes more than a dollar tomorrow. For instance, if the interest rate is 10 percent and you save $100 today, a year from now you would have $110. Thus there is no difference between receiving $100 today or $110 one year from now; hence the statement that a dollar today is worth more than the same dollar one year from now.

One characteristic of the technique requires further discussion. The R_t represents the benefits of a project at different points in time (t). These benefits are measured over time but they consider only "private" benefits for profit-seeking firms. Costs and the benefits are normally measured as market prices. These market prices, however, do *not* reflect social costs and social benefits, a significant characteristic of the output of NFP firms. In the absence of externalities, the prices people pay for goods and services in the profit-seeking sector reflect the marginal economic value (or benefit) they receive from those goods and services. Likewise, the prices of the inputs used to produce those goods and services provide a correct measure of their opportunity cost. The market itself in such instances serves to maximize the net benefits as firms compete to produce the best "bottom line." In the profit-seeking sector of the economy the market makes the calculations necessary to gauge efficiency, but only private costs (expenses) and private benefits (revenue/profit) are taken into account.

In order to evaluate a project that has receipts or expenditures in future years, the firm multiplies those receipts and expenditures by the discount factor $(1/(1+K)^t)$ that makes those future receipts and payments just equal in worth to current receipts and payments. The discount factor becomes smaller the further out into the future receipts and expenditures are projected.

Consider a three-year project being evaluated by a profit-seeking firm that employs a discount rate of 12 percent. The project is expected to return the following benefits:

Time period	Expected benefits
1	$100
2	$200
3	$300

The costs of the project are $400 paid at the beginning of the first year (i.e., time period). The calculation using the *NPV* equation above would be:

$$NPV = \frac{\$100}{(1+0.12)^1} + \frac{\$200}{(1+0.12)^2} + \frac{\$300}{(1+0.12)^3} - \$400$$

$$NPV = \$100(0.893) + 200(0.797) + 300(0.712) - 400$$

$$NPV = \$462.30 - 400$$

$$NPV = \$62.30$$

The discount factors in the above calculation are 0.893, 0.797, and 0.712; note that the discount factors are smaller the further into the future the benefits are projected. This is the "time value of money" at work. In this particular instance, the positive net present value (*NPV*) of $62.50 indicates that the project is a candidate for investment since its benefits exceed its costs. The positive *NPV* does not insure that the firm will make the investment; there may be other, more attractive, investments with even higher *NPV*s and these projects would be the first to be implemented. There are projects, having positive *NPV*s, not implemented because the firm has already reached its credit limit. In no case does a firm implement a project with a negative *NPV*. Doing so would diminish profits.

Private cost–benefit analysis (also called net present value analysis) is much simpler than the type we use with NFP firms. However, as previously mentioned, some NFP firms, such as hospitals considering whether or not to purchase a piece of equipment, will decide based on straight forward private cost–benefit analysis. Will the firm be better off with or without the equipment? As of today, will the projected discounted revenue derived from having the machine equal or exceed the present and future discounted expense of providing it? In summary, there are four steps to an investment decision:

1   Identify possible alternatives. The firm lists projects or programs suitable for investment.
2   Identify the consequences of each alternative identified; that is, identify the costs and benefits. In doing this it is essential not to double count. Focus only on cost and benefits created by the project.
3   Compute the costs of each input. This is easy when market prices accurately measure the true costs the firm will incur. Compute expected benefits in terms of prices at which the outputs will be sold. Again, this is simple when market prices accurately reflect the benefits the firm will directly receive. Net benefits for each time period are discounted using a market interest rate chosen by the firm.
4   Add up the discounted costs and benefits to determine if the project is truly profitable and thus a candidate for implementation. If multiple projects are available, the firm will implement the most profitable project first followed by the next most profitable and so on. The firm will not invest in projects with negative net present values.

11.3   COST–BENEFIT ANALYSIS IN THE NOT-FOR-PROFIT SECTORS

Although the process of *social cost–benefit analysis* as performed by NFP firms appears to be the same as its profit-seeking version, there are two critical differences.

First, the only outcomes considered in profit-seeking cost–benefit analysis are those that affect the firm's profit. NFP firms, however, must be concerned with a wider measurement of a project's costs and benefits. The safety and steady supply of a NFP blood bank goes beyond legal and profit considerations. A government agency concerned with building "affordable housing" is more concerned with social benefits (e.g., children of low-income homeowners are much less likely to drop out of school) than financial return on investment.

Second, when profit-seeking firms evaluate projects, market prices are commonly available. But NFP firms and government agencies often have no market prices available to use as measuring sticks. In most instances, the output of the NFP is not sold at market price; the client fee represents only part of the value created. Our definition of a NFP firm is one in which the client payment is subsidized by a sponsoring agency. Therefore, it makes little sense to value benefits at administered or nonmarket fees. For example, the value of real resources allocated to a state university class exceeds the nominal cost of tuition. Because it is subsidized with tax revenue, it must be at least worth what students *and* taxpayers are willing to pay. Likewise, NFP opportunity costs, generally more easily calculated than benefits, are not always apparent and can only be approximated. For example, what is the market value of food, donated to a nonprofit food bank, as it approaches its expiration date?

Most NFP programs extend beyond a year and perhaps even beyond the current generation of the target population (i.e., intergenerational investments); in these instances the complete range of impacts are quite difficult to measure or estimate. Nevertheless, social cost–benefit analysis is the valuation technique of choice. This is true even when market prices are not available or do not reflect true social costs and benefits. It may actually be the case that the item or service is not traded at all and thus has no market value. We now analyze cost–benefit analysis step by step and consider extended real world examples.

Benefits ratio

The decision to engage in any project compares benefits to costs. We define the *benefits ratio* as:

Benefits ratio $= B/C$

Where

$B =$ Benefits
$C =$ Costs

Multiple projects often compete one with another. In this case, the private non-profit firm or government agency should if possible undertake the project in which the total net benefit is highest (that is, the project that maximizes the difference between the benefits and the costs). Note, carefully, that the project that maximizes the difference between benefits and costs is not the same as choosing the project that maximizes the benefits ratio! Small projects with minuscule net benefits might have very high benefits ratios ($3/2 = 1.5$ compared with $25/20 = 1.25$). However, the project having the greatest net benefits ($25 - 20 = 5$ compared with $3 - 2 = 1$) is preferred.

A NFP firm should obviously direct resources to projects yielding the greatest net benefits, but first we eliminate worthless projects from consideration. We start, for example, using data to assess the folly of building "a bridge to nowhere." The first rule is to eliminate projects for which the benefits ratio fails to exceed unity:

$B/C < 1$

11.4   COST–BENEFIT FRAMEWORK

A consistent generalized framework is needed to determine if net benefits exist and to choose between projects. NFP project expenditures involve effects (both costs and benefits) extending well beyond the present timeframe and affecting different groups of individuals. Some effects may be positive, while others may be negative.

To set up a cost–benefit framework, an administrator must address each of the following:

- *Alternatives.* Consider all potential projects, policies, or programs, including the option of "the status quo."
- *Costs.* Determine the opportunity cost (or proxy opportunity cost) for each project.
- *Benefits.* Determine benefits for each project.
- *Identify cost bearers and beneficiaries.* Determine groups affected by the project.
- *Evaluate cost, benefits, and any transfer payments.* Determine the pattern of benefits reception and cost bearing.
- *Consider distributional impact.* Evaluate the effects of expected outcomes on different groups.
- *Choose a discount rate.* Determine the present value of costs and benefits over time.

Consider the type of data and the consistent methodology required to evaluate a project in terms of the above points. Table 11.1 provides the scaffolding or framework for structuring a cost–benefit analysis. Relevant non-overlapping groups are listed across the first row. Categories of costs and benefits are listed in the left-hand column. The present value of all the project's costs and benefits, by group, fit into each relevant cell.

Costs and benefits are not identical to and should not be confused with revenue and expenses. Note that costs represent the real opportunity cost of resources and are not limited to financial transactions. Public administers act in trust for donors/taxpayers/clients to ensure that all resources allocated to a project are used to create services of equal or greater value. Volunteer services, donations, and the use of facilities owned by an agency are considered costs. When market values for these costs do not exist, proxy values are estimated. Benefits and costs, impossible to estimate with any degree of accuracy, are recognized and identified with a plus or minus. Be warned, that benefits generally are more difficult to estimate, more subject to bias, and more complicated to discount than costs.

Each row under transfers considers costs and benefits between groups and must necessarily equal zero. Transfers on net may leave some individuals worse off and some better off than the status quo, but these transfers do not enter into the equation for determining net benefits. In some cost–benefit studies, transfers are not calculated because the CBA focuses on determining the extent to which real resources are allocated to a specific project relative to the total benefits derived from the project.

Considering alternatives

It is obvious, although often overlooked, that the first step in any cost–benefit analysis is to list all alternative courses of action. Cost–benefit analysis was first used in public settings to evaluate water projects (i.e., dams, flood control programs, etc.); in these situations there was often more than one method available to achieve desired outcomes. In 1936 Congress passed the Federal Navigation Act containing this charge to government agencies: "The Federal Government should improve or participate in the improvement of navigable waters or their tributaries

Table 11.1   The cost–benefit framework

	Group 1	Group 2	Group 3	Group 4	Group 5	All society
PV of costs						
Cost a						
Cost b						
Cost c						
Cost d						
Cost e						
Cost f						
Cost g						
PV of benefits						
Benefit h						
Benefit i						
Benefit j						
Benefit k						
Benefit l						
Benefit m						
PV of transfers						
Transfer n						
Transfer o						
Total benefit						
Total cost						
Net benefit						
Net qualitative benefit						

. . . if the benefits are in excess of the estimated costs." The Army Corps of Engineers followed the prescriptions of the Act by developing an analysis of public investments. Cost–benefit analysis (as it has come to be called) is presently widely used in NFP decision-making.

The search for alternatives is often the least emphasized, though perhaps the most important, cost–benefit steps. The search for alternatives should go beyond technical and engineering considerations to capture the relative effectiveness of different approaches.

11.5   IDENTIFYING COST BEARERS AND BENEFICIARIES

In some projects, such as roadways, benefits and costs apply to the same individuals or groups; that is, the costs are borne by those receiving the benefits. This assumption, however, is not true in most NFP situations. When the issue of how benefits are distributed and how costs are borne is injected into the analysis, we realize that not everyone in a community will be affected in the same way by a particular project or process. Because NFP provision by definition involves a subsidy, there are few projects directly benefiting exactly the same group ultimately funding the project. The distribution of costs and benefits may be as important as the calculation of the net costs and benefits. Subsidized classical concerts in the park yield enormous benefits to some, yet fail to benefit or reflect the tastes of the general public.

Government and private nonprofit firm projects are usually designed to target one group or another; we should not expect the benefits and costs to be equally shared in most situations. In a mass vaccination program, for example, the rhetoric implies that the benefit will accrue to the entire society. But just exactly what does the phrase "entire society" mean? If the vaccination is for measles, there will be a clear and significant benefit to pregnant women and their unborn children. Birth defects are reduced by there being fewer opportunities to contract a disease particularly dangerous to fetuses. However, a small number of those vaccinated suffer severe reactions to the vaccine; for these individuals there are no net benefits. For most, the inoculations protect from measles and complications from the disease; thus, they are more comfortable and lose less time off from work or school. All outcomes are probabilistic; that is, nobody can know for certain exactly how any group will be affected.

Measuring costs and benefits involves:

1   Risks about the existence and sizes of future benefits and costs.
2   The chronological distribution of benefits and costs over time.
3   Identification of the groups receiving benefits and those paying the costs.

Consider a town setting up a sheltered workshop to train and employ mentally challenged adults. Table 11.2 provides a cost–benefit framework differentiating groups

Table 11.2   Monetary valuations required for a proposed sheltered workshop

		Participants	Sponsor/ donors	Volunteers	Other citizens
PV of costs					
	Salaries and benefits		Negative		
	Supplies and services		Negative		
	Facility use				Negative
	Volunteer time			Negative	
	Participant costs	Negative			
PV of benefits					
	Participant income	Positive			
	Income from products sold				Positive
	Reduced social service costs				Positive

bearing some of the costs and benefits. Table 11.2 makes no attempt to quantify the costs or benefits but merely indicates potential values as being positive (benefit) or negative (cost).

Transfer payments are a feature of many projects; this is simply the concept that one group transfers benefits or costs to another group with no net change in the total costs and benefits. Viewed from the standpoint of a particular group in society, these transfer payments look exactly like costs or benefits. But viewed from the standpoint of an entire society or population, these transfer payments are simply an accounting convention that allocates the costs and benefits without changing the total net benefit or net cost at all. This is an important point because transfer payments are not counted as net benefits to society as a whole. They may appear to be benefits or costs to a single group but from a total society standpoint they most certainly do not affect the net situation. In Table 11.2, for example, subsidies are transferred from taxpayers/donors to participants. There is a remote possibility that taxes from participants' future income due to the workshop go to other citizens. Transfers are correctly not included in total benefits or total costs and have no bearing on whether the project creates benefits exceeding costs; some analysts do not even explicitly include them. The piling on of dubious benefits, such as those transmitted to participants' parents or the macroeconomic multiplier effects, may "sell" the project to the general public. However, they are misleading and should be excluded from the analysis.

11.6   MEASURING COSTS AND BENEFITS

A decision-making process like cost–benefit analysis offers a formal method to analyze complicated situations. Recall, however, that cost–benefit analysis, while similar to net discounted present value calculation (private cost–benefit analysis), seeks to quantify the societal benefits and societal costs as well as those that are privately borne. In the public arena due to externalities, true costs borne by society are not evident in the market prices; there is a huge distinction between private competitive market situations and nonmarket provision of public and quasi-public goods and services. The prices you pay for a good in a private competitive market, in the absence of externalities, generally reflect all of the costs incurred in bringing the good to the marketplace, and as the buyer you receive the benefits. This must be so in the long run or the firm providing the good would soon find itself financially unable to continue providing the good and it would become unavailable. Each production input in private competitive markets is paid its marginal value. If factor scarcities arise, prices reflect this change and the market moves to a new equilibrium.

In the public and private nonprofit sectors no such "automatic" mechanism exists. Quite the opposite may be the case; prices may not exist and quoted fees are not market determined and fail to represent marginal values. Economists measure value in such situations by estimating the **shadow price**. Shadow prices are proxies which are estimates or mathematically derived substitutes for market prices. They are not real prices; nowhere will you see shadow prices quoted in *The Wall Street Journal*.

Shadow prices are designed to reflect the true social value or cost of a resource. They are used to estimate such costs and benefits as the value of a volunteer's services or the worth of "free" recreational activities at a public park. Fortunately, many expected social costs and benefits of projects can be directly derived from labor and product markets. But when there is no market, then analysts need a shadow price – for example, the value of a human life saved, the cost of various types of injuries, the social cost of a robbery, or the value of an hour of travel time saved. Application 11.1 discusses how the Outdoor Recreation Review Commission, established by the U.S. Congress, places values on recreational activities.

APPLICATION 11.1
Outdoor Recreation

Outdoor recreation is a major land use involving a quarter of a billion acres of U.S. public land plus about as much private land. Over 90 percent of Americans participate yearly in outdoor recreation. Conservatively, $20 billion is spent by the public on outdoor recreation with $1 billion being spent by the government annually.

Generally, public outdoor recreation is not sold for a price. As a result, there is no direct measure of the worth of recreation experiences at public sites (we do have such information for private sites such as Disneyworld). What is the value to a person of bathing in the Atlantic along the Jersey shore or hiking the Rockies in Idaho? Or, passively seeing the sun rise over Lake Michigan from a bench on Navy Pier in Chicago or enjoying a wetland or sand dune from a wheelchair accessible boardwalk? What is the value to you of knowing that the Grand Canyon is being preserved even if you never have the opportunity to see it? Measurement makes it difficult to judge primary direct benefits accruing to people engaged in outdoor recreation. In turn, this hampers efforts to allocate scarce resources among competing uses.

However, if we refuse to measure the benefits accrued to outdoor recreation seekers, how can we form any reasonable idea of superior alternatives to the present? With what assurance can we arrive at a reasonably efficient use of public resources? To answer these questions since 1962, Federal agencies have devised methods for measuring individual values of publicly provided outdoor recreation.

One method has been to more or less arbitrarily value all visits to federal water related recreational facilities at 50 cents per day, $1 per day, or $1.60 per day; different schedules are proposed if fishing takes place. Fixed-value estimates like these do not measure differences in quality at various sites or in the activities available at those sites. The estimated value will always be a "judgment value" placed on the activity by the researcher.

A second method that has attracted attention is to develop demand schedules based on the client cost of travel to the recreation area. The implied assumption here is that average client travel costs reflect benefits received. However, basing the entire estimate of benefits on the location of the recreation area ignores the quality of recreation provided.

A third approach is to place a value on public recreation provided in terms of the opportunity cost of using the resources in some other way. That is, recreational resources are valued at their highest alternative. The difficulty here, of course, is that some resources such as the Grand Canyon have at present no alternative use and would thus be undervalued. Alternatively, some sites, such as a modest bird-watching reserve, might be considered highly valued simply because they are on flat land with fertile soil and would be quite productive in alternative agricultural use.

A fourth approach is to conduct market surveys of the perceived economic value of outdoor recreation. People are asked to select among several suggested prices that might be charged for a recreational site offering specific activities located within stated distances. Private recreation facilities in the same geographic area would also be taken into account.

A final technique involves the use of market simulations or controlled laboratory experiments to assess people's preferences. These techniques are gaining greater favor in the profit-seeking sectors as research tools and they may be able to be adapted to measuring the value of public resources.

Cost data are as important as benefit estimation, because costs vary with the level of usage. The problem of assessing cost in public recreation becomes one of estimating accurately the development costs (land and capital) as well as the annual operating costs needed for planned capacity at different levels of use.

Source: Alan Ewert, "Outdoor Recreation at 40! Research: An Essential Ingredient in the Outdoor Recreation Mix," *Parks and Recreation*, 37 (8), 2000, 64–72.

Because shadow prices play a key role in determining the outcome of cost–benefit analysis, care should be taken in arriving at any approximation of valuation. How, for example, would you derive a figure for the future income of participants in a sheltered workshop? Or the social benefits? Table 11.3 is a useful classification of market versus shadow prices (Boardman, et al., 1997).

Table 11.3 divides all possible private nonprofit firm and governmental projects into one of three categories displayed across the top of the table. These three categories are:

Table 11.3   Cost–benefit valuations: market and shadow prices

	Transportation/ infrastructure	*Natural resources/ environment*	*Human resources/ technological/social*
Valuations can be based on market prices	Construction resources: materials land labor equipment Operations resources: labor maintenance Fuel and operating cost savings Product outputs Increased tourism	Extraction/development resources: equipment labor materials water Product outputs Process changes	Program resources: staff facilities equipment Product outputs Process changes
Valuations require shadow prices	*Lives saved Injuries avoided Accidents avoided Time saved* *Air quality changes* *Noise level changes Recreational improvements Marginal excess tax burden* Social discount rate	*Air quality changes Water quality changes Species preserved Recreational improvements Marginal excess tax burden* Social discount rate	*Crimes avoided Lives saved Injuries avoided* Health improvements Productivity improvements *Marginal excess tax burden* Social discount rate

Source: Anthony E. Boardman, David H. Greenberg, Aidan R. Vining, and David L. Weimer, " 'Plug-in' Shadow Price Estimates for Policy Analysis," *Annals of Regional Science*, 31, 1997, 299–324.

1   transportation or infrastructure projects;
2   natural resources or environmental projects;
3   human resources and technological/social projects.

The two methods of determining impacts are listed down the left-hand side of the table:

1   valuations that can be based upon market prices;
2   valuations that require a shadow price.

A few examples make clear exactly how useful this taxonomy is. Consider a municipality that has decided to build an addition to its public transportation infrastructure; the city wishes to construct a new bus terminal in the city center. The costs of construction need to be estimated as a step in the cost–benefit analysis. How will incurred costs be estimated? According to Table 11.3 this is a transportation project involving construction resources (i.e., materials, land, labor, and equipment). Because these resources are routinely used in the same city by private construction firms, it is reasonable to use their market prices as representative in building the new bus terminal. Measuring benefits is generally more difficult. Because the bus terminal project provides a "safer" environment for passengers, planners wish to include some measure of these benefits. Market determined measures are not available, but a shadow price reflecting "injuries avoided" or "lives saved" ought to be included in the calculation of benefits.

Another example is a proposed dam to prevent frequent flooding of a particular locality and to create an artificial lake for recreation. Constructing such a dam requires financing a bond placing a burden on future generations. This type of project falls under the natural resources column in Table 11.3. Once again, construction costs are represented quite well by the prices charged in competitive markets for labor and equipment. The tax cost and the expected recreational benefits are, however, not easily measured. In these cases, shadow prices are once again needed.

In Chapter 10, we used "full-time market equivalent" calculations for volunteer services as a type of shadow price. Shadow rent for a program in a NFP's deteriorating or single-purpose facility might be the potential earned income if the building were demolished, the land sold, and the proceeds invested. Calculating values for the social benefits category is particularly challenging. Economists have developed two procedures for estimating these elusive shadow prices. One of these procedures is contingent valuation and the other is the hedonic approach.

Contingent valuation uses surveys. These consist of a series of questions asking the respondent to place a value on benefits received from a particular project. Consider a municipality trying to value the services offered at a local library. The contingent valuation technique asks questions that lead a library patron or potential patron to place a value on these services. The technique is called contingent valuation because the question itself may influence the answer; hence, the answer is "contingent" upon included information. Example questions like the following were actually used by the Institute of Museum and Library Services in Washington, DC. How much would you pay to retain access to the library? Supposing that public libraries did not exist, how much would your household be willing to pay each year to establish your public library as it exists today? These values, even when quite small, add up when used to represent the total population. Contingent valuation is not without its critics; people often have little incentive to tell the truth on surveys and/or have little incentive to take the effort to formulate a realistic answer. Nobel Prize winners Robert Solow of MIT and Kenneth Arrow of Stanford recommend cautious use of contingency valuation.

A second method uses market data; this procedure eliminates the direct questioning of individuals and instead observes how potential clients reveal their preferences in the marketplace. Most economists are much more comfortable with this technique for collecting valuations. It is sometimes called the *hedonic approach to valuation*.

The hedonic approach could be used to determine how much less people are willing to pay for a home subject to air traffic noise or how much more they are willing to pay for one fronting a park. It could also be used to assess the value of a proposed bus terminal project, previously discussed. A new terminal results in significant time savings to individuals, but we need dollar estimates for a cost–benefit analysis. How do we make the conversion without an "exchange rate" for time and dollars? How much is an hour of someone's time worth in dollars? One common approach is to measure the average wages of those using the bus terminal; the implied assumption is that if the individuals were not waiting for buses they could be working and earning this wage rate. The wage, in one sense, provides an individual's own estimate of the value of their time as reflected in an actual market transaction (they freely contracted to work for this wage). Wages are not arrived at by surveying the individuals directly but through observation.

There are drawbacks to the hedonic approach to valuation. Obviously, we are making the heroic assumption that an individual would work the extra time saved by the new terminal and also that the individual has the opportunity to do so at the given wage rate. Both assumptions may not apply and hence our estimates of value are suspect.

The economic value of life

At the risk of seeming macabre and provoking all sort of emotional conflict, CBA is forced to deal with the benefits and costs of lives put at risk, saved, or extended. One often hears the statement, "No economic value can be placed on a human life." Yet, every day you place a value on your life by taking risks. Whenever you cross a busy street, you weigh the small chance that you will be hit by an automobile with the benefits of having crossed the street. However distasteful the valuation of human life seems, in practice it is done when making choices between goods and services with public-good characteristics.

Limitless funds could be expended in making buildings safe from fire; there is always some extra device that is safer than current fire protection measures. Likewise, some expenditure could be made to make highways safer for motorists. When do these extra expenditures exceed the gains to making them? It is simply not sensible to repeat the mantra that "there can be no value placed on a human life." If that were so, fire-safe buildings, given existing technology, would cost up to half of our yearly national income. Similarly, the safest possible highways would be so expensive that few could afford the tolls needed to build them. Values are placed on human lives all the time. The more reasonable question for us to ask is, "How do we determine the correct expenditure on fire protection or highway safety equipment?"

There are two methods used to value life in common practice. One is the *human capital approach* and the other is the *willingness-to-pay approach*. The human capital approach is also called the "constructive method" because it equates the market value of a life with what the individual would have earned in their expected lifetime. The human capital method is objectionable to many and represents a legitimate criticism of CBA. It is objectionable because it places a different value on individual lives depending on their earning potential. That is, we assess the value of a saved life as equal to the monetary value of what that person would have earned in their remaining lifetime. The present value of future discounted earnings accounts for the fact that potential earnings are distributed throughout time. Expected wages and fringe benefits are discounted and a monetary value produced depending upon the age, education, health, etc. of the person at the time of death. The value of stay-at-home spouses is calculated similarly, begging the question of a homemaker's "worth." The human capital approach fails to consider nonmarket returns and is biased toward labor market compensation. In the extreme, the human capital approach values the life of a permanently unemployed individual near zero.

The second approach to valuing a life is called the "willingness-to-pay approach." This indirect method recognizes the desire of individuals to extend their lives. It is based on estimates of how much people are willing to pay to gain a small reduction in the probability of dying. This information, however, is usually not based on surveys. Once again, economists observe what people do and not what they say. If people fail to install smoke detectors in their houses, if they choose "safe" professions such as college teaching over relatively risky professions such as combat pilot, if they decide not to wear seat belts, then we can make estimates of the values they place on their own lives. By choosing one or the other of the above situations, the individual signals what they are willing to pay to achieve a longer expected life. To see this, consider an individual deciding whether to order optional side-impact airbags on a new automobile. The benefit of the side-impact airbags is that they reduce the probability of dying in the event of an accident. In such a situation assume the now reduced probability of dying is P, the cost of the airbags is C, and the value of a person's life is V. A rational individual will continue purchasing safety devices until the marginal benefits are just zero; another way of saying the same thing is to say that the person will purchase the device if the benefit $(P \times V)$ just compensates for the cost, C.

$$P \times V = C$$

Solving this equation for V gives:

$$V = C/P$$

This implies that the value of a life for this individual is equal to cost divided by the reduced probability of dying. Note that we are observing how the individual behaves in an actual market and trying to deduce the value that person places on his or her own life; we are not asking the individual directly what value they place on their life. The distinct advantage of this method is that it does not just value the market wages the person may earn as their human value, but measures the total value of human life as displayed by the individual's actions. The willingness-to-pay approach will generally result in higher human life valuations than the human capital approach.

Consider the decision by a parent to purchase a car safety seat. While most states now require the use of such devices, when Carlin and Sandy studied the question there were few such laws and the decision was left to the parent. Carlin and Sandy used the equation above to estimate the value of the child's life as reflected in the mother's purchase of a safety seat. The benefits received by purchasing a car seat at approximately $180 were measured by the decrease in the probability of the child dying in a collision (approximately a reduction of 4.3 in 10,000). Based upon these estimates the estimated value of a young child's life (to a mother) was $418,597 (Carlin and Sandy, 1991).

11.7   CHOOSING THE DISCOUNT RATE

The rate used to discount costs and benefits received in the future may itself be thought of as a shadow price. The discount rate chosen for a cost–benefit analysis is related to market interest rates but can be adjusted to reflect social concerns. In this section, we must first understand the effect on the benefit–cost ratio of a particular discount rate and then discuss how discount rates are chosen.

The time length of the project being evaluated increases the importance of the chosen discount rate. For short-term projects the discount rate has little effect, but for longer-term projects the discount rate choice can easily mean the difference between approval and rejection. A project that looks reasonable at a discount rate of 5 percent may be rejected at a discount rate of 9 percent.

Suppose that the ongoing cost of staff salaries of the sheltered workshop, outlined in Table 11.2, is expected to be $50,000 per year over the next three years of the project. Assume the single cost is staff salaries and the single benefit is the reduced need for psychological services. Suppose that the social benefits to adult participants are $10,000 a year in social services otherwise required over the next 30 years in the absence of the program. Using a 5 percent discount rate, the present value of the salaries is $136,162 (the cost) and of the social benefits are $153,725. Using a 10 percent discount rate, the values are $124,343 and $94,269 respectively. Note that with a discount rate of 10 percent net benefits are negative. This reverses the positive benefits with a 5 percent discount rate.

The size and timing of the benefits and costs as well as the size of the discount rate affect the attractiveness of projects. If a project has large costs early on and receives benefits much later, a higher discount rate makes the project less attractive (because you pay "expensive" dollars now and receive "cheaper." i.e., discounted, benefits later).

To illustrate the distribution of benefits over time consider the following two projects, A and B in Table 11.4. Note that Project A receives most of its benefits later in the project (in years 4 and 5) while project B receives most of its returns earlier in the project (years 1 and 2).

Both projects yield the same dollar benefits and pay the same dollar costs. Costs are paid when the project is initiated. The significant difference lies in the timing of benefits. Project A is **rear-end loaded**. That is, a rear-end loaded project receives its largest benefits toward the end of the project. On the other hand, project B is **front-end loaded**, receives most of its benefits early in the 5-year time horizon. If a 10 percent discount rate is selected, project A has a negative net present value, and a benefit–cost ratio of less than one. Project B has a positive net

Table 11.4 Two projects with differing benefits schedules

Year	Project A	Project B
0	($3,500)	($3,500)
1	$200	$1,970
2	$500	$1,300
3	$800	$800
4	$1,300	$500
5	$1,970	$200
NPV at 10%	($192.77)	$432.03
NPV at 5%	$448.12	$814.46
B/C ratio at 10%	0.9449	1.123
B/C ratio at 5%	1.128	1.2327

present value and a benefit–cost ratio greater than one. Project *B* will be chosen. If the discount rate chosen is 5 percent, then project *A* has a positive benefit–cost ratio, but project *B* is still preferred. Application 11.2 indicates that when the Expanded Food and Nutrition Education Program of Virginia used 10 percent rather than 5 percent as a discount rate, the benefit/cost ratio of their project was reduced from 10.64 to 2.77. *Sensitivity analysis* is the study of how costs and benefits respond to different discount rates and other critical assumptions affecting cost–benefit conclusions. Most studies supply figures using at least two discount rates.

APPLICATION 11.2
Nutrition Education

The state of Virginia provides a nutrition education program entitled the "Expanded Food and Nutrition Education Program (EFNEP)" to selected residents. In 1996, a cost–benefit analysis was done by the state to determine its cost effectiveness. EFNEP primarily targeted low-income homemakers, defined as families at 150 percent of the poverty level and below.

These homemakers tended to be predominantly ethnic or minority, had limited education, and were generally considered culturally, socially, and geographically isolated. The average homemaker's age was 23 years. Seventeen percent were teenagers.

The focus of EFNEP was nutrition education. The goal was to assist homemakers with limited incomes in "acquiring the knowledge, skills, attitudes, and changed behaviors necessary for nutritionally sound diets." Funded through the United States Department of Agriculture, the program was delivered as a set of lessons available either in the form of flip charts or, later, as a set of videos.

The CBA study used various measures of tangible and intangible benefits. Tangible benefits related to targeted disease, such as efforts to reduce the effects of heart disease on homemakers (and their children). Decreased sodium intake (salt) was a measured proxy for better heart care and, hence, program effectiveness. Likewise, decreased fat intake and increased physical activity were used as a measure of program effectiveness (and therefore measured benefits).

Obesity was among the other diseases and conditions targeted. The increased intake of fiber, complex carbohydrates, fruits, and vegetables was used as a proxy for obesity reduction, along with decreased caloric intake. Some indirect benefits, associated with the program, were much more difficult to measure. One program goal was "improved self-image." This was proxied in actual measurements by improved stamina and an improved sense of wellbeing.

Costs included in the study were more predictable. These included personnel costs, office space, travel expenditures, training costs, and support costs (e.g., secretarial staff, computer support, etc.).

The dollar value of benefits was monetized in two ways. First, health-care costs associated with treating nutrition-related diseases and conditions (like heart disease) were used. Second, earnings forgone due to lost workdays or death were estimated.

The formula for monetizing tangible program benefits follows:

$$\text{Benefit} = A * B * C * D * E$$

Where:

A = annual number of program graduates of EFNEP
B = Incidence rate of disease/condition in low-income population
C = Incidence of the disease/condition related to diet
D = Percent of graduates practicing optimal nutritional behaviors related to avoiding or delaying the disease/condition
E = Present value of appropriate benefits for the disease/condition

A sample calculation of benefits might look as follows:

$A = 3,100$ Graduates of EFNEP.

$B = (0.10 \times 3,100) = 310$ Graduates affected with the targeted health conditions.

$C = (0.25 \times 310) = 77$ There is a probability that 25 percent of those with the disease/condition could control it through specific diet related behaviors.

$D = (0.05 \times 77) = 4$ There is a probability that 5 percent of graduates practice optimal behaviors.

$E = (\$3,000 \times 4) = \$12,000$ Present value of appropriate benefits for the disease/condition is $3,000.

Thus, $12,000 is the discounted benefit associated for one disease/condition under consideration. Similar calculations were made for each targeted disease/condition.

Calculating the number of EFNEP graduates was done conservatively. A questionnaire called the Family Record was required at the beginning and end of the program. A part of the questionnaire was a 24-hour food recall in which participants had to indicate the number of servings they had eaten of all foods in the last 24 hours. Nutrient intakes were compared to recommended dietary allowances. To be a graduate, practicing optimal nutritional behaviors, the individual needed to achieve a threshold high score where a positive response was desired and also be below a low threshold where a negative response was desired. "Graduates" that were already practicing good nutritional habits at the beginning of the program were not included (i.e., the program did nothing additional to help them).

Once costs were computed (and their compilation was a much easier and straightforward task than dealing with the benefits), two distinct measures of effectiveness were used. First a benefits ratio was calculated. Secondly, an *internal rate of return* was calculated. For the overall program (taking into account all the target disease/ conditions) the benefits ratio was 10.64.

The initial benefits ratio of 10.64 indicated a substantial return to the state of Virginia. However, one critical assumption the study observed was that graduates were assumed to practice good nutritional habits indefinitely. The study did attempt to document the experience of 5-year graduates from the program and believed the assumption was actually a reasonable one. Because this was by no means certain, they chose to decrease the retention of behavior rate from 100 percent to 50 percent and 25 percent and recalculate. In a sense, they were performing a sensitivity analysis to ascertain if the retention rate was a dominant determinant of outcome. At a 25 percent retention rate the benefits ratio had fallen to 2.66. With a retention rate of 50 percent the benefits ratio was 5.3. The researchers, even assuming the most pessimistic assumption (only 25 percent of graduates continued with good dietary behaviors), concluded that "EFNEP is a program that generates significant net returns on investments."

The discount rate used in the study was 5 percent. The authors did, however, also run the calculations again with a discount rate of

386 Input Markets and Cost–Benefit Analysis

10 percent in order to determine sensitivity to the discount rate. The benefits ratio in this case decreased substantially from 10.64 to 2.77.

Source: Michael Lambur, Radhika Rajgopal, Edwin Lewis, Ruby H. Cox, and Michael Ellerbrock, *Applying Cost Benefit Analysis to Nutrition Programs: Focus on the Virginia Expanded Food and Nutrition Education Program*, Virginia Cooperative Extension, no. 490–403, January 2003.

The choice of a discount rate, then, is all important in net discounted present value and cost–benefit analysis. Profit-seeking firms generally discount with a current market interest rate, representing their time value of money. But what interest rate/ discount rate should be adopted for NFP analysis?

If a public investment project displaces private consumption then the appropriate discount rate would be the taxpayers' after-tax time preference. On the other hand, if private investment is displaced, the before-tax rate of return suggests that a higher discount rate be used. The actual discount rate chosen represents the societal view toward a preference for public investment. In general, the higher the discount, the lower is the value being placed on the future benefits.

For comparison purposes it is useful to note that the United States Office of Management and Budget (OMB) generally directs federal agencies to use a 7 percent discount rate as its basic guideline. This probably reflects the opinion that the average rate of return on investments across the economy is about 7 percent. Lower discount rates are permitted for very long projects involving environmental impacts.

11.8   LIMITATIONS OF COST–BENEFIT ANALYSIS

Economics is the science of trade-offs, and trade-offs are nowhere more evident than in a NFP firm choosing between projects. Usually, there are more projects than resources to fund them. The goal of cost–benefit analysis is to provide a method for ranking alternative projects in terms of net benefits. However, whenever any project is undertaken there is a trade-off implied; the funds that a NFP expends on any new project will either (1) reduce current projects, or (2) reduce present assets or increase the firm's indebtedness (or both).

There are project alternatives that cost–benefit analysis is incapable of handling. It cannot assess a set of compatible alternatives (non-mutually exclusive projects). Consider, for example, projects dealing with the goal of outfitting prisoners: project *A* – new prison uniforms and project *B* – a uniform repair center. Projects *A* and *B* are too closely related to a single goal and cannot be separated for cost–benefit analysis. Similarly, cost–benefit analysis cannot work when a continuous choice must be made. For example, it cannot provide insight into the appropriate size of a new prison.

The goal of cost–benefit analysis is to uncover projects with the greatest net benefits. In the profit-seeking sector, funds are available at some interest rate, and firms can concentrate on projects with the greatest net benefits. NFP firms are more constrained in borrowing. The benefit to cost ratio may be high for changing the washing detergent used to launder prison uniforms, but the goal is to maximize net benefits such as air conditioning the facility. However, even if cost–benefit analysis indicates that air conditioning yields the highest net benefits, the bond issue needed for construction may be voted down or exceed a legal borrowing constraint. The relevant choice may indeed be to change laundry detergents!

Another weakness of cost–benefit methodology is that it cannot automatically distinguish between private and/or society-wide public benefits. For example, cost–benefit analysis, considering all of a town's subgroups, might indicate that a skateboarding park has a positive benefit ratio. It ignores, however, the decrease in revenue to private skateboarding parks, a subgroup beyond the scope of the analysis.

There are additional dangers in the misuse of cost–benefit analysis. When used as a justification for condemning private property, it violates property rights. Eminent domain is appropriately used in benefit tests of "public use" property, such as for the construction of bridges and highways. However, fundamental constitutional protections indicate that property transfers, even those meeting a "public benefits" test, may be illegal. Condemning property and forcing individuals to move involuntarily fails to meet the Pareto Optimal condition discussed in Chapter 1. Net benefits may be insufficient to compensate the displaced homeowner.

Finally, cost–benefit analysis, although a logical tool for decision-making, is only as good as its assumptions. As we indicated earlier in this chapter, shadow prices must be constructed and these are based on assumptions that may or may not be realistic.

In the case of *Corrosion Proof Fittings v. EPA (1999)* on asbestos-regulation, the court criticized the EPA for discounting only the costs of regulation and not the benefits, for using an unreasonably high valuation for life, and for calculating costs and benefits over a short period rather than the life of the regulation. These, however, are technical issues. One economist questions a strict division of labor, "Should agencies have the minimal task of determining the effect of projects on overall well-being and elected officials and courts enforce moral commitments [Kuziemko, 2007]?" Kuziemko applauds CBA for increasing the transparency of decision-making within agencies but recommends that agencies, as well as courts and officials, use judgment in CBA preparation, submit their results to peer review, use a standardized uniform statistic for the value of life, and improve the culture of agencies to become more open to economic analysis in general and CBA in particular.

In the following two examples, we will see how cost–benefit analysis is implemented and how sensitivity analysis can be used to test the underlying assumptions that critically affect conclusions.

11.9 USING COST–BENEFIT ANALYIS: PUBLIC LIBRARY CASE

In the fall of 2002 the City of Skokie, Illinois, embarked on cost–benefit analysis as part of a nationwide project funded by the Institute of Museum and Library

Services, an independent federal agency. The purpose of the study was to estimate the net dollar value of benefits from services provided by Skokie public library. The study was a social cost–benefit analysis lacking market prices. The impetus for the study was the budgetary crisis facing public libraries at the time; libraries were asked to cut budgets if they could not "prove" that the excess in benefits produced exceeded the production cost. The Skokie Library decided that the best way to do this would be to employ a standard cost–benefit analysis.

The institute sought to develop a practical, conservative, transportable methodology to estimate a lower bound for libraries' direct return on taxpayer investment. In particular, they wished to answer two questions:

1   How much benefit do public library patrons receive for each dollar of annual tax support?

2   What return do citizens get for the capital invested in their public library?

The study hoped to calculate a benefits ratio that could be used to explain the "value" of the library to its sponsors. The cost–benefit analysis was meant to be quite conservative with few imputed values or assumptions of value.

Researchers compiled a matrix of services and users showing which users employed the various services. This is reproduced in Table 11.5.

Contingent valuation and a stylized hedonic index were used to make estimates of both direct benefits to current patrons and indirect benefits to future generations.

The contingent valuation portion of the analysis was carried out by using a questionnaire approach with Internet and telephone surveys. A random sample conducted by a university survey research center used a branching technique to gain the required information from the various client groups. Both categorical and open-ended questions were used. The contingent valuation approach sought to obtain an estimate of how much households would pay to retain library services. An example of such a question would be:

Suppose that public libraries did not exist. How much would your household be willing to pay per year to establish your public library as it exists today?

A hedonic index or consumer surplus technique seeks to define market substitutes. In Chapter 3, we introduced the concepts of consumer surplus and producer

Table 11.5   Service–user matrix: public library case

Taxonomy	Households	Teachers	Business
Books	X	X	X
Repair manuals	X		
Staff help	X	X	X
Financial			X
Computer	X	X	X

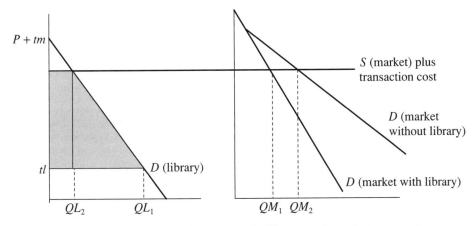

Figure 11.1   The consumer surplus approach: library and market purchases/rentals as substitute goods. The left graph represents the patron's demand for library books and the right diagram represents the demand for purchasing books.
Source: Courtesy of Donald Elliott, Ph.D., Southern Illinois University, an author of Elliot et al. (2003).

surplus. Each concept can be used to help classify and measure benefits of proposed projects and programs. Cost–benefit analysis tries to measure the increase to all beneficiaries resulting from a specific project. In some projects there are both producer surplus and consumer surplus effects; the sum reflects the total surplus to be considered as benefits of any policy change on the part of a NFP firm.

Clients are subsidized and organizations experience increased functionality from certain programs. In the library case, we concentrate on consumer surplus ignoring the loss of producer surplus due to public libraries.

Most patrons actually purchase as well as borrow similar services. Library clients were asked to "price" a list of market substitutes, such as books, journals, encyclopedias, and DVDs. Figure 11.1 shows a patron's demand for borrowing books on the left and for purchasing books on the right. Note that the shaded area in the diagram on the left represents the consumer surplus from borrowing books. We can approximate the value of this surplus in terms of how many additional books, tapes, etc. the client would purchase privately in the absence of a library.

Even though borrowing privileges are free to city residents, the patron faces an average transaction cost, such as downtown parking, in accessing the library. The diagram on the right shows the patron's demand for purchasing books. At a gross price of $P + tm$, where tm is the transaction cost of purchasing a book, the patron purchases QM_1 books per period in addition to borrowing QL_1 books per period from the library. Borrowing books and purchasing books are close substitutes. While the gross price of borrowing is usually less than the gross price of purchasing a book, sometimes purchasing is more convenient (lower gross cost due to lower transaction costs), satisfies a more urgent need, or satisfies the need for ownership of the book.

If their local library did not exist, clients would face a price of $P + tm$ for all access to books. This former library patron would add QL_2 books per period to the market demand of QM_1 for a total of QM_2 books purchased per period. The consumer surplus for library borrowing privileges would be the area of the trapezoid lying under D (library) between tl and $P + tm$. For simplicity we assume that tl and tm are approximately equal. If the library did not exist, the change in price of books that the patron otherwise would have borrowed would be $P + tm - tl = P$. Hence, the consumer surplus is the area of the trapezoid, which is equal to one half of the product of P and $(QL_1$ and $QL_2)$.

In practice, to measure the benefit of a specific library service, we identify a close market substitute for the library service, determine the price of the substitute, and survey patrons in contingent analysis to measure QL_1 and QL_2. QL_1 is factual – "How many books does your household borrow per month from your local public library?" QL_2 is counter-factual – "If your household could not borrow books from your local public library, how many more books would your household purchase each month at a price of \$7 each?" Given the responding household's answers, we can calculate consumer surplus for the library service.

As usual for projects of this type, costs are more easily measured. Capital assets such as land, buildings, furnishings, collections, computers, and vehicles are included in the analysis as well as annual operating costs (annual revenues less capital outlays less end-of-year surplus). Capital assets are valued at replacement cost rather than at original expenditure. Both benefits and costs are appropriately discounted.

The results

What were the results of this library study? First, the library learned a great deal about the demographics of its actual patrons. While the variation in demographics is substantial for the library coverage area, variation in demographics for actual library patrons is less distinct, especially so with respect to income, poverty rates, and education. For instance, while population demographics for Skokie showed that per capita income was \$27,136, the per capita income of library patrons was \$47,318. For library clients, not surprisingly considering their income levels, 33 percent held an advanced degree and 83 percent owned a personal computer. Both figures far exceeded the comparable estimates for the population as a whole.

Based upon the contingent valuation approach to measuring benefits, the study estimated that the benefits ratio was between 1.04 and 1.24. The same estimate based on consumer surplus gave a benefits ratio between 1.22 and 1.87. Using either valuation, the benefits ratio exceeds one and suggests that "the project" should be considered. In this case the library is already in existence and the study was instead used to justify its existence and quantify the net benefits to the community. With either measure, the benefits to the citizens of Skokie appear to be in excess of dollars spent yearly.

This study measured as well the distributional aspects of a library between different users. Households enjoy the greatest breadth in the use of library services. On the other hand, educators tend to value different services (children's books, audio/visual media, and electronic information services) and are less likely than others to use staff help. The estimated yearly value to the average household of the library was estimated to be between \$235 and \$389. For teachers, the estimated value of the library was about \$700.

11.10   USING COST–BENEFIT ANALYSIS: HEALTH WARNINGS ON TOBACCO PRODUCTS

The Australian Commonwealth Department of Health and Ageing examined new health warnings to appear on tobacco products starting in 2004. The proposed regulation required that 14 rotating messages cover 50 percent of the front and back of cigarette packages; the same set of warnings would apply to pouch tobacco as well but cigars would receive a different set of health warnings. Present warnings required that 25 percent of the front and 33 percent of the back be devoted to health warnings. Various studies (for example, Elliott and Shanahan, 2003) indicated that the impact of current warnings was declining.

The government study projected the costs and benefits of new health warnings from 2004 through 2030. Expected costs were printing costs, loss of income to the tobacco industry, and loss of government revenue from tobacco taxes collected. Expected benefits were individuals' health improvement, cost savings for health-care, and income gained by the non-tobacco industry.

The Australian government had traditionally used a discount rate of about 7 percent, perceived as the approximate marginal rate of return to alternative uses of capital. At the time of the study interest rates were low, so they initially chose an appropriate rate of 5 percent. Governments in general prefer using lower discount rates for health and environmental projects that offer long-term benefits.

Benefits

Benefits as usual are more difficult to calculate than costs. Overall, 10 percent of all individuals who quit smoking cited health warnings as a contributing factor. Size of message was found to be quite important, increasing until about 60 percent of the package surface area was covered. With status quo regulations, rates of decline in tobacco consumption were expected to slowly decay. The study expected the new warnings to restore the decline to recent trend rates (about 3 percent per year).

The primary expected benefit is the value of lives extended by increased warnings. Its calculation depended on two steps: a calculation of life years increased by the program and an estimation of their dollar value.

Mortality estimates were based on a reference population of Australian smokers. A measure of disability-adjusted life years (*DALY*) lost due to smoking was employed. One *DALY* equals one year lost of healthy life; a disability of 0 represents perfect health and 1 represents death. Obviously, the degree of disability is represented by some value between 0 and 1. Years lost due to smoking equals the sum of two components: first, the years lost due to premature death (*YLL*) and, second, the equivalent years of life lost due to disability (*YLD*). The *DALY* calculation used was then:

$$DALY = YLLs + YLDs$$

Where:

$DALY$ = disability-adjusted life year
YLL = years of life lost due to premature death
YLD = effective years of life lost due to disability

This cost–benefit study, however, requires dollar estimates for the "value of a life." The Commonwealth study uses a standard approach to derive the value of a healthy year of life. For example, if the estimated value of a life is $2 million and the average healthy working life is 40 years then the present value of a healthy year would be $118,000, using a 5 percent discount rate.

$$\$2,000,000 = \$118,000/1.05 + \$118,000/(1.05)^2 + \$118,000/(1.05)^3 \ldots + \$118,000/(1.05)^{40}$$

The Commonwealth study set its full life value equal to $1.5 million, assumed a 40 year healthy working life, and used a 5 percent discount rate. With these assumptions, the yearly value of a healthy life is $87,000. To estimate the value of life lost in any particular year, of course, it became necessary to estimate the present discounted value. For example, the loss of 8 years would result in a discounted value of $566,000 while the loss of 9 years would result in a discounted loss of $622,000.

There are other benefits associated with the program. The Commonwealth would save health treatment costs (including hospital, medical, pharmaceutical, and other costs) with reduced tobacco-related morbidities. These savings were estimated at $3,150 per $DALY$. Non-tobacco industries would also receive some benefits with a decline in the use of tobacco products.

Some social benefits were not included because of measurement difficulties. These include the reduction of other smoking-related morbidities such as burns, low-weight births, and diabetes complications. The study did not include the benefits of reduced passive smoking (i.e., reduced inhalation of secondary smoke) or the reduced pain and suffering of relatives and friends of smokers. While the study recognized that these benefits would be quite significant, there was an absence of a solid basis for estimating the true magnitude.

Results

Recall that the study ran from 2004 through 2030 and used a 5 percent discount rate. The key assumption that the new program would induce a 3 percent fall in tobacco consumption led to a forecast of 332 fewer deaths in 2006 and 488 fewer deaths in 2021. The Commonwealth estimated that the present value of the aggregated benefits exceeded the present value of the costs by $2.9 billion and the benefits ratio was calculated as 2.4.

To check their assumptions, the Commonwealth used two separate sensitivity tests. They placed their results in perspective by varying their most controversial assumptions. In the first sensitivity analysis the following assumptions were used:

- the 3 percent reduction in tobacco consumption was not changed;
- a higher 7 percent discount rate was employed;
- the evaluation period was shortened to 2004 through 2021.

This first sensitivity analysis resulted in a reduction of the benefits ratio from the original 2.4 to a new benefits ratio of 1.3.

The second sensitivity analysis changed only the assumption regarding the reduction in tobacco consumption; it was changed from the original assumption of 3 percent to a new assumption of 1 percent. This resulted in a new benefits ratio of 2.2 as compared with the original ratio of 2.4.

In both sensitivity analyses the Commonwealth found that there remained significant net benefits to employing the plan. In neither case did the benefits ratio fall below 1. Since they believed that their estimates of benefits in the study were quite conservative these sensitivity analyses were all the more impressive in supporting the implementation of the program.

CONCLUDING NOTES

- Cost–benefit analysis seeks to answer, "What value is gained in return for costs incurred for a given project?" It is a method to determine if benefits exceed costs and enables a sponsor to compare net returns between projects.

- The concepts of consumer and producer surplus assist in assessing the benefits of proposed projects.

- Firms in all three sectors adopt a form of cost–benefit analysis in using net present value (*NPV*). A positive difference between a project's present value of its discounted future stream of revenue (*R*) and its cost (*C*) identifies projects contributing to net income/profit.

- Cost–benefit analysis as compared with net discounted present value is characterized as: (1) Less concerned with how a project affects net income/profit and more concerned with identifying worthwhile projects in terms of NFP mission. (2) Less likely to have the same group incurring costs and receiving benefits. (3) Providing more of a challenge in determining the value of costs and benefits. Market prices are not always available for NFP costs and benefits, and shadow prices must be substituted.

- The benefit to cost ratio (B/C) compares the positive outcomes of a project with its costs. Any project for which the benefit ratio exceeds 1 is worthy of consideration. Given alternative competing projects, a NFP firm should undertake the project that maximizes net benefits, the difference between benefits and costs.

- A consistent cost–benefit framework, listing all costs and benefits and subgroups of cost bearers and beneficiaries, is determined for each alternative project.

- Transfers between subgroups of costs and benefits are identified but not included in quantifying net benefits of a project.

- Benefits are more difficult to calculate than costs.

- The discount rate used affects the net benefits of a particular project. Size and timing as well affect the relative attractiveness of competing projects. A lower discount rate favors all projects.

- Sensitivity analysis tests benefit–cost ratios by changing assumptions such as the discount rate.

- Cost–benefit analysis is a limited tool. It is not useful for choosing between a set of compatible (non-mutually exclusive) projects. It cannot overcome problems associated with uncovering alternative projects or budget limitations. It cannot be used for making choices concerning the size of a specific project.

KEY TERMS

Compensating variation
Cost–benefit analysis (CBA)
Private cost–benefit analysis
Social cost–benefit analysis
Benefits ratio
Transfer payments
Shadow price
Contingent valuation

Hedonic approach to valuation
Human capital approach
Willingness-to-pay approach
Rear-end loaded
Front-end loaded
Sensitivity analysis
Internal rate of return

SUGGESTED READINGS

Boardman, Anthony E., Greenberg, David H., Vining, Aidan R., and Weimer, David L. 1997: " 'Plug in' Shadow Price Estimates for Policy Analysis," *Annals of Regional Science*, 31, 299–324.

Carlin, Paul S. and Sandy, Robert 1991: "Estimating the Implicit Value of a Young Child's Life," *Southern Economic Journal*, 58 (July), 186–202.

Downing, Paul B. 1984: *Environmental Economics and Policy*, Boston, MA: Little, Brown.

Elliott and Shanahan Research 2003: *Evaluation of the Health Warnings and Explanatory Health Messages on Tobacco Products*, prepared for the Tobacco and Alcohol Strategies Section of the Department of Health and Aged Care, Australian Commonwealth Department of Health and Aging, *Cost–Benefit Analysis of Proposed New Health Warnings on Tobacco Products*, December.

Elliott, Donald, Holt, Glen E., and Moore, Amonia 2003: *Results of the Cost/Benefit Analysis Survey of Skokie Public Library in 2002*, Institute of Museum and Library Services, October.

Harberger, Arnold and Jenkins, Glen P. (eds.) 2002: *Cost–Benefit Analysis*, Williston, VT: Edward Elgar.

Kuziemko, Ilyana 2007: "Review: *New Foundations of Cost–Benefit Analysis* by Matthew D. Adler and Eric A. Posner, Cambridge and London: Harvard University Press, 2006," *Journal of Economic Literature*, 45 (4), 1028–9.

McTigue, Maurice P. 2004: "Rolling Back Government," *Imprimus*, 33 (4), 1–7.
Young, Dennis and Steinberg, Richard 1995: *Economics for Nonprofit Managers*, New York: Foundations Center.

END OF CHAPTER EXERCISES

Exercise 11.1
The table on p. 396 represents a cost–benefit analysis for an adult sheltered workshop proposed for the next *three years* for a cohort of 20 developmentally challenged adults. A rate of 15 percent is used to discount all future costs and benefits.

   a. Use the benefit–cost ratio to determine if the project is acceptable. Show your work.
   b. What type of sensitivity analysis would you use to test its assumptions? How do you expect this to affect your conclusions?
   c. Explain the rows of "positive" and "negative" entries.

Exercise 11.2
(*Advanced analysis.*) Refer to the table in Exercise 11.1. Use a 5 percent discount rate, rather than 15 percent presently used, to calculate the present value of the following:

   a. Salaries costing $50,000 per year.
   b. Supplies costing $10,000 per year.
   c. Facilities costing $6,000 per year.
   d. Five full-time equivalent volunteers working two hours per week, 40 weeks each year. An hourly rate of $20 represents the sum of the opportunity cost of volunteers plus training costs. (*Hint*: 80 hours a week * $20 * 5.)
   e. Participants' costs for transportation totaling $1,600 per year.
   f. Future income of 10 of the 20 participants. Ten participants are expected to earn approximately $5,000 a year more as a result of completing the program. It is assumed that their 30 year careers will start 10 years after the program starts.
   g. Work produced in the sheltered workshop. Each year 600 objects produced in the shop, such as wood pallets, will be sold for $5 each.
   h. The social benefits from a reduced need for psychological services. This is estimated at $10,000 each year over the next 30 years.
   i. Stipends awarded yearly to participants. Each of the 20 participants receives a yearly stipend of $200 for attending the workshop.
   j. Future tax payments generated from the increase in income of the 10 participants who go on to work in the general economy. This total of $10,000 a year starts 10 years after the program begins and extends for 30 years.

Exercise 11.3
Enter the information calculated in Exercise 11.2 in the table on p. 397 and solve to indicate if the project has positive net benefits.

Cost–benefit matrix framework

0.15 discount rate

	Participants	Donors/taxpayers	Volunteers	Other citizens	All society
PV of costs					
Salaries and benefits		($114,161.26)			($114,161.26)
Supplies and services		($22,832.25)			($22,832.25)
Facility use				($13,699.35)	($13,699.35)
Volunteer time			($18,265.80)		($18,265.80)
User cost	($3,653.16)				($3,653.16)
Opportunity cost of time	Positive				Positive
PV of benefits					
Participant income	$81,150.49				$81,150.49
Products sold				$6,849.68	6,849.675351
Reduced social services				$65,659.80	65,659.79637
Enjoyment	Positive				Positive
Satisfaction		Positive	Positive		Positive
PV of transfers					
Stipends	$9,132.90	($9,132.90)			$0.00
Tax payments	($16,230.10)			$16,230.10	$0.00
Total benefit	$90,283.39			$88,739.57	$153,659.96
Total cost	($19,883.26)	($127,860.61)	($18,265.80)	($13,699.35)	($172,611.82)
Net benefit	$70,400.13	($127,860.61)	($18,265.80)	$75,040.22	($18,951.86)
Net qualitative benefit	Pos. or neg.	Positive	Positive		Pos. or neg.
	($328,298.98)		($686.06)		
	($65,659.80)				
	4.045557736				

Cost–benefit matrix framework   *0.05 discount rate*

		Participants	Donors/taxpayers	Volunteers	Other citizens	All society
PV of costs						
	Salaries and benefits		a.			
	Supplies and services		b.			
	Facility use				c.	
	Volunteer time			d.		
	User cost	e.				
	Opportunity cost of time	Positive				Positive
PV of benefits						
	Participant income	f.				
	Products sold				g.	
	Reduced social Services				h.	
	Enjoyment	Positive				Positive
	Satisfaction		Positive	Positive		Positive
PV of transfers						
	Stipends	i.	i.			
	Tax payments	j.				j.
Total benefit **Total cost** **Net benefit** **Net qualitative benefit**		Pos. or neg.	Positive	Positive		

Exercise 11.4

A donor has approached the town manager offering a $100,000 contribution toward building a $300,000 swimming pool on 10 percent of land presently allocated to the town's park. The town manager decides to commission a cost–benefit analysis.

a. Should the contribution of the donor be considered a cost or benefit? Explain.
b. How would you calculate the opportunity cost of land used for the pool?
c. What benefits other than those represented by entrance fees should be considered? How can these benefits be quantified?
d. As a public facility, the pool is designed for the use of all residents. Would all taxpayers benefit? Explain.
e. Justify the decision to eliminate or include the potential increase in private property values around the pool and subsequent increase in local property taxes in the list of benefits.

Index